GALATIANS

This commentary offers a concise, incisive view of Galatians, Paul's most polemical letter. Here, Paul is fighting for the spiritual life and loyalty of some of his hard-won converts. Taking advantage of a range of persuasive rhetorical approaches, his letter appears to bristle with anger at the interlopers and the anguish of spurned affection. In this commentary, Craig Keener mines insights from the ancient world to highlight Paul's persuasive tactics and how the Galatian Christians would have heard his intense yet profound message. In so doing, Keener also helps readers confront Galatians afresh today, so they can hear more closely what Paul is and is not saying for the church universal. Drawing on a wide range of ancient Mediterranean sources to reconstruct the context of Galatians, Keener helps us grasp the issues that Paul was addressing, the reasons that Paul wrote the letter, and its continuing relevance for contemporary audiences.

Craig S. Keener is the author of twenty-two books, seven of which have won national or international awards. He is known especially for his detailed research in the world of the New Testament, bringing to light aspects of New Testament background that are often unfamiliar to modern readers.

NEW CAMBRIDGE BIBLE COMMENTARY

The New Cambridge Bible Commentary (NCBC) aims to elucidate the Hebrew and Christian Scriptures for a wide range of intellectually curious individuals. While building on the work and reputation of the Cambridge Bible Commentary popular in the 1960s and 1970s, the NCBC takes advantage of many of the rewards provided by scholarly research over the past four decades. Volumes utilize recent gains in rhetorical criticism, social scientific study of the Scriptures, narrative criticism, and other developing disciplines to exploit the growing advances in biblical studies. Accessible jargon-free commentary, an annotated "Suggested Readings" list, and the entire New Revised Standard Version (NRSV) text under discussion are the hallmarks of all volumes in the series.

PUBLISHED VOLUMES IN THE SERIES
Mark, Darrell Bock
Psalms, Walter Brueggemann and William H. Bellinger Jr.
Matthew, Craig A. Evans
Genesis, Bill T. Arnold
Exodus, Carol Meyers
Judges and Ruth, Victor H. Matthews
1–2 Corinthians, Craig S. Keener
The Gospel of John, Jerome H. Neyrey
James and Jude, William F. Brosend II
Revelation, Ben Witherington III

FORTHCOMING VOLUMES
Deuteronomy, Brent Strawn
Joshua, Douglas A. Knight
1–2 Chronicles, William M. Schniedewind
Isaiah 1–39, Jacob Stromberg
Jeremiah, Baruch Halpern
Hosea, Joel, and Amos, J. J. M. Roberts
The Gospel of Luke, Amy-Jill Levine and Ben Witherington III
The Letters of John, Duane F. Watson

Galatians

Craig S. Keener
Asbury Theological Seminary

CAMBRIDGE
UNIVERSITY PRESS

University Printing House, Cambridge CB2 8BS, United Kingdom

One Liberty Plaza, 20th Floor, New York, NY 10006, USA

477 Williamstown Road, Port Melbourne, VIC 3207, Australia

314–321, 3rd Floor, Plot 3, Splendor Forum, Jasola District Centre, New Delhi – 110025, India

79 Anson Road, #06-04/06, Singapore 079906

Cambridge University Press is part of the University of Cambridge.

It furthers the University's mission by disseminating knowledge in the pursuit of education, learning, and research at the highest international levels of excellence.

www.cambridge.org
Information on this title: www.cambridge.org/9781108445573
DOI: 10.1017/9781108642392

First published 2018

Printed in the United States of America by Sheridan Books, Inc.

A catalogue record for this publication is available from the British Library.

Library of Congress Cataloging-in-Publication Data
Names: Keener, Craig S., 1960– author.
Title: Galatians / Craig S. Keener, Asbury Theological Seminary, Kentucky.
Description: New York: Cambridge University Press, 2017. |
Series: New Cambridge Bible Commentary | Includes bibliographical references and index.
Identifiers: LCCN 2017045620 | ISBN 9781108426817 (hardback) |
ISBN 9781108445573 (paperback)
Subjects: LCSH: Bible. Galatians – Commentaries.
Classification: LCC BS2685.53.K44 2017 | DDC 227/.407–dc23
LC record available at https://lccn.loc.gov/2017045620

ISBN 978-1-108-42681-7 Hardback
ISBN 978-1-108-44557-3 Paperback

To John Barclay, Richard Bauckham, James D. G. Dunn, and N. T. Wri

scholars and friends who are never afraid to think outside the box

Contents

Acknowledgments

I am grateful to Ben Witherington for inviting me to write a brief commentary on Galatians for Cambridge University Press, and indebted both to Ben and to Beatrice Rehl at the Press for allowing me to produce a larger, more documented version of the commentary for Baker Academic. The present version is the more readable and concise version of the work (although Cambridge has graciously allowed me much more space for Galatians than was available for my earlier 1–2 Corinthians commentary). Because this is a commentary and will normally be used for reference, however, some repetition of major ideas will be necessary at various critical points.

I am grateful also to both Ben Witherington and Beatrice Rehl for their guidance and patience on this project and to one of Ben's and my brilliant PhD students, Judith Odor, for reviewing this commentary before my final submission. A second set of eyes is always helpful, especially when it is eyes as skilled as those of Judith. I am grateful to Judith also for the extensive task of indexing the work. Thanks also to Ramesh Karunakaran, project manager, and Ami Naramor, copyeditor.

Ancient Extrabiblical Abbreviations

Note that sources are cited by putative authors even when pseudepigraphic or debated.

EARLY JEWISH SOURCES

Apocrypha

Bar	Baruch
Ep Jer	Epistle of Jeremiah
1 Esd	1 Esdras
Jdt	Judith
1 Macc	1 Maccabees
2 Macc	2 Maccabees
3 Macc	3 Maccabees
4 Macc	4 Maccabees
Sir	Sirach
Tob	Tobit
Wis	Wisdom of Solomon

Dead Sea Scrolls

CD	Damascus Document
1QHa	1QHodayot
1QM	Qumran War Scroll
1QpHab	Qumran pesher commentary on Habakkuk
1QS	Qumran Manual of Discipline
4QMMT	Qumran Halakhic Letter
11Q19	Qumran Temple Scroll

Josephus

Ant.	*Antiquities of the Jews*
Ag. Ap.	*Against Apion*
Life	*Life*
War	*The Jewish War*

LXX	Septuagint (Greek translation of the Old Testament)
MT	Masoretic Text

Philo

Abr.	*On Abraham*
Agr.	*On Husbandry/Agriculture*
Alleg.	*Allegorical Interpretation*
Cher.	*On the Cherubim*
Conf.	*On the Confusion of Languages*
Cont.	*On the Contemplative Life*
Creation	*On the Creation*
Decal.	*The Decalogue*
Dreams	*On Dreams, That They Are God-Sent*
Drunk	*on Drunkenness*
Embassy	*Embassy to Gaius*
Flacc.	*Flaccus*
Flight	*On Flight and Finding*
Free	*Every Good Person Is Free*
Heir	*Who Is the Heir of Divine Things*
Immut.	*Immutable*
Jos.	*Joseph*
Migr.	*The Migration of Abraham*
Mos.	*Life of Moses (1–2)*
Names	*On the Change of Names*
Plant.	*Concerning Noah's Work as a Planter*
Post.	*On the Posterity of Cain and His Exile*
Prelim. St.	*Preliminary Studies*
Sacr.	*On the Birth of Abel and the Sacrifices Offered by Him and His Brother Cain*
Sobr.	*On the Prayers and Curses Uttered by Noah When He Became Sober*
Spec. Laws	*Special Laws (1–4)*

Virt.	*On Virtues*
Worse	*That the Worse Is Wont to Attack the Better*

Pseudepigrapha

Apoc. Mos.	Apocalypse of Moses
Apoc. Zeph.	Apocalypse of Zephaniah
Asc. Isa.	Ascension of Isaiah
2 Bar.	2 Baruch
3 Bar.	3 Baruch
4 Bar.	4 Baruch
1 En.	1 Enoch
2 En.	2 Enoch
3 En.	3 Enoch
4 Ezra	4 Ezra
L.A.B.	Pseudo-Philo *Biblical Antiquities*
Let. Aris.	Letter of Aristeas
Jos. Asen.	Joseph and Asenath
Jub.	Jubilees
Ps.-Phoc.	Pseudo-Phocylides
Ps. Sol.	Psalms of Solomon
Sib. Or.	Sibylline Oracles
T. Ab.	Testament of Abraham
T. Ash	Testament of Asher
T. Gad	Testament of Gad
T. Iss.	Testament of Issachar
T. Job	Testament of Job
T. Jos.	Testament of Joseph
T. Jud.	Testament of Judah
T. Levi	Testament of Levi
T. Mos.	Testament of Moses
T. Naph.	Testament of Naphtali
T. Reub.	Testament of Reuben
T. Sol.	Testament of Solomon

Rabbinic Sources

Ab.	Abot
Abod. Zar.	Abodah Zarah
Abot R. Nat.	Abot de Rabbi Nathan

b.	Babylonian Talmud
bar.	baraita
Bek.	Bekorot
Ber.	Berakot
B. Bat.	Baba Batra
B. K.	Baba Kamma
B. M.	Baba Mesia
Dem.	Demai
Eccl. Rab.	Ecclesiastes Rabbah
Erub.	Erubin
Exod. Rab.	Exodus Rabbah
Gen. Rab.	Genesis Rabbah
Ger.	Gerim
Git.	Gittin
Hag.	Hagigah
Hor.	Horayoth
Kel.	Kelim
Kip.	Kippurim
m.	Mishnah
Maas.	Maaserot
Mak.	Makkot
Meg.	Megillah
Mekilta Bah.	Mekilta Bahodesh
Mekilta Besh.	Mekilta Beshallah
Mekilta Nez.	Mekilta Nezikin
Mekilta Shir.	Mekilta Shirata
M. Q.	Moed Qatan
M. S.	Maaser Sheni
Naz.	Nazir
Num. Rab.	Numbers Rabbah
par.	parashah
Peah	Peah
Pesah.	Pesahim
Pesiq. Rab.	Pesiqta Rabbati
Pesiq. Rab Kah.	Pesiqta Rab Kahana
pq.	pereq
Qid.	Qiddushin
Rosh hash.	Rosh hashanah
Ruth Rab.	Ruth Rabbah
Sanh.	Sanhedrin

Shab.	Shabbat
Sheq.	Sheqalot
Sipra A. M.	Sipra Aharé Mot
Sipra Behuq.	Sipra Behuqotai
Sipra Qed.	Sipra Qedoshim
Sipra Sh.	Sipra Shemini
Sipra VDDeho.	Sipra Vayyiqra Dibura Dehobah
Sipre Num.	Sipre Numbers
Sipre Deut.	Sipre Deuteronomy
Song Rab.	Song of Solomon Rabbah
Sot.	Sotah
Suk.	Sukkot
t.	Tosefta
Taan.	Taanit
Tg. Neof.	Targum Neofiti
Tg. Ps.-Jon.	Targum Pseudo-Jonathan
Toh.	Toharot
y.	Jerusalem Talmud (Yerushalmi)
Yeb.	Yebamot

EARLY CHRISTIAN SOURCES

Ambrosiaster

Ep. Gal.	*On the Epistle to the Galatians*

Athenagoras

Plea for the Christians

Augustine

Cont.	*On Continence*
Ep. Gal.	*On the Epistle to the Galatians*
Nature	*On Nature and Grace*

Chrysostom

Hom. Cor.	*Homilies on 1–2 Corinthians*
Hom. Gal.	*Homilies on Galatians*

Hom. Rom.	*Homilies on Romans*
Pan. Ign.	*Panegyrics of Saint Ignatius*
1 Clem.	1 Clement
Did.	Didache
Diogn.	Epistle of Diognetus

Eusebius

H. E.	*Ecclesiastical History*
Hermas	Shepherd of Hermas

Hippolytus

Ref.	*Refutations*

Ignatius

Eph.	*Epistle to the Ephesians*
Magn.	*Epistle to the Magnesians*
Phld.	*Epistle to the Philadelphians*
Phili.	*Epistle to the Philippians*
Rom.	*Epistle to the Romans*

Jerome

Ep. Gal.	*On the Epistle to the Galatians*

Justin

Dial.	*Dialogue with Trypho*

Marius Victorinus

Ep. Gal.	*On the Epistle to the Galatians*

Origen

Cels.	*Against Celsus*
Comm. Rom.	*Commentary on Romans*

De princ.   *De principiis (On First Principles)*

Poly. *Phil.*   Polycarp *Letter to the Philippians*

Ps.-Clem. Hom.   Pseudo-Clement *Homilies*
Ep. Pet.   *Epistle of Peter*
Recogn.   *Recognitions*

Tertullian

Adv. Marc.   *Against Marcion*
De Car.   *On the Flesh of Christ*

Theodoret

Ep. Gal.   *On the Epistle to the Galatians*

OTHER GRECO-ROMAN SOURCES

Achilles Tatius

Leucippe and Clitophon

Aeschines

Ctes.   *Ctesiphon*
Embassy   *False embassy (De falsa legatione)*
Tim.   *Timarchus*

Aeschylus

Suppl.   *Suppliant Women*

Apollodorus

Bib.   *Bibliotheca*

Apollonius Rhodius

Argonautica

Appian

Bell. civ.	*Civil War*
Hist. rom.	*Roman History*

Apuleius

Apol.	*Apology*
De deo Socr.	*De deo Socratis*
Flor.	*Florida*
Metam.	*Metamorphoses*

Aristotle

E. E.	*The Eudemian Ethics*
N. E.	*Nicomachean Ethics*
Pol.	*Politics*
Rhet.	*Rhetoric*
V. V.	*Virtues and Vices*

Arrian

Alex.	*Anabasis of Alexander*

Arius Didymus

Epitome of Stoic Ethics

Artemidorus

Oneir.	*Oneirocritica*

Aulus Gellius

Attic Nights

Babr.   Babrius *Fable*

Caesar

Alex. W.	*Alexandrian War*
C. W.	*Civil War*

Chariton

Chaer.	*Chaereas and Callirhoe*

Cicero

Agr.	*De Lege agraria*
Amic.	*De Amicitia*
Att.	*Letters to Atticus*
Brut.	*Brutus or De claris oratoribus*
Cael.	*Pro Caelio*
Cat.	*In Catalinam*
De or.	*De Oratore*
Fam.	*Letters to Friends*
Fin.	*De finibus*
Flacc.	*Pro Flacco*
Inv.	*De Inventione*
Leg.	*De Legibus*
Mur.	*Pro Murena*
Nat. d.	*De Natura Deorum*
Or. Brut.	*Orator ad M. Brutum*
Phil.	*Orationes philippicae*
Pis.	*In Pisonem*
Prov. cons.	*De provinciis consularibus*
Quinct.	*Pro P. Quinctio*
Quint. fratr.	*Epistulae ad Quintum fratrum*
Resp.	*De Re Publica*
Rosc. Amer.	*Pro Sexto Roscio Amerino*
Rosc. com.	*Pro Roscio comoedo*
Scaur.	*Pro Scauro*
Sest.	*Pro Sestio*
Vat.	*In Vatinium*
Verr.	*In Verrem*

Crates

Ep.   *Epistle* (Ps.-Crates)

Demetrius [Ps.-Demetrius]

Style   *On Style*

Demosthenes

Cor.   *On the Crown*
Ep.   *Epistle*
Nic.   *Against Nicostratus*
Olynth. 2   *Olynthiaca* 2

Dio Cassius

Roman History

Dio Chrysostom

Or.   *Oration*

Diodorus Siculus

Library of History

Diogenes

Ep.   *Epistles*

Diogenes Laertius

Lives of Eminent Philosophers

Dionysius of Halicarnassus

Ant. rom.   *Roman Antiquities*
Comp.   *Literary Composition/De compositione verborum*

Demosth.	*Demosthenes*
Epid.	*Epideictic*
Isaeus	*Isaeus*
Lysias	*Lysias*
Pomp.	*Letter to Gnaeus Pompeius*
Thuc.	*Thucydides*

Epictetus

Diatr.	*Diatribai*
Ench.	*Encheiridion*

Euripides

Bacch.	*Bacchanals*
Cretans	*Cretans*
Cycl.	*Cyclops*
El.	*Electra*
frg.	*fragment*
Hec.	*Hecuba*
Hel.	*Helen*
Heracl.	*Children of Heracles*
Med.	*Medea*

Fronto

Ad Am.	*Ad Amicos*
Ad Ant. Imp.	*Ad Antoninum Imperator*
Ad M. Caes.	*Ad Marcus Caesarem*
Ep. Graecae	*Epistulae Graecae*
Nep. Am.	*De Nepote Amisso*

Gaius

Inst.	*Institutes*

Gorgias

Hel.	*Encomium of Helen*

Heraclitus

Ep.   *Epistles*

Hermog.Hermogenes

Issues   *On Issues*
Inv.   *[Invention]*
Method   *[Method in Forceful Speaking]*
Progymn.   *Progymnasmata*

Herodotus

Histories

Hesiod

W. D.   *Works and Days*

Homer

Il.   *Iliad*
Od.   *Odyssey*

Horace

Sat.   *Satires*

Iamblichus

Myst.   *Mysteries*
Pyth. Life   *Pythagorean Life*

IsaeusIsaeus

Cleon.   *Cleonymus*
Dic.   *Dicaeogenes*
Menec.   *Menecles*
Nicost.   *Nicostratus*

Isocrates

| *Antid.* | *Antidosis* |
| *Demon.* | *Demonicus* |

Julian the Apostate

| *Ep.* | *Epistle* |

Justinian

| *Inst.* | *Institutes* |

Juvenal

| *Sat.* | *Satires* |

Libanius

| *Topics* | *Common Topics* |

Livy

Ab Urbe Condita Libri

Longinus

| *Sublime* | *On the Sublime* |

Lucan

| *C. W.* | *Civil War* |

Lucian

Affairs	*Amores/Affairs of the Heart*
Alex.	*Alexander the False Prophet*
Critic	*The Mistaken Critic*
Dem.	*Demonax*

Eunuch	*Eunuch*
Gout	*Gout*
Hist.	*How to Write History*
Lover of Lies	*The Lover of Lies/Doubter/Philopseudes*
Peregr.	*The Passing of Peregrinus*
Phil. Sale	*Philosophies for Sale*
Prof. P.S.	*A Professor of Public Speaking*
Syr. G.	*Syrian Goddess*
Tyr.	*The Tyrannicide*
Z. Cat.	*Zeus Catechized*

Lucretius

Nat.	*De Rerum Natura*

Lysias

Or.	*Orations*

Marcus Aurelius

Meditations

Martial

Epig.	*Epigrams*

Maximus of Tyre

Or.	*Oration*

Musonius Rufus

Discourses (Cora Lutz ed.)

Ovid	Ovid
Am.	*Amores*
Fasti	*Fasti*
Metam.	*Metamorphoses*
Tristia	*Tristia*

Petronius

Sat.   *Satyricon*

Philodemus

Crit.   *On Criticism*
Prop.   *On Property Management*

Philostratus

Ep. Apoll.   *Epistles of Apollonius*
Vit. Apoll.   *Life of Apollonius of Tyana*
Vit. soph.   *Lives of the Sophists*

Pindar

Ol.   *Olympian Odes*

Plato

Prt.   *Protagoras*

Plautus

Mer.   *Mercator*

Pliny

Ep.   *Epistles* (Pliny the Younger)
Nat.   *Natural History* (Pliny the Elder)

Plutarch

Aem. Paul.   *Aemilius Paulus*
Alc.   *Alcibiades*
Alex.   *Alexander*
Arist.   *Aristides*
Caes.   *Caesar*

Cam.	*Camillus*
Cat. Min.	*Cato Minor*
Cic.	*Cicero*
Contr. A.	*On the Control of Anger*
Demosth.	*Demosthenes*
Educ.	*On the Education of Children*
Envy	*On Envy and Hate*
Flatt.	*How to Tell a Flatterer from a Friend*
Lect.	*On Lectures*
M. Cato	*Marcus Cato*
Mor.	*Moralia*
Praising	*Praising Oneself Inoffensively*
Profit by Enemies	*How to Profit by One's Enemies*
R. Col.	*Reply to Colotes*
Rom. Q.	*Roman Questions*
Sign Soc.	*Sign of Socrates*
Sulla	*Sulla*
Superst.	*Superstition*
Thes.	*Theseus*
T. T.	*Table Talk*
Vat.	*In Vatinium*

Porphyry

Marc.	*To Marcella*

Ps.-Callisthenes

Alex.	*Alexander Romance*

Publilius Syrus

Moral Sayings

Quintilian

Decl. Declamations (Ps.-Quintilian)
Inst.   *Institutes of Oratory*

Quintus Curtius Rufus *Alexander*

| Rhet. Alex. | Rhetorica ad Alexandrum |
| Rhet. Her. | Rhetorica ad Herennium |

Sallust

| *Ep. Caes.* | *Letter to Caesar* |
| *Pomp.* | *Letter of Gnaeus Pompeius* |

Seneca the Elder

| *Controv.* | *Controversies* |

Seneca the Younger

Ben.	*On Benefits*
Dial.	*Dialogues*
Ep. Lucil.	*Epistles to Lucilius*
Nat. Q.	*Natural Questions*
Troj.	*Trojan Women*

Sextus Empiricus

| *Pyr.* | *Outlines of Pyrrhonism* |

Silius Italicus

Punica

Socrates

| *Ep.* | *Epistle* (Ps.-Socrates) |

Socratics

| *Ep.* | *Epistles* |

Sophocles

Oed. Col.	*Oedipus at Colonus*
Philoc.	*Philoctetes*
Wom. Tr.	*Women of Trachis*
Soranus *Gynec.*	Soranus *Gynecology*

Stobaeus

Anth.	*Anthology*
Strabo *Geography*	

Suetonius

Aug.	*Augustus*
Claud.	*Claudius*
Dom.	*Domitian*
Jul.	*Julius*
Otho	*Otho*
Tib.	*Tiberius*

Symmachus

Ep.	*Epistles*

Tacitus

Ann.	*Annals*
Dial.	*Dialogues*
Hist.	*History*

Thebaid

Frg.	Fragment

Theon

Progymn.	*Progymnasmata*

Theophrastus

Char.   *Characters*
   Valerius Maximus *Memorable Deeds and Sayings*

Virgil (= Vergil)

Aen.   *Aeneid*
Ecl.   *Eclogues*

Vitruvius

Arch.   *Architecture*

Xenophon of Athens

Anab.   *Anabasis*
Apol.   *Apology*
Cyr.   *Cyropaedia*
Hell.   *Hellenica*
Lac.   *Constitution of Lacedemonians*
Mem.   *Memorabilia*

INSCRIPTIONS AND PAPYRI

B. G. U.   *Berliner griechische Urkunden (Ägyptische Urkunden aus den Königlichen Museen zu Berlin)* (Berlin 1895–)
CIJ   *Corpus Inscriptionum Iudaicarum*, ed. Frey
CPJ   *Corpus Papyrorum Judaicarum*, ed. Tcherikover
I. Eph.   *Inschriften von Ephesos*
P. Cairo Zen.   Zenon Papyri. Edited by C. C. Edgar, O. Guéraud, and P. Jouguet. 5 vols. *Catalogue général des antiquités égyptiennes du Musée du Caire.* Cairo: Institut Français d'Archéologie Orientale, 1925–40.
P. Giess.   *Griechische Papyri zu Giessen*, ed. E. Kornemann, O. Eger, and P. M. Meyer
P. Lond.   *Greek Papyri in the British Museum*, ed. F. G. Kenyon and H. I. Bell

P.Oxy.	Oxyrhynchus Papyri
P.Ryl.	*Catalogue of the Greek Papyri in the Rylands Library,*
	ed. A. S. Hunt, J. de M. Johnson, and V. Martin
P.S.I.	*Papiri della Società Italiana*, ed. G. Vitelli et al.

OTHER SOURCES

Calvin
Inst.   *Institutes*

Hammurabi   Code of Hammurabi
Lipit-Ishtar   Code of Lipit-Ishtar

Abbreviations for Secondary Sources Cited

AB	Anchor Bible
ABD	Anchor Bible Dictionary
ABIG	Arbeiten zur Bibel und ihrer Geschichte
ABR	Australian Biblical Review
ABRL	Anchor Bible Reference Library
ACCS	Ancient Christian Commentary on Scripture
ALGHJ	Arbeiten zur Literatur und Geschichte des Hellenistichen Judentums
ANET	*Ancient Near Eastern Texts Relating to the Old Testament*, ed. J. B. Pritchard, 1955 edn.
ANRW	*Aufstieg und Niedergang der Römischen Welt*
ArchRep	*Archaeological Reports*
AsJ	*Asbury Journal*
ASV	American Standard Version
AThR	*Anglican Theological Review*
BA	*Biblical Archaeologist*
BBR	*Bulletin for Biblical Research*
BDAG	Bauer, W., F. W. Danker, W. F. Arndt, and F. W. Gingrich. *Greek-English Lexicon of the New Testament and Other Early Christian Literature.* 3rd rev. edn. Chicago: University of Chicago, 1999
BDF	Blass, F. and A. Debrunner. *A Greek Grammar of the New Testament and Other Early Christian Literature.* Revised and translated by Robert W. Funk. Chicago: University of Chicago Press, 1961.
BECNT	Baker Exegetical Commentary on the New Testament
B.G.U.	*Berliner griechische Urkunden (Ägyptische Urkunden aus den Königlichen Museen zu Berlin)* (Berlin 1895–)
Bib	*Biblica*

BibInt	Biblical Interpretation
BibT	The Bible Today
BJS	Brown Judaic Studies
BNTC	Black's New Testament Commentaries
Bray	*Galatians, Ephesians.* Ed. G. Bray; *Reformation Commentary on Scripture, New Testament* 10; Downers Grove, IL: IVP Academic, 2011.
BSac	*Bibliotheca Sacra*
BT	*Bible Translator*
BTB	*Biblical Theology Bulletin*
BZ	*Biblische Zeitschrift*
CBC	Cambridge Bible Commentary
CBET	Contributions to Biblical Exegesis and Theology
CBQ	*Catholic Biblical Quarterly*
CCWJCW	Cambridge Commentaries on Writings of the Jewish and Christian World 200 BC to AD 200
CNS	*Cristianesimo nella Storia*
ConcC	Concordia Commentary
CQ	*Classical Quarterly*
CTJ	*Calvin Theological Journal*
CurBR	*Currents in Biblical Research*
DhDeep	*Dharma Deepika*
DNTB	*Dictionary of New Testament Background.* Ed. Craig A. Evans and Stanley E. Porter. Downers Grove, IL: InterVarsity, 2000
Edwards	M. J. Edwards, ed., *Galatians, Ephesians, Philippians.* ACCS, NT 8. Downers Grove, IL: InterVarsity, 1999
ÉPROER	Études préliminaires aux religions orientales dans l'empire romain
ESV	English Standard Version
EvQ	*Evangelical Quarterly*
EvT	Evangelische Theologie
ExpT	*Expository Times*
GRBS	*Greek, Roman and Byzantine Studies*
HeyJ	*Heythrop Journal*
HTKNT	Herders Theologischer Kommentar zum Neuen Testament
HTR	*Harvard Theological Review*
HUCA	*Hebrew Union College Annual*

IBC	Interpretation, a Bible Commentary for Teaching and Preaching
ICC	International Critical Commentaries
Int	*Interpretation*
ITS	*Indian Theological Studies*
IVPNTC	InterVarsity Press New Testament Commentary
JANESCU	*Journal of the Ancient Near Eastern Society of Columbia University*
JBL	*Journal of Biblical Literature*
JBLMS	Journal of Biblical Literature Monograph Series
JETS	*Journal of the Evangelical Theological Society*
JGRChJ	*Journal of Greco-Roman Christianity and Judaism*
JJS	*Journal of Jewish Studies*
JPFC	*The Jewish People in the First Century: Historical Geography, Political History, Social, Cultural and Religious Life and Institutions.* 2 vols. Edited by S. Safrai and M. Stern with D. Flusser and W. C. van Unnik. Section 1 of Compendia Rerum Iudaicarum ad Novum Testamentum. Vol. 1: Assen: Van Gorcum & Comp., B.V., 1974; Vol. 2: Philadelphia, PA: Fortress Press, 1976
JRA	*Journal of Roman Archaeology*
JRS	*Journal of Roman Studies*
JSJ	*Journal for the Study of Judaism in the Persian, Hellenistic, and Roman Periods*
JSNT	*Journal for the Study of the New Testament*
JSNTSup	Journal for the Study of the New Testament Supplement Series
JTInt	*Journal of Theological Interpretation*
JTS	*Journal of Theological Studies*
KJV	King James Version
LCL	Loeb Classical Library
LEC	Library of Early Christianity
Levy	I. C. Levy, translator and editor. *The Letter to the Galatians.* The Bible in Medieval Tradition. Grand Rapids, MI: Eerdmans, 2011
LNTS	Library of New Testament Studies
MAMA	*Monumenta Asiae Minoris Antiqua*
MBCBSup	Mnemosyne, bibliotheca classica batava: Supplementum
NASB	New American Standard Bible

Neot	*Neotestamentica*
NET	New English Translation
NETR	*Near East School of Theology Theological Review*
New CBC	New Cambridge Bible Commentary
NIB	New Interpreter's Bible
NICNT	New International Commentary on the New Testament
NIGTC	New International Greek Testament Commentary
NIV	New International Version
NovT	*Novum Testamentum*
NovTSup	Supplements to Novum Testament
NRSV	New Revised Standard Version
NTS	*New Testament Studies*
NTTS	New Testament Tools and Studies
OBT	Overtures to Biblical Theology
*OCD*³	*The Oxford Classical Dictionary: The Ultimate Reference Work on the Classical World.* 3rd rev. edn. Ed. Simon Hornblower and Antony Spawforth. Oxford: Oxford University Press, 2003
OEANE	*The Oxford Encyclopedia of Archaeology in the Near East.* Ed. Eric M. Meyers. 5 vols. New York: Oxford University Press, 1997
OJRS	*Ohio Journal of Religious Studies*
PBSR	*Papers of the British School at Rome*
PRSt	*Perspectives in Religious Studies*
RB	*Revue Biblique*
ResQ	*Restoration Quarterly*
RevExp	*Review and Expositor*
RevistB	*Revista Bíblica*
RevQ	*Revue de Qumran*
SBFA	Studii Biblici Franciscani Analecta
SBLDS	Society of Biblical Literature Dissertation Series
SBLIMI	Society of Biblical Literature and Its Modern Interpreters
SBLMS	Society of Biblical Literature Monograph Series
SBLRBS	Society of Biblical Literature Resources for Biblical Study
SBLSBS	Society of Biblical Literature Sources for Biblical Study/ SBL Resources for Biblical Study
SBLSymS	Society of Biblical Literature Symposium Series
SBT	Studies in Biblical Theology
ScrB	*Scripture Bulletin*

SHBC	Smyth & Helwys Bible Commentary
SJT	*Scottish Journal of Theology*
SJTOP	Scottish Journal of Theology Occasional Papers
SNTSMS	Society for New Testament Studies Monograph Series
SNTU	*Studien zum Neuen Testament und seiner Umwelt*
SP	Sacra Pagina
SR	*Studies in Religion/Sciences religieuses*
StBibLit	Studies in Biblical Literature
TJ	*Trinity Journal*
TLG	*Thesaurus Lingua Graecae: Canon of Greek Authors and Works*
TynBul	*Tyndale Bulletin*
TZ	*Theologische Zeitschrift*
UNDCSJCA	University of Notre Dame Center for the Study of Judaism and Christianity in Antiquity
VT	*Vetus Testamentum*
WBC	Word Biblical Commentary
WEB	World English Bible
WTJ	*Westminster Theological Journal*
WUNT	Wissenschaftliche Untersuchungen sum Neuen Testament
ZECNT	Zondervan Exegetical Commentary on the New Testament
ZNW	*Zeitschrift für die Neutestamentliche Wissenschaft*

I Introduction

Galatians is more ad hoc than many of Paul's letters, leaving unstated many assumptions shared between Paul and the Galatians.[1] Most scholars agree that we can learn something about Paul's challengers in Galatia from Paul's letter to the Galatians.[2] That we have only one side of the conversation, however, warns us not to think that we know more than we really do.[3] In keeping with ancient polemical conventions,[4] Paul sometimes reduces his opponents' principles to absurdity and puts a worse face on their intentions than they would have conceded.

GALATIANS IN EARLY CHRISTIAN CONTEXT

Galatians has long occupied center stage in theological debates, particularly since the period of the Protestant Reformation. Because some modern negative depictions of Paul's view of the law purport to derive their inspiration from Luther, it is helpful to observe that Luther retained valid uses for the law as Scripture.[5]

Luther did depend too heavily on the interpretive grid supplied by his early reading of Galatians. Still, his appeal to Romans to fill the gaps in

---

[1] G. D. Fee, *Galatians: Pentecostal Commentary* (Blandford Forum, Dorset, UK: Deo Publishing, 2007), 1.
[2] See, e.g., E. P. Sanders, *Paul: The Apostle's Life, Letters, and Thought* (Minneapolis, MN: Fortress, 2015), 477 (with cautions on 165–66).
[3] On mirror-reading Galatians, see J. M. G. Barclay, "Mirror-Reading a Polemical Letter: Galatians as a Test Case," *JSNT* 31 (1987): 73–93.
[4] Smearing opponents was the norm (e.g., Isaeus *Dic.* 46; Fronto *Ad M. Caes.* 3.3); for reducing arguments to the absurd, see, e.g., Rom 3:6, 8; Lysias *Or.* 4.5–6, §101; Cicero *Phil.* 8.5.16; Seneca *Ep. Lucil.* 83.9; 113.20; Apuleius *Apol.* 29–30, 58, 102.
[5] E.g., Luther, *Second Lectures on Galatians* on 3:21 (from *Galatians, Ephesians* [ed. G. Bray, *Reformation Commentary on Scripture, New Testament* 1; Downers Grove, IL: IVP Academic, 2011]).

Galatians' more ad hoc arguments[6] is probably helpful. If we appeal to any background at all, surely Paul's own developed thought is the closest available background for Galatians.

Nevertheless, precisely *because* Romans is more developed, we must recognize differences between the letters. Luther and most of his contemporaries thought that Galatians abridged Paul's earlier argument in Romans,[7] whereas most scholars today deem Romans the later, more mature work. Galatians is much harsher toward Jewish tradition and the law, whereas Romans is clearer in differentiating the law from its abuse.

Theologically, the letters basically cohere,[8] opposing not works per se but boasting in them. Yet Romans is more nuanced, and is helpful for qualifying, by means of Paul's more comprehensive theology just several years later, some striking statements found in Galatians. Galatians is more direct and polemical because, unlike Romans, it addresses an immediate threat from opponents.

At many points Acts also supplies information that coincides with or fills gaps in our understanding of Galatians. Because Acts functions as a historical monograph, because "we" material in Acts suggests that its author traveled with Paul at times, and because I have argued these matters at length elsewhere, I will cite Acts where I believe it relevant.[9]

Nevertheless, when one compares Acts with Galatians, not only omissions but differences of perspective are obvious. For example, writing with the benefit of hindsight, Luke puts the best face on differences between Paul and the Jerusalem apostles (cf. Acts 15:2–32), whereas Paul is at pains in Galatians to emphasize his independence from those apostles (Gal 1:18–20; 2:6). Sharing ancient historians' appreciation for an appearance of a degree of neutrality, Luke has apparently incorporated some Jerusalem perspectives for which Paul had little use when writing Galatians (cf. Acts 15:20, 29; Gal 2:6, 10). Such differences of perspective are helpful for us to keep in mind when comparing the accounts.

---

6   T. Wengert, "Martin Luther on Galatians 3:6–14: Justification by Curses and Blessings," pages 91–116 in *Galatians and Christian Theology: Justification, the Gospel, and Ethics in Paul's Letter* (ed. M. W. Elliott et al.; Grand Rapids, MI: Baker Academic, 2014).

7   G. Bray, "Introduction to Galatians, Ephesians," pages xxxvii–liii in *Galatians, Ephesians* (ed. G. Bray; *Reformation Commentary on Scripture, New Testament* 10; Downers Grove, IL: IVP Academic, 2011), xxxviii, xli.

8   See esp. H. Boers, *The Justification of the Gentiles: Paul's Letters to the Galatians and Romans* (Peabody, MA: Hendrickson, 1994), 223–24.

9   See C. S. Keener, *Acts: An Exegetical Commentary*, 4 vols. (Grand Rapids, MI: Baker Academic, 2012–2015), 90–319.

THEOLOGY OF GALATIANS AND SOME DOMINANT THEMES

Many interpreters read Galatians against the backdrop of Paul's "apocalyptic" worldview, more explicit in, e.g., 1 Thessalonians or 1 Corinthians than in Galatians.[10] Some scholars, however, warn against an apocalyptic reading that neglects prior salvation history.[11] The extent to which "apocalyptic" can characterize Galatians is largely a matter of definition: Galatians is far from the technical definition of an apocalypse as a visionary text,[12] but like Paul's other letters, it does embrace elements of the apocalyptic eschatological worldview.[13]

In the letter's body, the theme of *the gospel* dominates Paul's apologetic narrative section (Gal 1:6–9, 11, 16, 23; 2:2, 5, 7, 14; cf. 4:13); here Paul invokes his personal accounts of receiving and defending the gospel God gave him. The themes of law (2:16, 19, 21; 3:2, 5, 10–13, 17–19, 21, 23–24; 4:4–5, 21; cf. 5:3–4) and promise (3:14, 16–19, 21–22, 29; 4:23, 28) dominate the letter's direct argumentative section, and here Paul repeatedly invokes Scripture (most explicitly in 3:6, 8, 10–13, 16; 4:22, 27, 30), although he also appeals to their experience (3:1–5; 4:8, 13–14) and stirs pathos (4:12–20).

Although law continues to appear (5:14, 18, 23; 6:2, 13) in the body's final section and the Spirit was introduced earlier (3:2–5, 14; 4:6, 29), the theme of the Spirit tends to dominate the letter's ethical section (5:16–18, 22–23, 25; 6:1, 8). It is the Spirit, not external laws, that enables true righteousness (cf. Ezek 36:27). In its distinctively negative or inadequate sense that contrasts with the promised Spirit, *flesh* (*sarx*) is introduced in 3:3, appears in the contrast between the Spirit-promised (prophetically promised) heir and the child born by natural means (4:23, 29), and features heavily in the continued contrast with the Spirit in 5:13, 16–17, 19–21, 24; and 6:8, 12–13.

Paul insists that because his gentile converts have embraced Christ and received the Spirit just like Jewish believers, they are no less full heirs of Israel's promises. In my view, this means that Paul envisions gentile believers

[10]   See J. L. Martyn, *Galatians: A New Translation with Introduction and Commentary* (New York: Doubleday, 1997), 97–105, esp. helpful regarding 1:4; 3:23–25; 4:4, 6.

[11]   E.g., N. T. Wright, *Paul and the Faithfulness of God* (Minneapolis, MN: Fortress, 2013), 781; Wright, *Pauline Perspectives: Essays on Paul, 1978–2013* (Minneapolis, MN: Fortress, 2013), 481–82; R. B. Hays, "Apocalyptic Poiêsis in Galatians: Paternity, Passion, and Participation," pages 200–19 in *Galatians and Christian Theology: Justification, the Gospel, and Ethics in Paul's Letter* (ed. M. W. Elliott et al.; Grand Rapids, MI: Baker Academic, 2014).

[12]   See J. J. Collins, *The Apocalyptic Imagination: An Introduction to Jewish Apocalyptic Literature* (Grand Rapids, MI: Eerdmans, 1998).

[13]   See J. M. G. Barclay, *Obeying the Truth: Paul's Ethics in Galatians* (Vancouver, BC: Regent College Publishing, 1988), 100.

as spiritual proselytes (see Gal 3:29; cf. Rom 2:28–29; 11:17), whereas his competitors viewed them as merely sympathizers or God-fearers (cf. Acts 15:20), still needing marks of the covenant to become full children of Abraham.

AUTHOR, PROVENANCE, AND DATE

Nearly all scholars affirm that Paul wrote Galatians.[14] It is too closely connected with the local situation and too close in style to other letters with local connections to be pseudepigraphic.

Ancient writers often thought that Paul wrote Galatians late, from Rome.[15] Modern scholars usually prefer a provenance of Corinth or Ephesus. If Paul's rivals proceeded to Galatia shortly after the Jerusalem Council, Paul could even write the letter from Antioch, describing recent events in 2:11–14. The question of Galatians' provenance makes little difference in interpreting the letter, however, in contrast to the question of the location of its addressees (treated in the later section "North or South Galatia").

Date: After the Jerusalem Council

Scholars today vary in the date they assign to the letter's composition, although the entire range of debated dates is generally less than a decade, from ca. 48[16] to the mid-50s,[17] a common median (which I accept as a working hypothesis) being about 51.[18] Earlier tradition, followed by most Reformers, favored a late date for Galatians, believing that Paul composed it after Romans.[19] Whereas scholars today debate whether 2:1–10 refers to the council depicted in Acts 15 or to an earlier occasion, Luther applied it to an occasion even later than Acts 15.[20]

---

[14] E.g., J. B. Lightfoot, *Saint Paul's Epistle to the Galatians: A Revised Text with Introduction, Notes, and Dissertations* (New York: Macmillan and Co., 1896), 57–62; H. D. Betz, *A Commentary on Paul's Letter to the Churches in Galatia* (Hermeneia Commentaries; Philadelphia, PA: Fortress, 1979), 1.

[15] E.g., Theodoret *Ep. Gal.* 6.18 (Edwards).

[16] E.g., W. Ramsay, W. Neil, F. F. Bruce, C. Hemer, B. Witherington, D. Moo.

[17] See, e.g., M. Hengel, G. W. Hansen, G. Fee, S. Eastman, E. P. Sanders, A. M. Schwemer.

[18] J. D. G. Dunn, *The Epistle to the Galatians* (Black's New Testament Commentary; London: A&C Black, 1995), 19 (late 50 through early 51); Martyn, *Galatians*, 19–20, esp. 20n20 (ca. 50); M. C. de Boer, *Galatians: A Commentary* (Louisville, KY: Westminster John Knox, 2011), 5–11; cf. P. Oakes, *Galatians* (Paideia; Grand Rapids, MI: Baker Academic, 2015), 22.

[19] G. Bray, "Introduction to Galatians" (2011), xxxviii, xli.

[20] Luther, *Second Lectures on Galatians*, on Gal 2:1 (Bray).

Because Galatians could not be written before the events it reports, the date of the incident in Gal 2:1–10 is a primary crux in the debate concerning a possible early date of Galatians. Scholars most often identify this incident with the time of either (1) Paul's famine visit of Acts 11:30 and 12:25; or, more commonly (2) the Jerusalem Council of Acts 15. Proponents of both views offer plausible arguments. Many respected scholars support the first view,[21] though a greater number of scholars, including myself, favor the second.[22]

I shall first list several of the arguments that scholars have advanced for the first (famine visit) view, following each argument with my response supporting the second (Jerusalem Council) view. Then I shall turn to remaining arguments for the Jerusalem Council view not already treated in my responses.[23]

First, supporters of the famine visit view doubt that Paul would have omitted mention of the famine visit in Galatians. This argues from silence, however; in Galatians, Paul addresses only occasions on which he met the *apostles* in Jerusalem (1:17–20; 2:1–2); most of the apostles may have been in hiding when he came (Acts 11:30; 12:1–3, 17).

Second, some consider it "inconceivable" that Paul would not mention the Jerusalem decree in Galatians had the council of Acts 15 already occurred. All scholars acknowledge, however, that 1 Corinthians postdates any event depicted in Acts 15; but 1 Corinthians appeals to no decree to settle the questions of sexual immorality or food offered to idols, issues that the Jerusalem decree expressly addressed (Acts 15:20).

Further, on a post–Jerusalem Council date for Galatians, Paul had *already* delivered these decrees to south Galatia (Acts 16:4) – apparently before insistence on circumcision became an issue there (note the geographic range in 15:1, 23) – and it had not silenced his challengers. Moreover, Paul may effectively *appeal* to the decree in Gal 2:6–10 (see comment there).

[21] E.g., W. Ramsay (eventually), W. Knox, C. Williams, R. Longenecker, W. Larkin, P. Trebilco, B. Witherington, R. Bauckham, S. Mitchell, D. Bock (very tentatively), D. Moo, A. Das; see especially the detailed cases of E. J. Schnabel, *Early Christian Mission,* 2 vols. (Downers Grove, IL: InterVarsity; Leicester, UK: Apollos, 2004), 988–92; D. Wenham, "Acts and the Pauline Corpus, II: The Evidence of Parallels," pages 215–58 in *The Book of Acts in Its Ancient Literary Setting* (ed. B. W. Winter and A. D. Clarke; Grand Rapids, MI: Eerdmans; Carlisle, UK: Paternoster, 1993), 234–43.
[22] E.g., J. B. Lightfoot, R. B. Rackham, J. Knox, F. Stagg, R. Stein, H. D. Betz, G. Lüdemann, H. Ridderbos, S. Kistemaker, C. K. Barrett, J. Fitzmyer, F. Mussner, M. Hengel, C. Hill, A. M. Schwemer, J. Dunn, K.-S. Krieger, R. Pervo, P. Nepper-Christensen, G. Fee, R. Hays, S. Eastman, G. Lyons, M. de Boer, P. Oakes, B. Chance, *Acts,* 250, E. P. Sanders. Earlier, see, e.g., Bede *Comm. Acts* 15.2.
[23] See further Keener, *Acts,* 2195–2206, 2258–79.

Third, some find discrepancies between Gal 2:1–10 and Acts 15. Most such discrepancies, however, involve omissions of detail in one account or the other, such as is common in ancient historical texts as well as modern eyewitness testimony.[24] The account in Acts 11:30, by contrast, is simply too bare to *offer* many discrepancies – or parallels.

Fourth, the "revelation" in Gal 2:2 could fit the prophetic reason for the famine visit (Acts 11:28–30). In Galatians, however, Paul applies revelatory language specifically to his personal revelation of the gospel (Gal 1:12, 16; cf. 3:23; Rom 1:17; 16:25). In context, then, Paul's revelation was the gospel message for the gentiles that he presented to the Jerusalem leaders, as suggested even in the verse itself (Gal 2:2).

Fifth, some contend that the agreement reached in Acts 11:30/12:25 and Gal 2:1–10 was incomplete, requiring it to be later revisited in Acts 15. But in logic, the simplest solution is generally the best one available. Since Acts 11:30/12:25 do not mention any agreement or even any meeting with Jerusalem apostles, and since Acts 15 includes both these features, is it not simpler to conclude that Gal 2:1–10 reflects events also reported in Acts 15?

Even right before the Jerusalem council, when Paul debated with circumcisionists in Antioch (Acts 15:1–2), the issue had not yet traveled north from Syria-Cilicia to Galatia (Acts 15:23, 41).

Additional considerations confirm that Paul wrote Galatians after the Jerusalem Council. First, numerous features in common between Gal 2:1–10 and Acts 15 suggest that they refer to the same event.[25]

Commonalities	Acts 15:6–22	Gal 2:1–10
The same basic object	Acts 15:5	Gal 2:4
The same basic outcome	Acts 15:19–21, 28–29	Gal 2:5–6
Paul's mission is recognized	Acts 15:12	Gal 2:2
Leaders agree that gentiles need not be circumcised	Acts 15:19–20	Gal 2:7–9
Peter agreed	Acts 15:7–11	Gal 2:9
James agreed	Acts 15:13–21	Gal 2:9

I believe that it strains plausibility to suppose these are coincidentally two completely separate events, one recorded by Luke and the other by Paul.

The accounts emphasize different features, but so long as we recognize that Luke's and Paul's reports are independent and from different perspectives,

---

[24] Cf. Keener, *Acts*, 194–96; regarding Acts 15, see 2195–2202.
[25] I borrow the following chart from Keener, *Acts*, 2200. See also comparisons in Lightfoot, *Galatians*, 123–24.

their points of agreement provide multiple attestation for memories of an important event.[26]

James was already influential earlier (Gal 1:19), but in Gal 2:9, 12, he is listed first and appears to be the most prominent leader in the Jerusalem church.[27] Insofar as we can tell from Acts, he did not achieve this rank before the famine visit and Peter's departure from the city (Acts 11:30; 12:17; cf. 15:13, 19; 21:18; 1 Cor 9:5).

Because Gal 2:1–10 probably refers to the event later depicted in Acts 15, this commentary adopts a date some time after the Jerusalem Council (ca. 48), but probably before the collection (about which most scholars believe that Galatians is silent), so perhaps ca. 50–52 CE.

Paul's Audience in Galatia

At least the strong majority of Paul's audience was gentile;[28] they were not yet circumcised (Gal 5:2; 6:12) and they once worshiped non-gods (4:8). Many gentiles were attracted to Judaism in areas where some Jews lived,[29] so some sympathetic polytheists may have had some acquaintance with the synagogue before their conversion (cf. Acts 13:43; 14:1).

Nevertheless, they would be ill prepared to match the circumcisionist teachers from Judea with whom Paul finds himself in theological conflict in this letter.

Galatia's religious environment offers some valuable insights, discussed at Gal 4:8–10 and, regarding one cult, at 5:12. More recently, a number of scholars have viewed Galatians through an anti-imperial lens,[30] in view of strikingly prominent imperial temples in this region.[31] In this letter, however, Paul is probably too concerned with the immediate issue to be focused

[26] With, e.g., J. A. Fitzmyer, *The Acts of the Apostles: A New Translation with Introduction and Commentary* (AB 31; New York: Doubleday, 1998), 540. On the differences, cf. Lightfoot, *Galatians*, 125–28.
[27] What was named first was often deemed greater (Dionysius of Halicarnassus *Comp.* 5; Mekilta Pisha 1.28; Bah. 8.28–30).
[28] Noted also by Jerome *Gal.* 2.5.2 (Edwards).
[29] See, e.g., Epictetus *Diatr.* 2.9.20; Juvenal *Sat.* 5.14.96–106.
[30] See helpfully on this element B. Kahl, *Galatians Re-imagined: Reading with the Eyes of the Vanquished* (Minneapolis, MN: Fortress, 2010); J. K. Hardin, *Galatians and the Imperial Cult* (WUNT 2.237; Tübingen: Mohr Siebeck, 2008).
[31] In Antioch, see S. Mitchell, *Anatolia: Land, Men, and Gods in Asia Minor*, 2 vols. (Oxford: Clarendon, 1993), 1:101, 104–06; 2:10; Mitchell, "Archaeology in Asia Minor, 1990–1998," *ArchRep* 45 (1998–99): 125–92, here 178; in Phrygia generally, MAMA 1.19, 23, 24, 24a, 416, 429.

on the larger setting of Roman oppression.[32] Still, Paul is concerned with his rivals imposing their cultural (and they believed scriptural) strictures on his converts, so one could still speak of a sort of cultural and theological imperialism.

One frequently offered aspect of background involves the people from whom the Galatian province derived its name.[33] Many Gauls, or Celts, had settled in Phrygian and Cappadocian territories in Asia Minor.[34] Outsiders stereotyped Galatians as ignorant, although Galatians themselves worked hard to challenge this prejudice.[35] Erasmus follows Jerome in deeming them stupid, providing Erasmus (though not Jerome) an occasion for anti-French prejudice.[36]

The relevance of this Celtic backdrop depends to some extent on whether Paul addresses ethnic Gauls (on the north Galatian view) or simply inhabitants of the Galatian province (on the south Galatian view). Yet the character of Paul's letter suggests that even if he addressed north Galatia, he addressed its hellenized and romanized urban residents, not the stereotypical Celtic invaders of earlier generations.[37]

North or South Galatia?

Commentators divide between those who argue that Paul's primary audience consisted of ethnic Galatians in the northern part of the province of Galatia[38] and those who argue that Paul simply employs the provincial

---

[32] Against overemphasis on the imperial cult in Paul, see, e.g., A. A. Das, *Paul and the Stories of Israel: Grand Thematic Narratives in Galatians* (Minneapolis, MN: Fortress, 2016), 179–215; C. Miller, "The Imperial Cult in the Pauline Cities of Asia Minor and Greece," *CBQ* 72 (2, 2010): 314–32; K. Galinsky, "The Cult of the Roman Emperor: Uniter or Divider?" pages 1–21 in *Rome and Religion: A Cross-Disciplinary Dialogue on the Imperial Cult* (ed. J. Brodd and J. L. Reed; Atlanta, GA: Society of Biblical Literature, 2011).

[33] For details on the Celts who settled in Asia, see Lightfoot, *Galatians*, 1–17, 239–51; and esp. Mitchell, *Anatolia*, 1:11–58.

[34] Livy 38.17.2; W. M. Ramsay, *A Historical Commentary on St. Paul's Epistle to the Galatians* (New York: G. P. Putnam's Sons, 1900), 25, 45–52. Cf. Callimachus *Hymn* 4.173, 184; Seneca *Dial.* 12.7.2.

[35] Mitchell, *Anatolia*, 2:84.

[36] Desiderius Erasmus, *Paraphrases*, on Galatians' introduction, following Jerome *Gal.* 1.1.1 (Bray, *Galatians*, 1). Luther and others also deemed Galatians foolish as a people (*Gal.* 1535 on 3:1; see comment on Gal 3:1).

[37] Betz, *Galatians*, 2.

[38] E.g., Lightfoot, K. Lake, Meeks, Reicke, Mussner, F. Watson, de Boer, Koch, Soards and Pursiful.

label, which allows that his audience could be (and for various reasons probably was) in southern Galatia.[39] The latter are probably the majority today.

Historically, most commentators favored the north Galatian hypothesis.[40] The weight of historical opinion is thus behind the north Galatian hypothesis, ironically (given recent scholarship) making this a more "conservative" (and certainly traditional) view. This was the case, however, because patristic commentators assumed the provincial boundaries and population patterns of their own day, being generally unaware of those of Paul's day.[41]

Arguments for the North Galatian Hypothesis

Following are some key arguments traditionally offered for the north Galatian hypothesis, followed by my responses, and then arguments for the south Galatian hypothesis. One significant argument in favor of the north Galatian hypothesis is its antiquity, already addressed earlier. Another argument is that Luke employs the title Galatia only in Acts 16:6 and 18:23, there in connection with Paul's mission in the north. This argument, however, proves vulnerable to several criticisms. First, Luke mentions no evangelization occurring in connection with these travels. Second, Luke's usage cannot determine Paul's. Third, ancient usage suggests that in 16:6 Luke probably refers to Phrygian Galatia, not to northern Galatia.[42] Indeed, the route depicted in Acts 16:6–8 might not even pass through northern Galatia.[43] Finally, if we are to appeal to Acts, Luke devotes not two verses but the better part of two chapters to the evangelization of the southern part of the Galatian province.

---

[39]   E.g., Ramsay, W. Knox, Burton, Neil, Breytenbach, J. Scott, R. Riesner, Rackham, C. Williams, Arrington, G. W. Hansen, P. Barnett, J. Bligh, Bruce, Fung, E. Yamauchi, J. Finegan, B. Witherington, T. Schreiner, D. deSilva, P. Oakes, A. Das, S. Porter; see esp. C. J. Hemer, *The Book of Acts in the Setting of Hellenistic History* (ed. C. H. Gempf; WUNT 49; Tübingen: Mohr Siebeck, 1989), 278–307; T. Witulski, *Die Adressaten des Galaterbriefes: Untersuchungen zur Gemeinde von Antiochia ad Pisidiam* (Forschungen zur Religion und Literatur des Alten und Neuen Testaments 193; Göttingen: Vandenhoeck & Ruprecht, 2000).

[40]   Lightfoot, *Galatians*, 239, cites "the universal tradition of ancient writers."

[41]   With Oakes, *Galatians*, 19.

[42]   See the primary sources in C. J. Hemer, "The Adjective 'Phrygia,'" *JTS*, n.s., 27 (1, 1976): 122–26; Hemer, "Phrygia: A Further Note," *JTS*, n.s., 28 (1, 1977): 99–101.

[43]   See R. Riesner, *Paul's Early Period: Chronology, Mission Strategy, Theology* (trans. D. Stott; Grand Rapids, MI: Eerdmans, 1998), 282–86; Mitchell, *Anatolia*, 2:3.

Orators addressing mixed communities usually used provincial titles. Unlike Luke's descriptions in this region, Paul's letters regularly refer to regions by their provincial titles (Rom 15:26; 16:5; 1 Cor 16:5, 15, 19; 2 Cor 1:1, 8, 16; 2:13; 7:5; 8:1; 9:2, 4; 11:9–10; Gal 1:21; Phil 4:15; 1 Thess 1:7–8; 4:10). More important, in direct address he speaks to the "Corinthians" (using a geographic, not ethnic, designation in direct address) in 2 Cor 6:11, and Philippians in Phil 4:15. If he were using instead ethnic designations, he would probably call them "Roman citizens" and (more typically for Paul's usage) "Greeks"!

Many doubt that Paul would have risked offending Lycaonians and Phrygians by calling them "Galatians," with its often negative connotations (Gal 3:1).[44] Had Paul been concerned with offense, however, he might have dispensed particularly with the adjective "foolish" that immediately precedes this title.

A more compelling argument for the north Galatian hypothesis is that the letter's audience are former pagans (Gal 4:8–9), a situation that need not be exclusively true in Phrygia.[45] Luke reports that some Jewish people (Acts 14:1; cf. 13:42) and proselytes (Acts 13:43) in Phrygia became followers of Jesus, and Galatians seems to leave no trace of them. But perhaps Paul simply addresses the group most at risk from his rivals (Paul never objected to circumcision of fellow Jews); after all, his arguments about circumcision address only males, but this does not indicate that there were no females among his converts (Gal 3:28).[46]

It is further possible that Paul addresses primarily the gentile believers because most Jewish believers who remain have gone over to the side of his rivals, who claimed Jerusalem backing. Moreover, it appears that the majority of converts in the chief city of the region were gentiles, opposed by the local synagogue (13:45–50); this was apparently true also in Lystra (14:11–20) and surely true of the outlying areas (13:49; 14:6). Luke speaks of just two synagogues in the region (13:14, 43; 14:1; in both cases articular, as if these were the only ones), though there were apparently some Jews in Lystra (even if at least some of them were fairly lax in observing the Torah; Acts 16:1).

---

[44]   E.g., W. A. Meeks, *The First Urban Christians: The Social World of the Apostle Paul* (New Haven, CT: Yale University Press, 1983), 42.

[45]   Martyn, *Galatians*, 15; de Boer, *Galatians*, 5.

[46]   D. A. deSilva, *Global Readings: A Sri Lankan Commentary on Paul's Letter to the Galatians* (Eugene, OR: Cascade, 2011), 22.

Arguments for the South Galatian Hypothesis

Today, the south Galatian hypothesis probably represents the majority view among scholars.[47] Indeed, Stephen Mitchell, possibly today's best-known scholar concerning ancient Anatolia, regards the matter as "beyond dispute."[48] People in the middle of the first century CE called the entire province "Galatia";[49] its boundary ran south of both Pisidian Antioch and Iconium.[50] This area thus includes the regions that Paul and Barnabas evangelized in Acts 13–14.[51]

Southern Galatia had better roads and was far more populated in the first century, and its residents used Greek much more widely than did those of north Galatia. As Stephen Mitchell points out, north Galatia had very few cities to evangelize in Paul's day.[52] At this time North Galatia was sparsely populated, apart from Pessinus or Ancyra, and given the prevalence of local languages Paul could have communicated only with the hellenized upper classes even there.[53]

Although some Jews lived in central Anatolia,[54] there were more Jews in Phrygian (south) Galatia than in the interior.[55] There were enough law-observant Jewish communities in south Galatia (cf. Acts 13:14; 14:1) to make plausible the opponents' arguments that real followers of Israel's God

---

[47] With R. P. C. Hanson, *The Acts in the Revised Standard Version, with Introduction and Commentary* (Oxford: Clarendon, 1967), 19–20; Wright, *Faithfulness*, 808n109, 1304.

[48] S. Mitchell, "Galatia," *ABD* 2:870–72, here 871; cf. Mitchell, *Anatolia*, 2:3.

[49] Mitchell, "Galatia," 871; Mitchell, *Anatolia*, 1:99; 2:155; William Moir Calder and Stephen Mitchell, "Galatia," *OCD*³ 621; B. M. Levick, *Roman Colonies in Southern Asia Minor* (Oxford: Clarendon, 1967), 122, 163.

[50] Levick, *Roman Colonies*, 163n2.

[51] Mitchell, *Anatolia*, 2:4, 155; K. Strobel, "Galatia: Roman Province," *Brill's New Pauly* 5: 650–51; S. Dmitriev, "Observations on the Historical Geography of Roman Lycaonia," *GRBS* 41 (4, 2000): 349–75; G. W. Hansen, "Galatia," pages 377–95 in *The Book of Acts in Its Graeco-Roman Setting* (ed. D. W. J. Gill and C. Gempf; Grand Rapids, MI: Eerdmans, 1994), 378.

[52] Mitchell, *Anatolia*, 1:96.

[53] R. Riesner, *Paul's Early Period*, 282–83; C. Breytenbach, "Probable Reasons for Paul's Unfruitful Missionary Attempts in Asia Minor (A Note on Acts 16:6–7)," pages 157–69 in *Die Apostelgeschichte und die hellenistische Geschichtsschreibung: Festschrift für Eckhard Plümacher zu seinem 65. Geburtstag* (ed. Cilliers Breytenbach and Jens Schröter; Leiden: Brill, 2004), 160.

[54] Betz, *Galatians*, 4–5. De Boer, *Galatians*, 5, notes that none of this evidence belongs to the first century.

[55] See Josephus *Ant.* 12.149; Mitchell, "Galatia," 2:33, 35; M. Stern, "The Jewish Diaspora," 117–83 in *JPFC*, 148–50; E. M. Meyers and A. T. Kraabel, "Archaeology, Iconography, and Nonliterary Written Remains," pages 175–210 in *Early Judaism and Its Modern Interpreters* (ed. R. A. Kraft and G. W. E. Nickelsburg; SBLIMI 2; Atlanta, GA: Scholars Press, 1986), 191.

needed to observe Jewish practices. Why would Paul bypass the region nearer the coast, with a larger Jewish population, for a region where he would have less immediate access to those clearly interested in his God? Perhaps more tellingly, why would Paul's circumcisionist rivals follow him to "the remote interior of Anatolia" when south Galatia "was both accessible and settled by Jews"?[56]

If both the Corinthians (1 Cor 16:1) and Paul's opponents (Gal 1:7; 3:1; 4:17; 5:10–12; 6:12–13) knew the churches of Galatia, how likely is it that Luke, whose itinerary for Paul fairly closely matches the itinerary we can reconstruct from Paul's letters,[57] would be oblivious to them? Yet Luke's narrative includes only Paul's ministry in the southern part of the province.[58] The churches of Galatia that Paul directly addresses are therefore likely centered in the south Galatian area of Pisidian Antioch, Iconium, Lystra, and possibly Derbe.[59] This commentary will therefore periodically note possible connections with Acts 13–14.

OPPONENTS

Whether Paul's rivals initially viewed him as an "opponent" is disputed, but there can be no doubt that he considered them his opponents as well as his rivals for the Galatian believers' allegiance.

Reconstructing opponents by "mirror-reading" can be a precarious exercise, so we should be humble about what we actually know.[60] On the other end of the spectrum, some doubt that any of Paul's negations respond to charges, real or suspected,[61] and maintain that Paul is simply establishing his *êthos*, or character. Moreover, although some rhetoricians suggested that one should not try to anticipate opponents' arguments with counterarguments,[62] such anticipation was

---

[56] Riesner, *Paul's Early Period*, 286.

[57] See T. H. Campbell, "Paul's 'Missionary Journeys' as Reflected in His Letters," *JBL* 74 (2, 1955): 80–87, here 87; C. H. Talbert, *Reading Luke-Acts in Its Mediterranean Milieu* (NovTSup 107; Leiden: Brill, 2003), 203–04.

[58] This includes in Acts 16:6–7; see e.g., Hemer, "Phrygia"; Hemer, "Further Note"; Keener, *Acts*, 2324–30.

[59] Derbe had historic ties with Galatia (Strabo 12.6.3 with 12.5.1; Hansen, "Galatia," 389), though it was not always part of the province (see Mitchell, *Anatolia*, 1:99).

[60] See esp. J. L. Sumney, *Identifying Paul's Opponents: The Question of Method in 2 Corinthians* (JSNTSup 40; Sheffield, UK: JSOT Press, 1990).

[61] Cf. G. Lyons, *Pauline Autobiography: Toward a New Understanding* (SBLDS 73; Atlanta, GA: Scholars Press, 1985), 82–121.

[62] Quintilian *Decl.* 338.6.

common,[63] so at some points Paul may merely try to head off further objections.

But while Paul clearly works to establish his character, he lingers over some potential objections in unusual detail.[64] For example, why does he highlight his limited association with the Jerusalem apostles, even though, given different sorts of charges, such association might count in his favor? In forensic rhetoric, one worked to establish one's character, particularly in matters relevant to the case.[65] The same could be true in other forms of apologetic as well.[66]

Which Opponents?

Although scholars propose a range of identities for Paul's opponents, most scholars believe that Paul's opponents were circumcisionist Jewish Jesus followers[67] but lacked direct support from the movement's leaders in Jerusalem[68] (analogous to those circumcisionists already criticized in Acts 15:24). Probably the opponents saw themselves as motivated by zeal for the law (cf. Paul's experience in Gal 1:14); Paul saw them as succumbing to peer pressure or even threats of persecution (6:12). They were sensitive to non-Christian Jewish hostility over the issue of circumcision (Gal 5:11; 6:12).[69]

Can we discover more specific information about this hostility? Some suggest that the opponents were sensitive to pressure from local synagogues.[70] On the south Galatian hypothesis, this position is tenable and could be correct (see Acts 13:45, 50; 14:2, 4–5, 19). Nevertheless, there are clearly some specific agitators among them, whom Paul appears to treat

---

[63] See e.g., *Rhet. Alex.* 18, 1432b.11–1433b.16; 33, 1439b.2–14; 36, 1442b.4–6; 36, 1443a.6–1443b.14; R. D. Anderson Jr., *Glossary of Greek Rhetorical Terms Connected to Methods of Argumentation, Figures, and Tropes from Anaximenes to Quintilian* (Leuven: Peeters, 2000), 104; Anderson, *Ancient Rhetorical Theory and Paul* (rev. edn. CBET 18; Leuven: Peeters, 1999), 235.

[64] On rhetorical "lingering," see, e.g., Euripides frg. 866; *Rhet. Her.* 4.45.58; Hermogenes *Method* 5.417–18 (for diatribe); Anderson, *Glossary*, 48–49, 53.

[65] E.g., *Rhet. Alex.* 36, 1443b.34–38; Xenophon *Mem.* 4.8.4; *Apol.* 3; Aeschines *Tim.* 181; Lysias *Or.* 19.24, §154; Isaeus *Cleon.* 12.36; 27.37; Cicero *Sull.* 24.68–28.77; *Rosc. com.* 7.21; *Vat.* 10.25–26; Appian *Hist. rom.* 11.7.40–41.

[66] Cf. Josephus's *Ag. Ap.* passim.

[67] E.g., J. L. Martyn, "A Law-Observant Mission to the Gentiles: The Background of Galatians," *SJT* 38 (3, 1985): 307–24; Martyn, *Galatians*, 121–23; T. R. Schreiner, *Galatians* (ZECNT; Grand Rapids, MI: Zondervan, 2010), 49–51.

[68] E.g., C. B. Cousar, *Galatians* (IBC; Atlanta, GA: John Knox, 1982), 5.

[69] So e.g., Cousar, *Galatians*, 5.

[70] A position opposed in Barclay, *Obeying*, 51.

not as errant members of the congregations he planted (1:7; 4:17; 5:10, 12; 6:12–13).

While local Jewish Christian[71] agitators are possible, where would they have come from if they did not belong to the congregations Paul founded? Paul treats them as outside agitators, not members of his communities (Gal 1:6–7; 6:12–13; contrast, e.g., 1 Cor 15:12; 2 Thess 3:11). Paul's opponents apparently claimed more direct links to Jerusalem (cf. Gal 4:25–26 and Paul's emphasis on Jerusalem in 1:17–18; 2:1); given what we know of opposition to Paul in Jerusalem (2:3–4) and the greater concentration of Jewish believers there, it seems likelier that (and more scholars currently argue that) they came from there.

Although the image can be exaggerated, the idea of opponents following one's travels, at least to some locations, in order to undermine a person is not far-fetched. Josephus cites opponents who did just that, seeking to undermine his influence in each city and town, and claiming to represent the leadership in Jerusalem. Josephus had to keep traveling and winning people back.[72] Moreover, other evidence supports the thesis that Jerusalemite believers who insisted on gentile converts' circumcision were propagating their understanding in the Diaspora (Acts 15:1, 24).

If so, they might have been sensitive to local synagogue opposition, but they may have been especially concerned about how other Jerusalemites were perceiving their movement, and what sort of reports local travelers might carry with them to Jerusalem about the gentile-corrupted Jesus movement.

The "false believers" of Gal 2:3–4 had enough of a following in the Jerusalem church to try to force Titus's circumcision, and it is not likely that their ideological conflict with Paul ended when he departed.[73] Martyn contends that "The Teachers' claim to represent the Jerusalem gospel implies a significant connection with a powerful part of the Jerusalem church."[74] That "Jerusalem" appears five times in Galatians – as much as in the rest of his extant letters put together (Rom 15:19, 25–26, 31; 1

---

[71]   Again, given statements such as 1:6–7 and 6:12, these Jewish persons must define themselves as somehow members of Jesus's movement; they are clearly not Jews who dispute Jesus's Messiahship.

[72]   Josephus *Life* 272–75.

[73]   Martyn, *Galatians*, 218.

[74]   Martyn, *Galatians*, 218. Sanders thinks that some Jewish Christians, noting the influx of gentiles, wanted to "take the movement back" (Sanders, *Paul*, 472).

Cor 16:3) – suggests the degree to which this connection remains an issue here (see esp. Gal 4:25–26).

BACKGROUND OF THE ISSUES IN GALATIANS

In the first century, few Jews would consider someone an apostate or a betrayer of one's people for believing that a particular person was a Messiah, controversial as that notion may have been. Treating half-converted gentiles as full members of God's people, however, comes much closer to appearing such a betrayal.[75]

Jews in general held varying views about gentiles, and so apparently did Jesus-believing Judeans.[76] Some Jewish people expected the coming eschatological time to destroy or subjugate gentiles; some expected their conversion.[77] Diaspora Jews who interacted with gentiles more regularly usually held less hardline sentiments than wilderness pietists and rural Judeans.

Various factors gave rise to increasing Judean nationalism in the 40s and 50s, the period of the Antioch conflict (Gal 2:11–14) and the writing of Galatians. This was a time when, not surprisingly, more conservative elements likely gained ground in the Jerusalem church as well (cf. Acts 15:5; 21:20–21).[78]

In the Diaspora, gentile sympathizers often attended synagogues. Apparently, mainstream Jewish thinkers even in Judea believed that gentiles who honored the true God alone and avoided sexual immorality would ultimately share in the world to come. Gentiles who wished to become Jews, however, and thus children of Abraham and heirs of Israel's promised covenant blessings, had to convert, starting with the initiation ritual of circumcision. In cases where such full conversion could generate a backlash against Jews, some Jews might affirm that fearing God was sufficient. Others, however, insisted on circumcision.[79]

---

[75] Cf. D. Ravens, *Luke and the Restoration of Israel* (JSNTSup 119; Sheffield, UK: Sheffield Academic, 1995), 247–49.

[76] Because Galatians is a Diaspora document, "Judea" in this commentary normally designates greater Judea, including Galilee (cf., e.g., Acts 10:37; Pliny *Nat.* 5.15.70), in contrast to my narrower usage in my Gospels commentaries.

[77] See esp. E. P. Sanders, *Jesus and Judaism* (Philadelphia, PA: Fortress, 1985), 213–17; T. L. Donaldson, *Paul and the Gentiles: Remapping the Apostle's Convictional World* (Minneapolis, MN: Fortress, 1997), 52–74.

[78] See, e.g., Josephus *Ant.* 19.326–27, 331–34; Keener, *Acts*, 1869–70, 1875–76.

[79] See Josephus *Ant.* 20.34–48.

In the 30s and early 40s, some leaders of the Jesus movement already recognized, albeit initially reluctantly, that God granted the eschatological Spirit even to gentile believers (Acts 10:45–47; 11:15–18). Thus they received in Christ the restoration-era privilege promised for people of the covenant of which circumcision was the historic physical sign. At the time, gentile converts to the movement were exceptional,[80] but in cosmopolitan Antioch large numbers of gentiles joined the movement (11:19–21). The line between sympathetic observers and full participants is not always clearly defined, and in a city already known for many Jewish sympathizers and proselytes (Acts 6:5),[81] many gentile believers probably became full participants without anyone enforcing the requirement of circumcision.

In Jerusalem, by contrast, more hardline views were coming to the fore, and some teachers from there began chiding Antioch's believers for being too lax (Acts 15:1). Antioch thus sent a delegation, which included the influential Paul and Barnabas, to consult with Jerusalem's leaders (15:2). In his pastoral role, Jesus's younger brother James, leader of the Jesus movement in Jerusalem, had greater concern for preserving the movement's unity at home than for what happened abroad. He and the other top leaders of the movement nevertheless risked strife at home by accommodating the Antioch delegation's position that gentile believers did not have to be circumcised (Gal 2:3, 7–9; Acts 15:5–6, 19–20; 21:25).

In return, Paul was clear that he was not undercutting circumcision for Jews or the Torah-observant mission (Gal 2:7–9; cf. Acts 15:21; 21:21–26; 1 Cor 7:18–19). Jerusalem also expected, however, that gentile believers would meet basic standards that Jews expected of righteous gentiles (Acts 15:20; cf. Gal 2:10). Paul and perhaps other members of the Antioch delegation regarded gentile believers as full converts (cf. Gal 3:29), but for the agreement it was sufficient that they be regarded as righteous gentiles, like Jewish sympathizers who attended synagogues.

The compromise satisfied the chief leaders on both sides who brokered the agreement, but some prominent, well-educated, Torah-observant Jerusalem Jesus believers, probably including some of the elders, had wanted more (Acts 15:5–6; Gal 2:4). Their concerns must have seemed confirmed when some Judean travelers close to James found Peter himself, a

---

[80] Luke emphasizes Cornelius as a model from hindsight, but at the time he was probably considered an anomaly (J. D. G. Dunn, *Beginning from Jerusalem* [Grand Rapids, MN: Eerdmans, 2009], 446, 456).

[81] Josephus *War* 7.45.

respected leader in the mission among his own people (Gal 2:7–9), compromising scrupulous Judean standards of table fellowship in Antioch (Gal 2:12). Undoubtedly hoping to keep peace (cf. 1 Cor 9:20–21), Peter and his fellow Judeans returned to the more scrupulous Judean practice for the sake of the new visitors.

An accommodation probably meant to prevent offending Judean conservatives, however, confused and hurt the gentile believers. Table fellowship was an important mark of acceptance and friendship. If accommodating Jewish visitors took precedence over long-standing ties among fellow believers in Antioch, then gentile Christians were in effect second class, merely sympathizers and not full members of God's people.

This behavior implied that to *really* be *full* members of God's people, gentiles would have to become Jews (Gal 2:14). Short of that, it shattered the Antioch church's unity along ethnic lines – and shattered it severely. In the ancient Mediterranean world, rejecting friendship ties typically created enmity,[82] and enmity after enjoying table fellowship was deemed a particularly heinous form of betrayal.[83]

Paul naturally saw this behavior as breaching the Jerusalem agreement and even undercutting the understanding of the gospel that he and Peter shared (Gal 2:14, 16). The issue was so important that Paul broke normal protocol (valued even by himself, 6:1) and rebuked Peter publicly. Whatever the immediate outcome, Paul undoubtedly alienated the Judean visitors, who probably took a bad report back to Jerusalem. Rumors spread in Jerusalem: if Paul embraced gentiles without giving them the law and making them Jews, it did not seem far-fetched to them that he was also turning Jews from practicing the law (Acts 21:20–21), and therefore undercutting biblical morality (Rom 3:8; cf. 2 Cor 6:8).

At the time of Antioch's agreement with Jerusalem regarding circumcision, Judean circumcision conservatives had gotten no farther than Syria-Cilicia (Acts 15:23), Paul's earlier sphere of ministry (Gal 1:21–23), and its capital, Antioch (Acts 14:26–15:1). By the time Paul writes Galatians, however, some had crossed the Taurus mountains into the region of Paul's

---

[82]   P. Marshall, *Enmity in Corinth: Social Conventions in Paul's Relations with the Corinthians* (WUNT 2.23; Tübingen: Mohr Siebeck, 1987), 13–21. At the least such a refusal could show contempt (Pliny *Ep.* 8.6.9).

[83]   E.g., Homer *Il.* 21.76; *Od.* 4.534–35; 11.414–20; 14.404–5; Hesiod *W.D.* 327; Euripides *Cycl.* 126–28; *Hec.* 25–26, 710–20, 850–56; Apollonius Rhodius 3.377–80; Ovid *Metam.* 1.144; 10.225–28; Livy 25.16.6.

Galatian mission, following up his work by offering "sounder" teaching to his churches.

What Did These Opponents Believe?

We can attempt to reconstruct the beliefs of Paul's opponents in Galatia only by cautiously mirror-reading his letter. This strategy is precarious because Paul is not presenting them as they would present themselves, because Paul's informants may not have given him a fully complete or balanced picture, and because Paul's responses could be understood as addressing various issues. Nevertheless, we have a fair sense of their ultimate short-range objective – circumcising Galatian believers. We also have good reason to believe that Paul's scriptural argumentation in 3:6–5:1 responds to their arguments, since many of the texts chosen appear on the surface more persuasive for their position than for his.[84] That Paul can respond to opponents on this level of detail suggests that Paul probably had a supportive informant, further suggesting that not literally *everyone* in the church was succumbing to his rivals' teachings.

Presumably Paul's opponents believed that Paul had compromised the message of Jesus by not explaining that following the Jewish Messiah entailed keeping the Jewish law.

Apparently central to the argument of Paul's rivals, and undoubtedly particularly persuasive, circumcision was the essential sign of the covenant from Abraham forward (Gen 17:9–14).[85] It was not required for gentile sojourners but it was necessary for those wanting to become part of God's people (Gen 34:22; Exod 12:48).[86] Those who wished to commit themselves fully to Israel's God must therefore be circumcised (Gal 5:3). Paul's teaching to the Galatians had therefore been incomplete.[87] Indeed, in contrast to Israelites born in the covenant of grace, *gentile converts* had to adopt

---

[84] Barclay, *Obeying*, 53; Martyn, *Galatians*, 306; Das, *Stories*, 221; cf. Schreiner, *Galatians*, 34–35.

[85] With, e.g., E. P. Sanders, *Paul, the Law, and the Jewish People* (Philadelphia, PA: Fortress, 1983), 18; Barclay, *Obeying*, 53; Fee, *Galatians*, 113; slightly more tentatively, see Schreiner, *Galatians*, 34–35. Although some suggest that they also appealed to Moses (cf. 2 Cor 3:7–15; B. H. Brinsmead, *Galatians, Dialogical Response to Opponents* [SBLDS 65; Chico, CA: Scholars Press, 1982], 200), Galatians strongly focuses on Abraham, only hinting at Moses (Gal 3:19–20).

[86] With, e.g., Sanders, *Paul, the Law and the Jewish People*, 18; Cousar, *Galatians*, 4.

[87] Cf. J. S. Vos, "Paul's Argumentation in Galatians 1–2," *HTR* 87 (1, 1994): 1–16.

elements of a culture foreign to them, which might even seem like having to *earn* salvation.[88]

Paul will respond that Christ has brought a stage in salvation history beyond the law, a stage in continuity with (by fulfillment of) the promise to Abraham (3:17–25). The law's stipulations were needed like a pedagogue or guardian to discipline God's immature children (3:22–4:4), but the era of fulfillment provides maturity for God's children, rendering superfluous literal adherence to all the law's stipulations. The law was never designed to save (Gal 2:21; 3:21), only to preserve Israel's identity and to instruct in moral principles. But gentile believers did not need that distinctive ethnic identity, and the Spirit makes less relevant the law's particulars as an external standard, since it inscribes in believers' hearts the essential moral and spiritual message to which the law attested (cf. 5:14, 16, 18, 22–23; 2 Cor 3:3; Jer 31:33; Ezek 36:26–27). For Paul, the Spirit confirmed gentile believers as members of the eschatological covenant people (cf. Isa 44:3; Ezek 36:27; 37:34, 39; Joel 2:28–29).

Paul's rivals, however, believed that Paul had compromised. If God gave gentiles the Spirit, it was to invite them into covenant practice. Like some other strict interpreters from the holy land, they believed that any special concessions about circumcision violated a chief commandment.[89] Paul may have fancied himself an apostle, but he did not follow Jesus during his earthly ministry like the Twelve real apostles (cf. Gal 1:17–19; 2:9). Not only did he see Jesus only long after the first resurrection appearances (cf. 1 Cor 15:8), but he had persecuted Jesus's followers until that point (cf. 1 Cor 15:9; Gal 1:13)! Worst of all, Paul's law-free gospel undermined biblical morality, a charge to which Paul must respond briefly in Gal 2:16–21 and, at greatest length, in chs. 5–6.

Like Paul, his rivals apparently knew the Torah. They may have claimed that many in Jerusalem, the mother city, supported them and mistrusted Paul. This does not mean that they were authorized by the chief apostles (cf. earlier Acts 15:24); Paul would probably mention any kind of letters of authorization or recommendation (2 Cor 3:1). They could, however, appeal to the law-observant *behavior* of Peter and especially James in Jerusalem.[90]

---

[88] Although this idea was rarely articulated so explicitly, in the late source Num. Rab. 8:9, proselytes had no ancestral merits on which to rely, but had to gain the world to come by their own merit.

[89] See Josephus *Ant.* 20.43–45.

[90] Cf. also Barclay, *Obeying*, 59. Later rabbis could even appeal to the behavior of earlier rabbis for halakhic precedent; see e.g., t. Piska 2:15–16; Sipre Deut. 221.1.1. Christians even in the Pauline circle continued to cede a special authority or relevance to Jerusalem (Rom

Barclay, Obeying, 68–69, citing Josephus Ag. Ap. 2.282.

(Paul, by contrast, will have a different side of the story to recount about Peter in Antioch – Gal 2:12!)

Paul did, however, have some advantages over his rivals: he was the one who had ushered them into the faith and their undeniable experience of the Spirit (3:1–3; 4:19). Further, willing as the Galatians may have been to undergo circumcision if it was necessary, they would likely be happy to be persuaded that it was not.

Paul's rivals probably did not just try to supplement his teaching; they also tried to undermine his authority that stood behind his teaching.[91] "From now on, let no one make trouble for me" (Gal 6:17) suggests that his critics had been doing just that. Challenging the êthos, or character, of one's opponents was conventional polemic.[92] This is one reason that we should not play off Paul's defense of his êthos in 1:13–2:21 against the idea that he defends himself against charges. That Paul accuses his antagonists of not keeping the law themselves (Gal 6:13) is a natural reply to those who deemed him antinomian (Acts 21:21; Rom 3:8); it was standard practice to return the accusations of one's accusers in kind.[93]

Why the Opponents' Arguments Appealed to Galatian Christians

How could gentiles initially persuaded by apostolic signs and their experience with the Spirit now be swayed? Several factors may be involved. One may be the opponents' Jerusalem connection, if they claimed one.

Ancient sources also suggest another possible social factor. Judaism was popular with many gentiles, who sometimes adopted various practices such as special days, lamps, and some food customs.[94] If male gentile sympathizers wanted to follow the full path to Jewish practice, they would embrace circumcision. Diaspora Jews' success in gaining converts in many locations sometimes inflamed pagan sentiment against them; most polytheists did

---

15:19, 25–27; Gal 2:1) or to Jerusalem leaders or other "authentic" Jewish Christians (2 Cor 11:22; Gal 1:17, 22; 2:9; Phil 3:5; cf. 1 Cor 1:12; Col 4:11; 1 Thess 2:14).

[91] So most scholars, e.g., J. B. Tyson, "Paul's Opponents in Galatia," NovT 10 (1968): 241–54, here 249; Schreiner, Galatians, 34.

[92] E.g., Lysias Or. 10.2, §116; 12.1, §120; Rhet. Alex. 4, 1426b.29–35; Cicero Scaur. 13.29; Verr. 2.2.48.118; Tacitus Ann. 3.12; Apuleius Apol. 1, 25; Hermogenes Inv. 1.1.99; 1.2.102–03; 1.3.104; Method 5.418.

[93] E.g., Euripides Cretans frg. 472e.33–35; Xenophon Hell. 2.3.37; Aeschines Embassy 3, 69; Ctes. 113, 156, 259; Tim. 179; Thucydides 3.61.1; Rhet. Alex. 36, 1442b.6–9; Cicero Sest. 37.80; Quinct. 3.11–9.33; Rosc. Amer. 30.82–45.132; Pliny Ep. 3.9.29; 4.9.20; 6.22.2, 4; 7.33.7.

[94] Barclay, Obeying, 68–69, citing Josephus Ag. Ap. 2.282.

not appreciate what they viewed as intolerant repudiation of other gods and ethnic realignment.[95]

Christians who did not belong to synagogues did not fit anywhere on the social grid.[96] Circumcision was costly, but so was the social isolation that left them as a celebratory community of only other Christians (perhaps not all of them friendly, Gal 5:15). Circumcision also had another possible benefit: by explaining why these gentiles could no longer participate in civic cults, including that of the emperor, it removed their responsibility for doing so.

STRUCTURE

For a letter as grammatically disordered as Galatians sometimes is, its structure appears remarkably well organized. The letter body, the only part of the structure reasonably open to dispute, naturally divides into three sections: narrative (1:6–2:21, or at least 1:13–2:14); more direct proofs (3:1–5:12; or, in some outlines, 3:1–5:1); and exhortation and ethics (5:13–6:10, or, in some outlines, 5:1–6:10).[97] The arguments of the central section include appeal to past experience (3:1–5; and, with intense pathos, 4:12–20), two lines of argument that employ Scripture (3:6–4:11; 4:21–5:1) and Paul's strongest confrontation (5:2–12; this last section, 5:2–12 or 5:1–12, is often included instead in the hortatory section).

Those who read Galatians as a sort of written oration arrange the letter the way they would a speech of a given (usually deliberative or judicial) rhetorical genre.[98] Because much of Paul's letter is argumentation, characteristic features of many speeches do appear in Galatians, more clearly than in many of his other letters, particularly in an introductory narrative followed by proofs. Those who read it simply as a letter naturally structure it according to basic epistolary conventions, such as prescript, body, and

---

[95]   See J. G. Gager, *The Origins of Anti-Semitism: Attitudes toward Judaism in Pagan and Christian Antiquity* (New York: Oxford University Press, 1983), 55–56; M. Whittaker, *Jews and Christians: Graeco-Roman Views* (CCWJCW 6; Cambridge: Cambridge University Press, 1984), 85–91; Z. Yavetz, "Judeophobia in Classical Antiquity: A Different Approach," *JJS* 44 (1993): 1–22.

[96]   Sanders, *Paul*, 115–17, 198–203, 312.

[97]   With, e.g., Lightfoot, *Galatians*, 65–67.

[98]   See, e.g., Betz, *Galatians*, 16. For a survey of proposals, see S. E. Porter, "Paul of Tarsus and His Letters," pages 533–85 in *Handbook of Classical Rhetoric in the Hellenistic Period, 330 B.C.–A.D. 400* (ed. S. E. Porter; Leiden: Brill, 1997), 541–47.

conclusion (an obvious arrangement perhaps no more enlightening than it is controversial).[99]

One particularly noteworthy aspect of the structure for almost anyone's account is the turn to ethics in 5:13–6:10. If Paul's opponents promote law-observance as anything like a path to liberation from passion, Paul must offer an alternative and superior ethical path through the Spirit in Christ (see 5:16–18, 25; 6:2).[100] Both may have seen obedience as a response to grace, but for Paul grace has inaugurated an eschatological new creation, in which obedience is the fruit of God-implanted desire for divine matters that reflects God's character of love.

RHETORIC AND GALATIANS

Despite grammatical lapses, Galatians is full of conventional rhetorical devices such as antithetical word pairs (devices familiar even to those without any necessary training in rhetoric).[101] Still, it exhibits fewer of such devices than any of Paul's undisputed letters except for the personal letter to Philemon.[102] Most rhetorical elements in Paul had long been part of Greek language without requiring formal knowledge of rhetoric.[103]

Regarding more formal rhetorical elements, scholars' views diverge more widely.[104] Many scholars have offered rhetorical analyses of Galatians.[105] Ancient Christian thinkers trained in rhetoric, such as Chrysostom, also took rhetorical principles into account when reading Galatians, though

---

[99] With R. B. Hays, "The Letter to the Galatians: Introduction, Commentary, and Reflections," 11:181–348 in *The New Interpreter's Bible* (12 vols.; Nashville, TN: Abingdon, 2000), 187–88. But see J. L. White, *The Form and Function of the Body of the Greek Letter: A Study of the Letter-Body in the Non-literary Papyri and in Paul the Apostle* (SBLDS 2; Missoula, MT: Society of Biblical Literature, 1972), 154, 159.

[100] Cf. Barclay, *Obeying*.

[101] J. D. Harvey, *Listening to the Text: Oral Patterning in Paul's Letters* (Grand Rapids, MI: Baker, 1998), 217–30.

[102] Harvey, *Listening*, 286.

[103] C. J. Classen, *Rhetorical Criticism of the New Testament* (Boston, MA: Brill Academic, 2002), 29.

[104] For surveys, see D. E. Aune, *The Westminster Dictionary of New Testament and Early Christian Literature and Rhetoric* (Louisville, KY: Westminster John Knox, 2003), 192–94; esp. Anderson, *Rhetorical Theory*, 129–42.

[105] E.g., W. B. Russell, "Rhetorical Analysis of the Book of Galatians, Parts 1 and 2," *BSac* 150 (1993): 341–58, 416–39; Vos, "Argumentation"; L. L. Cranford, "A Rhetorical Reading of Galatians," *Southwestern Journal of Theology* 37 (1, 1994): 4–10; Anderson, *Rhetorical Theory*, 142–89. For a synchronic, nonclassical rhetorical analysis, see R. N. Longenecker, *Galatians* (WBC 41; Grand Rapids, MI: Zondervan, 1990), cxiv–cxix.

they recognized that Paul was not an orator.[106] Nevertheless, ancient rhetorical critics who found rhetorical devices in Paul's letters did not claim wholesale rhetorical structures (macrorhetoric).[107]

Some scholars try to classify the letter according to one of the major three rhetorical categories treated in typical rhetorical handbooks: epideictic, forensic, or deliberative. Following Betz, who inaugurated contemporary rhetorical criticism of Galatians, some contend that the letter is forensic, given Paul's defense of himself against detractors. The hortatory section (5:13–6:10), however, does not fit expectations for forensic rhetoric.[108] More often, scholars treat Galatians as deliberative, noting that Paul is seeking to persuade the Galatian believers to change their course of action.[109]

To some degree, the division of even speeches into these three major rhetorical categories is too artificial.[110] The categories proved most useful for rhetorical students or professional declaimers whose speeches would be evaluated by category, but theory did not always influence practice. Most important, these genres are rarely relevant for *letters*. Put simply, letters were not speeches.[111] Later epistolary handbooks treat them differently.[112]

Speech outlines do not fit letters even in collections from orators such as Cicero, Pliny, and Fronto. Thus rhetorical critic David deSilva notes that "most attempts at outlining" letters "are forced," though he recognizes that "Galatians comes *closer* to fitting this overall outline than any other

---

[106] M. Heath, "John Chrysostom, Rhetoric and Galatians," *Biblical Interpretation* 12 (2004): 369–400. For patristic and Reformers' rhetorical approaches to Paul, see C. J. Classen, "St. Paul's Epistles and Ancient Greek and Roman Rhetoric," *Rhetorica* 10 (1992): 319–44; Harvey, *Listening*, 22–23.

[107] S. A. Cooper, "Narratio and Exhortatio in Galatians According to Marius Victorinus Rhetor," *ZNW* 91 (2000): 107–35.

[108] G. A. Kennedy, *New Testament Interpretation through Rhetorical Criticism* (Chapel Hill: University of North Carolina Press, 1984), 145; Witherington, *Grace*, 28; R. F. Hock, "Paul and Greco-Roman Education," pages 198–227 in *Paul in the Greco-Roman World: A Handbook* (ed. J. P. Sampley; Harrisburg, PA: Trinity Press International, 2003), 214.

[109] Kennedy, *Interpretation*, 145–46; R. G. Hall, "The Rhetorical Outline for Galatians: A Reconsideration," *JBL* 106 (1987): 277–87; D. E. Aune, *The New Testament in Its Literary Environment* (LEC 8; Philadelphia, PA: Westminster, 1987), 206–07; Witherington, *Grace*, 31 (noting Quintilian *Inst.* 3.8.12); Hays, "Galatians," 189.

[110] For mixed genres, see Aune, *Dictionary of Rhetoric*, 419.

[111] Anderson, *Rhetorical Theory*, 114–21 (esp. 114–17), 280–81; J. T. Reed, "The Epistle," pages 171–93 in *Handbook of Classical Rhetoric in the Hellenistic Period, 330 B.C.–A.D. 400* (ed. S. E. Porter; Leiden: Brill, 1997).

[112] Classen, *Rhetorical Criticism*, 6.

New Testament text."[113] Indeed, Philip Kern's particularly detailed study of Galatians finds no clear relationship of this letter to conventional rhetorical genres or structures.[114]

Rhetoric affected letters' style more than structure,[115] but even here there were limits. Generally ancient letters were supposed to be conversational.[116] Cicero used common language in his letters; for "What similarity is there between a letter, and a speech in court or at a public meeting?"[117]

Thus some scholars severely question studies of macrorhetoric in Paul.[118] Many recognize rhetorical elements in Paul's letters, while stopping short of outlining them as if they were speeches per se.[119] But the matter remains disputed. Even given all the preceding caveats, just as ancient epistolography helps us understand the epistolary character of Paul's letters, ancient rhetoric helps us to appreciate the character of Paul's argumentation.[120]

Paul's letters are plainly not speeches. Nevertheless, apart from Philemon, they also differ from ordinary letters, which averaged roughly eighty-seven words long, whereas Paul's letters average 2,495 words (and 7,114 for Romans).[121] Ancient critics would regard such long letters as more like essays than letters.[122] Moreover, the level of Greek in Paul's letters far exceeds the level found in typical papyri.[123] Unlike most other letters, Paul's letters usually contain argumentation, which naturally includes conventional rhetorical elements.

---

[113] deSilva, *Readings*, 48.
[114] P. H. Kern, *Rhetoric and Galatians: Assessing an Approach to Paul's Epistle* (SNTSM 101; Cambridge: Cambridge University Press, 1998), esp. 258–59.
[115] Porter, "Paul and Letters," 567–68, 585.
[116] So Seneca *Ep. Lucil.* 75.1–3.
[117] Cicero *Fam.* 9.21.1 (trans. W. G. Williams, LCL 2:261).
[118] E.g., J. A. D. Weima, "What Does Aristotle Have to Do with Paul? An Evaluation of Rhetorical Criticism," *CTJ* 32 (1997): 458–68; M. P. Surburg, "Ancient Rhetorical Criticism, Galatians, and Paul at Twenty-five Years," *Concordia Journal* 30 (2004): 13–39.
[119] E.g., Anderson, *Rhetorical Theory*, 127; Classen, "Rhetoric."
[120] Recognizing the value of both, see e.g., A. C. Thiselton, *The First Epistle to the Corinthians: A Commentary on the Greek Text* (Grand Rapids, MI: Eerdmans, 2000), 42–46.
[121] Anderson, *Rhetorical Theory*, 113. Cicero's letters average roughly 300 words and Seneca's about 1,000 (L. Morris, *The Epistle to the Romans* [Grand Rapids, MI: Eerdmans, 1988], 1).
[122] See Demetrius *Style* 4.228.
[123] See E. A. Judge, *The First Christians in the Roman World: Augustan and New Testament Essays* (ed. J. R. Harrison; WUNT 229; Tübingen: Mohr Siebeck, 2008), 710–11; Anderson, *Rhetorical Theory*, 113–14.

LETTERS AND GALATIANS

Whatever else Paul's letter to the Galatians is, it is a letter. Many scholars therefore rightly appeal to epistolary theory to interpret Paul's letters.[124] Although epistolary theory's key insights shed the most light on the openings and closings of Paul's letters, various features and characteristics of ancient letters shed light on Paul throughout his letters, as references to them in this commentary will illustrate.

Still, epistolary analysis of Paul's letters has its limitations; as noted earlier, Paul's letters are quite unlike most letters found in the papyri and even literary letter collections. Exhortation, which is common in Paul's letters, is much more characteristic of moral philosophy than of the interests addressed in rhetorical handbooks;[125] the closest analogy to this particular feature, then, might be letters such as Seneca's letters to Lucilius or the pseudepigraphic Cynic epistles.

Many scholars regard Galatians as a letter of blame, a characteristic certainly present in the letter.[126] Galatians may include elements of blame, reproach, and apologetic, depending on the definitions employed.[127] Still, ancient moral philosophy provides more examples of harsh rebukes (such as Gal 3:1) than does ancient epistolary theory.[128]

But just as it is premature to assume that Paul's letters must fit standardized genres of ancient rhetoric, it is also premature to assume that they will fit handbooks' overlapping and potentially arbitrary epistolary classifications.

A letter the length of Galatians would have taken several hours to copy,[129] plus several hours more to produce the backup copy (and still more if he produced earlier drafts on reusable material).[130] It would have consumed

---

[124] E.g., A. A. Das, *Galatians* (ConcC; Saint Louis, MO: Concordia Publishing House, 2014), 63; see esp. J. A. D. Weima, *Paul the Ancient Letter Writer: An Introduction to Epistolary Analysis* (Grand Rapids, MI: Baker Academic, 2016).

[125] S. K. Stowers, *Letter Writing in Greco-Roman Antiquity* (LEC 5; Philadelphia, PA: Westminster, 1986), 52.

[126] Stowers, *Letter Writing*, 133–34.

[127] Cf. rebuke-request in G. W. Hansen, *Abraham in Galatians – Epistolary and Rhetorical Contexts* (JSNTSup 29; Sheffield: Sheffield Academic Press, 1989), 22–44, esp. 34–43.

[128] Anderson, *Rhetorical Theory*, 161. Even most moralists, however, sought to avoid inflicting more pain than necessary (see Plutarch *Statecraft* 14, *Mor.* 810C; Stowers, *Letter Writing*, 133–34; D. E. Fredrickson, "Paul, Hardships, and Suffering," pages 172–97 in *Paul in the Greco-Roman World: A Handbook* [ed. J. P. Sampley; Harrisburg, PA: Trinity Press International, 2003], 176).

[129] E. R. Richards, *Paul and First-Century Letter Writing: Secretaries, Composition, and Collection* (Downers Grove, IL: InterVarsity, 2004), 165.

[130] For production of second copies of important letters for personal records, see Richards, *Letter Writing*, 158–59.

almost half a "standard" sized papyrus roll;[131] the cost for the papyrus and a scribe for writing for both copies may be estimated at roughly 6.56 denarii, or in today's currency, roughly \$722.[132] As opposed to a short note on a scrap of papyrus or an oral greeting, Galatians was a significant task undertaken to address a significant problem.

POLEMIC

Chrysostom noted Paul's passion in Galatians, and that such "vehemence" was sometimes needed.[133] However we classify Galatians specifically, it seethes with negative emotion.[134] Paul either simulated anger for rhetorical purposes[135] or, more likely, was genuinely angry – an anger mixed with hurt and fear for his converts (Gal 4:11; cf. 2 Cor 7:5; 11:28; 1 Thess 3:5).

Some of Paul's critiques in Galatians are harsh (esp. 5:12), though – against a significant line of Christian tradition – their object is not ethnic Judaism but a group of fellow Jewish Christians who were imposing their customs on gentiles.[136] Following ancient rhetorical practice, Paul caricaturizes his opponents, reducing their positions to the absurd. Readers today must take this practice into account when reading Galatians, comparing Paul's theology expressed in his less polemical letters. Paul would have surely recoiled to learn that a later gentile-dominated church exploited his words against his own people, whom he loved (cf. Rom 9:1–5; 11:1–5, 17–31).[137]

Scholars too often extrapolate Paul's theology about the law or the Jewish people from Galatians without recognizing that on some points Galatians presents only Paul's most extreme position. In the face of his opponents' accusations, he could afford to argue only one side of the case. His later

---

[131] Richards, *Letter Writing*, 169.
[132] Richards, *Letter Writing*, 169, using 2004 costs.
[133] Chrysostom *Hom. Gal.* 1.1–3, on Gal 1:1 (Edwards).
[134] Indeed characteristic of invective rhetoric (blame; Quintilian *Inst.* 6.2.20).
[135] Cf. Isocrates *To Nicocles* 23.
[136] With Martyn, *Galatians*, 36–37; W. Campbell, "Paul, Antisemitism, and Early Christian Identity Formation," pages 301–40 in *Paul the Jew: Rereading the Apostle as a Figure of Second Temple Judaism* (ed. G. Boccaccinni and C. A. Segovia; Minneapolis, MN: Fortress, 2016), 310.
[137] Cf., e.g., C. A. Segovia, "Discussing/Subverting Paul: Polemical Rereadings and Competing Supersessionist Misreadings of Pauline Inclusivism in Late Antiquity: A Case Study on the Apocalypse of Abraham, Justin Martyr, and the Qur'an," pages 341–61 in *Paul the Jew: Rereading the Apostle as a Figure of Second Temple Judaism* (2016), 341.

arguments in Romans are more nuanced and tell us more about how Paul would argue when he was in a less urgent situation.[138]

Was Paul's letter to the Galatians effective?

Many scholars suggest that believers in Galatia rejected Paul's pleas and followed the path of circumcision. Thus, they note, although Paul mentions Galatian involvement in the collection in 1 Cor 16:1, he omits them in 2 Cor 8–9 and Rom 15:25–27.[139] Against this argument from silence, however, Paul also omits Asia in those passages, yet Luke's list of representatives for Paul's Jerusalem visit includes members from Asia and possibly from Derbe and (clearly in the Galatian province) Lystra (Acts 20:4).

Others respond that the very fact that Galatian believers preserved Paul's letter suggests that they honored it.[140] Whatever the short-term effect in Galatia, however, Paul's letter was effective in the long run for the wider gentile church, which followed Paul in allowing admission to the covenant community without circumcision.

---

[138] Barclay, *Obeying*, 210–11; T. G. Gombis, "Arguing with Scripture in Galatia: Galatians 3:10–14 as a Series of Ad Hoc Arguments," pages 82–90 in *Galatians and Christian Theology: Justification, the Gospel, and Ethics in Paul's Letter* (ed. M. W. Elliott et al.; Grand Rapids, MI: Baker Academic, 2014), 82–83.

[139] E.g., de Boer, *Galatians*, 411.

[140] With, e.g., Dunn, *Galatians*, 277; Das, *Galatians*, 19.

II Select Suggested Readings on Galatians

Works on Galatians continue to be published regularly.[1] It is therefore possible only to engage select recent commentators here. Those wanting fuller
surveys of earlier commentators will find them in the major academic commentators I am engaging.

HEAVILY ACADEMIC COMMENTARIES

H. D. Betz, *A Commentary on Paul's Letter to the Churches in Galatia*
(Hermeneia; Philadelphia, PA: Fortress, 1979).

M. C. de Boer, *Galatians: A Commentary* (Louisville, KY: Westminster John
Knox, 2011).

F. F. Bruce, *The Epistle to the Galatians* (NIGTC; Grand Rapids, MI:
Eerdmans, 1982).

E. W. Burton, *A Critical and Exegetical Commentary on the Epistle to the
Galatians* (Edinburgh: T. & T. Clark, 1921).

A. A. Das, *Galatians* (ConcC; Saint Louis, MO: Concordia Publishing
House, 2014).

R. Y. K. Fung, *The Epistle to the Galatians* (NICNT; Grand Rapids MI:
Eerdmans, 1988).

J. B. Lightfoot, *Saint Paul's Epistle to the Galatians: A Revised Text with
Introduction, Notes, and Dissertations* (New York: Macmillan and
Co., 1896).

R. N. Longenecker, *Galatians* (WBC 41; Grand Rapids, MI: Zondervan, 1990).

---

[1]   See, e.g., M. A. Seifrid, "A Select Bibliography of Commentaries on Galatians," *Review and
Expositor* 91 (1994): 219–24; D. F. Tolmie, "Research on the Letter to the Galatians: 2000–
2010," *Acta Theologica* 32 (2012): 118–57.

J. L. Martyn, *Galatians: A New Translation with Introduction and Commentary* (New York: Doubleday, 1997).

D. J. Moo, *Galatians* (BECNT; Grand Rapids, MI: Baker Academic, 2013).

F. Mussner, *Der Galaterbrief* (5th edn.; HTKNT 9; Freiburg: Herder, 1988).

T. R. Schreiner, *Galatians* (ZECNT; Grand Rapids, MI: Zondervan, 2010).

LESS TECHNICAL COMMENTARIES

J. Bligh, *Galatians: A Discussion of St Paul's Epistle* (London: St Paul, 1970).

A. M. Buscemi, *Lettera ai Galati: Commentario esegetico* (SBFA 63; Jerusalem: Franciscan Printing Press, 2004).

C. B. Cousar, *Galatians* (IBC; Atlanta, GA: John Knox, 1982).

J. D. G. Dunn, *The Epistle to the Galatians* (BNTC; London: A&C Black; Peabody, MA: Hendrickson, 1995).

S. Eastman, "Galatians," pages 825–32 in *The New Interpreter's Bible One Volume Commentary* (ed. B. R. Gaventa and D. Petersen; Nashville, TN: Abingdon, 2010).

G. D. Fee, *Galatians: Pentecostal Commentary* (Blandford Forum, Dorset, UK: Deo, 2007).

G. W. Hansen, *Galatians* (IVPNTC; Downers Grove, IL: InterVarsity Press, 1994).

R. B. Hays, "The Letter to the Galatians: Introduction, Commentary, and Reflections," 11:181–348 in *NIB*.

G. Lyons, *Galatians: A Commentary in the Wesleyan Tradition* (New Beacon Bible Commentary; Kansas City, MO: Beacon Hill Press, 2012).

F. J. Matera, *Galatians* (SP 9; Collegeville, MN: Liturgical Press, 1992).

W. Neil, *The Letter of Paul to the Galatians* (CBC; Cambridge: Cambridge University Press, 1967).

P. Oakes, *Galatians* (Paideia Commentaries on the New Testament; Grand Rapids, MI: Baker Academic, 2015).

M. Silva, "Galatians," pages 785–812 in *Commentary on the New Testament Use of the Old Testament* (ed. G. K. Beale and D. A. Carson; Grand Rapids, MI: Baker Academic, 2007).

M. L. Soards and D. J. Pursiful, *Galatians* (SHBC; Macon, GA: Smith & Helwys, 2015).

B. Witherington III, *Grace in Galatia: A Commentary on St Paul's Letter to the Galatians* (Edinburgh: T&T Clark; Grand Rapids, MI: Eerdmans, 1998).

HISTORY OF INTERPRETATION

Many ancient and medieval sources in this commentary are from Bray, Edwards, or Levy.[2]

G. Bray, ed., *Galatians, Ephesians* (Reformation Commentary on Scripture, NT 10; Downers Grove, IL: IVP Academic, 2011).

M. J. Edwards, ed., *Galatians, Ephesians, Philippians* (ACCS, NT 8. Downers Grove, IL: InterVarsity, 1999).

I. C. Levy, translator and editor. *The Letter to the Galatians* (The Bible in Medieval Tradition; Grand Rapids, MI: Eerdmans, 2011).

J. Riches, *Galatians through the Centuries* (Malden, MA: Wiley-Blackwell, 2013).

READINGS FROM SOME PARTICULAR SOCIAL LOCATIONS

B. R. Braxton, "Galatians," pages 333–46 in *True to Our Native Land: An African American New Testament Commentary* (ed. B. K. Blount; Minneapolis, MN: Fortress, 2007).

D. A. deSilva, *Global Readings: A Sri Lankan Commentary on Paul's Letter to the Galatians* (Eugene, OR: Cascade, 2011).

R. T. George, *Paul's Identity in Galatians: A Postcolonial Appraisal* (New Delhi: Christian World Imprints, 2016).

A. C. Niang, *Faith and Freedom in Galatia and Senegal: The Apostle Paul, Colonists and Sending Gods* (BibInt 97; Leiden, Boston, MA: Brill, 2009).

H. Le Cornu with J. Shulam, *A Commentary on the Jewish Roots of Galatians* (Jerusalem: Academon, Netivyah Bible Instruction Ministry, 2005).

S. M. Ngewa, *Galatians* (Africa Bible Commentary; Grand Rapids, MI: Hippo, 2010).

F. Philip, "Galatians," pages 1615–30 in *South Asia Bible Commentary* (ed. B. Wintle; Udaipur, India: Open Door, 2015).

SOME OF THE STUDIES OFTEN CITED IN THE COMMENTARY
OR IN GALATIANS RESEARCH

J.-N. Aletti, "Galates 1–2: Quelle fonction et quelle démonstration?" *Biblica* 86 (3, 2005): 305–23.

---

[2]   Regarding patristic commentaries on Galatians, see J. B. Lightfoot, *Saint Paul's Epistle to the Galatians: A Revised Text with Introduction, Notes, and Dissertations* (New York: Macmillan and Co., 1896), 227–36.

R. D. Anderson Jr., *Ancient Rhetorical Theory and Paul* (rev. edn.; CBET 18; Leuven: Peeters, 1999).

R. D. Anderson Jr., *Glossary of Greek Rhetorical Terms Connected to Methods of Argumentation, Figures, and Tropes from Anaximenes to Quintilian* (Leuven: Peeters, 2000).

C. E. Arnold, "'I Am Astonished That You Are So Quickly Turning Away!' (Gal 1.6): Paul and Anatolian Folk Belief," *NTS* 51 (2005): 429–49.

D. E. Aune, *The New Testament in Its Literary Environment* (LEC 8; Philadelphia, PA: Westminster, 1987).

D. E. Aune, *The Westminster Dictionary of New Testament and Early Christian Literature and Rhetoric* (Louisville, KY: Westminster John Knox, 2003).

J. M. G. Barclay, *Jews in the Mediterranean Diaspora: From Alexander to Trajan (323 BCE–117 CE)* (Berkeley: University of California Press, 1996).

J. M. G. Barclay, "Mirror-Reading a Polemical Letter: Galatians as a Test Case," *JSNT* 31 (1987): 73–93.

J. M. G. Barclay, *Obeying the Truth: Paul's Ethics in Galatians* (Vancouver, BC: Regent College Publishing, 1988).

J. M. G. Barclay, *Paul & the Gift* (Grand Rapids, MI: Eerdmans, 2015).

B. H. Brinsmead, *Galatians, Dialogical Response to Opponents* (SBLDS 65; Chico, CA: Scholars Press, 1982).

A. A. Das, *Paul and the Stories of Israel: Grand Thematic Narratives in Galatians* (Minneapolis, MN: Fortress, 2016).

W. D. Davies, *Paul and Rabbinic Judaism: Some Rabbinic Elements in Pauline Theology* (4th edn.; Philadelphia, PA: Fortress, 1980).

M. C. de Boer, "The Meaning of the Phrase τὰ στοιχεῖα τοῦ κοσμοῦ in Galatians," *NTS* 53 (2007): 204–24.

T. L. Donaldson, *Paul and the Gentiles: Remapping the Apostle's Convictional World* (Minneapolis, MN: Fortress, 1997).

J. D. G. Dunn, *Beginning from Jerusalem* (Grand Rapids, MI: Eerdmans, 2009).

J. D. G. Dunn, *The Theology of Paul the Apostle* (Grand Rapids, MI: Eerdmans, 1998).

M. W. Elliott, S. J. Hafemann, N. T. Wright, and J. Frederick, eds., *Galatians and Christian Theology: Justification, the Gospel, and Ethics in Paul's Letter* (Grand Rapids, MI: Baker Academic, 2014).

S. M. Elliott, "Choose Your Mother, Choose Your Master: Galatians 4:21–5:1 in the Shadow of the Anatolian Mother of the Gods," *JBL* 118 (1999): 671–76.

S. M. Elliott, *Cutting Too Close for Comfort: Paul's Letter to the Galatians in its Anatolian Cultic Context* (LNTS 248; New York: T&T Clark, 2003).

P. F. Esler, "Making and Breaking an Agreement Mediterranean Style: A New Reading of Galatians 2:1–14," *BibInt* 3 (3, 1995): 285–314.

G. D. Fee, *God's Empowering Presence: The Holy Spirit in the Letters of Paul* (Peabody, MA: Hendrickson, 1994).

B. R. Gaventa, *Our Mother Saint Paul* (Louisville, KY: Westminster John Knox, 2007).

G. W. Hansen, *Abraham in Galatians – Epistolary and Rhetorical Contexts* (JSNTSup 29; Sheffield: Sheffield Academic Press, 1989).

J. K. Hardin, *Galatians and the Imperial Cult* (WUNT 2.237; Tübingen: Mohr Siebeck, 2008).

J. R. Harrison, *Paul's Language of Grace in Its Graeco-Roman Context* (WUNT 2.172; Tübingen: J. C. B. Mohr, 2003).

J. R. Harrison, "Why Did Josephus and Paul Refuse to Circumcise?" *Pacifica* 17 (2004): 137–58.

R. B. Hays, *Echoes of Scripture in the Letters of Paul* (New Haven, CT: Yale University Press, 1989).

M. Hengel and A. M. Schwemer, *Paul between Damascus and Antioch: The Unknown Years* (trans. Bowden; London: SCM; Louisville: Westminster John Knox, 1997).

J. D. Hester, "The Use and Influence of Rhetoric in Galatians 2:1–14," *TZ* 42 (1986): 386–408.

R. Jewett, "The Agitators and the Galatian Congregation," *NTS* 17 (1971): 198–212.

B. Kahl, *Galatians Re-imagined: Reading with the Eyes of the Vanquished* (Minneapolis, MN: Fortress, 2010).

C. S. Keener, *Acts: An Exegetical Commentary* (4 vols.; Grand Rapids, MI: Baker Academic, 2012–2015).

C. S. Keener, "A Comparison of the Fruit of the Spirit in Galatians 5:22–23 with Ancient Thought on Ethics and Emotion," pages 574–98 in *The Language and Literature of the New Testament: Essays in Honor of Stanley E. Porter's 60th Birthday* (ed. L. K. Fuller Dow, C. A. Evans, and A. W. Pitts; Leiden: Brill, 2016).

C. S. Keener, *The Mind of the Spirit: Paul's Approach to Transformed Thinking* (Grand Rapids, MI: Baker Academic, 2016).

C. S. Keener, "The Pillars and the Right Hand of Fellowship in Galatians 2:9," *JGRChJ* 7 (2010): 51–58.

G. A. Kennedy, *New Testament Interpretation through Rhetorical Criticism* (Chapel Hill: University of North Carolina Press, 1984).

P. H. Kern, *Rhetoric and Galatians: Assessing an Approach to Paul's Epistle* (SNTSM 101; Cambridge: Cambridge University Press, 1998).

B. W. Longenecker, *Remember the Poor: Paul, Poverty, and the Greco-Roman World* (Grand Rapids, MI: Eerdmans, 2010).

D. J. Lull, *The Spirit in Galatia: Paul's Interpretation of Pneuma as Divine Power* (SBLDS 49; Chico, CA: Scholars Press, 1980).

G. Lyons, *Pauline Autobiography: Toward a New Understanding* (SBLDS 73; Atlanta, GA: Scholars Press, 1985).

P. Marshall, *Enmity in Corinth: Social Conventions in Paul's Relations with the Corinthians* (WUNT 2.23; Tübingen: Mohr Siebeck, 1987).

J. L. Martyn, "A Law-Observant Mission to the Gentiles: The Background of Galatians," *SJT* 38 (3, 1985): 307–24.

S. Mitchell, *Anatolia: Land, Men, and Gods in Asia Minor* (2 vols.; Oxford: Clarendon, 1993).

S. Mitchell, "Galatia," *ABD* 2: 870–72.

S. E. Porter, "Paul of Tarsus and His Letters," pages 533–85 in *Handbook of Classical Rhetoric in the Hellenistic Period, 330 B.C.–A.D. 400* (ed. S. E. Porter; Leiden: Brill, 1997).

E. R. Richards, *Paul and First-Century Letter Writing: Secretaries, Composition, and Collection* (Downers Grove, IL: InterVarsity, 2004).

G. O. Rowe, "Style," pages 121–57 in *Handbook of Classical Rhetoric in the Hellenistic Period, 330 B.C.–A.D. 400* (ed. S. E. Porter; Leiden: Brill, 1997).

E. P. Sanders, *Paul: The Apostle's Life, Letters, and Thought* (Minneapolis, MN: Fortress, 2015).

E. P. Sanders, *Paul and Palestinian Judaism: A Comparison of Patterns of Religion* (Philadelphia, PA: Fortress, 1977).

E. P. Sanders, *Paul, the Law, and the Jewish People* (Philadelphia, PA: Fortress, 1983).

S. K. Stowers, *Letter Writing in Greco-Roman Antiquity* (LEC 5; Philadelphia, PA: Westminster, 1986).

B. R. Trick, *Abrahamic Descent, Testamentary Adoption, and the Law in Galatians: Differentiating Abraham's Sons, Seed, and Children of Promise* (NovTSup 169; Leiden: Brill, 2016).

J. B. Tyson, "Paul's Opponents in Galatia," *NovT* 10 (1968): 241–54.

J. A. D. Weima, *Neglected Endings: The Significance of the Pauline Letter Closings* (JSNTSup 101; Sheffield, UK: JSOT Press, 1994).

J. A. D. Weima, *Paul the Ancient Letter Writer: An Introduction to Epistolary Analysis* (Grand Rapids, MI: Baker Academic, 2016).

W. N. Wilder, *Echoes of the Exodus Narrative in the Context and Background of Galatians 5:18* (StBibLit 23; New York: Peter Lang, 2001).

N. T. Wright, *Paul and the Faithfulness of God* (vol. 4 of Christian Origins and the Question of God; book 2; Minneapolis, MN: Fortress, 2013).

III Commentary

1:1–5: GOSPEL GREETINGS

1:1 Paul an apostle – sent neither by human commission nor from human authorities, but through Jesus Christ and God the Father, who raised him from the dead –

1:2 and all the members of God's family who are with me, To the churches of Galatia:

1:3 Grace to you and peace from God our Father and the Lord Jesus Christ,

1:4 who gave himself for our sins to set us free from the present evil age, according to the will of our God and Father,

1:5 to whom be the glory forever and ever. Amen.

In antiquity, many sorts of works contained narrative introductions.[1] Most scholars contend that Paul's frequent denials of negative points about him respond to and thus reveal some of his rivals' complaints about him.[2] Many scholars offer other explanations for Paul's opening, such as that Paul was defending his gospel, contrasting himself with his rivals, or offering a model for imitation. Such explanations are not, however, mutually exclusive. Certainly autobiographic material could also function apologetically.[3]

The letter's opening contains the most essential elements characteristic of letter openings, although Paul here elaborates two of them in distinctive ways: author, addressee(s), and a salutation or blessing. The opening fulfills

---

[1]   E.g., Rev 1:13–20; Fronto *Ad Amicos* 1.1–2; Kennedy, *Interpretation*, 145; older covenants in G. E. Mendenhall, "Covenant Forms in Israelite Traditions," *BA* 17 (3, 1954): 50–76, here 58–60.

[2]   E.g., Martin Luther *Gal.* 1.1; Fee, *Galatians*, 14.

[3]   See, e.g., Josephus *Life* 336–67. On apologetic historiography more generally, see G. E. Sterling, *Historiography and Self-Definition: Josephos, Luke-Acts, and Apologetic Historiography* (NovTSup 64. Leiden: Brill, 1992).

the standard function of any persuasive opening (in speeches, this could be called an *exordium*)[4] by preparing the audience for what follows.[5]

Unlike the Twelve, Paul did not follow or receive a commission from Jesus during the latter's public ministry. But some early Christian writers who recognize the Twelve as apostles also employ the designation more broadly (Rev 2:2; 18:20; 21:14; *Did.* 11.3–6),[6] as do Paul (Rom 16:7; 1 Cor 15:5–7; Gal 1:19; 1 Thess 2:7) and apparently some of his rivals (2 Cor 11:5, 13; 12:11).[7] Paul may apply the label *apostle* to those whom Christ authorizes in a special way for establishing new foundations of some sort (Rom 15:20; 1 Cor 3:10; cf. Eph 2:20). Many scholars cite as a (limited) analogy the Jewish conception of the commissioned agent (a *shaliach*) who accurately represents the sender.[8] Sometimes Jewish sources treat as agents Moses, Aaron, or biblical prophets.[9]

His rivals apparently suggest that Paul's apostleship or commission was merely *by human commission* or *from human authorities* (Gal 1:1);[10] Paul responds to a related charge about his message in 1:11–12. They may view him as a mere emissary of the Antioch church (Acts 11:30)[11] or as having gotten his message from the Jerusalem apostles (cf. Gal 1:17–20; 2:1–2, 6).

Paul responds that, by contrast, he was authorized *through Jesus Christ and God the Father, who raised him from the dead* (Gal 1:1). Paul further elaborates on this direct commissioning in Gal 1:15–16. Paul may also contrast his own direct authorization with his opponents' lack of such.[12]

That Paul did not receive his commission *from human authorities* (lit., from a human) but *through Jesus Christ and God the Father* (1:1) suggests that Paul understands Jesus as more than human (while also affirming his humanity, 4:4);[13] see comment on 1:3.

---

4   E.g., Betz, *Galatians*, 44–45.
5   Rhet. Alex. 29, 1436a.33–39; Polybius 11.1.4–5; Dionysius of Halicarnassus *Thuc.* 19; *Lysias* 24; Cicero *Or. Brut.* 40.137; Virgil *Aen.* 1.1–6; Aulus Gellius preface 25; Lucian *Hist.* 53; Soranus *Gynec.* 1.1.3; 2.5.9 (25.78); Hippolytus *Ref.* Bk 1.proem.
6   Cf. Eusebius *H.E.* 1.12.4.
7   For early Christianity's broad use of *apostle*, see further Lightfoot, *Galatians*, 92–101.
8   See esp. m. Ber. 5:5; for fuller discussion, see C. S. Keener, *The Gospel of John: A Commentary* (2 vols.; Grand Rapids, MI: Baker Academic, 2003), 310–15.
9   Mekilta Pisha 1.87 (Lauterbach 1:8); Sipra Behuq. pq. 13.277.1.13–14; Sipra Sav Mekhilta DeMiluim 98.9.6.
10 With, e.g., Jerome *Epistle to the Galatians* 1.1.1; Dunn, *Galatians*, 25–26; Schreiner, *Galatians*, 74.
11 Early Christians sometimes used *apostle* simply for commissioned agents of churches, as in 2 Cor 8:23; Phil 2:25.
12 Cf. Luther, *Galatians* on 1:1.
13 E.g., Wolfgang Musculus *Commentary on Galatians* 1:1; Rudolf Gwalther *Sermons on Galatians* (on Gal 1:1; Bray); de Boer, *Galatians*, 24; Oakes, *Galatians*, 38.

As in 1:2, Paul often lists coauthors in his letters (1 Cor 1:1; 2 Cor 1:1; Phil 1:1; Col 1:1; 1 Thess 1:1; 2 Thess 1:1; Phlm 1), which was sometimes apparently simply a way of sending special greetings from people the audience knew.[14] Here Paul mentions the support of fellow believers (*all the members of God's family*; Gal 1:2) so the Galatians will understand that, though he was not commissioned by other mortals, many others do stand with him.[15]

The churches of Galatia (Gal 1:2) include multiple house churches in multiple cities. By this period *Galatia* was the title of an entire province as well as the name of a smaller region dominated by ethnic Galatians. In his letters, Paul normally designates regions by their provincial titles rather than ethnic ones (Rom 15:19, 26; 16:5; 1 Cor 16:5, 15, 19; 2 Cor 1:8, 16; 2:13; 7:5; 8:1; 9:2; 11:9–10; Gal 1:21; Phil 4:15; 1 Thess 1:7–8; 4:10). Elsewhere Paul may address both a province and its chief locale (2 Cor 1:1), but Paul had planted churches in multiple cities in south Galatia (see Acts 13:52; 14:20–23), so here he names the province only (see introduction).

Unfortunately, southern Galatia lay directly on the route across the Taurus mountains from Cilicia, making the Galatians a natural target for those who, already in Syria and Cilicia (Acts 15:23, 41), wanted to correct Paul's gentile converts.

Although Paul could use such phrases as *the churches of Galatia* elsewhere (1 Cor 16:1), in his opening greetings he elsewhere sometimes designates churches by their relation to Christ (1 Cor 1:2; 2 Cor 1:1; 1 Thess 1:1; 2 Thess 1:1). Moreover, he so designates the churches of Judea just a few paragraphs later (*churches … in Christ*, Gal 1:22); Paul may have hesitated here to designate them as *God's* churches.[16] *Churches* translates a Greek term that could refer to any sort of assemblies, including civic ones; designating a church as "of God" specified what kind of assembly, linking the assembly more clearly to the people of God often so designated in the Greek version of the Law.

The common Pauline and early Christian blessing of *grace and peace* adapts the standard Greek greeting, *chairein* (Acts 15:23; 23:26; James 1:1; "grace" is *charis*), and the Jewish greeting "Peace" (e.g., Judg 19:20); some other Jewish sources also combined such language.[17] Jews used "Peace" as

---

[14]   See, e.g., Cicero *Fam.* 16.1.title; 16.3.title; 16.4.title; 16.5.title; 16.6.title; 16.9.title; 16.11.1.

[15]   With, e.g., Chrysostom *Hom. Gal.* 1.1–3; Marius Victorinus *Ep. Gal.* 1.1.1; Luther, *Galatians*, 1:2; F. J. Matera, *Galatians* (SP 9; Collegeville, MN: Liturgical Press, 1992), 38; Dunn, *Galatians*, 29; de Boer, *Galatians*, 25.

[16]   See also Chrysostom *Gal.* 1.2; Das, *Galatians*, 80.

[17]   2 Macc 1:1; cf. 2 Bar. 78:2.

more than a greeting, however; it was a blessing formally addressed to the recipient but implicitly functioning as a request (or at least hope) that God would bless the person with well-being (cf. Num 6:26; Matt 10:13; Luke 10:5). Here Paul prays for the spiritually needy Galatians to receive well-being (*peace*) and God's generosity (*grace*).

Prayers or wishes for a recipient's well-being were extremely common in ancient letters (e.g., 3 John 2).[18] What is striking is the deity whom Paul and other early Christian writers invoke in these blessings: *God our Father and the Lord Jesus Christ* (Gal 1:3).[19] They regularly invoke Jesus as divine alongside the Father in the way that other works invoked deities such as Serapis.[20] This practice certainly fits Paul's Christology (e.g., 1 Cor 8:6, where "God" and "Lord" echo the Shema; Phil 2:6–11).

Paul then elaborates Jesus's gracious work in ways more specific to the message of this letter (Gal 1:4). Jesus *gave himself,* an act of self-sacrificial love (2:20; cf. Eph 4:19; 5:2, 25). Because of *our sins* might evoke Isa 53, as it most likely does in a text where Paul summarizes his (and his predecessors') gospel according to the Scriptures (1 Cor 15:1–4).[21]

If it evokes Isa 53, "for [*huper*] our sins" might evoke Isa 53:6. The phrase can also apply to sin offerings,[22] which is how a majority of commentators believes Paul uses the similar phrase "concerning [*peri*] sin" in Rom 8:3. Paul probably here articulates Jesus's death in terms of what has come to be called "substitutionary atonement,"[23] as in the probably analogous phrasing in 1 Cor 15:3.[24]

He gave himself *to free us from the present evil age.* Especially in Judea and Galilee, many Jews believed that the present age was under the dominion of evil forces, but that God would exalt his people in the age to come.[25]

---

[18]   E.g., P. Oxy. 292; P. Lond. 42; P. Giess. 80.13; CPJ 1:244–45, §132; Cicero *Fam.* 14.8.1; Seneca *Ep. Lucil.* 10.4; 2 Macc 9:19; 3 Macc 7:1–2, 9. Cf. further C.-H. Kim, *Form and Structure of the Familiar Greek Letter of Recommendation* (SBLDS 4; Missoula, MT: SBL, 1972), 15–16, 25–34; Stowers, *Letter Writing*, 20, 74; J. A. D. Weima, *Neglected Endings: The Significance of the Pauline Letter Closings* (JSNTSup 101; Sheffield, UK: JSOT Press, 1994), 34–39.

[19]   Noted also by Luther, *Galatians* 1:3.

[20]   On early Jesus veneration, see, e.g., L. W. Hurtado, *Lord Jesus Christ: Devotion to Jesus in Earliest Christianity* (Grand Rapids, MI: Eerdmans, 2003); A. T. E. Loke, *The Origins of Divine Christology* (SNTSMS 169; Cambridge: Cambridge University Press, 2017).

[21]   S. Gathercole, *Defending Substitution: An Essay on Atonement in Paul* (Acadia Studies in Bible and Theology; Grand Rapids, MI: Baker Academic, 2015), 55–79, esp. 61–69.

[22]   Mic 6:7; Ezek 40:39; 43:22, 25; 44:29; 45:17, 22, 25; 46:20; 1 Esd 7:8; so also Barn. 7.3, 5.

[23]   Oakes, *Galatians*, 40.

[24]   See again Gathercole, *Substitution*, 55–79.

[25]   E.g., CD 4.12–13; 1QM 14.4–7, 10–15; 1 En. 46:5–6; 96:8; 104:2; 2 Bar. 15:8; 4 Ezra 4:27; t. Ber. 6:21.

Paul here declares that believers no longer belong to this age, an age characterized by the present world system (cf. Rom 12:2; Eph 2:2).[26] In Galatians (5:5) and elsewhere Paul emphasizes that the Spirit provides believers a foretaste, a proleptic experience, of the coming age (Gal 5:5; Rom 8:23; 14:17; 1 Cor 2:9–10; 2 Cor 1:22; 5:5). In Galatians, this means that believers should no longer serve old laws, principles, or powers (3:23–25; 4:1–5, 8–10); like Paul, they have died to the world because a new creation has come (6:14–15). Fitting the theme of divine rather than human initiative elsewhere in Galatians, Jesus's sacrifice to deliver us from evil was *according to the will of our God and Father* (1:4).

The Galatians' religious past was morally rigorous. Distinctively Phrygian deities from the Galatian Christians' preconversion past included the paired deities "Holy and Just."[27] A God who loved and sacrificially redeemed those who trusted him, by contrast, was extraordinarily good news.[28]

As in Gal 1:5, Paul often pauses to honor God in his letters (Rom 1:25; 9:5; 2 Cor 1:3; 11:31; Eph 1:3), including attributing to him the *glory forever* (Rom 11:36; 16:27; Eph 3:21; Phil 4:20). "Amen" was a common affirmation, especially for blessings, curses, and prayers.[29]

1:6–12: NO OTHER GOSPEL

1:6 I am astonished that you are so quickly deserting the one who called you in the grace of Christ and are turning to a different gospel –

1:7 not that there is another gospel, but there are some who are confusing you and want to pervert the gospel of Christ.

1:8 But even if we or an angel from heaven should proclaim to you a gospel contrary to what we proclaimed to you, let that one be accursed!

1:9 As we have said before, so now I repeat, if anyone proclaims to you a gospel contrary to what you received, let that one be accursed!

---

[26] Cf. C. S. Keener, *The Mind of the Spirit: Paul's Approach to Transformed Thinking* (Grand Rapids, MI: Baker Academic, 2016), 153–55, 176–80.

[27] See Mitchell, *Anatolia*, 2:25–26; A. C. Niang, *Faith and Freedom in Galatia and Senegal: The Apostle Paul, Colonists and Sending Gods* (BibInt 97; Leiden, Boston, MA: Brill, 2009), 51.

[28] C. E. Arnold, "'I Am Astonished That You Are So Quickly Turning Away!' (Gal 1.6): Paul and Anatolian Folk Belief," *NTS* 51 (2005): 429–49, esp. 444.

[29] E.g., Deut 27:15–26; Ps 41:13; Tob 8:8; 1QS 1.20; 2.10, 18; t. Ber. 3:26; Sipre Deut. 320.3.1; CIJ 1:434, §599; 1:466, §650.

1:10 Am I now seeking human approval, or God's approval? Or am I trying to please people? If I were still pleasing people, I would not be a servant of Christ.

1:11 For I want you to know, brothers and sisters, that the gospel that was proclaimed by me is not of human origin;

1:12 for I did not receive it from a human source, nor was I taught it, but I received it through a revelation of Jesus Christ.

Galatians is the only undisputed letter in which Paul omits a thanksgiving. Even Paul's blessing is brief (Gal 1:3) and is quickly followed by a curse (1:8–9). As has long been recognized,[30] Paul conspicuously skips formal niceties and gets right down to business – in this case, the business of rebuking them.

In rhetoric, one normally opened by establishing rapport and praising the audience;[31] in severe cases, however, one could also begin with reproof.[32] Reproving and reproaching letters often include "*I am astonished*" (as here in 1:6).[33]

Here, as often in his letters to local churches (cf. 3:2–5; 1 Cor 2:1–5; Phil 1:5–6; 1 Thess 1:2–10), Paul invokes the memory of the church's beginning. What astonishes him is how *quickly* they are *deserting* the gracious Lord. This is strong language: *quickly* might evoke the speed at which ancient Israel turned aside to false religion (Exod 32:8; Judg 2:17).[34] In 2 Macc 7:24, the term here translated *deserting* involves abandoning ancestral Jewish customs; Paul here applies it to those who thought that they were embracing these very customs![35] The Galatians thus risk betraying the Lord *who*

[30]   E.g., Origen *Comm. Rom.* on 1:8; Ramsay, *Galatians*, 249–51.
[31]   See, e.g., Rhet. Alex. 29, 1436b.33–39; 36, 1441b.36–1442b.27; Cicero *De Or.* 1.31.143; *Inv.* 1.15.20; *Sest.* 1.2; Ps.-Dionysus *Epideictic* 1.256–57; Quintilian *Inst.* 3.7.24; 4.1.16; 4.1.23; Dio Chrysostom *Or.* 34.7–8; 39.1; 41.1. In letters, see, e.g., Let. Aris. 1–2; Cicero *Fam.* 13.66.1.
[32]   Witherington, *Grace*, 80; cf. Quintilian *Inst.* 4.1.11. For threatening a curse, see Betz, *Galatians*, 46.
[33]   See Demosthenes *Ep.* 3.11, 23; Stowers, *Letter Writing*, 139; esp. Hansen, *Abraham*, 28, 33–43.
[34]   With F. Mussner, *Der Galaterbrief* (5th edn.; HTKNT 9; Freiburg: Herder, 1988), 53n54; Hays, "Galatians," 204; Schreiner, *Galatians*, 85; G. Lyons, *Galatians: A Commentary in the Wesleyan Tradition* (New Beacon Bible Commentary; Kansas City, MO: Beacon Hill Press, 2012), 60.
[35]   With Matera, *Galatians*, 45; Dunn, *Galatians*, 39–40; D. J. Moo, *Galatians* (BECNT; Grand Rapids, MI: Baker Academic, 2013), 77.

called them (1:6).[36] The language of "calling" may evoke gracious inclusion among God's people, as in some other Pauline passages.[37]

Non-Jewish Greek speakers applied the term here translated *gospel* (Gal 1:6–7; meaning "good news" or "glad tidings") to news of victories, weddings, imperial accessions, and other sorts of happy announcements. Normally the term included celebratory information previously unknown to an audience; Paul thus applies it most often for the message when he has brought it to a new audience.[38] Ancient writers usually used the plural form of the term here translated *gospel*, "good tidings," but Paul and other early Christian writers used it in the singular, for the one "good news" message above all others.

Early Christians borrowed the term especially from the use of the related verb in the Greek translation of the Old Testament.[39] Early Christian expressions such as good news of peace (Acts 10:36; Eph 2:17; 6:15), of salvation (Eph 1:13; cf. Rom 1:16), and of God's kingdom or reign (e.g., Mark 1:15; Matt 4:23; 9:35; Luke 8:1; Acts 8:12) evoke Isa 52:7, presumably the original source of this language. Paul elsewhere cites Isa 52:7 (Rom 10:15), and is well aware that it closely precedes Isa 53 (which he quotes in Rom 10:16).

After speaking of a different gospel, Paul corrects himself to speak with more technical accuracy. When Paul warns that his hearers are turning *to a different gospel*,[40] one that is not really a gospel,[41] he presumably evokes the language that he believes his rivals are using;[42] perhaps they also envision Isaiah's good news of Israel's restoration, but with gentiles being admitted

---

[36] Oakes, *Galatians*, 43, noting that communities were expected to be loyal to and to reverence founders, suggests they are deserting Paul. Paul, however, applies this "call" verb with respect to conversion especially to God (1:15; 1 Cor 1:9; 7:17–18; 1 Thess 2:12; 4:7; 5:24).

[37] See Rom 9:7, 12, 25; 11:29; cf. Isa 49:1; 51:2. It may evoke a "chosen" people (Deut 4:37; 7:6; 10:5; 14:2; Ps 33:12; 105:6; Isa 41:8–9; 43:10, 20; 44:1, 2; 45:4; Jer 33:24; Ezek 20:5; Amos 3:2) related to Abraham (cf. Gen 18:19; Neh 9:7).

[38] See J. P. Dickson, "Gospel as News: Εὐαγγελ – from Aristophanes to the Apostle Paul," *NTS* 51 (2, 2005): 212–30.

[39] See, e.g., A. D. Nock, "The Vocabulary of the New Testament," *JBL* 52 (2–3, 1933): 131–39, here 132.

[40] Although some scholars still distinguish here Paul's terms translated *different* (1:6) and *another* (1:7), they were usually interchangeable by this period of Greek, including normally in Paul.

[41] Persuaders would sometimes make and then immediately and deliberately correct a statement to drive home a point more forcefully, as here; see Rhet. Her. 4.26.36; Hermogenes *Inv.* 4.12.203–04; cf. G. O. Rowe, "Style," pages 121–57 in *Handbook of Classical Rhetoric in the Hellenistic Period, 330 B.C.–A.D. 400* (ed. S. E. Porter; Leiden: Brill, 1997), 141; Porter, "Paul and Letters," 581; Anderson, *Rhetorical Theory*, 146; Anderson, *Glossary*, 71; 1 Cor 1:16.

[42] Dunn, *Galatians*, 10; Martyn, *Galatians*, 121.

on different terms than Paul affirms. That is, they may expect the nations to serve Israel (e.g., Isa 49:22; 54:3; 60:5, 11–16; 61:6; 64:2; 66:20), and only the circumcised to become part of God's people. Presumably emphasizing different promises such as Isa 2:3–4; 11:10; and especially 19:19–25; 56:3–8; as well as Zech 2:11, Paul believed that the true message was already good news for gentiles who embraced Christ.

Elsewhere Paul associates a different gospel with a different Jesus and a different spirit (2 Cor 11:4), presumably a demonic one[43] (cf. 11:13–15). A gospel different than the one Paul proclaims is not a true gospel (Gal 1:7); a gospel of circumcision is hardly gospel – literally, "good news" – for gentiles.

The true gospel that Paul proclaims (1 Cor 15:1)[44] emphasizes Christ's death and resurrection (15:3–7), the same message that other apostles also proclaimed (15:11).

It is doubtful that Paul's rivals were denying Jesus's death or resurrection, which seems not to have been at issue in Galatia. Paul did insist, however, that they were missing the theological implication of those events: if Christ died "for our sins" (1 Cor 15:3), he did so to free us from the present evil age (Gal 1:4). The law proclaimed by his rivals, by contrast, lacked this power (3:21–22). As one called to preach this good news among gentiles (1:16; 2:2), Paul recognized that his rivals' message was no longer good news for gentiles.

The true gospel was connected with *the one who called you in the grace of Christ* (1:6), the same one who also *called* Paul *through his grace* (1:15). That is, this gospel involved a transforming gift to which the outward signs of the covenant merely pointed.[45] This was a grace that cost God his Son's death. Thus the true gospel gave them new life at God's initiative; by trying to take back the salvific initiative, Paul's rivals would *pervert the gospel of Christ* (1:7).[46]

Paul may display disdain here for these *some*, these "certain persons" (Greek *tines*; cf. perhaps 1:9; 3:1; 5:7).[47] These rivals are now *confusing* or

---

[43] On ancient demonology, see E. Ferguson, *Demonology of the Early Christian World* (Symposium Series 12; New York: Edwin Mellen, 1984); C. S. Keener, *Miracles: The Credibility of the New Testament Accounts* (Grand Rapids, MI: Baker Academic, 2011), 769–87.

[44] Luke mentions Paul preaching "good news" (using the verb form) in this region (Acts 13:32; 14:7, 15, 21) as often as everywhere else together.

[45] For grace as empowering gift, as benevolence with expectations, see J. M. Barclay, *Paul & the Gift* (Grand Rapids, MI: Eerdmans, 2015).

[46] *Pervert* here can mean simply "turn" or "change," but changing something good to something bad perverts it (as also in Sir 11:31).

[47] Damning opponents with anonymity was common practice.

disturbing the Galatian believers (1:7).[48] The Greek term translated here as *confusing* had a range of meaning that included sowing division.[49] It is probably no coincidence that the same Greek term also appears in the Jerusalem Council's public disavowal of some law-demanding Jerusalemite believers (*tines,* "certain persons") who had earlier disturbed believers in the province directly to Galatia's south and east (Acts 15:24). By speaking of *some who are confusing you,* Paul may directly evoke the language of the widely circulated Jerusalem decree that he either had delivered or soon would deliver among them (Acts 16:4). Paul uses this Greek term again – the only other time in his extant letters – in Gal 5:10, where he notes that *whoever it is that is confusing you* will face divine judgment.

Quickly after his customary epistolary blessing (1:3–5) Paul turns to a curse, although happily not against the Galatians themselves. Curses (1:8–9) and blessings (6:16) also frame the letter's body, posing a stark choice like the blessings and curses of Deuteronomy.[50] The curse is against those who pervert the gospel, a curse applicable in principle even against himself or an angel if they proclaimed a different gospel. That is, no authority stands above the divine message.

The Greek term *anathema* often means simply "a votive offering," but it appears on curse tablets,[51] which could be relevant for ancient magical rituals (see discussion of putative witchcraft language in Gal 3:1; 5:20). Curses were widely used, including against rivals. Indeed, imprecations were the most frequent "type of appeal to the gods" in Asia Minor.[52] The Dead Sea Scrolls also include curse rituals against God's enemies.[53]

More relevantly here, the LXX uses the term for devoting to complete destruction people or things contaminated with evil (e.g., Lev 27:28–29;

---

[48] The term can refer to bringing needless disorder (e.g., Josephus *War* 9.79, 88). In 1 Macc 3:5 and 7:22, it applies to both gentiles and Jews who disturbed God's people by unfaithfulness to God's law; in Josephus *Life* 134, a disturber exploits the law unjustly.
[49] E.g., Dio Chrysostom *Or.* 34.19; Josephus *Ant.* 16.278; 17.325; 1 Macc 3:5; 7:22; Acts 17:8, 13.
[50] H. D. Betz, "In Defense of the Spirit: Paul's Letter to the Galatians as a Document of Early Christian Apologetics," pages 99–114 in *Aspects of Religious Propaganda in Judaism and Early Christianity* (ed. E. S. Fiorenza; UNDCSJCA 2; Notre Dame, IN: University of Notre Dame Press, 1976), 112, although going too far in speaking of Galatians as a "magical letter."
[51] See BDAG. Cf. 1 En. 95.4. Nock, "Vocabulary," 135, finds an unexplained use for cursing to be distinctively Jewish.
[52] W. M. Calder, "Introduction, 7," pages ix–xliii in vol. 7 of *Monumenta Asiae Minoris antiqua* (ed. W. M. Calder et al.; Manchester: Manchester University Press; London: Longmans, Green, 1928–), xxxv–xxxvi; cf. MAMA, 1, §§25, 126, 294, 425, and 437.
[53] 1QS 2.4; 1QM 13.1–5; 4Q257 2.1; 4Q266 f11.17; 4Q286 f7ii.2–11.

Deut 7:26; Josh 6:17–18), including communities polluted by false prophets
(Deut 13:15, 17). We might translate Paul here colloquially, "*Damn* them" or
"To *hell* with them," so long as we recognize that Paul means it more literally
than do most who utter such curses today.[54]

Probably Paul's warning about angels in 1:8 is hyperbolic, like his mention of himself as a false teacher: Christ's gospel, through which they unde-
niably experienced God's Spirit (3:2), takes precedence over the greatest
figures under God or the very one who first evangelized you.

But why does Paul choose these particular examples for hyperbole? On
the one hand, Paul may simply select the most extreme examples possible.
On the other, perhaps his rivals made claims relevant to one or both of
these examples. Paul's rivals may have suggested that he himself preached
differently (5:11). Moreover, many Jewish visionaries claimed to receive revelations from angels.

Nevertheless, if Paul has in mind a particular angelic referent, it is probably not his rivals' subjective spiritual experiences, but their insistence on
the law mediated through angels (Gal 3:19).[55] Even if such angels demanded
compliance with the law, the gospel of the Lord Christ was of greater import.

Scholars often suggest that 1:9 refers back to Paul's and his companions'
instruction to this effect in the past, but he probably simply refers to what
he has just declared in 1:8. Paul's explicit repetition of the literal point of 1:8
in 1:9 is a way of highlighting the point with greater emphasis.[56]

Paul frequently resorts to rhetorical questions (e.g., Rom 2:3–4; 3:1–9;
1 Cor 9:1–13);[57] in the case of Gal 1:10, however, scholars divide regarding
what answers he implies. The word that is translated *seeking … approval*
(*peithô*) here has a wide range of potential meaning. It most often means
something like "persuade," "cause to believe" (2 Cor 5:11), "believe/be persuaded" (Gal 5:10), or (accordingly) "obey," but it can also include trying
to please or pacify someone (BDAG). Grammatically, one could possibly
answer Paul's opening question four different ways: Paul seeks to please
both humans and God (cf. Rom 12:17; 2 Cor 8:21); Paul seeks to persuade
just humans (God not needing persuasion); Paul seeks to persuade God

---

54   Some argue that Paul here proposes excommunication (cf. Gal 4:30; 1 Cor 5:5; Betz,
     Galatians, 53; Martyn, *Galatians* [1997], 114); others, noting that God is implicitly
     invoked, demur (Lightfoot, *Galatians*, 78; Schreiner, *Galatians*, 87–88).
55   E.g., Dunn, *Galatians*, 45. Others demur here; Moo, *Galatians*, 81.
56   In rhetoric, cf. *anadiplosis* and *mimetikon* (Anderson, *Glossary*, 18, 77; cf. 116).
57   On rhetorical questions, see, e.g., Anderson, *Glossary*, 51–52.

alone (human opinion being unimportant; cf. Gal 2:6; 2 Cor 6:8–9); or Paul, disdaining human rhetoric,[58] seeks to persuade neither.[59]

Many scholars here find a contrast to Paul depending on human persuasion earlier, before his conversion (versus the emphatic *now* or "still" in Gal 1:10; cf. 1 Cor 2:1–5). Before his conversion, which he is preparing to recount, he sought to persuade people to observe the law (cf. Gal 1:13–14; 5:11).[60] This allusion would implicitly condemn the approach of his law-supporting adversaries, who lack Paul's converting revelation and do seek to please people (6:12).[61]

Alternatively, Paul's *now* in 1:10 may refer back to his *now I repeat* in 1:9; that is, what Paul is *seeking* to do relates to his curses in 1:8–9. In that case it might mean something closer to its more common meaning, "persuade." Perhaps Paul seeks to persuade God to carry out the curse he invoked in 1:8–9; people sometimes tried to persuade God to take their side or honor their curses.[62] Alternatively, when used with God as the object in the LXX, the verb means "rely on" him.[63] Paul surely does seek to rely on God.

All these options are grammatically conceivable. However one construes the grammar, however, Paul's basic point remains clear from the context. Whether or not Paul is trying to persuade God (God might not need persuading on this matter), Paul has implicitly invoked God in the curse (1:8–9). Paul does want to persuade people (1 Cor 10:33), including the Galatians, whether or not he does so in *this* passage; yet he would never do so at the expense of compromising dependence on God.

Paul is not here seeking to please people (1:10).[64] Sometimes Paul notes the importance of pleasing (i.e., serving) others (Rom 15:1–3), and that he tried to please people for the sake of winning them to Christ (1 Cor 10:33).[65] Unfortunately such language may have been used against him by his detractors; persuading people by "pleasing" them was the behavior of a

---

[58] By Paul's day "persuading people" defined rhetoric (Betz, *Galatians*, 54–55). Philosophers, esp. in earlier times, sometimes claimed to disdain rhetoric (Plato *Theaetetus* 164CD; Epictetus *Disc.* 3.23).

[59] See esp. Das, *Galatians*, 111–12.

[60] Barclay, *Gift*, 356.

[61] Luther *First Lectures on Galatians* (on Gal 1:10; Bray); Das, *Galatians*, 113.

[62] De Boer, *Galatians*, 63; Das, *Galatians*, 111–12.

[63] 2 Kgs 18:22; 2 Chron 14:10; 16:7–8; Job 27:8 (LXX only); Ps 118[117]:8; 125[124]:1; Prov 28:25; 29:25; Isa 8:17; 10:20; 36:7; 58:14; Zeph 3:2.

[64] Usage would suggest a contrary-to-fact conditional sentence (Fee, *Galatians*, 34; Schreiner, *Galatians*, 89), though context could prove more decisive.

[65] Noting different contexts, Augustine recognized that Paul both pleased others and did not please others (Augustine *Ep. Gal.* 5 [1B.1.10]; Edwards).

demagogue.[66] Moralists condemned flattery and warned that true friends spoke truth even when it seemed painful (cf. Gal 4:16; 1 Thess 2:5).[67] Flattery was a form of hypocrisy, a charge that Paul will associate instead with those who compromised the true gospel to please Judean hardliners at gentiles' expense (2:13–14). Such flatterers were viewed as servile,[68] but Paul protests here that he is instead a slave of Christ (Gal 1:10).

When any conflict between pleasing God and pleasing people existed, Paul wanted to please God rather than people (1 Thess 2:4). In this context, by harshly invoking a curse (Gal 1:8–9), Paul was surely not trying to please people! His rivals in Galatia *were* concerned with pleasing people (4:16–17; 6:12),[69] but Paul was a servant of Christ. Pleasing God rather than people meant that he moved from persecutor to persecuted (1:13; 4:29; 5:11). Accordingly, he would obey the divine revelation to preach to the gentiles, including those in Galatia (1:11–16), regardless of the cost (5:11).[70]

Paul elsewhere calls himself (Rom 1:1; Phil 1:1) or fellow workers (Col 4:12) slaves of God or Christ, echoing Old Testament language for prophets and other divine agents (e.g., 2 Kgs 9:7, 36; 18:12; 24:2; Josh 24:29; Judg 2:8; Neh 10:29). Moreover, slaves of powerful persons sometimes wielded considerable prestige or authority themselves.[71] Such a role can sometimes be contrasted in principle with being a slave of people (1 Cor 7:22; Eph 6:6), unless at the Lord's bidding (2 Cor 4:5).

Paul uses expressions such as *I want you to know* (1:11) to hold attention or to highlight some important points (1 Cor 12:3; 15:1; 2 Cor 8:1).[72] In 1:11–12, Paul articulates the thesis that he will elaborate by way of illustration in 1:13–24 and perhaps beyond it.[73] His focus is *the gospel that was proclaimed by me* to the Galatians.[74]

---

[66]   Betz, *Galatians*, 55.
[67]   See, e.g., Isocrates *To Nicocles* 28 (*Or.* 2); Seneca *Dial.* 10.15.2; Plutarch *Profit by Enemies* 6, *Mor.* 89B; *Flatt.* 17–37, *Mor.* 59A–74E.
[68]   E.g., Velleius Paterculus 2.83.1; Musonius Rufus 7, p. 58.3; Dio Chrysostom *Or.* 51.1; 66.13–14.
[69]   As, in Gal 2:11–14, is Peter, in contrast to Paul; see Dodd, "Slave."
[70]   Cf. D. Hunn, "Pleasing God or Pleasing People? Defending the Gospel in Galatians 1–2," *Bib* 91 (1, 2010): 24–49.
[71]   Epictetus *Disc.* 1.19.19; 4.7.23; D. B. Martin, *Slavery as Salvation: The Metaphor of Slavery in Pauline Christianity* (New Haven, CT: Yale University Press, 1990), 47–49.
[72]   Such disclosure formulas also appear in some other ancient letters (see Hansen, *Abraham*, 28).
[73]   Cf. J.-N. Aletti, "Galates 1–2: Quelle fonction et quelle démonstration?" *Bib* 86 (3, 2005): 305–23; A. M. Buscemi, *Lettera ai Galati: Commentario esegetico* (SBFA 63; Jerusalem: Franciscan Printing Press, 2004), 76.
[74]   Fitting Semitic idiom but perhaps reinforcing his focus in Greek, Paul's noun and verb here are cognate (*euangelion … euangelisthen*).

Not of human origin translates the phrase *kata anthropon*, which Paul elsewhere uses for imprecise, "human" illustrations (Rom 3:5; Gal 3:15) or what is merely human (1 Cor 3:3; 9:8; 15:32; cf. Philo *Virt.* 217).

In 1:1, Paul insisted that God rather than humans commissioned him; now in 1:11–12 he shows the same for *the gospel* that his commission involved. This contrast dominates the following narrative: he received this gospel through a revelation of Christ narrated in 1:13–16a, and did not depend on human sources for it, as shown in 1:16–21.[75] Indeed, he had to defend this gospel even when the Jerusalem leadership seemed uncommitted, ambivalent, or confused (2:2, 5, 7, 14).

This revelation is relevant to the Galatians because this is *the gospel that was proclaimed by me* (1:11), i.e., to them (*what we proclaimed to you*, 1:8–9) – a gospel from which they have been turning to a human gospel that is *not* from Christ (1:6–7).

Although they *received* the gospel from Paul (1:9), Paul himself received it through Christ rather than human agents (1:12).[76] (*From a human source*, Greek *para anthrōpou*, means from no mere human.) When involving human agents, "received" often implies receiving traditions that have been passed on, including elsewhere in Paul (1 Cor 11:2, 23; 15:1, 3).[77] It is therefore likely no coincidence that Paul quickly mentions *the traditions of my ancestors* (1:14), since *traditions* literally mean "matters passed on." Once Paul had followed human traditions – the sort of traditions now probably followed by his rivals (cf. Col 2:8; Mark 7:8). Now, however, he no longer proclaims traditions received from mortals, but the gospel he received directly from Christ.

Paul is not denying contact with other Christians (1 Cor 15:3–4), but rather is claiming that he first encountered this reality independently and directly from Jesus Christ (cf. 1 Cor 15:8). To emphasize this point, he elaborates it in three ways, with two negations and one affirmation: *I did not receive …, nor was I taught …, but I received ….*[78]

---

[75] The centrality of *gospel* and its cognates in this section cannot be missed; it appears in 1:6–9, 11, 16, 23; 2:2, 5, 7, 14, and afterward in Galatians only with reference to his first preaching to them in 4:13.

[76] Ancient readers sometimes found an allusion to Christ's deity in this contrast; see Marius Victorinus *Ep. Gal.* 1.1.11 (tentatively); Pamphilus *Apology for Origen* [PG 17:585] (Edwards); cf. comment on Gal 1:1.

[77] E.g., Thucydides 1.85.1; Dio Chrysostom *Or.* 18.10; Lucian *Alex.* 61; Iamblichus *Pyth. Life* 28.148–49; Josephus *Ant.* 13.297, 408; Mark 7:3, 5; Luke 1:2; 1 Cor 11:23; 15:3; see also BDAG.

[78] For lingering on a point, see, e.g., Hermogenes *Method* 5.417–18.

Grammatically, the *revelation of Jesus Christ* could mean a revelation "from" him or, more likely here, a revelation "about" him. Here God is the direct source of the revelation (1:15) and Jesus is the content (1:16). Jesus usually appears as the content of the revelation (although 2 Cor 12:1 and Rev 1:1 are debatable), as is usual with nouns in the genitive following "revelation" in Paul.

1:13–17: GOD REVEALS THE GOSPEL TO PAUL

1:13 You have heard, no doubt, of my earlier life in Judaism. I was violently persecuting the church of God and was trying to destroy it.

1:14 I advanced in Judaism beyond many among my people of the same age, for I was far more zealous for the traditions of my ancestors.

1:15 But when God, who had set me apart before I was born and called me through his grace, was pleased

1:16 to reveal his Son to me, so that I might proclaim him among the Gentiles, I did not confer with any human being,

1:17 nor did I go up to Jerusalem to those who were already apostles before me, but I went away at once into Arabia, and afterwards I returned to Damascus.

The entire narrative section (1:13–2:14 or 2:21) almost certainly follows chronological sequence.[79] Introductory narratives summarizing the events leading up to the matter under discussion were common, including in speeches. Although normally despised, self-praise was considered justifiable under appropriate circumstances.[80]

As noted in the commentary introduction, Paul responds to the suspicion that his calling is subordinate to and dependent on the apostles who knew Jesus during his earthly ministry. He accordingly also reestablishes his *êthos*, or character, which is necessary for his credibility.

Contrary to some modern Western religious approaches,[81] Paul readily argues here from experience, both his own (1:11–2:14) and that of

[79] *Rhet. Her.* 1.9.15 recommends this practice for setting forth a case's facts; cf. also Hermogenes *Issues* 47.8–11 (for prosecution).
[80] C. Forbes, "Comparison, Self-Praise, and Irony: Paul's Boasting and the Conventions of Hellenistic Rhetoric," *NTS* 32 (1, 1986): 1–30; Marshall, *Enmity*, 124–29.
[81] Paul's revelations presuppose an epistemology foreign to most modern Westerners; see C. S. Keener, *Spirit Hermeneutics: Reading Scripture in Light of Pentecost* (Grand

the Galatians (3:1–5). These experiences are, however, incontrovertible ones – the Galatians', because it was their own, and Paul's, because it was not purely subjective.[82]

Paul distinguishes the more distinctive experience to which he alludes here from his typical visions (cf. 2 Cor 12:1–4).[83] He believes that he met the risen Christ in the same way that other apostles and witnesses had (1 Cor 9:1; 15:8), and Paul envisions resurrection as involving the body in some way (*sôma*; 1 Cor 6:13–14; 15:44; Phil 3:21). Scholars may debate how *much* of Paul's theology derived from this initial experience,[84] but certainly it transformed Paul's perspective on key concepts.

Using the sociological definition of conversion, Paul was converted.[85] In contrast to those who argue that Paul was only converted or only called, he was both converted (Phil 3:4–11) *and* called (1 Cor 9:1; 15:8–11; Gal 1:11–23).[86] The most emphatic point in Galatians, however, is that Christ commissioned Paul to reach gentiles (Gal 1:16; cf. Acts 9:15; 13:47; 22:21; 26:17). Galatian Christians could not question Paul's call to gentiles, for they were among the fruits of that call.

Given the discussion Paul will soon undertake (see esp. 2:14), Paul has good reason to explain his former lifestyle in the terms he will employ in

---

Rapids, MI: Eerdmans, 2016), 153–204; esp. W. J. Abraham, "The Offense of Divine Revelation," *HTR* 95 (3, 2002): 251–64. They disturbed even some who shared Paul's epistemology but not his experience (D. C. Sim, "The Appearances of the Risen Christ to Paul: Identifying Their Implications and Complications," *ABR* 54 [2006]: 1–12).

[82] Pace the NRSV's interpretive *no doubt*, Paul presumably recounted his story early in his preaching in Galatia; it would have proved particularly relevant where there were conflicts with advocates of more traditional Jewish approaches (cf. Acts 13:45, 50; 14:2–5, 19). Paul apparently told his stories often (1 Cor 15:8–9, 32; 2 Cor 1:8–11; 11:32–33; Phil 3:4–7), and word about his conversion spread even apart from him (Gal 1:23).

[83] Cf. Tob 12:19; Acts 1:3; Luke 24:39–40; E. Schweizer, *Jesus* (trans. D. E. Green; London: SCM, 1971), 48–49; J. D. G. Dunn, *Jesus and the Spirit: A Study of the Religious and Charismatic Experience of Jesus and the First Christians as Reflected in the New Testament* (London: SCM, 1975), 97–103; L. Goppelt, *Apostolic and Post-apostolic Times* (trans. R. Guelich; Grand Rapids, MI: Baker, 1980), 18–19; E. P. Sanders, *The Historical Figure of Jesus* (New York: Penguin, 1993), 280.

[84] For Paul's encounter shaping his theology, see S. Kim, *The Origin of Paul's Gospel* (Tübingen: J. C. B. Mohr, 1981).

[85] See, e.g., A. F. Segal, *Paul the Convert: The Apostolate and Apostasy of Paul the Pharisee* (New Haven, CT: Yale University Press, 1990), 32–33.

[86] With, e.g., Witherington, *Grace*, 112–13. For discussion of Paul's conversion experience, see further Keener, *Acts*, 1614–17.

1:13–14. When Paul speaks of his *earlier life*[87] *in Judaism* in terms of per-secuting God's church, he does not mean by the term translated *Judaism* (*Ioudaismos*) what modern readers might suppose. It refers not to a former ethnicity or faith, as if Paul became a gentile or stopped following the God of Israel when he became a Christian. It refers to Jewish practice, and appears especially in contexts of nationalistic resistance against foreign cul-tural impositions (2 Macc 2:21; 8:1; 14:38), even when some tried to "compel" abandonment of Jewish practice (4 Macc 4:26).[88] The cognate verb means for gentiles to practice Jewish customs[89] – something that Paul now fiercely opposes (Gal 2:14)!

Persecuting (from *diôkô*, 1:13, 23) foreshadows what his rivals are doing spiritually to Galatians who hold to the truth (Gal 4:29). At the time, Paul undoubtedly saw himself as following the model of the Maccabees, who pursued or persecuted (*diôkô*) those who broke (1 Macc 2:47;[90] 3:5) or militarily opposed (3:24; 5:22; 10:49) God's law. They courageously fought for the Jewish way of life (*Ioudaismou*) and pursued their foes (2 Macc 2:21).

Yet ironically what Paul persecuted was *the church of God*. The term translated *church* can refer to any assembly, but the assembly *of God* in the Old Testament was the community of his people Israel (see, e.g., Judg 20:2; 1 Chron 28:8), to which some kinds of foreigners could not belong (Deut 23:3, 8; Neh 13:1). Blinded by nationalistic zeal to purify the Lord's own commu-nity, Paul had in fact been opposing that community! He had been pleasing some among his people, but not his God (Gal 1:10).

He adds that he *was trying to destroy* the community (using *portheô*, 1:13). Yet this was what a persecutor of God's people might do (*portheô* in 4 Macc 4:23; 11:4), while murdering those who circumcised their sons (4:25) and torturing Jews to force them to eat unclean foods and to renounce the Jewish way of life (4:26)! In his zeal to defend Jewish traditions, Paul had acted like those remembered for repressing Jewish tradition!

[87] Although the term *anastrophê*, "way of life," was in common use by the time Paul wrote Galatians, in this context it might possibly evoke 2 Macc 6:23, which describes another devoted pietist's faithfulness to the law from his childhood.

[88] Y. Amir, "The Term Ἰουδαισμος (*Ioudaismos*): A Study in Jewish-Hellenistic Self-Identification," *Immanuel* 14 (1982): 34–41; Dunn, *Galatians*, 56–57; M. V. Novenson, "Paul's Former Occupation in *Ioudaismos*," pages 24–39 in *Galatians and Christian Theology: Justification, the Gospel, and Ethics in Paul's Letter* (ed. M. W. Elliott et al.; Grand Rapids, MI: Baker Academic, 2014), 32–34, 39; Oakes, *Galatians*, 53.

[89] CIJ 694 in Novenson, "Occupation," 33. See discussion of LXX Esth 8:17 at Gal 2:14.

[90] In 1 Macc 2:46, they "circumcised all the uncircumcised boys" in Judea.

Paul declares that he *advanced … beyond many among my people of the same age* (1:14). This idea of making progress naturally appears often in discussions of education,[91] and became very prominent in discussions of virtue.[92]

The focus of Paul's training, however, was *the traditions of my ancestors* (1:14).[93] This sort of advance would have made him a young person of note in Jerusalem, where wisdom was typically defined by prowess in their ancestral laws.[94] Thus in describing his own background as a child prodigy, Josephus notes how he quickly advanced in learning.[95]

For Philo, someone advancing would go beyond the elementary stage of "Hagar" learning.[96] Only after his conversion did Paul realize that his own prior learning dealt with merely elementary matters (Gal 4:3, 9; see comment on Hagar in 4:24–25).

That Paul was advancing *among my people of the same age* makes sense, since hellenistic education involved peer groups. Still, people often associated youth not only with vigor but with violence,[97] which fits some of Paul's activity in this context.[98]

The focus of Paul's training was in *the traditions of my ancestors* (1:14). The term translated *traditions* normally refers to what is passed on and received (to be passed on again). Pharisees were known for their meticulous faithfulness to ancestral traditions.[99] Both Paul (Phil 3:5; cf. Acts 23:6) and at least some advocates for gentile circumcision (Acts 15:5) were Pharisees, and Paul would have gotten his Pharisaic training in Jerusalem, where Pharisees predominated. *The traditions of my ancestors* (1:14) are not

---

[91] E.g., Quintilian *Inst.* 2.7.1; Lucian *Sham Sophist or Solecist* 6; Marcus Aurelius 1.17.4.

[92] E.g., Isocrates *Demon.* 12 (*Or.* 1); Diogenes Laertius 7.1.91; see E. A. Judge, *Jerusalem and Athens: Cultural Transformation in Late Antiquity* (ed. A. Nobbs; Tübingen: Mohr Siebeck, 2010), 261.

[93] On Jewish education, see, e.g., S. Légasse, "Paul's Pre-Christian Career According to Acts," pages 365–90 in *The Book of Acts in Its Palestinian Setting* (ed. R. Bauckham; Grand Rapids, MI: Eerdmans, 1995), 375–77; D. F. Watson, "Education: Jewish and Greco-Roman," *DNTB* 308–13, here 312; discussion in Keener, *Acts*, 1387, 3208–15.

[94] Josephus *Ant.* 20.264; cf. Sir 15:1.

[95] Josephus *Life* 8–12.

[96] *Flight* 202.

[97] E.g., Seneca *Troj.* 250–51; Dio Chrysostom *Or.* 2.1–2; Maximus of Tyre *Or.* 26.5.

[98] See further discussion in Keener, *Acts*, 1388–89, 1446–53.

[99] Mark 7:3, 8–9; Josephus *Ant.* 13.297, 408. Because they often saw many of their traditions already implicit in the law of Moses (m. Ab. 1:1; Sipre Deut. 313.2.4), some successors of Pharisaic teachers suggested that the oral traditions even equaled (Sipra Behuq. par. 2.264.1.1; pq. 8.269.2.14; Sipre Deut. 115.1.1–2; 306/25.1; 351.1.2–3) or outranked (m. Sanh. 11:3) the written law.

inherently negative,[100] but they are passed on from people, in contrast to the gospel he received, which *is not of human origin* (1:11). In the present context, Paul's zeal for them probably also implies nationalistic fervor.[101]

Paul's reference in Gal 1:14 to being *zealous* might evoke ideas associated with his persecuting activities in 1:13. The Greek term here is *zêlôtês*. *Zêlôtês* is not inherently negative, including in Paul's letters (1 Cor 14:12). A wise young person would show zeal and make progress in wisdom by following the law meticulously (Sir 51:13, 17–19, using three of Paul's key terms in Gal 1:14).[102]

Nevertheless, violence characterized Paul's early role as *zêlôtês* (Acts 22:3; his zeal in Phil 3:6). In that respect, Paul was like those who associated *zêlôtês* with the law in a violent way: following the traditions of the Maccabees, they were zealous for the purity of their ancestral customs against contamination from sinful, foreign ways.

Zeal for the law could be aroused by others' disobedience (Ps 119:139; cf. Ps 69:9).[103] Philo praises the zeal of the Israelites who slew their fellow Israelites for idolatry.[104] He also praises those who express zeal for the laws in his own day by their readiness to execute those who break them.[105] Various models of zeal, such as that of Elijah, were used to support violent suppression of sin in the land.[106]

Most influential was Phinehas's act of "zeal," which appeased God's "zeal" (in its other sense as jealousy), in the noun's first use in the LXX (Num 25:11–13). Other texts plainly use the zeal of Phinehas as a model.[107] Philo takes Phinehas's zeal as a model for angrily dispatching even gentile transgressors without trial![108] The Maccabees took his zeal (1 Macc 2:26, 54) as a biblical model for their own zeal for God's law expressed in revolt (1 Macc 2:24–27, 50).[109]

The Maccabees themselves became models of zeal, including for the Zealots, one of the militant nationalist groups during the impending

---

[100]   Cf. 1 Cor 11:2; 2 Thess 2:15; 3:6; Papias 3.7–8, 11, 14 Holmes; 1 Clem. 7.2; Diogn. 11.6.
[101]   Cf., e.g., 1 Macc 2:50; 2 Macc 6:1; 7:2, 8, 24, 30, 37.
[102]   F. Philip, *The Origins of Pauline Pneumatology: The Eschatological Bestowal of the Spirit upon Gentiles in Judaism and in the Early Development of Paul's Theology* (Tübingen: Mohr Siebeck, 2005), 131–32. For zeal for the law, see also, e.g., 2 Macc 4:2; 1QS 9.23.
[103]   In what follows I condense material from Keener, *Acts*, 3222–25; cf. 744–46.
[104]   Philo *Mos.* 1.303; *Spec. Laws* 3.126.
[105]   *Spec. Laws* 2.253.
[106]   1 Macc 2:58; Sir 48:2.
[107]   Sir 45:23; 4 Macc 18:12; Philo *Conf.* 57; *Mos.* 1.304.
[108]   *Spec. Laws* 1.54–57.
[109]   Also Josephus *Ant.* 12.271.

Judean revolt. Josephus associates negative zeal with robbers or social bandits, whom he ultimately depicts as the main cause of the Judean revolt of
66.[110] By that time, some revolutionaries claimed special zeal[111] and therefore
called themselves Zealots.[112]

Many scholars believe that the Maccabees' and Phinehas's "zeal" for God,
which led to violence, is the model for Paul's pre-Christian persecution of
Christians. Such zeal was not impossible for a Pharisee like Paul (Phil 3:5–
6). Judas the Galilean, author of the Judean revolutionary movement, was
largely Pharisaic in his outlook except for his violent nationalism.[113]

Scholars debate whether a specific party *named* "Zealots" existed as early
as Galatians,[114] but whenever that party emerged it probably reflects the
same ideal of nationalistic zeal that Paul did. Paul may link his zeal (Gal
1:14) with persecuting (1:13), as in Phil 3:6 (cf. also Acts 22:3–4). This was
probably directed especially against those who undermined nationalistic
agendas, such as he understood Hellenist Jewish Christians to be doing
(Acts 6:13–14; 8:1–3; 11:19–20).[115]

Paul's vision of Christ includes a *call* (Gal 1:15), as often in the biblical
prophets.[116] As nearly all commentators recognize, Paul's *before I was born
and called* (lit., "from my mother's womb and called") echoes Isa 49:1 and
Jer 1:5. The dominant Greek version of Isa 49:1 uses precisely the same
words for "from my mother's womb" and the indicative form of "called."
Jer 1:5 includes the words "womb" and "from [my] mother" but addition-
ally speaks of the calling to be "a prophet to the nations," just as Paul in Gal
1:16 is called to *proclaim him among the Gentiles* (the same Greek word also
translated *nations*; cf. Rom 11:13).

Instead of simply noting that God "called" Paul from his mother's womb,
Paul adds "set apart," which resembles Jeremiah's "consecrated" (Jer 1:5),
although Paul employs a different Greek term (contrast Sir 49:7).[117] Paul has

[110] Josephus *War* 2.56.
[111] *War* 4.161; 7.270.
[112] *War* 2.651; 4.160, 162, 193–579 passim; 5.3, 5, 7, 101, 250, 358, 528; 6.92, 148; 7.268.
[113] Josephus *Ant.* 18.4, 9, 23. Some Pharisees also were martyred for challenging foreign
       decorations on the temple (*War* 1.648–55; *Ant.* 17.149–63).
[114] See R. A. Horsley and J. S. Hanson, *Bandits, Prophets, and Messiahs: Popular Movements
       in the Time of Jesus* (Minneapolis, MN: Winston, 1985), 214–17.
[115] Donaldson, *Gentiles*, 287; Dunn, *Beginning*, 341–46.
[116] K. Ehrensperger, *Paul and the Dynamics of Power: Communication and Interaction in the
       Early Christ-Movement* (LNTS 325; New York: T&T Clark, 2007), 83–85, 93.
[117] Some are consecrated from the womb for the day of slaughter in 1QHa 7.30; cf. more pos-
       itively being established for the covenant from the womb in 7.28; possible consecration
       from the womb in 1QHa 17.30 (reconstructed).

a special reason to employ this different term, however; it contrasts here
with the use of the same Greek term in 2:12 (its only other use in Galatians),
where Peter separates from gentiles. God separated Paul from his mother's
womb (i.e., allowing him to be born), ultimately for the purpose of *reaching*
gentiles, setting him apart for his mission for the gospel (Rom 1:1, using the
same term). Paul's mission was, originally unknown to Paul, the purpose
for which he was born.

In keeping with this context, Paul was thus *called through* God's *grace*
(1:15), by God's initiative rather than by his prior zeal for his people's traditions (1:14). God had likewise *called* the Galatian believers by *grace* (1:6).

Scholars debate the precise sense of 1:16's first clause. Did God graciously
reveal Christ *in* Paul (ASV, NASB, NET text, NIV, WEB),[118] *by* him, or *to*
him (NRSV, ESV text)?[119] The Greek term *en* here often means "in" or "by,"
and the same ambiguity between those two options appears elsewhere
when Paul uses it with "reveal."[120] Because all three renderings are true in
Paul's thought, a decision here is both difficult on the one hand and probably theologically unnecessary on the other.

Paul received his gospel through Jesus Christ being revealed *to* him
(1:12). Similarly, in Paul's ministry to the gentiles, God's Son is revealed *in*
Paul (2:20) and thereby revealed through him (2:8; cf. Phil 4:9). God's Son
was revealed in Paul so that people could witness Christ's life and suffering
in Paul (Gal 2:20; 3:1; 6:14–15, 17; 2 Cor 4:6, 10–12); God's Son likewise would
be revealed in all believers (Gal 4:6, 19; 5:22–23), who are thus also God's
"sons" (i.e., children; 3:26; 4:7).

What is clear is that this revelation is followed by a purpose clause: God
revealed his Son in Paul not primarily for Paul's sake, but *so that I might
proclaim him among the Gentiles*. The term *proclaim* here is the verb form of
bringing the gospel, the good news revealed to Paul (Gal 1:11) and by which
God had called them (1:6).

Proclaiming Jesus to *gentiles* was Paul's direct commission (1:16); it was
not what the Jerusalem apostles were doing, so there was no need to consult

[118] Longenecker, *Galatians*, 32; Fee, *Galatians*, 45–46; Witherington, *Grace*, 106; Das, *Galatians*, 132–33.
[119] Schreiner, *Galatians*, 100 (emphasizing that Paul saw Christ; cf. 1 Cor 15:8); Oakes, *Galatians*, 57. But as Dunn, *Galatians*, 64, rightly notes, elsewhere Paul expresses revela-tion *to* someone with the dative (1 Cor 2:10; 14:30; Phil 3:15), without using *en*.
[120] In Paul, the verb "revealed" (*apokaluptô*) with "in" (*en*) can mean "revealed in" (Rom 1:17; cf. Ezek 16:36 LXX) or "revealed by means of" (1 Cor 3:13), to the extent that there is a difference.

them (1:16–17). This information also means that the Galatians belonged to *Paul's* commission – not to that of the Jerusalem apostles (2:7–9; cf. Rom 1:13; 11:13). Thus *proclaim him among the gentiles* (1:16) echoes the *gospel … we proclaimed to you* (1:8) that the Galatians received (1:9) and that was *not of human origin* (1:11).

The agitators may claim that Paul's gospel was secondary to that of Jerusalem's true apostles. Paul, however, emphasizes that he did not even confer with humans, including those apostles, at the beginning (1:16–17). Paul employs this term translated *confer* just one other time in his extant letters (indeed, in biblical Greek), and that instance belongs to this introductory narrative: Jerusalem's chief apostles added nothing more to his gospel (Gal 2:6). As Chrysostom noted, Paul is implying that he did not get his message from the other apostles (1:18–19).[121] Like Peter (Matt 16:17), who is Paul's peer (Gal 2:7), Paul's understanding of the gospel did not depend on flesh and blood.[122]

Jews outside *Jerusalem* (1:17) accorded that city special respect, and even travelers from there might be given special respect because they originated from there.[123] Paul may have initially commanded some respect in Galatia because he came from Judea (see Acts 13:15), though such background would not help him in this instance because his rivals also likely hailed from there (cf. Acts 15:1; 2 Cor 11:22). Paul instead emphasizes his independence from Jerusalem; what his foes would have meant as a criticism he turns to his advantage.[124] Far from immediately seeking instruction from Jerusalem, Paul in fact remained far away, in *Arabia*.

Yet *Arabia*, the land of the Arabs, encompassed a vast breadth of territory.[125] Scholars thus debate which part Paul means here. Does he refer to

---

[121]   *Hom. Gal.* 1.15–16; contrast Jerome *Ep. Gal.* 1.1.16.

[122]   D. Wenham, "Paul's Use of the Jesus Tradition: Three Samples," pages 7–37 in *The Jesus Tradition outside the Gospels* (ed. D. Wenham; Sheffield, UK: JSOT Press, 1984), 26. Whether the Galatians would have heard this tradition about Peter is uncertain; despite its single attestation in Matthew; however, it does have claim to be early (W. D. Davies and D. C. Allison, *A Critical and Exegetical Commentary on the Gospel According to Saint Matthew* [3 vols.; ICC; Edinburgh: T&T Clark, 1988–1997], 2:609–15).

[123]   E.g., Josephus *Life* 198.

[124]   A respected manner of argumentation; see, e.g., M. Heath, "Invention," pages 89–119 in *Handbook of Classical Rhetoric in the Hellenistic Period, 330 B.C.–A.D. 400* (ed. S. E. Porter; Leiden: Brill, 1997), 97; Rowe, "Style," 145–46.

[125]   As far south as the Red Sea (Josephus *Ant.* 1.239), it also lay south (*War* 3.51), north (*Ant.* 12.233), and east (*Ant.* 14.83; *War* 1.161; 3.47; 5.160) of Judea. Nabatea thus extended from the Euphrates to the Red Sea (*Ant.* 1.221), and might even be viewed as stretching toward India (perhaps Apuleius *Flor.* 6.2). Pliny E. *Nat.* 6.32.142–62 counts Arabians as widespread, though he counts only the Arabian peninsula as Arabia proper (6.32.143).

the Arabia of Mount Sinai, as in Paul's only other mention of Arabia (Gal 4:25), or, with most scholars, to the lands of Nabatean Arabs especially to the southeast of Damascus? Luke offers us no direct help here; he either did not know of Paul's time there or deems it too irrelevant to his narrative to recount it. (Such compression or omission was acceptable historical and rhetorical practice.)[126]

Geographically speaking, it seems far more probable that Paul remained in Nabatea before "returning to" Damascus (1:17). As E. P. Sanders observes, it probably would have taken Paul more than a month and roughly 400 miles (more than 600 km) to trudge from Damascus to Sinai, and he would need to travel with a caravan or equip an expedition that could carry food and water and protect against bandits.[127] Nabatean Arabia, meanwhile, was comparatively next door. Moreover, Paul did *something* significant among Nabateans, since ethnarchs did not normally hunt down random passersby (2 Cor 11:32–33, an occasion also near Damascus, so probably chronologically related to the one in Gal 1:17). There is little reason for Paul to have returned to Damascus in particular afterward unless it was nearby.[128]

Nabatea was included in the title *Arabia* in the first century.[129] Josephus spoke of Sinai as lying between Egypt and Arabia,[130] but identified Petra, the leading city of Nabatea,[131] as the chief city of Arabia.[132] The Nabatean king Aretas was king of Petra and Arabia,[133] and Nabateans were among the residents of Arabia.[134]

Why Arabia? Did Paul go to Arabia to *confer* with God rather than *with any human being* (1:16)? Or did Paul go there, as a majority of scholars thinks, to begin his mission to *proclaim* Christ *among the Gentiles* (also 1:16)? Luther, as usual, left no doubt of his view on the subject: "It is silly for

[126] See M. L. W. Laistner, *The Greater Roman Historians* (Berkeley: University of California Press; London: Cambridge University Press, 1947), 58–59; P. E. Satterthwaite, "Acts against the Background of Classical Rhetoric," pages 337–79 in *The Book of Acts in Its Ancient Literary Setting* (ed. B. W. Winter and A. D. Clark; Grand Rapids, MI: Eerdmans, 1993), 345; M. R. Licona, *Why Are There Differences in the Gospels? What We Can Learn from Ancient Biography* (New York: Oxford University Press, 2017), 2, 20, 51, 56, 72, 75, 77, 95, 109.
[127] Sanders, *Paul*, 90.
[128] E. W. Burton, *A Critical and Exegetical Commentary on the Epistle to the Galatians* (Edinburgh: T. & T. Clark, 1921), 58.
[129] See, e.g., Strabo 16.4.2.
[130] Josephus *Ag. Ap.* 2.25.
[131] See Strabo 16.4.21; Pliny E. *Nat.* 6.32.144.
[132] Josephus *Ant.* 4.82, 161; 14.80, 362; *War* 1.125, 159, 267; 4.454.
[133] *Ant.* 17.287; 18.109, 112; *War* 1.124.
[134] *Ant.* 1.221; 13.10, 179.

Jerome to ask what Paul did in Arabia. What else would he have done but preach Christ?"[135] If Paul's ministry began in Nabatea, it could have targeted fellow Jews, who were abundant in the region.[136] Paul is explicit that after Jerusalem (1:18) he preached in Syria and Cilicia (1:21–23), but he does not specify what he did before visiting Jerusalem. Whether Paul evangelized Jews or Nabateans or both in Nabatea, he probably preached within Nabatea to Judea's south and east, as in Syria and Cilicia to the north (1:21).[137]

Paul clearly did something active to provoke the hostility of the Nabatean ethnarch in Damascus (2 Cor 11:32–33), and that was probably what Luke suggests that he also did to provoke the hostility of Judeans in Damascus and Jerusalem: preaching (cf. Acts 9:19–24). No letters survive from this period in Paul's ministry, and we have no evidence of Paul's success, but he certainly did not go unnoticed.

Nevertheless, it may be no coincidence that the only two mentions of *Arabia* in the New Testament appear in this letter; like Moses (cf. 2 Cor 3:7–18), Paul has received revelation, and he knows the limitations of the land of the Ishmaelites (encompassing all Arabia)[138] better than do his opponents (Gal 4:24–25). Although Paul's actual Arabia is further north than Sinai, for the Galatians it could still evoke Sinai.

That Paul *afterward returned to Damascus* indicates that after his conversion he left for Nabatea *from* Damascus, comporting well with Luke's depiction of his conversion as somewhere in the vicinity of Damascus (Acts 9:2–3; 22:5–6; 26:12, 20).

A Closer Look: Damascus

Both Acts and Paul (Gal 1:17, which claims that he "returned" there) state that Paul was in Damascus after his conversion (which presumably happened near there; 2 Cor 11:32) before traveling again to Jerusalem.[139]

---

[135] Luther *Second Lectures on Galatians* on Gal 1:17, responding to Jerome *Comm. Gal.* 1.1.17 (Bray).

[136] M. Hengel and A. M. Schwemer, *Paul between Damascus and Antioch: The Unknown Years* (trans. Bowden; London: SCM; Louisville, KY: Westminster John Knox, 1997), 112; M. Hengel, "Paul in Arabia," *BBR* 12 (1, 2002): 47–66.

[137] C. Burfeind, "Paulus in Arabien," *ZNW* 95 (1–2, 2004): 129–30; cf. S. Kim, *Paul and the New Perspective: Second Thoughts on the Origin of Paul's Gospel* (Grand Rapids, MI: Eerdmans, 2002), 103.

[138] Arabia is the land of Ishmael's descendants in Josephus *Ant.* 1.214; 2.32, 213.

[139] With Riesner, *Paul's Early Period*, 263. This excursus is adapted and condensed from Keener, *Acts*, 1627–30.

Damascus was about 135 miles north of Jerusalem, a journey of roughly six days by foot (though it could be covered two or three times as fast by horse). Its pagan religion included elements both old and new; it boasted a massive temple of the Damascene Jupiter, the largest temple we know of in the region of Roman Syria.[140]

Most relevant for Paul's preconversion persecution of fellow Jews, many Jews and also proselytes lived in Damascus; Josephus even claims that a generation later Damascus slaughtered 10,000 to 20,000 Jewish residents.[141] Some scholars estimate that 30,000 to 40,000 Jews lived there in this period. Luke mentions multiple synagogues here (Acts 9:2, 20).[142] Jewish Christians there eventually would have attracted God-fearers, just as local synagogues in Damascus were doing in large numbers.[143] ****

1:18–24: FAR FROM JUDEA

1:18 Then after three years I did go up to Jerusalem to visit Cephas and stayed with him fifteen days;

1:19 but I did not see any other apostle except James the Lord's brother.

1:20 In what I am writing to you, before God, I do not lie!

1:21 Then I went into the regions of Syria and Cilicia,

1:22 and I was still unknown by sight to the churches of Judea that are in Christ;

1:23 they only heard it said, "The one who formerly was persecuting us is now proclaiming the faith he once tried to destroy."

1:24 And they glorified God because of me.

Undoubtedly against the idea that Paul is an inferior, a purveyor of secondhand information from the original apostles in Jerusalem, Paul emphasizes that his direct source is Jesus rather than the Jerusalem apostles.[144] He elaborates a chronology that illustrates the impossibility of depending on the Jerusalem apostles for his knowledge. In doing so, Paul is not discounting their mission or support; he will in fact mention their affirmation that he has an equal and parallel calling from God (2:7–9). But Paul does not

---

[140] W. T. Pitard, "Damascus," *OEANE* 2:103–06, here 104.
[141] Josephus *War* 2.561; 7.368; cf. *Life* 27.
[142] Hengel and Schwemer, *Between Damascus and Antioch*, 51, 54.
[143] Hengel and Schwemer, *Between Damascus and Antioch*, 53, 83; cf. Josephus *War* 2.462–63, 465.
[144] Cf., e.g., Tyson, "Opponents," 249.

regard ties with the Twelve or with Jerusalem as necessary for his direct commission from God.

What did Paul's visit to Peter (1:18)[145] involve? Paul says he went *to visit* him, and he uses the term *historeō*. As with *apokalupsis* and *apokalyptō* in Gal 1:12, 16, we need to be careful not to read a term's later influence into its earlier meaning; Paul only mentions that he went to make Peter's acquaintance, not that he went to get a "history" lesson. Paul's interest here is precisely in dissociating himself from any alleged secondhand dependence on Jerusalem apostles.

Nevertheless, if we ask, on the historical level, why Paul would have interest in visiting Peter in particular, the answer would presumably be Peter's role in the church, which in turn rested on Peter's relationship with Jesus during the latter's public ministry. It is inconceivable that the two did not discuss their respective experiences with Jesus.[146] Indeed, this brief yet intense period of learning from Peter could well be the basis for the rumor of Paul's dependence that Paul must here combat.

Whatever else Paul might have done besides getting to know Peter, however, is beside Paul's own point. The emphasis rests more on the time: no one could sensibly accuse Paul of getting his gospel from Peter. He had already been preaching it for up to three years. Moreover, he spent with Peter only fifteen days inclusive, or about two weeks. As an eleventh-century commentator observed, the point is, "For even if I were in need of instruction, I could hardly have learned enough in so short a period of time."[147]

Nearly all scholars acknowledge that the three years is reckoned inclusively;[148] parts of a year counted as a whole, so this is between thirteen and thirty-six months. Some count the three years from Paul's return to Damascus, and others from Paul's conversion. If, as a greater number of scholars think, the latter is the case, we cannot calculate how much time was spent in each of the two locations.

---

[145] Peter is simply the Greek version of *Cephas*, referring to the same person (D. C. Allison, "Peter and Cephas: One and the Same," *JBL* 111 [3, 1992]: 489–95).

[146] E.g., W. Neil, *The Letter of Paul to the Galatians* (CBC; Cambridge: Cambridge University Press, 1967), 30; Dunn, *Galatians*, 110–13; Matera, *Galatians*, 66–69.

[147] Bruno the Carthusian on Gal 1:18 (Levy); cf. earlier Marius Victorinus *Ep. Gal.* 1.1.18 (Edwards).

[148] H. Koester, *Introduction to the New Testament* (2 vols.; Philadelphia, PA: Fortress, 1982), 2:102; Betz, *Galatians*, 76n190; Matera, *Galatians*, 66; Hengel and Schwemer, *Between Damascus and Antioch*, 107; Schreiner, *Galatians*, 109; de Boer, *Galatians*, 7; Moo, *Galatians*, 108; Das, *Galatians*, 137; Sanders, *Paul*, 92.

As for the other apostles, Paul did not really see any other apostle except James the Lord's brother (Gal 1:19). (In Greek, the name rendered into English as "James" is always "Jacob," the popular Jewish name borrowed from Israel's ancestor.) Whereas Paul came *to visit* Peter (1:18), he only "saw" James (1:19), suggesting even less possible dependence on James than on Peter. Despite some detractors, the text probably does include James as an apostle,[149] a conclusion probably supportable also by Paul's usage in 1 Cor 15:5–7.

James is *the Lord's brother* (Gal 1:19). After the tradition of Mary's perpetual virginity developed, James came to be seen as Joseph's son by a prior marriage or, most often, as Jesus's cousin rather than his half-brother. Most scholars today agree, however, that the earliest sources depict James as Jesus's brother, son of Joseph and Mary.[150]

Unanimous testimony of our early sources agrees that Peter was leader of Jesus' disciples in the early church;[151] by 2:12, however, James (there listed first) seems to be the chief leader in the Jerusalem church (cf. Acts 12:17; 15:13, 19; 21:18), with a role perhaps modeled after Alexandria's Jewish ethnarch. Making a relative as sort of a successor made sense to those familiar with royal and priestly dynasties.[152]

Acts 9:27 declares that Paul met "the apostles." Paul wants to emphasize his partial independence, whereas Luke writes after Paul's approach to gentiles has prevailed and Paul's connections with Jerusalem fit Luke's emphasis on continuity.[153] Paul's specificity here, though apologetically motivated, offers greater precision. In both cases, however, Paul's encounter with Jesus and his gospel preceded his meeting with Jerusalem apostles.[154]

Though Paul's stay in Jerusalem at this time was brief, Luke is undoubtedly correct that Paul preached there (Acts 9:28), since he counts his own mission starting from Jerusalem, the theological center of the world (Rom 15:19). On many matters, Luke's report overlaps substantially with Paul's:[155]

---

[149]   Lightfoot, *Galatians*, 85; Burton, *Galatians*, 60; Moo, *Galatians*, 110.

[150]   Lightfoot, *Galatians*, 252–91; J. P. Meier, "The Brothers and Sisters of Jesus in Ecumenical Perspective," *CBQ* 54 (1, January 1992): 1–28; Meier, *A Marginal Jew: Rethinking the Historical Jesus* (4 vols.; ABRL; New York: Doubleday, 1994-), 1:318–32; see also Tertullian *Adv. Marc.* 4.19; *De Car.* 7.

[151]   See, e.g., Schnabel, *Mission*, 395–98.

[152]   E.g., Josephus *Ant.* 9.45, 160, 233, 257; 18.95; 20.93; *War* 1.664; 2.31, 248; cf. Philostratus *Vit. Apoll.* 2.19.599.

[153]   With Matera, *Galatians*, 110.

[154]   De Boer, *Galatians*, 100.

[155]   I borrow this chart from Keener, *Acts*, 1668; cf. 1687.

Event in Galatians	Gal 1:17–2:1 (and other epistles fitting Galatians' chronology)	Acts 9:19–30; 15:2 (Acts 9:27 presumably corresponds with Gal 1:18 19)
Paul persecuted Christians	Gal 1:13–14; cf. 1 Cor 15:9; Phil 3:6; 1 Tim 1:13	Acts 7:58; 8:1–3; 9:1–2
Conversion near the city of Damascus	Gal 1:17 (implied)	Acts 9:3, 19
Conversion through encountering the risen Christ	Gal 1:12; cf. 1:15–16; 1 Cor 15:8	Acts 9:3–6
Time in Arabia	Gal 1:17; cf. 2 Cor 11:32	–
Damascus three years later	Gal 1:17	Acts 9:23 ("many days later")
Escapes Damascus, let down in a basket from the wall	2 Cor 11:32–33	Acts 9:25
Visits Jerusalem	Gal 1:18–19	Acts 9:26–29
Syro-Cilicia	Gal 1:21	Acts 9:30 (Caesarea, probably briefly; Tarsus); 11:26; 13:1 (Syrian Antioch)
Paul's ministry accepted on a par with Peter's in Syrian Antioch	Cf. Gal 1:21; Gal 2:11 (Paul a well-known minister in Antioch)	Acts 11:26; 13:1; 14:26; 15:22–23, 30, 35; 18:22
Evangelism in south Galatia	Gal 4:13–14; cf. 1 Cor 16:1; cities in 2 Tim 3:11	Acts 13:14–14:24
Troubles with advocates of gentile circumcision in Antioch	Gal 2:11–14 (by implication; this event probably occurs after 2:1–10)	Acts 15:1–2
Return to Jerusalem after fourteen years' absence[156]	Gal 2:1	Acts 15:2 (some prefer Acts 11:30)

Paul emphatically swears an oath to the veracity of his claim of his limited time with the apostles (Gal 1:20). Swearing by a deity invited judgment from the deity if one did not speak the truth. (If Paul knew the tradition against all swearing that appears in Matt 5:33–37, he seems to have understood it as hyperbole.) That Paul goes so far as to call God as witness to the truth suggests that his detractors had presented a different picture,[157] perhaps with some basis in (but a different interpretation of) the facts. Paul's visit may have been summarized generally as a visit to the apostles (a Jerusalem report

---

[156] Riesner, *Paul's Early Period*, 232 (noting that the Antioch incident in Gal 2:11–12 *could* be chronologically before the Jerusalem Council of Gal 2:1–10, but that this is debated; Paul is certainly in Antioch earlier, 11:26; 13:1; 14:26).

[157] So, e.g., Luther *First Lectures on Galatians* on Gal 1:20.

perhaps behind Acts 9:27, if it is not simply an independent generalization), which was then interpreted in line with Paul's dependence on Jerusalem.

In Gal 1:21–22, Paul emphasizes that he *could* not have received training or commissioning from the Jerusalem apostles subsequent to the limited visit to which he has sworn in 1:18–20. Paul was far away from Judea throughout that period prior to his ministry that the Galatians themselves first experienced. Here Luke's summary supplies just a little more information about Paul's ministry in Syria and Cilicia, specifically in Tarsus, Cilicia's capital (Acts 9:30), and Antioch, Syria's capital (Acts 11:25–30; 12:25–13:3).

From the official Roman standpoint Cilicia was joined to Syria as one province in this period.[158] Although Paul as a Tarsian might have viewed Syria and Cilicia as distinct, he probably had reason to mention Cilicia specifically, apart from simply Syria, only if he had spent time in both. (The plural *regions* also implies more than one location.)

Given Syria's massive size and large Jewish population,[159] it was natural for Paul to minister there and to name it in the text first here. Greater Syria's population may have been nearly 4 million by this period,[160] and Syria's leading metropolis, Antioch on the Orontes, was probably the third city of the empire (see comment at Gal 2:11–14).[161] Cilicia was simply one of many possible destinations. Luke's report that Paul was originally from Tarsus helps explain why Paul also evangelized there (Acts 9:11).[162]

Although silent on any details regarding Paul's time in Cilicia, the churches that reportedly existed there by the time of the Jerusalem conference (Acts 15:23, 41) suggest someone's success in evangelizing.[163] Paul's preaching in these regions was sufficiently noteworthy that churches in Judea heard about it (Gal 1:23), probably because of travelers between Jerusalem and Antioch (cf. Acts 11:22–26; Gal 2:11–12), despite the long journey of more than 300 miles.

---

[158]   Ramsay, *Galatians*, 275–78.
[159]   See Josephus *Ag. Ap.* 2.39; *War* 7.43–44; C. H. Kraeling, "The Jewish Community at Antioch," *JBL* 51 (1932): 130–60, here 131–36; W. A. Meeks and R. L. Wilken, *Jews and Christians in Antioch in the First Four Centuries of the Common Era* (SBLSBS 13; Missoula, MT: Scholars Press, 1978), 8–9. On Judaism in Roman Syria, see J. M. G. Barclay, *Jews in the Mediterranean Diaspora: From Alexander to Trajan (323 BCE–117 CE)* (Berkeley: University of California Press, 1996), 249–58.
[160]   See D. Kennedy, "Demography, the Population of Syria, and the Census of Q. Aemilius Secundus," *Levant* 38 (2006): 109–24.
[161]   Josephus *War* 3.29; Herodian 4.3.7.
[162]   On Tarsus, see Keener, *Acts*, 1646–51.
[163]   See further discussion in Hengel and Schwemer, *Between Damascus and Antioch*, 156–57; M. Wilson, "Cilicia: The First Christian Churches in Anatolia," *TynBul* 54 (1, 2003): 15–30.

Far from depending on Jerusalem, as his critics alleged, Paul in fact was unknown by sight to the Judean churches (1:22). That Paul was not physically recognizable to them does not imply that they knew nothing about him; they knew that he was *[t]he one who was formerly persecuting us* (1:23). Moreover, he cannot mean that *no* one would have recognized him, since he was in Jerusalem in 1:18–19 and had to pass through parts of Judea to reach it and to leave it.[164] He simply means that he had little contact with Judea again until 2:1.

Many in the Judean churches may have once seen Paul, since the report mentions "the one who persecuted *us*" (1:23); perhaps Paul means that he simply remained unknown by sight to them in this period. Nevertheless, in an era without television or the Internet, surely only a minority of Judean believers would recognize him by sight. Even in Acts, Ananias, presumably one of those dispersed by Paul's persecution (Acts 8:4), had only *heard* about him (9:13). Given the movement's apparently rapid expansion after Paul's persecution stopped (Acts 9:31; 21:20), many new members would have joined.[165]

Although false rumors may have later circulated about Paul in Jerusalem (Acts 21:21), initially his conversion and subsequent ministry were a cause for celebration there (Gal 1:23–24). Some suggest that Paul echoes some pre-Pauline elements of the report heard in Judea; while this might be true, Paul especially frames this summary in his own words to echo 1:13. The Galatian Christians had *heard* of how Paul in his *earlier* (Gr. *pote*) days was *persecuting the church of God and was trying to destroy it*; now *the churches of Judea* also *heard* about *the one who formerly* (Gr. *pote*) *was persecuting us* and had *tried to destroy* the faith. Moreover, as God called Paul to *proclaim* Christ *among the Gentiles* (1:16), Paul was *now proclaiming* the faith in Syria and Cilicia.

In 1:24, Judean believers *glorified God because of me* [*edoxazon en emoi*]: Paul, i.e., they praised God because of what God had done in converting Paul from persecutor to proclaimer. In light of God perhaps revealing his Son *in* Paul (1:16), some would translate, "honored God *in* me," but "because of" communicates Paul's point better. In the Septuagint, this verb or cognates with *en* followed by a dative noun often refer to God being glorified or honored by some means (e.g., Judg 9:9, *en emoi*

---

[164] Cf. Hengel and Schwemer, *Between Damascus and Antioch*, 38; de Boer, *Galatians*, 101.
[165] With Das, *Galatians*, 144. On the movement's growth, see C. S. Keener, "The Plausibility of Luke's Growth Figures in Acts 2.41; 4.4; 21.20," *JGRChJ* 7 (2010): 140–63.

edoxasen), including through (*en*) those he judged (LXX Exod 14:4, 17; Lev 10:3). Perhaps more relevantly in view of the Isa 49 echo in Gal 1:15, God tells his servant in LXX Isa 49:3, "in you I will be honored" (*en soi doxasthêsomai*).

If Paul's critics cited widespread Judean knowledge of Paul as evidence that he got his gospel from there, Paul could easily refute this. He was not in Judea for much of the time in question (in a court of law this would function like an alibi),[166] and most Judean knowledge about him was second-hand and, unlike the opinion of his critics, positive.

2:1–10: CONSENSUS IN JERUSALEM

2:1 Then after fourteen years I went up again to Jerusalem with Barnabas, taking Titus along with me.

2:2 I went up in response to a revelation. Then I laid before them (though only in a private meeting with the acknowledged leaders) the gospel that I proclaim among the Gentiles, in order to make sure that I was not running, or had not run, in vain.

2:3 But even Titus, who was with me, was not compelled to be circumcised, though he was a Greek.

2:4 But because of false believers secretly brought in, who slipped in to spy on the freedom we have in Christ Jesus, so that they might enslave us –

2:5 we did not submit to them even for a moment, so that the truth of the gospel might always remain with you.

2:6 And from those who were supposed to be acknowledged leaders (what they actually were makes no difference to me; God shows no partiality) – those leaders contributed nothing to me.

2:7 On the contrary, when they saw that I had been entrusted with the gospel for the uncircumcised, just as Peter had been entrusted with the gospel for the circumcised

2:8 (for he who worked through Peter making him an apostle to the circumcised also worked through me in sending me to the Gentiles),

2:9 and when James and Cephas and John, who were acknowledged pillars, recognized the grace that had been given to me, they gave to Barnabas and me the right hand of fellowship, agreeing that we should go to the Gentiles and they to the circumcised.

---

[166] Thus, for example, Cicero shows that his client was far from the scene and could not have made a 700-mile trip in two to three days (*Quinct.* 25.78–80).

2:10 They asked only one thing, that we remember the poor, which was actually what I was eager to do.

Scholars debate whether and to what extent 2:1–10 reflects the events of the Jerusalem Council reported in Acts 15. A significant minority of scholars (including such respected authorities as Ramsay, Bauckham, Bruce, and Trebilco) identify it instead with Paul's trip to deliver famine relief mentioned briefly in Acts 11:30 and 12:25; the "revelation" of Gal 2:2 would then correspond nicely with the prophecy in Acts 11:28. Taken as a whole, however, the correspondences between this passage and Acts 15 are more numerous, and I believe that the problems of the famine visit view outweigh its advantages. With the majority of scholars, therefore (including Lightfoot, Barrett, Betz, Fee, and Kistemaker), I believe that Gal 2:1–10 and Acts 15 reflect the same events, although from the standpoint of different interests. For much fuller comment, see my introduction to Galatians (under the heading, "Date: After the Jerusalem Council").

Certainly Paul recounts the features that he considers relevant to the matter at hand and from his own perspective. One might report even in detail the dialogue when a delegation met with other leaders, but one would naturally report it in such a way that one's hearers would appreciate one's role in it.[167]

Some interpreters have found here the basis for a fierce conflict between Paul and the pillars, the Jerusalem apostles. Far from displaying any direct conflict with these apostles in 2:1–10, however, Paul seems at pains to emphasize their support of his noncircumcision policy. It is this very agreement that makes Peter's about-face in 2:12 appear so hypocritical (2:13). Paul does confront and publicly embarrass Peter in 2:11–14, but in 2:1–10 merely prepares to recount that confrontation. Even in 2:11–14, the nineteenth-century Tübingen approach that reads second- through fourth-century schisms into the debate at Antioch is ill advised; Paul is silent about any enduring schism and continues to recognize that God uses Peter's ministry (1 Cor 3:22; 9:5; 15:5; Gal 2:7–8).[168]

Paul's point is that his message does not depend on Jerusalem: he visited Peter for only two weeks (Gal 1:18) and then went away to Syria and Cilicia (1:21), returning to the Jerusalem apostles only some fourteen years later (2:1). Some count the fourteen years from Paul's conversion; a large number

---

[167] See Rhet. Alex. 30, 1438a.6–19.
[168] See, e.g., Lightfoot, *Galatians*, 292–74, especially 346–74.

of scholars, however, count it as fourteen years after his last meeting with Peter and James in 1:18–19. (On the view articulated in the introduction, Paul does not here count his famine visit in Acts 11:30/12:25, which did not involve meeting with the apostles and would only unnecessarily complicate his account.)

Paul mentions *Barnabas* and *Titus* as if they are known to the Galatians (2:1); Barnabas ministered with Paul in Galatia (Acts 13:13–14:25). Although *revelation* (*apokalupsis*; 2:2) can refer to personal prophetic experience (1 Cor 14:6, 26, 30; 2 Cor 12:1, 7), the uses of the term *revelation* in the context of Galatians refer to the *revelation of Jesus Christ* that God showed to and in Paul, especially with respect to its implications for the gentiles (Gal 1:12, 16; cf. 3:23). Likewise, the phrase *kata apokalupsin* elsewhere refers to the revelation of the gospel (Rom 16:25; Eph 3:3). Paul is thus not going up *in response to a revelation*, as the NRSV translates, but rather in accordance with the specific revelation of the gospel to the gentiles that he had received.

Thus Paul presented in Jerusalem *the gospel that I proclaim among the Gentiles* (2:2), that is, the gospel that was revealed to and in him (1:11, 16), which he has been defending (1:6–9) and preaching (1:23) and would be defending also in the next scene/paragraph (2:14). Paul did not get this gospel from Jerusalem; even at the time he consulted them, he already had his revelation and had already been preaching this gospel for years.

Paul made this presentation privately *with the acknowledged leaders*, literally, to those who were "recognized" (from *dokeô*, 2:2), a term that Paul uses twice more in this passage. Being "recognized" is not a negative description in Greek; it relates to public honor, applicable here to those "recognized" (the same Greek term) as pillars in 2:9. Some suggest that Paul even derives this title from his opponents, who may boast in their own Jerusalem connections and the great apostles there. Certainly his opponents *acknowledged* these *leaders*.

The term can, however, also mean "seemed," and Paul, who sometimes plays on words and their senses (cf. 3:15; 5:12), will point out that their status means nothing to him or to God (2:6). Even in 2:6, however, such language is not hostile; Paul discounted human honor generally (1 Cor 1:26–29), rejecting celebrity status for all Christian leaders, including himself (1 Cor 3:4–9). In effect, Paul is saying that he needed the pillars' approval for the sake of his gospel's credibility (i.e., for the sake of public relations or marketing purposes), but as far as God was concerned Paul's gospel remains true regardless of anyone's approval. Paul remained polite and respectful, humbling himself, despite not respecting human opinions, *until* his hand was forced in 2:11–14. (One needed to employ care when criticizing a respected person.)[169] Paul revisits the term *dokeô* once more in Galatians, where he puts boasters, possibly his opponents, in their place (Gal 6:3).

Nevertheless, Paul's meeting was not exclusively a private meeting with the three major pillars, since someone brought in others whom Paul did not consider even true believers (Gal 2:4). Probably Paul has in mind a meeting of some or all of the apostles and elders present in Jerusalem as opposed to the entire assembly of believers there (cf. Acts 15:6).[170] Our sources do not specify whether the false believers at this point were actually elders (cf. Acts 20:17, 30) or were other influential persons whom some overly tolerant elders simply brought in contrary to the agreement (cf. Gal 2:4a).

It is not fully clear whether Paul's concern about *running ... in vain* (2:2) is the reason that he presented his gospel in Jerusalem or the reason that he did so privately; if the latter, he trusted the judgment of the leaders more than that of the Jerusalem church generally. Paul's concern about *running ... in vain* does not imply that he was uncertain about his gospel himself; he in fact defended it on this occasion (2:5). But if those who had greater influence disagreed, they could undercut Paul's mission and lead some of his converts away from the faith (cf. 5:4), so that his mission proved *in vain*. His ministry would be *in vain* if his converts did not persevere in the true gospel for eternal life (4:11; 1 Cor 15:2, 10, 14, 58; 2 Cor 6:1; 1 Thess 3:5; for running in vain, see Phil 2:16).

Paul often uses such athletic images (Phil 1:30), including running (Gal 5:7; Rom 9:16; 1 Cor 9:24, 26; Phil 2:16; cf. Acts 20:24; 2 Tim 4:7),[171] to depict his striving and unwillingness to give up without achieving the goal. Paul's converts originally were also *running well*, but his rivals had tripped them up (Gal 5:7). Other ancient speakers in the Greco-Roman world commonly employed athletic images,[172] including running.[173] Some argue that Paul's

---

[169] Hermogenes *Method* 18.434.
[170] Luke apparently conflates by condensing into one what were at least two audiences; see Acts 15:12, 22.
[171] See V. C. Pfitzner, *Paul and the Agon Motif: Traditional Athletic Imagery in the Pauline Literature* (NovTSup 16; Leiden: Brill, 1967), 99; cf. Heb 12:1.
[172] E.g., Aeschines *Ctes.* 179; Isocrates *To Nicocles* 11, *Or.* 2; *Rhet. Her.* 4.3.4; Cicero *Att.* 13.21; Seneca *Ep. Lucil.* 80.3; *Ben.* 5.3.1; *Dial.* 1.2.3; 4.15.2; Epictetus *Diatr.* 1.2.25–26; 1.4.13; 1.18.21–23; 2.5.15–17; 2.17.29; 2.18.27–29; 3.20.9–10; 3.22.52; 4.4.30; Dio Chrysostom *Or.* 9.11–12; Philo *Worse* 32; *Free* 88; 4 Macc 17:12, 15; *Sib. Or.* 3.738–39; see further Pfitzner, *Agon Motif*, 23–72 (esp. 28–35).
[173] Diogenes in Dio Chrysostom *Or.* 9.10–12 and Diogenes Laertius 6.2.34; Cicero *Brutus* 67.236; Menander Rhetor 2.7, 406.14–24; Porphyry *Marc.* 32.500.

image also echoes the Old Testament (esp. Isa 65:23), which is probably true at least in passages where Paul speaks of laboring in vain (Phil 2:16).

That *even Titus … was not compelled to be circumcised* (2:3) suggests what the meeting was likely intended to be about, and indicates beyond question what the meeting came to be about: determining whether gentiles needed to be circumcised (Acts 15:1, 5).[174] Paul chooses these words carefully, because in the next paragraph he will accuse *Peter* of de facto compelling gentiles to convert to Judaism (2:14), and in 6:12 he denounces those now trying to compel the Galatian believers to be circumcised. These are three of the only four uses of the term *compel* (*anagkazô*) in the Pauline corpus.

Paul's words reflect a tension in Judean culture. Roughly a decade after Paul wrote Galatians, some Judeans reportedly tried to "compel" gentiles wishing to remain among the holy people to be circumcised.[175] Although such behavior may have once appeared honorable among Judeans,[176] Josephus knows that his own resistance to those insistent on circumcision will appear more honorable to his own Diaspora audiences. In the same way, Diaspora audiences would likely recoil at Paul's description of the circumcisionists, while respecting Paul's stand for gentiles' freedom.

A Closer Look: Images of Freedom and Slavery[177]

In Diaspora sources, "compulsion" (Gal 2:3) often contrasts with "freedom" (2:4; 5:1, 13).[178] Greek thinkers quite often warned against being enslaved by false ideologies[179] or, most often, by passions.[180]

Jews who emphasized circumcising gentiles (2:3) and appreciated Paul's earlier zeal for ancestral traditions (cf. 1:13) might think of *freedom* in terms

[174] A minority of scholars argues that Titus chose to be circumcised voluntarily (or that some words are missing and Titus was circumcised), but 2:5 and Paul's emphasis on apostolic support in this passage undermine the cogency of this reading.
[175] Josephus *Life* 113. For comparisons and contrasts between this episode and Paul, see J. R. Harrison, "Why Did Josephus and Paul Refuse to Circumcise?" *Pacifica* 17 (2004): 137–58.
[176] *Ant.* 13.257–58, 318–19. 1 Macc 2:46 might also be relevant, if it includes gentiles and not just Jewish boys who had not been circumcised.
[177] Much of this excursus is condensed from Keener, *Mind,* 39–41; see more fully, Keener, *John,* 750–51.
[178] Philo *Free* 36, 95–96; *Dreams* 2.196; Josephus *Ant.* 14.77; Musonius Rufus 16, p. 106.8 (Lutz).
[179] E.g., Seneca *Ep. Lucil.* 8.7; 27.4; Plutarch *Lect.* 1, *Mor.* 37E; *Superst.* 5, *Mor.* 167B.
[180] E.g., Plato *Phaedrus* 238E; Cicero *Amic.* 22.82; *Off.* 1.29.102; 1.38.136; 2.5.18; Seneca *Ben.* 3.28.4; *Ep. Lucil.* 14.1; 39.6; 47.17; 110.9–10; 116.1; *Nat. Q.* 1.16.1; Musonius Rufus 3, p. 40.19; Epictetus *Diatr.* 3.24.70–71, 75.

of nationalistic liberation, recalling fondly the Maccabean resistance.[181] God grants political liberty for obedience to laws,[182] and freedom includes freedom to practice God's laws.[183] Philo applies it to liberation from passion[184] and for reasoning not bound to the body but (verb *eleutheroô*) liberated from its constraints.[185] ★★★

Because Paul fiercely resisted Titus's circumcision in Galatians, some scholars challenge the plausibility of him supervising Timothy's in Acts 16:3. Perhaps Paul's contemporaries noted the apparent inconsistency as well (see comment on Gal 5:11). Nevertheless, the alleged inconsistency appears only at a surface level, for the circumstances are quite different, as commentators have long noted.[186] Timothy's mother was Jewish (Acts 16:1; so also 2 Tim 1:5); the circumcision was for mission (Acts 16:3) rather than salvation or spiritual benefit (cf. Acts 15:1); and Timothy did not face compulsion. If Paul writes Galatians after Timothy's circumcision in south Galatia (Acts 16:1–3), however – a case his Galatian audience would have surely known – it would not be surprising that the Galatians might need some clarification from him, which the Titus episode could provide.

The circumstances of the Titus incident, in some way analogous to the Galatians' current situation, obviously stirred Paul. As commentators regularly note, Paul's grammar becomes unusually careless in 2:3–5, which is grammatically disconnected from its context. Such anacolutha are not uncommon in Paul, but this passage offers the most obvious example and has generated a wide range of interpretations.[187] The lapses here appear to reveal Paul's angry state; de Boer suggests that "The memory of the encounter causes his grammar to break down."[188] The situation might also be too urgent for Paul to have reworked this letter's dictated rough draft.

People understood that haste or emotion could affect grammar,[189] and forensic speech, as opposed to epideictic, was even *supposed* to display some

[181] Cf. Dunn, *Galatians*, 100.
[182] Josephus *Ant.* 12.281.
[183] *Ant.* 12.281; 13.198.
[184] E.g., *Alleg.* 3.17; *Heir* 271.
[185] *Heir* 68.
[186] E.g., Chrysostom *Hom. Gal.* 5.11 (Edwards); Rudolf Gwalther *Sermons on Galatians* on Gal 2:3 (Bray); F. J. A. Hort, *Judaistic Christianity* (ed. J. O. F. Murray; 1894; repr., Grand Rapids, MI: Baker, 1980), 84–85; Betz, *Galatians*, 89.
[187] See, e.g., B. Orchard, "The Ellipsis between Galatians 2,3 and 2,4," *Bib* 54 (1973): 469–81; A. C. M. Blommerde, "Is There an Ellipsis between Galatians 2,3 and 2,4?" *Bib* 56 (1975) 100–02.
[188] De Boer, *Galatians*, 112.
[189] Cf., e.g., Virgil *Aen.* 1.135; Fronto *Ad M. Caes.* 4.2.3; on ellipsis signifying emotion, see Anderson, *Glossary*, 41.

clumsy constructions.[190] Writers and speakers communicating rebukes were expected to adopt an angry attitude; while this could be feigned, many argued that feeling the passions that one sought to convey was far more effective than merely simulating them.[191]

Others suggest that Paul leaves unsaid something about their motives to insinuate their guilt, a rhetorical move that was more effective than articulating the guilt explicitly in ways more open to challenge (cf. similarly Acts 24:19; Phlm 19).[192] (For that matter, in an informal letter even an orator could change his mind about something in mid-sentence, deciding not to finish the thought.)[193]

Paul speaks of his challengers, who sought to circumcise Titus, as *false believers* (lit., false siblings, as in 2 Cor 11:26; Gal 2:4). That is, unlike the Galatians who remain spiritual siblings (repeatedly in Galatians: 1:11; 3:15; 4:12, 28, 31; 5:11, 13; 6:1, 18), and unlike Peter, who is merely inconsistent (and thus hypocritical) in 2:11–14, these critics are followers of a false and damnable gospel (1:6–10). They were *secretly brought in*, perhaps slipped into the assembly of apostles and elders by some leaders who tolerantly wished their voice to be heard – or perhaps they earlier slipped into the assembly of believers though they were in reality *false believers*. Evidently they and whoever smuggled them in regarded them as genuine believers, in contrast to Paul's estimate. Paul, however, sees them as foreshadowing the sort of false teachers who have now invaded Galatia in his absence.

Their covert entrance appears particularly devious in connection with their mission *to spy* (2:4). Depending on how far Paul presses the metaphor, Paul might imply that the false believers were ultimately in cahoots with nonbelieving Judeans who pressured Judean believers (cf. 6:12).

Ancient writers sometimes used the image of spying figuratively.[194] This is not the only place where Paul uses the image of spiritual warfare or battle (Rom 7:23; 13:12; 2 Cor 10:3–6; Eph 6:11–17; 1 Thess 5:8). Such warfare

---

[190]   Fronto in Naber p. 211 (trans. C. R. Haines, LCL 1:40).

[191]   For simulating, see Isocrates *To Nicocles* 23 (*Or.* 2); Fronto *Ad M. Caes.* 3.6; for the orator feeling the emotion, Cicero *De or.* 2.46.189–91; cf. Pliny *Ep.* 6.33.10.

[192]   Dunn, *Galatians*, 97. For this rhetorical move of *insinuatio* and related tactics, see Demosthenes *Cor.* 268; Dionysius of Halicarnassus *Lysias* 24; Cicero *Verr.* 2.5.66.170; *Agr.* 24.63–64; *Cat.* 1.6.14; *Pis.* 2.3; Hermogenes *Method* 7.419–20; further examples in Keener, *Acts*, 3415–16.

[193]   Pliny *Ep.* 8.22.4; cf. Cicero *Att.* 7.18, 23; 13.2; 14.12.

[194]   See Seneca *Ep. Lucil.* 2.5 in H.-J. Klauck, *The Religious Context of Early Christianity: A Guide to Graeco-Roman Religions* (trans. B. McNeil; Minneapolis, MN: Fortress, 2003), 356.

imagery was common, including in oratory,[195] moral exhortations,[196] and especially philosophers.[197]

Paul, however, does envision genuine spiritual powers involved in genuine conflict, as in Eph 6:10–17 (cf. Rom 8:38; 16:20; 1 Cor 7:5; 1 Thess 2:18). Paul also elsewhere envisions Satan as deceptive (2 Cor 2:11; 11:14) and his opponents as agents of Satan (2 Cor 11:13–14). The surface level of conflict here, however, is with human adversaries Paul deems as treacherous.

Rather than accepting subjugation, Paul and his allies resisted these enslaving spies, not letting down their guard *even for a moment* (Gal 2:5). In a sense, then, Paul presents himself as now a *truer* Jewish nationalist than his adversaries, now contending for freedom in a more effective way than earlier in 1:13–14. Emphasizing consensus, Luke highlights the roles of Peter and James (Acts 15:7–11, 13–21), but at some point Paul evidently played a more directly argumentative role than simply offering testimonies (Acts 15:12). Paul was standing firm with the long-range effects on gentile believers in view – including his current audience in Galatia.

Although this passage's *false believers* are not Paul's opponents in Galatia – Paul surely would have afforded himself of the opportunity to specify the connection explicitly had the people been the same – from a literary standpoint they prefigure them and from a historical standpoint they may have influenced them.

Bridging the Horizons: What's Worth Fighting for

Those of us who were once in circles where minor details of belief were treated as gospel issues worth fighting for might wonder whether Paul here extends the implications of the gospel too far. After all, the heart of the gospel is Jesus's death for our sins and resurrection, according to the Scriptures (1 Cor 15:1–7). Could he not have been more gracious to those who differed on a secondary matter?

If we consider this matter secondary, however, we need only consider the likely outcome had Paul forfeited the argument. If gentiles needed to be circumcised to be full members of God's people, the Jesus movement's appeal to gentiles would not have extended further than the appeal of their

---

[195] E.g., Dionysius of Halicarnassus *Demosth.* 32; Cicero *De or.* 3.14.55; Seneca *Controv.* 9, pref. 4; Pliny *Ep.* 1.20.3; 4.22.5; 7.25.6.

[196] E.g., Cicero *Fam.* 4.7.2; *Brut.* 2.7; Dio Chrysostom *Or.* 49.10.

[197] E.g., Philodemus *Prop.* col. 4.6–15; Seneca *Ep. Lucil.* 96.5; 109.8; Epictetus *Diatr.* 1.14.15; 4.5.25–32.

contemporaries in the synagogues: it would remain an ethnic faith, a variation on the range of options that other Jewish circles already offered. Paul's divine mission to gentiles demanded freedom from encumbrances that would culturally alienate gentiles.

The specific situation here is imposing the law, but interpreters from Luther to the New Perspective have been right to find other implications as well. If imposing a law once given by God himself is wrong, how much more is it wrong to impose regulations that are not even God-given? For example, had the cultural situation been reversed, Paul certainly would have defended Jewish believers against gentile cultural impositions demanded by later anti-Semites (1 Cor 7:18–19; Gal 5:6).

These observations have serious implications for the history of Christian mission. When missionaries mix up their own culture with the gospel and impose this mixture in other cultures, they repeat the error of Paul's rivals in Galatia. Christian mission that follows Paul's model should contextualize the gospel in the ways that are most intelligible in the receiving culture.****

Paul is not impressed with leaders' status (2:6). He speaks of *what they actually were*, lit. "what they once [Gr. *pote*] were." Paul's other two uses of *pote* in Galatians refer to his own former life; here he thus probably refers to their special role as disciples of Jesus during his earthly ministry.[198] Subsequent generations might venerate them as saints, but that was plainly not always how all their peers experienced them.

Their status *makes no difference to* Paul (2:6). Ancient Mediterranean society heavily emphasized social status. Class and other social distinctions were crucial in how people related to one another,[199] and by the next century this was explicit even in matters of law[200] and dream interpretation.[201] Many philosophers disregarded status, at least in principle,[202] though ordinary Romans did so only during Saturnalia.[203]

---

[198]   With, e.g., Dunn, *Galatians*, 102; Das, *Galatians*, 179–80; Barclay, *Gift*, 365n36.
[199]   See, e.g., Polybius 26.1.1–3, 12; Livy 41.20.1–3; Suetonius *Dom.* 8.3; Pliny *Ep.* 9.5.2–3; Phaedrus 1.3; Babr. 101; Apuleius *Metam.* 3.11.
[200]   E.g., P. Garnsey and R. Saller, *The Roman Empire: Economy, Society, and Culture* (Berkeley: University of California Press, 1987), 115–16.
[201]   E.g., Artemidorus *Oneir.* 4.26.
[202]   See, e.g., Seneca *Ep. Lucil.* 47.16; Dio Chrysostom *Or.* 9.8–9; T. Engberg-Pedersen, *Paul and the Stoics* (Louisville, KY: Westminster John Knox; Edinburgh: T&T Clark, 2000), 76–77.
[203]   See J. Toner, *Popular Culture in Ancient Rome* (Malden, MA; Cambridge, UK: Polity, 2009), 93–94.

Perhaps Paul treated status the way Stoics viewed *adiaphora*, "matters of indifference."[204] Stoics regarded matters beyond their control[205] and matters that were neither good nor bad of themselves as indifferent matters.[206] Gentiles who respected popular philosophers who disdained status could also appreciate Paul's disregard for status here.[207]

Human status made *no difference* to Paul because it was irrelevant to God, whose perspective could be trusted as true. Jewish people widely emphasized the truth that *God shows no partiality* (Deut 10:17; 2 Chron 19:7);[208] Paul's wording reflects traditional Jewish idiom.[209] Although Paul applies the principle to status in 2:6, it informs even the thrust of his letter in terms of ethnic partiality (and by implication other roles as well; cf. 3:28), as in Rom 2:11 or Acts 10:34.[210]

In any case, Paul says, *those leaders contributed nothing to me* (2:6). The term *contributed* recalls the same Greek term in 1:16 (where it is translated *confer*). Just as Paul did not depend on the Jerusalem leaders for his gospel originally (1:16), he did not depend on them for the truth of his gospel now. He may also mean that they did not add any requirements to his gospel, such as circumcision; this thought picks up in verse 10, where they *asked only one thing*.[211] While they *contributed nothing to* Paul, however, they did recognize his mission and the truth of his gospel for the gentiles (2:7–9). God rather than human leaders called him, but (note the strong adversative *alla* in 2:7) human leaders recognized his calling.

They understood that (2:7) God gave Peter the gospel that he would preach among Jews (presumably including much of the gospel tradition that he witnessed), but God gave Paul (as noted in Gal 1:11–12, 16) the distinctive gospel that he would preach among gentiles (cf. "my gospel" in

204 Betz, *Galatians*, 94. On this topos in Paul, see J. L. Jaquette, *Discerning What Counts: The Function of the Adiaphora Topos in Paul's Letters* (Atlanta, GA: Scholars Press, 1995).

205 Lucian *Phil. Sale* 21.

206 Arius Didymus 2.7.7, p. 42.13–27.

207 See J. L. Jaquette, "Paul, Epictetus, and Others on Indifference to Status," *CBQ* 56 (1, 1994): 68–80.

208 Sir 35:15; Jub. 5:16; 21:4; 33:18; Ps. Sol. 2:18; Wis 6:7; see further J. M. Bassler, *Divine Impartiality: Paul and a Theological Axiom* (SBLDS 59; Chico, CA: Scholars Press, 1982), 7–119.

209 M. Silva, "Galatians," pages 785–812 in *Commentary on the New Testament Use of the Old Testament* (ed. G. K. Beale and D. A. Carson; Grand Rapids, MI: Baker Academic, 2007), 787.

210 As Barclay, *Gift*, 435, notes, God has different criteria of worth.

211 On the grammar here, see B. W. Longenecker, *Remember the Poor: Paul, Poverty, and the Greco-Roman World* (Grand Rapids, MI: Eerdmans, 2010), 196.

Rom 2:16; 16:25; similarly Eph 3:6–8). This distinctiveness cannot mean that they preached different gospels regarding Jesus's death and resurrection or its unique efficacy for salvation (1 Cor 15:1–4); a different gospel in that sense was no gospel at all (Gal 1:6–7). Instead, Paul's wording in 2:7 presumably implies the feature of his gospel for the gentiles that was most distinctive, or at least most relevant for the matter at hand: it was good news *for the uncircumcised*, precisely *as* those who were *uncircumcised*.[212] In Greek, these titles are literally "Uncircumcision" (i.e., gentiles) and "Circumcision" (i.e., Jews). This is *synecdoche* or metonymy,[213] but the language nevertheless could be shocking and offensive.[214]

Given his rivals' likely appeal to the authority of Jerusalem, Paul has reason to emphasize this agreement (2:7–9). The Jesus movement's top leaders shared the consensus that ministry to uncircumcised gentiles was *Paul's* divine commission, not that of the Jerusalem pillars. Jesus's followers in Galatia were Paul's responsibility, in his sphere of divine enablement (cf. Rom 1:5, 13–15; 11:13; 15:15–21; 2 Cor 10:13–15), not theirs. So why should Galatian believers let some Jerusalem interlopers modify Paul's gospel?

It was the way that God *worked through* Paul among gentiles in a manner analogous to how he worked through Peter among Jews (2:8) that assured the Jerusalem leaders that God entrusted Paul with the gospel (2:7). Although briefer than one would likely expect in a speech, this comparison of Peter and Paul would also appeal to ancient audiences accustomed to hearing rhetorical *synkrisis*, or comparison.[215] By comparing something favorably with something else known to be good, one rhetorically elevated the status of the component being compared;[216] placing Paul in Peter's category speaks favorably of Paul for those who respected Peter. Luke essentially follows the same practice by comparing Peter and Paul in Acts.[217]

Paul elsewhere uses the term translated *worked* (*energeô*) with reference to the effectiveness of the gospel (1 Thess 2:13; cf. Gal 5:6) and to God's activity in believers (Eph 3:20; Phil 2:13), empowering ministry (1 Cor 12:6, 11;

[212] With Fee, *Galatians*, 68.
[213] So Luther (1535) on 2:7. On this figure, see Rhet. Her. 4.32.43–4.33.45; Anderson, *Glossary*, 77, 112; Aune, *Dictionary of Rhetoric*, 453–54; Rowe, "Style," 126–27.
[214] See Barclay, *Gift*, 363, on the "good news of the foreskin."
[215] Theon *Progymn.* 2.86–88; 10.3–4; Forbes, "Comparison," 150–60.
[216] Dionysius of Halicarnassus *Demosth.* 33; Fronto *Ad Ant. Imp.* 1.2.4; Menander Rhetor 1.2, 353.9–10; 2.1–2, 376.31–377.2; 2.3, 380.21–22, 30–31; 2.10, 417.5–9, 13–17; Hermogenes *Progymn.* 8. On Syncrisis 19–20. Self-praise was acceptable if conducted in appropriate ways; see Plutarch *Praising*; Marshall, *Enmity*, 121–29, 266–67; Forbes, "Self-Praise."
[217] See Keener, *Acts*, 561–62, 568–73.

Col 1:29), sometimes including miracles (Gal 3:5).[218] Luke reports that at the Jerusalem council Paul and Barnabas reported concrete signs of God's blessing on their gentile mission (Acts 15:12). The coming of the Spirit through Paul's ministry (3:2; cf. 1 Cor 2:4; 1 Thess 1:5–6) was also a sign that paralleled him with Peter (Acts 10:44–46; 19:6).

This working (2:8) demonstrates God's *grace* (2:9) in the sense of his special empowerment or gifting.[219] So far as the apostles were concerned, the clear activity in Paul of the same Spirit who worked in them, even in ways different from *how* the Spirit worked in them, was proof enough of Paul's calling.

In 2:9, Paul designates as pillars the chief leaders, James, Cephas, and John.[220] In the earliest Christian sources, John often appears alongside Peter, always named subsequent to him and usually as his otherwise silent companion.[221] They belonged to the trio of Jesus's closest disciples;[222] some time after the martyrdom of John's brother James (Acts 12:2), Jesus's brother James assumed this role.

Pillars was a familiar designation for important persons,[223] similar to the modern idiom "pillars of our community." Lacking more specific indicators otherwise in the context, most of Paul's audience in Galatia would probably think in these terms.[224] Moreover, even such an understanding in Judea would have been lost on Paul's Galatian audience without further explanation.

---

[218] *Energeô* is not, however, a standard technical term; see, e.g., M. Hadas, ed., *Aristeas to Philocrates (Letter of Aristeas)* (New York: Harper & Brothers, 1951), 182, on Let. Aris. 210.

[219] Cf., e.g., Rom 1:5; 12:3, 6; 15:15; 1 Cor 1:4–5; 3:10; Eph 3:2, 7–8; 4:7. See Dunn, *Galatians*, 108, comparing *charismata*.

[220] 1 Clem. 5.2 seems to include Paul (5.5) as well as Peter (5.4) as pillars of the church (as here, without direct reference to a spiritual temple). For these chief leaders, including in subsequent tradition, see Lightfoot, *Galatians*, 292–374 ("St Paul and the Three").

[221] E.g., Mark 5:37; 9:2; 13:3; 14:33; Acts 3:1, 3–4, 11; 4:1, 13, 19; 8:14, 17, 25; cf. John 13:23–24; 20:2–4; 21:7, 20; keeping in mind the early decease of John's brother in Acts 12:2.

[222] Mark 5:37; 9:2; 14:33; cf. 13:3. Jerome *Ep. Gal.* 1.2.7–8 (Edwards) also notes this association, as do many more recent commentators (e.g., R. H. Gundry, *Matthew: A Commentary on His Literary and Theological Art* [Grand Rapids, MI: Eerdmans, 1982], 342). Some compare Qumran's use of twelve and three (e.g., Brinsmead, *Response*, 104–5), although at Qumran the three were separate from the twelve (G. R. Driver, *The Judaean Scrolls: The Problem and a Solution* [Oxford: Blackwell, 1965], 523).

[223] E.g., Pindar *Ol.* 2.81–82; Cicero *Verr.* 2.3.76.176.

[224] Some scholars note the application to the patriarchs in later Jewish sources; this connection in the Judean church is not impossible, but evidence for this specific tradition is not pervasive and this was only one Jewish way of applying the image of pillars to individuals. Cf., e.g., Ps 144:12; Jer 1:18; 4 Macc 17:3; Sir 36:24; 1QSa [= 1Q28a] 1.12; 4Q550[a-b] frg. 2–3, esp. 3.4; 2 Bar. 2:1–2; 4 Bar. 1:2.

It is possible that Paul presupposes the image of them as pillars in God's temple, as scholars often argue,[225] since Paul envisions the believing community as a temple (1 Cor 3:16–17; 2 Cor 6:16) and apostles as among those who lay its foundations (cf. Matt 16:18; Rom 15:20; 1 Cor 3:10–14; Eph 2:20–21; Rev 21:14).[226] The early nickname *Peter* (Aramaic *Cephas*), designating the "rock," could also support this idea.[227] If so, however, it is doubtful that Paul's Galatian audience would catch this narrower sense here, since Paul makes no temple allusions in the context. Early Christians continued the image in other writings without such allusions in the context.[228]

In the present context, giving Barnabas and Paul *the right hand of fellowship* indicates an agreement. (Some scholars even think that Paul quotes or, much more likely, echoes the agreement in some words in 2:7–10.) Giving *the right hand* and taking another's right hand could communicate a range of positive sentiments.[229] More specifically relevant here may be corporate, official uses. As here, clasping right hands was a way of establishing an agreement, friendship, or good faith,[230] including between peoples.[231] Perhaps relevant to the request to Paul in 2:10, the gesture could even function as a promise of assistance.[232]

Although some suggest that James later reneges on this agreement because no oath is sworn,[233] Paul is silent about both the lack of oath and

[225] E.g., already Jerome *Ep. Gal.* 1.2.7–8.
[226] For Jewish figurative temple imagery, see, e.g., Ps 114:2; 1QS 8.5–6; 4Q511 f35.2–3; Bertril Gärtner, *The Temple and the Community in Qumran and the New Testament: A Comparative Study in the Temple Symbolism of the Qumran Texts and the New Testament* (Cambridge: Cambridge University Press, 1965); among gentiles, see Porphyry *Marc.* 19.318–19; Keener, *Acts*, 1033–34; Keener, *Mind*, 147–49; P. N. Richardson, "What Are the Spiritual Sacrifices of 1 Peter 2:5? Some Light from Philo of Alexandria," *EvQ* 87 (1, 2015): 3–17; Richardson, "The Influence of Hellenistic Philosophy on Paul's Figurative Temple Language Applied to the Corinthians" (PhD diss., Asbury Theological Seminary, 2016).
[227] On the historical roots of this tradition, see further Davies and Allison, *Matthew*, 2:601–15; C. S. Keener, *The Gospel of Matthew: A Socio-rhetorical Commentary* (Grand Rapids, MI: Eerdmans, 2009), 423–30.
[228] 1 Clem. 5.2.
[229] See much fuller discussions in C. S. Keener, "The Pillars and the Right Hand of Fellowship in Galatians 2:9," *JGRChJ* 7 (2010): 51–58, esp. 51–55; Keener, *Acts*, 3316–17.
[230] E.g., Sophocles *Philoc.* 812–13; *Oed. Col.* 1632; Euripides *Heracl.* 307–08; Xenophon *Cyr.* 4.2.7, 17–19; 8.4.25–26; *Hell.* 4.1.38; Tacitus *Ann.* 2.71; 15.28; *Hist.* 15.1 (during adoption).
[231] E.g., Xenophon *Cyr.* 4.6.10; 5.2.14; 6.1.48; *Anab.* 2.3.28; 7.3.1; Dionysius of Halicarnassus *Ant. rom.* 6.84.4; Tacitus *Hist.* 1.54; 2.8; 2 Macc 12:12; Josephus *Life* 30.
[232] Quintus Curtius 4.2.17.
[233] Esler, "Agreement." One could swear an oath or promise while clasping right hands (Sophocles *Philoc.* 942; *Wom. Tr.* 1181; Euripides *Hel.* 838–39; *Med.* 21; Xenophon *Anab.* 2.3.28; Josephus *Ant.* 18.328, 334).

the alleged reneging.[234] It would be dishonorable for James to violate the agreement even if no oath were sworn (cf. Jas 5:12; Matt 5:33–37); breaking a pledge of the right hand was deemed perfidious.[235] Thus the psalmist laments the breach of covenant implied in "a right hand of falsehood" (Ps 144:8, 11).

Paul specifies that this *right hand* involves *fellowship* (*koinōnia*). For Paul, all members of Christ's body were in community with Christ and one another (1 Cor 1:9; 10:16; 2 Cor 6:14; 13:13; Phil 2:1; 3:10). Sometimes Paul uses this Greek noun and its cognate verb for believers sharing economic resources (Rom 12:13; 2 Cor 8:4; 9:13; Phil 4:15; Phlm 6–7; probably Gal 6:6), including for the saints at Jerusalem (Rom 15:26–27). Although unity in Christ, and perhaps recognition of a peer relationship, is the idea here, the pillars may have also thought of economic sharing (note Paul's caveat in Gal 2:10).

The leaders agree *that we* (Paul and Barnabas) *might go to the Gentiles, and they to the circumcised*. The agreement does not mean that Paul could not preach to Jews or Peter to gentiles. In fact, the NRSV's *we should go* does not appear in Greek, and the context invites us to infer a different sort of division of labor. It is not likely merely geographic, since more Jews lived in the Diaspora than in the holy land.[236] It may be primarily ethnic, but not in the sense of exclusive rights to preach.[237]

Rather, gentiles were in Paul's sphere of ministry, whereas the circumcised were in that of the pillars. The reason, in context, is that God entrusted Paul with the gospel for the uncircumcised (2:7) and particularly enabled him in this sphere (2:8). That is, it is a general division of responsibility and representative leadership.[238]

Although Paul insists that the pillars added nothing to his calling to the gentiles (2:6), such as no requirements for circumcision (2:3), from Jerusalem's perspective the agreement apparently did add something to his mission: the need to *remember the poor* (2:10). Benefaction demanded reciprocity, and the pillars may have seen Paul's commitment to the needy as

---

[234] Das, *Galatians*, 191, 200.
[235] Valerius Maximus 9.2.1; Josephus *War* 2.450–56; cf. Cicero *Phil.* 13.2.4.
[236] With Das, *Galatians*, 184. E. J. Schnabel, *Paul the Missionary: Realities, Strategies and Methods* (Downers Grove, IL: InterVarsity; Leicester, UK: Apollos, 2008), 48–49, argues that Gal 2:7–9 is *not* a turf division (a sort of comity agreement) along ethnic or geographic lines.
[237] Ambrosiaster *Ep. Gal.* 2.7.8 (Edwards); Witherington, *Grace*, 141.
[238] Cf. Dunn, *Galatians*, 111–12.

an appropriate response to their endorsement.[239] Certainly James is remembered for his emphasis on caring for the poor (Jas 1:9–11; 2:2–6, 15–16; 5:1–5).

The "poor" here are genuinely economically needy. Some suggest that the "poor" is a title for all believers in Jerusalem. But the later Jewish Christian tradition probably does not go back to the first century,[240] and the title "poor" usually includes economic need in the LXX. More important, Paul's other relevant uses of the term and its cognates imply economic need. Thus, whether the "poor" are located specifically in Jerusalem or not, what is distinctive about the title is their economic need.

When discussing the collection, Paul applies the term specifically for the saints at Jerusalem whom he was determined to help economically (Rom 15:26; 2 Cor 8:2).[241] Some argue that the Jerusalem apostles from the start had in mind *anyone* poor, not just those in Jerusalem;[242] given the most common focus of Paul's discussions about caring for the poor (Rom 15:26–27; 1 Cor 16:1–3; 2 Cor 8–9), I am less certain about this. Diaspora Jews also regularly sent money to Jerusalem,[243] although caring for the poor differs from the annual temple tax.

Whatever they had in mind, Paul is quick to note that he had already been *eager to do* this (2:10). Although current studies of Greek show the danger of reading too much into verb tenses, the contrast between the present tense of the word translated *remember* and the aorist of the word translated *was eager* might imply that the pillars were requesting a regular activity (rather than a single occasion, as exemplified in Acts 11:30).

If a regular activity is in mind, Paul's later collection for the needy in Jerusalem (Rom 15:25–27; 1 Cor 16:1–4; 2 Cor 8–9; cf. Acts 24:17) is simply the supreme fulfillment of his commitment to this understanding.[244] Caring

---

[239] On reciprocity for benefaction, see, e.g., Statius *Silvae* 4.9; Pliny *Ep.* 6.6.3; J. R. Harrison, *Paul's Language of Grace in Its Graeco-Roman Context* (WUNT 2.172; Tübingen: J. C. B. Mohr, 2003), 1, 15, 50–53, 196, 348, esp. here 40–43.

[240] L. E. Keck, "The Poor among the Saints in Jewish Christianity and Qumran," *ZNW* 57 (1–2, 1966): 54–78; Longenecker, *Remember the Poor*, 170–75.

[241] Arguing that the requirement was to help the *Judean* poor, see, e.g., Chrysostom *Hom. Gal.* 2.10; Jerome *Ep. Gal.* 1.2.10 (Edwards).

[242] Longenecker, *Remember the Poor*, 157–82.

[243] Josephus *Ant.* 16.171. See K. F. Nickle, *The Collection: A Study in Biblical Theology* (SBT 48; Naperville, IL: Alec R. Allenson, 1966), 87–89, 130, although more helpful regarding the analogous logistics than on some other points.

[244] With Dunn, *Beginning*, 934–35; D. J. Downs, *The Offering of the Gentiles: Paul's Collection for Jerusalem in Its Chronological, Cultural, and Cultic Contexts* (Grand Rapids, MI: Eerdmans, 2016), 36–37; Longenecker, *Remember the Poor*, 187.

for the poor, however, was a regular value of Jewish and biblical piety, and Paul undoubtedly viewed caring for the needy as an ethical duty (cf. Eph 4:28; 1 Thess 4:12), an inevitable corollary of loving one's neighbor (Rom 13:9–10; Gal 5:13–14). Caring for those in need was a nonnegotiably fundamental value of the Christian movement.[245]

Admittedly, Paul's small assemblies of believers lacked resources to care for everyone who was needy in the world around them. As Peter Oakes notes, probably "fewer than one in five of the letter's recipients are likely to be in control of a household's finances."[246] Nevertheless, they could at least care for one another, and there were hints that, where possible, this concern should extend beyond their communities (Rom 12:13, 16; 2 Cor 9:13; Gal 6:10; 1 Thess 5:14–15).[247] Paul's later collection for the poor in Jerusalem shows that this expectation transcended the local level; that Paul at one point can even suggest reciprocity in a time of their need (2 Cor 8:14) suggests that he did not envision the principle of caring for the poor as limited exclusively to the poor in Judea.

For the Jerusalem apostles, this requirement may have functioned as more than the mere proviso that Paul implies. First, insofar as at least some of the gifts could be directed toward the poor of Judea, they may have envisioned the eschatological ingathering of gentiles bearing gifts to Jerusalem (Isa 45:14; 60:5–17).[248] Paul himself expected the ingathering of gentiles to provoke the repentance of his own people (Rom 11:11, 14, 25–26, 31), and thus may have seen his later collection as a sort of foretaste of that eschatological promise.[249] This might be all the more the case for apostles who kept the Jerusalem church flourishing, perhaps expecting the nations to stream to Jerusalem as they led Jerusalem toward repentance (Isa 2:2–4; 60:3, 11; 62:2).

Second, and relevant to whether the proviso was limited to Jerusalem or not, requiring Paul to care for the poor may have implied a continuance of Jewish ethical standards among gentiles.[250]

---

[245] Longenecker, *Remember the Poor*, 104.

[246] Oakes, *Galatians*, 13; Longenecker, *Remember the Poor*, 291–92.

[247] Longenecker, *Remember the Poor*, 140–45, 292.

[248] Cf. Tob 13:11; 1QM 12.14; Nickle, *Collection*, 129–42, esp. 138.

[249] Cf. M. D. Nanos, *The Mystery of Romans: The Jewish Context of Paul's Letter* (Minneapolis, MN: Fortress, 1996), 18, 244, 249; Sanders, *Paul*, 686.

[250] D. E. Watson, "Paul's Collection in Light of Motivations and Mechanisms for Aid to the Poor in the First-Century World" (PhD diss., University of Durham, 2006), ch. 7; followed by Dunn, *Beginning*, 935n310; Longenecker, *Remember the Poor*, 161–63.

Despite exceptions, this biblical and early Jewish value proved much rarer among gentiles,[251] and so was worth mentioning explicitly. Laws concerning care for the poor constituted a major test of a proselyte's acceptance of Torah.[252] Jewish piety mandated giving to the poor as a central moral obligation.[253] Even gentiles recognized the high Jewish valuation on charity.[254]

Although at least some of the parties involved may have felt that caring for the poor required explicit mention, they and Paul may have understood some other standards as even more fundamental and therefore even more obviously required. That is, Paul's *only one thing* (Gr. *monos*) here may obscure for us some other extremely likely expectations from the Jerusalem perspective: the minimal requirements for foreigners or righteous gentiles in God's community, such as avoiding food offered to idols, meat from which blood had not been drained, and sexual immorality (Acts 15:20, 29).[255]

It is important for Paul's case, showing that he has a mission parallel rather than subordinate to the pillars, for him to emphasize that the pillars did not add any requirements that he had not already planned to carry out.[256] That is, Jerusalem laid nothing new on the gentile converts – certainly not circumcision, the most pressing matter here (Gal 2:3). Purely ethical matters that were not new expectations did not require explicit mention here; Paul notes here that he was already eager to care for the poor. He also regularly taught against food offered to idols (1 Cor 8–10)[257] and against sexual immorality (Gal 5:19; 1 Cor 6:9–20; 10:8; 2 Cor 12:21; 1 Thess 4:2–8). Paul always managed to do this without appealing to Jerusalem's

[251] W. D. Boer, *Private Morality in Greece and Rome: Some Historical Aspects* (MBCBSup 57; Leiden: Brill, 1979), 151–78; Watson, "Collection," chs. 2–4.
[252] L. H. Schiffman, "At the Crossroads: Tannaitic Perspectives on the Jewish Christian Schism," pages 115–56 in *Aspects of Judaism in the Graeco-Roman Period* (ed. E. P. Sanders with A. I. Baumgarten and A. Mendelson; vol. 2 of *Jewish and Christian Self-Definition*; ed. E. P. Sanders; Philadelphia, PA: Fortress, 1981), 124.
[253] E.g., Prov 29:7; Ezek 16:49; Tob 1:3; 2:14; 4:7; Sir 4:1–8; 17:22; Josephus *Ant.* 4.237; Ps.-Phoc. 23–24, 29; CD 6.21; 14.13–16; m. Abot 1:2, 5; 5:13; Sheq. 5:6; t. B.K. 11:3; B.M. 3:9; CIJ 1:142, §203; K.-J. Kim, *Stewardship and Almsgiving in Luke's Theology* (JSNTSup 155; Sheffield, UK: Sheffield Academic, 1998), 277–83; Watson, "Collection," 80–96, 106–19.
[254] Josephus *Ag. Ap.* 2.283.
[255] With Dunn, *Beginning*, 467.
[256] If Galatian believers envisioned Paul's collection as similar to the temple tax, they may have viewed Paul as subordinate to Jerusalem (L. W. Hurtado, "The Jerusalem Collection and the Book of Galatians," *JSNT* 1 [1979]: 46–62, here 48); but again, Paul likely wrote Galatians before the collection first mentioned in 1 Cor 16.
[257] Although Paul's social argument in 1 Cor 8:1–13 and 10:23–33 sounds moderate, the intervening theological argument of 10:1–22 is as "hard line" as Rev 2:14, 20; see C. S. Keener, *1 and 2 Corinthians* (New CBC; Cambridge: Cambridge University Press, 2005), 73, 84–88.

authority, a point about which, we may gather (cf. Gal 2:6), Paul may have disagreed, perhaps in polite silence, with the views of most Jerusalemite believers.

As far as avoiding meat with blood in it, it was true that gentile butchers were not as careful as Jewish kosher ones to drain out blood. Nevertheless, even gentiles sacrificing animals slit their throats; they did not hang them up to drain out all the blood, but the process of slicing apart the pieces would remove most of the remaining blood.[258] For urban Jesus-followers, the most convenient source of meat that was certainly not sacrificed to idols would be kosher butchers anyway.[259] Paul's converts, then, probably normally did not eat bloody meat in any case. Conservative Jerusalemites, though, may have been more suspicious of gentiles and may have held a higher standard for interpreting what was acceptable; "Some sages considered Diaspora Jews idolaters for eating with Gentiles even if they brought their own food (*t. Abod. Zar.* 4:6)."[260]

Paul undoubtedly felt satisfied that he had been keeping his end of the agreement, including regarding food during shared meals in Antioch. It may be, however, that some Judean visitors felt differently (cf. Gal 2:12–13).

Bridging the Horizons: We're All Different

When I was an undergraduate, a recent convert from unchurched atheism, I loved to join my friend Bruce when he would share his faith. Some non-Christians became Christians when I shared my faith, but non-Christians became Christians *regularly* when Bruce shared his faith. Today Bruce does evangelism on a significant scale in another country whereas I have become a Bible scholar. We respected one another's gifts, but we each flourished especially in the areas of our distinctive gifting. We cannot boast in gifts, since we are not the giver (1 Cor 4:7); but we can recognize those gifts and serve where God has gifted us (Rom 12:1–8).

The fruits of their ministries showed that God had gifted Peter and Paul in distinctive ways. As Paul emphasizes elsewhere in his letters (most obviously, Rom 12:4–8; 1 Cor 12:4–11, 27–30), God empowers different persons with different callings and gifts; some are more effective at reaching one

---

[258] E. P. Sanders, *Jewish Law from Jesus to the Mishnah: Five Studies* (London: SCM; Philadelphia, PA: Trinity Press International, 1990), 278–79; Klauck, *Context*, 16.
[259] Cf. B. W. Winter, *After Paul Left Corinth: The Influence of Secular Ethics and Social Change* (Grand Rapids, MI and Cambridge: Eerdmans, 2001), 6–7, 288–93.
[260] Keener, *Acts*, 1778.

group or another. Like Paul, believers should recognize their distinctive areas of divine gifting and, where possible, serve in those areas of gifting.

The narrative also, however, reveals that even the best of us have weaknesses. Readers generally find it difficult to approach this confrontation from a neutral perspective. The Ebionites condemned Paul's behavior in this account, whereas Marcion condemned Peter and his loyalty to Judaism. Meanwhile, ancient critics of Christianity used this account of the apostles' disunity to challenge their suitability to be true vehicles for divine revelation.[261] Apparently desperate to refute pagan criticism, some church fathers contended that Peter and Paul simply staged the confrontation to teach a point. Happily, Augustine argued against this position, persuading even Jerome.[262]

The Galatians obviously respect Peter, and Paul plays on that respect (esp. in 2:1–10) no less than he challenges it here. Yet all humans are fallible and God is no respecter of persons; the gospel is about God's work for us in Christ, not about human agents (1:1, 10–12; 2:6). Galatians 2:11–14 should warn us not to idealize or idolize the first apostles or any of Jesus's other agents, and if not then, neither anyone afterward. Had the Gospel of Mark not been sufficient to teach us that Jesus rather than his disciples is the only true human hero, Paul does so here. Both those we respect and we ourselves are fallible,[263] but the gospel is able to compensate for that fallibility and bring us back to truth.[264]****

2:11–14: CEPHAS COMPROMISES GOSPEL TRUTH

2:11 But when Cephas came to Antioch, I opposed him to his face, because he stood self-condemned;

2:12 for until certain people came from James, he used to eat with the Gentiles. But after they came, he drew back and kept himself separate for fear of the circumcision faction.

2:13 And the other Jews joined him in this hypocrisy, so that even Barnabas was led astray by their hypocrisy.

---

[261] Longenecker, *Galatians*, 64.
[262] Lightfoot, *Galatians*, 131; J. A. Myers, "Law, Lies and Letter Writing: An Analysis of Jerome and Augustine on the Antioch Incident (Galatians 2:11–14)," *SJT* 66 (2, May 2013): 127–39, here 138.
[263] See here Erasmus Sarcerius *Annotations on Galatians* on Gal 2:11 (Bray).
[264] Cf. Rudolf Gwalther *Sermons on Galatians* on Gal 2:11 (Bray), on reprimanding even those of higher worldly rank.

2:14 But when I saw that they were not acting consistently with the truth of the gospel, I said to Cephas before them all, "If you, though a Jew, live like a Gentile and not like a Jew, how can you compel the Gentiles to live like Jews?"

With most (but not all) scholars, the events of 2:11-14 surely are subsequent to the events of 2:1-10. Everything so far has been in chronological sequence, and this was the customary way to narrate one's case, often bringing events up to the current time.

What was the outcome of the confrontation recounted in 2:11-14? The view that Paul lost the debate with Peter and broke with Antioch here reads great significance into evidence that is ambiguous at best, since Paul's account of his challenge to Peter mentions a break neither with Peter nor with the church.[265] Notwithstanding lack of evidence in the text, many scholars believe, and some affirm with great assurance, that Paul lost the debate in Antioch.

Granted, Paul does not report Peter's response, which one might have expected had Peter complied. Some also contend that Antioch's failure to participate in Paul's later collection signals an implicit break. This suggestion, however, expects too much. We also do not hear of participation by churches of Phoenicia or Damascus. Paul's collection is from the churches he *founded*; Antioch had its own relationship with the Jerusalem church.

It is highly unlikely that the Antioch church abandoned Paul here. Why would Christians in Antioch, who earlier sent Paul as a representative rather than submit to Judean teachers of circumcision (Acts 15:2), suddenly repudiate their own spokesman and advocate? They may have accepted Peter's likely explanation that he was merely trying to keep peace with more conservative brothers and not trying to pressure Galatian gentiles into becoming Jews. Such acceptance would not, however, entail rejecting Paul; in fact, such a concession would mean that Paul had achieved his central objective. He does not appear to have viewed Peter himself as a subsequent threat (1 Cor 1:12; 3:22; 9:5; 15:5).

Moreover, unless we suppose that gentile Christians in Antioch then embraced circumcision or thereafter celebrated the Lord's supper, a fellowship meal, separately from Jewish believers, Paul's opinion must have

---

[265] Not all scholars see a major break between Paul and Antioch. See, e.g., Hengel and Schwemer, *Between Damascus and Antioch*, 218; Schreiner, *Galatians*, 145; more recently, S. E. Porter, *The Apostle Paul: His Life, Thought, and Letters* (Grand Rapids, MI: Eerdmans, 2016), 195.

won the day.[266] And how could it have been otherwise? Paul was close to the Antioch church; they did not know the visitors. Paul does not go on to denounce Antioch and highlight his own independence from them; instead it appears that the situation was resolved and local believers again ate together (whatever the Judean interlopers may have thought). Meanwhile, by the early second century, Antioch's bishop rejected gentile Christians becoming Jews much more vigorously than had Paul, making likely that Antioch had been in the Pauline camp for some time.[267] It is therefore likely that the confrontation in Antioch involved a single occasion in which Jewish believers withdrew, and that thereafter they returned to the practice they had maintained before the arrival of Jerusalemite critics.

Acts mentions a break with Barnabas, and it is reasonable to suppose that this incident may have contributed to the tensions also suggested in Gal 2:13, but Acts also shows Paul meeting with Antioch in Acts 18:22 and commended by that church in 15:40. Luke no longer depicts Paul as "sent" by Antioch after he has established bases in the Aegean region, precisely because by then he has other bases. The view that Gal 2:11–14 indicates Paul's break with Antioch is simply a scholarly tradition, one hypothetical way of reading the evidence selectively, not firmly grounded in the text. Whether Peter was persuaded or not, we lack evidence of a "break," and despite Paul's reservations Paul continues to respect him as an agent of the Lord (1 Cor 9:5; 15:5).

A Closer Look: Antioch[268]

Probably the empire's third largest city,[269] Antioch held a strategic position as the "mother city"[270] and the most powerful city in the massive province of

---

[266] The alternative perspective survived (cf. Phil 3:2; Titus 1:10–11, 14; 3:9) and may persist in the Pseudo-Clementine literature (cf. Gager, *Anti-Semitism*, 124–25), but not among dominant Christian leaders at Antioch; note explicit expressions of respect for Paul in Ignatius *Eph.* 12.2; *Rom.* 4.3; *Phili.* 3.2; 9.1; 11.2–3.

[267] Ignatius *Magn.* 8.1; 10.3; *Phld.* 6.1; see further Meeks and Wilken, *Antioch*, 19–20.

[268] On early Christianity in Antioch, see A. M. Schwemer, "Paulus in Antiochien," *BZ* 42 (2, 1998): 161–80; Meeks and Wilken, *Antioch*; Keener, *Acts*, 1834–40.

[269] Josephus *War* 3.29.

[270] Strabo 16.2.5; Josephus *War* 3.29; coins in R. Tracey, "Syria," pages 223–78 in *The Book of Acts in Its Graeco-Roman Setting* (ed. D. W. J. Gill and C. Gempf; Grand Rapids, MI: Eerdmans; Carlisle, UK: Paternoster, 1994), 238.

Syria.[271] Scholars lack consensus regarding its population, offering estimates from 150,000 to roughly 500,000.[272]

It was a "free" city, mostly permitted self-governance.[273] It had its own theater, amphitheater, and circus. Colonnades, wide walkways, and many shops lined its marble-paved main street, which ran for roughly two miles.[274]

Besides the usual smattering of pagan religion, Antioch was known for the nearby cult center of Daphnê.[275] But Josephus claims a very large Jewish population there;[276] rough estimates generally range from 20,000 to 40,000. Its ties to the east and the proximity of Judea, then governed as part of Syria, probably gave Antioch's Jewish community stronger Judean connections than most other Diaspora cities. Jews and Christians continued in active contact in Antioch at least into the fourth century.[277]

Josephus saw it as a mark of good Jewish–gentile relations there that, during the Judean–Roman war, Antioch spared its Jewish residents from the anti-Jewish slaughter that convulsed much of the region.[278] Anti-Judaism did persist there,[279] but apparently many Greeks also converted to Judaism there.[280]****

Although the scene in 2:11 is new, the topic is not. *But* here translates a weak conjunction (*de*, probably used adversatively as in the NRSV); it gives way to a contrast with the preceding agreement. *Cephas* was party to the Jerusalem agreement that recognized gentiles as the primary sphere of Paul's ministry rather than Peter's (2:7, 9). Jerusalem was not to add requirements to faith in Christ for gentiles. Now, however, Paul regards Peter (Cephas) as reneging on his commitment – even though Peter very well knew better. Because Paul claims to have addressed Cephas *before them all* (2:14), it appears likely that he confronted him even in front of those who *came from James* (2:12), and that the entire scene occurred during a single community meal.

---

[271] Syria's Roman governor resided there; see Josephus *Ant.* 18.95, 126; Tracey, "Syria," 243–46.
[272] Ancient estimates also varied; compare Strabo 16.2.5; Pliny E. *Nat.* 6.122; Chrysostom *Pan. Ign.* 4.
[273] Pliny *Nat.* 5.18.79.
[274] Dio Chrysostom *Or.* 47.16. See further J. Finegan, *The Archeology of the New Testament: The Mediterranean World of the Early Christian Apostles* (Boulder, CO: Westview; London: Croom Helm, 1981), 65, 68.
[275] Strabo 16.2.4–6; Josephus *War* 1.328.
[276] Josephus *Ag. Ap.* 2.39; *War* 7.43–44.
[277] Meeks and Wilken, *Antioch*, 21–24.
[278] Josephus *War* 2.479–80.
[279] Josephus *War* 7.100–11; *Ant.* 12.121–24; Hengel and Schwemer, *Between Damascus and Antioch*, 184–90, especially 189–90.
[280] Josephus *War* 7.45.

Paul's public confrontation of Cephas is dramatic and illustrates for his audience how fiercely committed Paul is to his gospel for the gentiles. Paul thus frames the entire scene by noting the confrontation (2:11, 14). Because the confrontation is difficult to comprehend without first exploring the situation it addresses, however, I will examine the situation depicted in 2:12–13 and then return to the confrontation only afterward.

Paul leaves unnamed those who came from James in 2:12, though we cannot be sure that they, like the *false believers* of 2:4, actually prefigure Paul's opponents. Nor does their coming *from James* indicate clearly that they come on an errand specified by James. The usual view that James sent them to encourage proper protocol in Antioch could be correct, but we cannot infer this conclusion simply from the language, because Paul does not actually say that James "sent" them. To "come from" someone can simply indicate geographic movement without indicating commissioning (2 Cor 1:16; 11:9; 1 Thess 3:6).

It is more likely, however, that James is mentioned because he is associated in some way with the ensuing conflict. Whether or not he commissioned those who came, the Jerusalemites would bring back the report of what they had seen and James would at least share the same concern as Peter – that this report would reflect negatively or even scandalously on Peter. Paul's sphere of ministry was gentiles, but Peter's sphere of ministry was Jews. Just as Paul became a Jew to Jews and outside the law to those outside it (1 Cor 9:20–21; Gal 4:12), Peter undoubtedly was seeking to do the same,[281] and Paul himself in fact says as much. Peter's previous eating with gentiles had compromised him (Acts 11:2–3) with conservatives in the church in a way that James had been spared, making James the safer leader to hold the Jerusalem church together (12:17). James and Peter probably both wished to prevent further undermining Peter's position in the increasingly conservative movement.

Peter *used to eat with the gentiles* – apparently regularly[282] – when there was no one present who would object (Gal 2:12), and thus behaved *like a gentile* (2:14). (Given his background, this probably presupposes some transformative experience such as the one that Luke depicts in Acts 10:1–48.)[283]

---

[281] See Tertullian *Adv. Marc.* 1.20; 4.3; Marius Victorinus *Ep. Gal.* 1.2.12–13; P. Richardson, "Pauline Inconsistency: I Corinthians 9:19–23 and Galatians 2:11–14," *NTS* 26 (3, 1980): 347–62.

[282] With, e.g., Matera, *Galatians*, 85; Hays, "Galatians," 233. One cannot of course rely on the imperfect tense to prove this.

[283] With, e.g., Sanders, *Paul*, 464–65.

Some praised flexibility and adapting to one's audience,[284] certainly in cross-cultural settings.[285] Others criticized such behavior as the domain of demagogues who enslave themselves (cf. 2:4) to the masses.[286] As Oakes suggests, Paul may portray Peter "as the waverer, the 'flatterer,' who instead of acting on principles, changes his actions to please different sets of people."[287]

Yet when more conservative Judeans who could report on his behavior to Jerusalem showed up, Peter *drew back and kept himself separate for fear of the circumcision faction* (2:12). Although we may be tempted to excoriate Paul for inferring Peter's motives, Peter may have even expressed something like this plainly: he did not wish to offend his own ministry constituency. As noted in the comment on 2:10, some in Jerusalem may have interpreted the agreement, particularly its culinary implications, differently from Paul; Jerusalem was also becoming increasingly conservative.[288] It was easier to conform to their expectations than to try to persuade his associates in Jerusalem that his behavior with gentiles in Antioch was acceptable. Readers thus often give Peter's motives the benefit of the doubt here.[289]

In any case, Peter probably felt that he had a legitimate concern, whether or not he would have worded that concern the way Paul did (*for fear*): his reputation in Jerusalem was at stake. This was a reputation that Paul has already noted in 2:6–9. Peter may have viewed it as influence for the gospel; Paul deemed the reputation worthless (2:6), an approach he apparently took regarding his own reputation as well (2 Cor 6:8–9).[290]

Peter's concern was the opinion *of the circumcision faction* (literally, "those from circumcision," 2:12). This could refer to the circumcision faction among Jerusalem believers (Acts 11:2, using the same Greek expression; 15:5). It could also refer to those Jews in general who insisted on circumcising gentiles; Judean believers had concerns about their witness to their nonbelieving peers, and those who were soft on gentiles might also face actual

---

[284] See, e.g., Quintilian *Inst.* 3.7.24; Diogenes Laertius 2.66; *Thebaid* frg. 8; cf. further C. E. Glad, "Paul and Adaptability," pages 17–41 in *Paul in the Greco-Roman World: A Handbook* (ed. J. P. Sampley; Harrisburg, PA: Trinity Press International, 2003), 19.

[285] On recognition of cultural differences, see, e.g., Sextus Empiricus *Pyr.* 3.198; Seneca *Ep. Lucil.* 88.44; Epictetus *Diatr.* 1.27.2, 15.

[286] See, e.g., Dio Chrysostom *Or.* 66.13–14; Martin, *Slavery*, 87–88, 93.

[287] Oakes, *Galatians*, 78–79; for excessive adaptation, cf. Glad, "Adaptability," 20–21; Marshall, *Enmity*, 71–78.

[288] Dunn, *Galatians*, 122–24.

[289] E.g., Theodoret *Ep. Gal.* 2.12–13; Robert of Melun on Gal 2:11 (Levy).

[290] Such considerations were not unique to apostles; ancient philosophers often disdained reputation, except insofar as it was useful to gain a hearing for their message (e.g., Crates *Ep.* 16; Arius Didymus 2.7.5a, p. 10.12–13; Diogenes Laertius 6.1.11; 6.2.58; 9.11.61).

hostility from some of those peers (see Gal 6:12 and comment there). The strictest of Judeans considered those who compromised Judean customs as damnable as gentiles themselves.[291] In this context, it almost certainly refers to the same group of people to whom Peter is called to minister, regularly called "the Circumcision" (*hê peritomê*; Gal 2:7–9, 12). Peter has a legitimate concern with maintaining his credibility within his sphere of ministry, but it is not sufficient excuse for alienating those within Paul's sphere (cf. Acts 21:20–25).

Jerusalem also had shared meals (Acts 2:42, 46), but obviously on different terms. Jewish prohibitions of eating with gentiles usually had to do with their status as idolaters (less relevant here).

Perhaps Antioch simply determined to ask fewer questions, trusting gentile hosts' sensitivity to their concerns (cf. 1 Cor 10:27). Perhaps the issue was treating uncircumcised gentiles as spiritual peers, as if they were full proselytes (and thus essentially Israelites) rather than merely God-fearers or righteous gentiles.[292]

Some Pharisees had joined the Jerusalem movement (Acts 15:5) and undoubtedly exerted disproportionate influence on account of their status. Pure table fellowship was a primary defining characteristic for them,[293] requiring scrupulous rules to be followed when dining with others.[294] "Pharisees" may have originally been "separatists,"[295] and some connect this idea here with Paul's former background as a non-Christian Pharisee. Peter may have wished to avoid offending this valuable element in the Jerusalem church, as well as to avoid offending precisely those members who, contrary to the wider and more generous view of most Jewish thinkers of antiquity, regarded uncircumcised gentiles as still "sinners" (see Acts 15:1, 5; Gal 2:15).[296]

---

[291] See Dunn, *Galatians*, 128, 133; cf. discussion of Jewish polemical rhetoric in L. T. Johnson, "The New Testament's Anti-Jewish Slander and Conventions of Ancient Rhetoric," *JBL* 108 (1989): 419–41.

[292] Nanos, *Mystery*, 349–53.

[293] J. Neusner, *From Politics to Piety: The Emergence of Pharisaic Judaism* (2nd edn.; New York: KTAV, 1979), 86; idem, *Judaism in the Beginning of Christianity* (Philadelphia, PA: Fortress, 1984), 27. This is not to argue that they intended to follow a *priestly* level of purity (see Sanders, *Jesus to Mishnah*, 131–254).

[294] E.g., t. Dem. 3:6; Abot R. Nat. 31, §68; 32, §72 B; b. Ber. 43b; y. Demai 2:3.

[295] For this suggested origin for their name, the majority view, see, e.g., S. J. D. Cohen, *From the Maccabees to the Mishnah* (LEC 7; Philadelphia, PA: Westminster, 1987), 162.

[296] If these were Pharisees, they likelier reflect the Shammaite wing of Pharisaism, which was traditionally less friendly toward gentiles (Donaldson, *Gentiles*, 275).

Pharisees were not the most conservative regarding culinary intercourse with gentiles. Some more extreme Judean voices insisted on separating even from the rest of Israel, the "perverse" community.[297] Only the strictest altogether forbade social contact or eating with gentiles,[298] but some were indeed so strict[299] and out of respect for their piety others might wish not to offend them. Such circles predominated in Judea more than in the Diaspora. Still, Israel's separation was biblical (Lev 20:26),[300] and even hellenized Jews warned against excess mingling with gentiles.[301]

The dominant popular reaction against gentiles was growing in the 40s and 50s, bringing the strictest and most ethnically exclusive values to the fore (see "A Closer Look"). Rising nationalism in Judea undoubtedly influenced believers there.[302] Unless they were sociologically unlike nearly all other culturally assimilated groups in history, Judean followers of Jesus probably shared the politics of most of their peers. Certainly they were zealous for the law and were susceptible to believing rumors about the gentile mission teaching Jews to abandon the law (Acts 21:20–21).

Whatever the specific reasons that Peter would separate from gentiles, this behavior was apparently calculated to appease more traditional Jerusalem believers. The pillars' agreement with Paul did not permit *Jewish* believers to abandon their purity customs.[303]

A Closer Look: Did Jews Eat with Gentiles?[304]

Did Jews eat with gentiles? The short answer is that some did and some did not.[305] Diaspora Jews in Antioch probably did; it would be less common

---

[297] See 1QS 5.1–2, 10; 8.13; 9.20; 4Q259 3.3–4; 4.1; CD 8.8; 19.20. Emphasizing a different term, Dunn, *Beginning*, 472, notes 4QMMT C7 = 92.

[298] See esp. Barclay, *Gift*, 368–69; Barclay, *Jews in Diaspora*, 434–37.

[299] See LXX Esth 14:17 = Ad. Esth. 4:17; Jdt 10:5; 12:2, 9, 19; Tob 1:10–13; Jub. 22:16; Jos. Asen. 7:1; Sanders, *Jesus to Mishnah*, 273–74; cf. Josephus *War* 2.591; *Ant.* 12.120; *Life* 74.

[300] See also Ezra 10:11; 1 Esd 8:70–71, 86–87; 2 Macc 14:3, 37–38; Jub. 2:19; Let. Aris. 138.

[301] Philo *Moses* 1.278; Josephus *War* 2.488; *Ag. Ap.* 2.257–61.

[302] See Keener, *Acts*, 1869, 1875–76, 3133, 3173; cf. 3269. For ultraconservative Jewish Christians working against Peter and Paul in the 40s and 50s, esp. in Jerusalem, see Brown in R. E. Brown and J. P. Meier, *Antioch and Rome: New Testament Cradles of Catholic Christianity* (New York: Paulist, 1983), 126.

[303] Cf. Dunn, *Galatians*, 125; Moo, *Galatians*, 148.

[304] I condense and adapt here material from Keener, *Acts*, 1769, 1777–78, 1787–91.

[305] For the wide range of Jewish views concerning Gentiles, see Donaldson, *Paul and Gentiles*, 52–74; G. Boccaccini, *Middle Judaism: Jewish Thought, 300 B.C.E. to 200 C.E.* (Minneapolis, MN: Fortress, 1991), 251–65.

with conservative Judeans. The question is thus not simply an ethnic one but a sociocultural one.

In the land of Israel, the more conservative pietists who wanted to restrict contact were particularly concerned about eating together. "Separate yourself from the gentiles," Jubilees warns, "and do not eat with them."[306] Even Diaspora Jews who hoped for gentile audiences could recognize that the purpose of purity laws, including those concerning food, was to separate Israel from other peoples.[307] Gentiles also complained even of Diaspora Jews' separatism regarding foods.[308]

Pharisees were not to eat the food of someone ignorant of the law, which one must presume untithed.[309] If Judean Pharisees limited their culinary intercourse with common Jews who ignored their precise legal interpretations, one would expect them (some of whom belonged to the Jerusalem church, Acts 15:5) to be no less concerned with gentiles. Even if Jewish people brought their own food when eating with gentiles, later rabbis feared that a gentile could contaminate the food if the Jews were not vigilant.[310] One Judean rabbi even deemed Diaspora Jews "idolaters" for attending gentiles' banquets, despite these Jews bringing their own food and drink.[311]

Gentiles were so impure that no gentile, including an uncircumcised God-fearer, could pass beyond the temple's outer court into the court of women.[312] Whatever they touched in a Jewish home became impure,[313] and rabbis debated whether proselyte immersion takes a day or a week to purify the convert from gentile impurity.[314]

While a God-fearer who abandoned idolatry (a status relevant to gentile Christians) would not be impure directly, such gentiles would carry contamination from contact with others; thus God-fearers were also immersed as well as circumcised when becoming full converts. Later rabbis might expect their food to be clean, but not the seating in their homes.[315]

---

[306]   Jub. 22:16 (trans. O. Wintermute).

[307]   Let. Aris. 139–42; Philo *Moses* 1.278.

[308]   3 Macc 3:4–7; J. N. Sevenster, *The Roots of Pagan Anti-Semitism in the Ancient World* (NovTSup 41; Leiden: Brill, 1975), 139.

[309]   So t. Dem. 3:6–7; on their untithed food, see also m. Dem. 2:2; 4:5; Maas. 5:3; M.S. 3:3.

[310]   M. Abod. Zar. 5:5.

[311]   E.g., t. Abod. Zar. 4:6.

[312]   Josephus *Ant.* 15.417; *War* 6.124–25; *Ag. Ap.* 2.103–04; Philo *Embassy* 212; m. Kel. 1:8.

[313]   See m. Toh. 7:6.

[314]   M. Pesah. 8:8 and t. Pisha 7:13–14. The practice is, against some, early enough and even known to some gentiles (Epictetus *Diatr.* 2.9.20); see Keener, *Acts*, 979–82.

[315]   H. Le Cornu with Joseph Shulam, *A Commentary on the Jewish Roots of Acts* (2 vols.; Jerusalem: Academon, 2003), 583, citing m. Ger. 3:1–2.

Moreover, casual observers might not distinguish between God-fearers and other gentiles. ****

Paul himself elsewhere quotes the most relevant text, using the LXX of Isa 52:11 to call for separation from paganism in 2 Cor 6:17. Concerned about perceptions, Peter now separates himself from his gentile siblings in Christ (Gal 2:12). From Paul's perspective, however, this separatism undercuts the gospel. In the time of restoration, according to Isaiah's context, the Lord will not "separate" foreigners joined to him (Isa 56:3, using the same LXX term). Paul's own separation by God to preach among the gentiles (Rom 1:1, 5; Gal 1:15–16) compelled him to oppose Peter's separation from some of God's people.

Gentiles typically viewed Jewish separatism, including at meals, as antisocial and anti-gentile.[316] The Roman historian Tacitus, for example, complains that Jewish separatism at meals reveals Jews' hatred of other peoples.[317] Such separatism among Jesus's followers would scandalize current and especially prospective gentile believers and thus disrupt the ethnic unity of the community for whom Christ died.

Scholars debate whether the meal that Peter *used to eat with the gentiles* (2:12) was the Lord's supper or just a common meal, but in this early period there seems little reason to doubt that believers' shared meal usually *was* (or at least often included) the Lord's supper (1 Cor 11:17–33, esp. 11:20–22; cf. Jude 12). Tension over social stratification (and insulted honor) often characterized ancient banquets,[318] but some held that the Greek friendship ideal invited egalitarian treatment at banquets.[319] Paul insisted on equality and unity at the Lord's supper (1 Cor 11:21–22, 29), so if the Lord's supper is in view here, division would be especially harmful.

In any case, regardless of the nature of the meal, one owed friendship and kindness to a host.[320] Eating together established a covenant of friendship,[321] and could effect reconciliation between estranged parties.[322] Those who entered this relationship thereby committed to permanent friendship; people were obligated to cherish hospitality ties.[323]

---

[316] Tacitus *Hist.* 5.5; Juvenal *Sat.* 14.102–03; Philostratus *Vit. Apoll.* 5.33; Josephus *Ag. Ap.* 2.148; Sevenster, *Anti-Semitism*, 89–145, esp. 143–44; Barclay, *Jews in Diaspora*, 272.

[317] Tacitus *Hist.* 5.5; cf. 3 Macc 3:4, 7.

[318] E.g., Pliny *Ep.* 2.6.2; Dio Chrysostom *Or.* 30.29; Plutarch *Table-Talk* 1.3, *Mor.* 619B–619F.

[319] E.g., Xenophon *Mem.* 3.14.1; Heraclitus *Ep.* 9; Pliny *Ep.* 2.6.3–5; Plutarch *T.-T.* 1.2.3, *Mor.* 616E; 1.2.5, *Mor.* 618A; 2.10.2, *Mor.* 644AB.

[320] Cicero *Verr.* 2.2.47.117.

[321] See Aeschines *Embassy* 22, 55; further discussion in Keener, *John*, 912–13.

[322] Plutarch *Cic.* 26.1.

[323] E.g., Homer *Il.* 6.212–31, esp. 224; Rhet. Her. 3.3.4; Cicero *Fam.* 13.34.1; 13.36.1; 13.73.2.

Antioch's believers had undoubtedly welcomed Peter sacrificially. Most
people felt honored to have a person of status visit their homes, and considered it an honor to entertain a noble friend as a guest. One refused hospitality to guests or from hosts only if the person was considered dishonorable;[324]
some later rabbis included gentiles in this category.[325] If believers could not
even eat together, bearing one another's burdens and loving the others as
oneself (Gal 5:14; 6:2) would be well-nigh impossible.

On the surface, Paul's public outburst at Peter might appear more a
breach of friendship than would Peter withdrawing from table. But from
the perspective of gentile believers in Antioch, Peter's action was serious: to
refuse to continue to share meals together when invited was akin to a declaration of enmity, breaking the bonds of friendship. Indeed, even refusing a
gift constituted a declaration of enmity.[326] Peter had now entered a situation
where he had to choose sides: he was going to offend someone either way,
and as a minister to his fellow Jews he chose to offend Paul's gentiles.

Whatever Peter's motives, Paul charges him here with *hypocrisy* (2:13).
Against the old Tübingen hypothesis, Paul does not indicate a *theological* difference with Peter here. This is a disagreement over behavior, not
over the content of the gospel message; that is why Paul charges Peter with
hypocrisy, of living differently from what he believes, not with believing
error. The point is not that Peter wrongly thinks it inappropriate to eat with
gentiles; the point is that Peter *knows* that it is not wrong to eat with gentiles
yet withdraws from them anyway to avoid criticism. It is acting differently
from what he knows to be true that earns the label of *hypocrisy*.[327]

Jewish teachers often condemned Jewish hypocrisy, so the charge was
also frequent in intra-Jewish polemic.[328] It can mean "acting the part"
(*hypokrinetai*), as in Epictetus *Diatr.* 2.9.20,[329] where one only pretends to be
a Jew, relevant to Peter's pretense for Jerusalemite visitors here. Ironically,
the Jewish martyr tradition honored one who refused to play the part by
simply *pretending* to eat gentile food (2 Macc 6:21, 24; 4 Macc 6:15, 17); by

[324] Aeschylus *Suppl.* 927; Sir 11:29, 34; 2 John 10–11.
[325] Sipre Deut. 1.10.1.
[326] See Marshall, *Enmity*, 13–21, 245–46. At the least such a refusal would display contempt (Cicero *Fam.* 14.3.1; Pliny *Ep.* 8.6.9).
[327] The term originally applied only to play-actors, but extension of the metaphor was now in common use (Epictetus *Diatr.* 2.9.20; Plutarch *Educ.* 17, *Mor.* 13B; Sir 1:29; 35:15; 36:2) including in the Jesus tradition for religious pretense (e.g., Mark 7:6; Matt 7:5//Luke 6:42).
[328] See J. D. G. Dunn, "Echoes of Intra-Jewish Polemic in Paul's Letter to the Galatians," *JBL* 112 (1993): 459–77; cf. Johnson, "Slander."
[329] Trans. W. A. Oldfather, LCL 1:272–73.

contrast, Peter pretends to honor conservative Jewish values but this is mere pretense and hypocrisy.[330]

Peter's status naturally carried great influence, and while he may not have intended others to follow his example, that was the result (2:13).[331] Probably most of the Antiochan Jewish believers decided that they should follow Peter's example for the sake of Jerusalem's perspectives.[332] Jews could speak of *the other Jews* without meaning to exclude themselves.[333]

Paul mentions Barnabas specifically as one who was *led astray* by the others (Gal 2:13), noting that *even* Barnabas was led astray. Why "even" Barnabas? The Galatians would know Barnabas as Paul's earliest main coworker in Galatia (Acts 13–14). Moreover, from this letter, if not from prior knowledge, the Galatians would also recognize that Barnabas was sent with Paul from Antioch and therefore knew the free rein the Jerusalem leaders had given Paul's gentile mission (2:1, 9). Of all people, Barnabas should have known better, so Paul had to take a stand that seemed virtually isolated from his colleagues at the time. That Paul did so exemplifies for the Galatians the strength of his commitment to this God-given gospel for the gentiles.

What Paul needed now was not Peter's or others' private assurances of support; he needed a public stand that would keep Jerusalem's distant agendas from splitting apart the ethnic and cultural unity of Antioch's present church.

For the sake of the long-range future of the church, Paul confronted Cephas (2:11).[334] But both standard Jewish ethics[335] and early Christian adaptation of those ethics (Matt 18:15–17), including by Paul in this letter (Gal 6:1), demanded that one reprove another privately first. Apparently the situation is so urgent, however, that Paul must act publicly; the separation and

---

[330]   Dunn, *Galatians*, 125.

[331]   One may compare the *sun*-compounded verbs in 2:12–13: Peter "ate *with*" gentiles (2:12), other Jews became "co-hypocrites *with*" him (2:13), and even Barnabas was "carried along *with*" them (2:13).

[332]   With Longenecker, *Galatians*, 75; J. M. G. Barclay, "Paul among Diaspora Jews: Anomaly or Apostate?" *JSNT* 60 (1995): 89–120, here 103.

[333]   Cf., e.g., W. A. Meeks, "'Am I a Jew?' – Johannine Christianity and Judaism," pages 163–86 in vol. 1 of *Christianity, Judaism, and Other Greco-Roman Cults: Studies for Morton Smith at Sixty* (ed. Jacob Neusner; 4 vols.; SJLA 12; Leiden: Brill, 1975), 181; cf. R. S. Kraemer, "On the Meaning of the Term 'Jew' in Greco-Roman Inscriptions," *HTR* 82 (1989): 35–53.

[334]   The NRSV translates the term here rendered as *opposed* in some other passages as "resist" (Rom 9:19; 13:2; 1 Pet 5:9) or "withstand" (Eph 6:13) and often involves standing against a strong person or force.

[335]   See, e.g., 1QS 6.26–27.9; 7.15–16; Josephus *Ant.* 3.67; *m. Ab.* 3:11.

offense are already occurring in public.[336] Scholars debate whether Cephas *stood self-condemned* (reading the participle as middle) or condemned by God (2:11). The charge of *hypocrisy* (2:13) might support the former understanding, but Paul's concern for God's true perspective (1:10; 2:6) might support the latter.

A Closer Look: Reproof[337]

Although some gentile moralists noted the importance of reproof,[338] this was especially a Jewish emphasis. Jewish tradition also emphasized proper giving and receiving of reproof. A sage could hyperbolically rule that publicly shaming one's fellow warrants exclusion from the coming age.[339]

The Qumran Scrolls, which include record-keeping of rebukes,[340] also emphasize the standard Jewish sequence: private reproof, then before witnesses, and finally before the gathered assembly.[341] That Josephus adds to Exodus 18:14 this principle of private correction in *Ant.* 3.67 reinforces the probability that Jewish people expected private reproof. Love and concern could demand reproof, at least toward those who might trust one enough to hear.[342] ****

The language of Paul's confrontation is strong: *I opposed him to his face* (2:11), language used in the Septuagint for military resistance.[343] Paul begins describing the confrontation in 2:14. Here "the truth of the gospel" echoes the same "truth of the gospel" for which Paul resisted the false brothers in 2:5, and for which he was now opposing his opponents in Galatia (1:6–9), the gospel revealed to him by God (1:11, 16) and that he preached (1:23; 2:2).

---

[336] That is, the matter is not a personal sin, as in Gal 6:1, but the church's faith; Luther *Second Lectures on Galatians* on 6:1 (Bray). Medieval commentators Haimo of Auxerre on Gal 2:14 (Levy) and Bruno the Carthusian on Gal 2:11 (Levy) opine here that public sin demands public reproof.

[337] Adapted from Keener, *Acts*, 2303.

[338] E.g., Publilius Syrus 10; Philodemus *Crit.* passim.

[339] E.g., m. Ab. 3:11; b. Sanh. 107a. Qumranites detested disrespect for fellow members of the community (e.g., 1QS 6.26–27.9; 7.15–16).

[340] For offenses like anger and pride; 4Q477; E. Eshel, "4Q477: The Rebukes by the Overseer," *JJS* 45 (1994): 111–22.

[341] Cf. L. H. Schiffman, *Sectarian Law in the Dead Sea Scrolls: Courts, Testimony, and the Penal Code* (BJS 33; Chico, CA: Scholars Press, 1983), 97–98.

[342] Cf. Prov 3:12; 13:24; 19:18; 23:13; 27:5; Sir 7:23; 18:13; 30:2, 13; Sipra Qed. pq. 4.200.3.3; Sipre Deut. 1.3.2; 173.1.2.

[343] See Deut 7:24; 9:2; 11:25; Judg 2:14; 2 Chron 13:7–8.

Peter and those who followed his behavior were *not acting consistently*[344] *with the truth of the gospel* (2:14), hence were acting as hypocrites (2:13).

Peter was living *like a gentile* (2:14), at least in the sense that he was eating *with the gentiles* (2:12), apparently without personal consideration of stricter Judean scruples. Some plausibly suggest that "living *like a gentile*" (2:14) may echo a complaint from men who came from James (2:12). Living like gentiles was common Jewish polemic against less strict Jewish sects.[345]

Yet Peter, who knew that there was nothing inherently wrong with this gentile sort of lifestyle, was now compelling gentiles to adopt a Jewish lifestyle. This compulsion violated the agreement that allowed both groups to follow their own cultures (2:9; Acts 15:29; 21:21, 25). Paul was not interfering with the Jewish mission (1 Cor 7:18–19; Gal 5:6), but Peter was adversely affecting Paul's ministry among gentiles.

The term translated *to live like Jews* (*ioudaizein*) applies to adopting Jewish customs or lifestyle. The term can apply simply to Jewish sympathizers who selectively adopted some Jewish customs,[346] but it could also go further. The Greek version of Esth 8:17 declares that many gentiles were circumcised and "judaized" because they feared the Jews. Likewise, a gentile soldier agreed to "judaize" to the point of circumcision to save his life.[347] In the last two examples, fear of Jewish fighters rather than personal conviction compels circumcision.[348]

It is no coincidence that Paul uses here a strong term, *compel* (2:14), the same term he used for the *false believers* who (in contrast to the pillars) tried to compel Titus's circumcision in 2:3 and the term he will use for his opponents trying to compel the Galatian believers to be circumcised in 6:12.

Peter no doubt would have insisted that he was not compelling gentiles to do anything; he was simply acting for himself to protect the integrity of the Judean mission. Paul saw the matter differently, with keen foresight recognizing where such an exclusivity would lead. To eat with Peter, to maintain fellowship with the mother church and to become part of the in-group, the

---

[344] *Acting consistently* translates a compound word that sometimes implied progress but could imply "walking uprightly," fitting the image, in different words, in Gal 5:16, 25.

[345] Dunn, *Galatians*, 128, cites Ps. Sol. 1:8; 8:13.

[346] As in Josephus *War* 2.463; Plutarch *Cic.* 7.6. See Dunn, *Galatians*, 129, 473. Many gentiles wanted to imitate some Jewish customs, such as resting on the sabbath, some food prohibitions, fasts and lighting lamps (Josephus *Apion* 2.282).

[347] Josephus *War* 2.454.

[348] Martyn, *Galatians*, 236. Compare perhaps "fear of the Jews" in Esth 8:17 with Peter's *fear of the circumcision faction* in Gal 2:12.

most committed gentile Christians would adopt circumcision. In the process, they would also alienate less committed gentile inquirers.[349]

Bridging the Horizons: Reflecting Our Political Milieu

In the face of rising nationalism in Judea, Judean believers in Jesus reflected the values dominant around them, closing ranks against generally hostile outsiders. In Acts, Paul had no problem identifying with Judean customs provided these were not imposed on gentiles (Acts 21:21–26). Yet Paul treated as betrayal Peter's similar accommodation of conservative Judean customs, because the setting in Antioch was very different.

The saying "When in Rome, do as the Romans do" (adapted from a saying attributed to Ambrose of Milan) somewhat communicates the thought. It is right to contextualize nonessentials for one's context – but positively dangerous to export that contextualization into a different context where it imposes hardship and violates local culture. The social unity of God's people is a fragile blessing, easily pulled and too often rent by our other allegiances. If we allow any other social allegiance – to culture, ethnicity, social status, gender, political party, or the like (cf. Gal 3:28) – to shatter our common unity in Christ, we cannot rightly call him Lord.

Unfortunately, contexts often overlap, somewhat complicating how we implement the principle. Within a span of a few months in 2016 the United Kingdom voted on the controversial Brexit referendum and the United States held a highly divisive election. In the States, immigrants and members of ethnic minorities had genuine reasons for anxiety about the election of one candidate; many felt that they could not trust Christian brothers and sisters whose votes revealed that they could accept as president someone often perceived at the time as an insensitive racist and misogynist. Some Christians who belonged to the dominant culture felt that a more pressing justice issue, if one had to choose, was abortion: if a fetus was genetically a live human being, then abortions have killed some 60 million persons in the United States since 1973. Some traded freely in accusations of fascism and genocide. Others, mistrustful of both

[349] Early second-century rabbis warned against imposing behavior, even by one's example, that most could not endure; see D. Daube, "Concessions to Sinfulness in Jewish Law," *JJS* 10 (1–2, 1959): 1–13, here 8.

candidates or their commitments, sat out the election or voted for a third-party candidate.

Because these and other concerns fell on different sides of the two-party political divide, Christians passionately divided as well. For example, if one defines "evangelical" by theological beliefs rather than by self-identification (in the United States, the label is more popular among white evangelicals), evangelicals were deeply divided. A strong majority of white evangelicals voted for one party, whereas a strong majority of black and Latino/a evangelicals (higher proportions of their respective populations) voted for the other. By exposing underlying divisions often avoided in polite, surface conversation, this election deepened mistrust across ethnic lines. Yet if we cannot love one another enough to listen and understand, a task typically less embraced by a dominant culture, our nationalistic or ethnic allegiances seem stronger than our membership in Christ's body.

Culture affects us. It is all too easy to denounce first-century Judean nationalism if we are unwilling to hear one another out in our own country. Dialogue across cultural lines might not produce immediate changes in partisan affiliations, but it can at least offer a sense of understanding why fellow-Christians acted the way they did. Confrontations such as the one Paul narrates between himself and Peter are inevitable insofar as the gospel engages multiple cultures. Their ultimate purpose, however, must not be deeper division but a knowledgeable unity in the gospel in the face of important cultural differences. ****

2:15–21: MADE RIGHT WITH GOD THROUGH CHRIST ALONE

2:15 We ourselves are Jews by birth and not Gentile sinners;

2:16 yet we know that a person is justified not by the works of the law but through faith in Jesus Christ. And we have come to believe in Christ Jesus, so that we might be justified by faith in Christ, and not by doing the works of the law, because no one will be justified by the works of the law.

2:17 But if, in our effort to be justified in Christ, we ourselves have been found to be sinners, is Christ then a servant of sin? Certainly not!

2:18 But if I build up again the very things that I once tore down, then I demonstrate that I am a transgressor.

2:19 For through the law I died to the law, so that I might live to God. I have been crucified with Christ;

2:20 and it is no longer I who live, but it is Christ who lives in me. And the life I now live in the flesh I live by faith in the Son of God, who loved me and gave himself for me.

2:21 I do not nullify the grace of God; for if justification comes through the law, then Christ died for nothing.

Paul's argument in 2:14–21 (esp. 2:17–19) is compact and complex, hence invites an introductory summary here. Although the matter is debated, it seems likely, with a majority of scholars, that Paul offers here a précis of the case he argued to Peter; in particular, verses 15 and 17 seem quite relevant to the situation in Antioch.[350] (Granted, Paul's argument summary here does not imply that nothing else was said.)

Thus Paul questions whether it is really a sin to eat with uncircumcised people. Peter's own conviction is obvious because Peter, though he is a Jew, acts like a gentile (as did Paul, 4:12; 1 Cor 9:21) in eating with gentiles. Yet Peter now expects gentiles to follow Jewish practices to be able to eat with Jews (2:14). Thus Paul could speak of "we Jews" (meaning here Jewish believers in Jesus, such as Peter and Paul), who were not gentile "sinners" (2:15). Yet because of Christ they became like gentiles in eating with them – and thus through Christ became "sinners" like them (2:17) – if in fact these gentiles were "sinners"!

The conclusion is absurd, which implies that the premise that it is sinful to eat with gentiles (because they alone are sinners) must also be absurd. Jewish *believers in Jesus* understood that all were sinners and all would be justified only by faith in Christ (2:16). It is absurd to suppose that those made right by Christward faith (2:16) will behave more sinfully (see 5:13; cf. Rom 6:1–2).

Paul argues further: if I rebuild the things that I once tore down (2:18) – ritual purity customs that separate me from Gentiles – then I am showing that I should not have torn them down to begin with, and admitting that I really am breaking the law by fellowshipping with Gentiles.

"In Christ," Paul says, "I died to the law" (2:19) – and thus to the need for ritual purity that supposedly separates Jews from Gentiles. Paul died with Christ so that he would have life in Christ (2:20; 3:11). He has been crucified with Christ (2:19–20) to the ways of the old age, which include passions (5:24), the world (6:14), and even in one sense the law (2:19), which Paul will equate with old ways (4:9–10). In Christ's risen life, he belongs to the realm of the new creation, where neither circumcision nor uncircumcision

---

[350]   Cf. fuller argument in Schreiner, *Galatians*, 150.

matters (6:15). It is Christ, not law, that makes one righteous (2:21); so on *theological* grounds, one should not withdraw from eating with Gentiles.

Paul reduces the social issue of table fellowship with gentile believers as equals to the theological issue of equal justification before God.

- 2:15–16: Jewish Christians are also justified by faith in Christ.
- 2:17–18: If the law condemns eating with justified gentiles, a practice that unity in Christ demands, this law cannot remain in force.
- 2:19–20: If the law executes Christ (2:17; 3:13), I have died with him to that law; my new life is Christ's life in me, which is truly righteous.
- 2:21: Righteousness is by Christ's life in us, not by the law.
- 3:1: The Galatians witnessed Christ crucified in Paul.
- 3:2: They received the Spirit.

Galatians receiving the Spirit (3:2) is not a new subject; Christ also lives in them (2:20). They, like the Jewish Christians who ate with them, are not under the law but can more than fulfill the righteous expectations of its heart by the reign of Christ and the Spirit in them (Gal 5:13–25).

Jews by birth (2:15) is literally "Jews by nature"; some Jewish tradition spoke of Jews having a special, inherited nature ancestrally freed from the impulse to idolatry,[351] but Paul's point here is undoubtedly more straightforward. Paul might believe that gentile Christians are spiritual proselytes grafted into Abraham's family (3:29), but he distinguishes ethnic Jews from gentiles "by nature" (Rom 2:14, 27; 11:21, 24).

Even more likely, Paul probably evokes scenes that Peter would have known firsthand: Pharisaic scribes challenged Jesus's disciples because Jesus ate with sinners (Mark 2:16; Matthew 11:19//Luke 7:34). Later, stricter elements in the church criticized Peter for eating with the uncircumcised (Acts 11:2–3), perhaps explaining Peter's anxiousness to avoid the appearance here.

Yet Jews who are not *Gentile sinners* (2:15) also were justified only through Christ; NRSV's *and we have come to believe* might mean something like, "*even* we have come to believe."[352] That is, if "even" Christian Jews could depend only on Christ for salvation, then surely this necessity applies also to Christian gentiles.

Galatians 2:16 is certainly a key statement of Paul's arguments; its complex of ideas is developed more fully in chapters 3–4.[353] Some suggest that

---

[351] Later rabbis in y. Qid. 4:1, §2; Song Rab. 7:8, §1; Pesiq. Rab. 41:4; lust in b. Shab. 145b–146a.
[352] Cf. D. Garlington, "'Even We Have Believed': Galatians 2:15–16 Revisited," *Criswell Theological Review* 7 (1, 2009): 3–28.
[353] Aletti, "Fonction."

Paul formulated justification by faith during the Galatian controversy, but this verse suggests otherwise. Although the exact formulation is missing in 1 Thessalonians, the basic idea of salvation only through Christ is already present (1 Thess 1:9–10; 5:9–10), dependent on their faith (3:5).[354] Although Paul highlights justification by faith especially when he must show that gentiles and Jews both come to God on the same terms, such as in Romans and Galatians, he continues to affirm its truth elsewhere (1 Cor 6:11; 2 Cor 3:9; Phil 3:9).[355]

More to the point here, the belief that people can be righted with God in Christ was apparently not unique to Paul. In the present passage, Paul appeals to a preexisting understanding shared with other Jewish Christians (*we know*);[356] some even believe that he appeals to a formula they already shared.[357] Still, their understanding could differ:[358] perhaps others took the *ean mê* – translated *but through* – as "except through,"[359] whereas Paul understands it as "but rather through." That is, they took for granted the need to keep Torah and added Christ. Paul thus will go on to force a choice between law-works and Christ-faith (3:9–13).[360]

A Closer Look: Justification

Although the NRSV translates *so that we might be justified in Christ* in 2:16, the Greek subjunctive here does not include the nuance of doubt that the English *might* could suggest.

English also does not capture well the connection in Greek between the terms that the NRSV translates as *justify* and *righteousness*; perhaps we could make the terminology clearer by rendering the verb "make/put right."[361] Scholarship today usually follows Ziesler's analysis of the terms: Paul uses

---

[354] Kim, *New Perspective*, 85–99.
[355] Interestingly, writing speech-in-character, Luke uses the verb only in Paul's speech in Galatia (Acts 13:38–39).
[356] With, e.g., Dunn, *Galatians*, 134; R. B. Hays, *The Conversion of the Imagination: Paul as Interpreter of Israel's Scripture* (Grand Rapids, MI: Eerdmans, 2005), 71; Hays, "Galatians," 236.
[357] E.g., M. C. de Boer, "Paul's Use and Interpretation of a Justification Tradition in Galatians 2.15–21," *JSNT* 28 (2, 2005): 189–216; de Boer, *Galatians*, 143.
[358] See A. A. Das, "Another Look at ἐὰν μή in Galatians 2:16," *JBL* 119 (3, 2000): 529–39.
[359] The usual sense of *ean mê*, by itself; see Donaldson, *Gentiles*, 113.
[360] Rhetorically, the forced choice between two alternatives can be called diairesis; see Aune, *Dictionary of Rhetoric*, 125. For *leges contrariae*, see comment on Gal 3:12.
[361] Some suggest "rectify"; Martyn, *Galatians*, 250; Hays, "Galatians," 237–38.

the verb *dikaioô* (typically translated *justify*) forensically but the noun *dikaiosunê* (normally translated *righteousness*, but sometimes *justification*) and the adjective *dikaios* (*righteous*) for righteous living. Emphasizing the verb, some scholars (more often in keeping with Protestant tradition) emphasize forensic righteousness: God has acquitted sinners. Emphasizing the noun, some (more often in keeping with Catholic tradition) emphasize behavioral righteousness. Often following Ziesler, many others believe that Paul always connotes something of both.[362]

Because Paul often uses the verb and the noun in the same contexts, it seems clear that he uses them in a related way. His key text is Gen 15:6 (Gal 3:6), which uses the noun *righteousness*. The presence of the noun might suggest that he uses both terms behaviorally, except that the verb *reckoned* may suggest a forensic verdict. The adjective *righteous* in his intertext, Hab 2:4 in Gal 3:11, suggests that when one is put right with God (*justified*), one receives a righteous status that also defines the person's identity. Galatians 2:11–21 itself addresses both forensic justification and union with Christ.[363]

With Paul depending on both such key terms, it seems likely that he welcomes readers to engage the fuller range of meaning. The verb normally does involve recognizing that someone is in the right or vindicating them.[364] In the Greek translation of the Old Testament, to "justify" someone was also to "render justice" on their behalf (2 Sam 15:4), e.g., defending the rights of the widow (Isa 1:17) and the poor (Ps 82:3). Yet Paul's language of God justifying *sinners* (Rom 4:5) suggests more than merely recognizing righteous behavior. Further, God who puts people in the right forensically also transforms them, whether or not (the debated issue) Paul uses *righteousness* to describe that transformation. The "transformative" righteousness view is the dominant view throughout most of church history.[365]

Paul certainly does not believe that righteous status (or transformation) are merited. Even in the Old Testament, God's servants could plead that he would forgive them according to his "righteousness" (Dan

---

[362] E.g., Longenecker, *Galatians*, 85; M. L. Soards and D. J. Pursiful, *Galatians* (SHBC; Macon, GA: Smith & Helwys, 2015), 88–89; Sanders, *Paul*, 505–11.

[363] Cf. Longenecker, *Galatians*, 85; M. A. Seifrid, "Paul, Luther, and Justification in Gal 2:15–21," *WTJ* 65 (2, 2003): 215–30.

[364] Barclay, *Gift*, 375–76.

[365] J. A. Fitzmyer, *Romans: A New Translation with Introduction and Commentary* (AB 33; New York: Doubleday, 1993), 118–19. On transformative righteousness in Augustine and Calvin but not Luther, see Barclay, *Gift*, 99–101, 124–27, 497.

9:16), though his judgments on them were just (9:7, 14). The Psalms often associate God's righteousness with his faithfulness and/or covenant love.[366] Israelites hoped for God to justify them someday (Isa 45:25; 50:8; 58:8; Mic 7:9). One who sinned might be justly punished and yet hope for God to vindicate him (using both *dikaioô* and *dikaiosunê*, Mic 7:9 LXX). In the time of restoration, God would vindicate his people, so that no one could challenge them (Isa 50:8, echoed in Rom 8:33). Probably the most important passage behind Paul's usage, however, is Isa 53:11, in which God's servant would bear his people's sins and therefore acquit them.[367]

In Galatians, righteousness comes by Christ rather than, as traditionally expected, the law (Gal 2:21, though the NRSV translates here *justification*; 3:21); the foretaste of this full righteousness is expressed in the present by faith working through love (5:5–6), displayed in the fruit of the Spirit (5:22–23). Because God speaks things into existence (cf. Rom 4:17; 2 Cor 4:6), when God acquits, he also brings into being a new creation, born from the Spirit (Gal 4:29). Although the sense of *dikaioô* is a legitimate lexical debate, theologically and on a larger literary level Gal 5:13–6:10 answer the probable claims of Paul's critics that Paul's gospel does not, without the law, produce righteousness.[368] Regeneration accompanies justification.

Perhaps in a similar way, lexically, justification does not include the idea of joining God's people.[369] Because Paul treats converted gentiles as spiritual descendants of Abraham, however (Gal 3:29), putting gentiles right with God has this consequence.[370] ****

---

[366] E.g., Ps 36:5–6, 10; 40:10; 88:11–12; 98:2–3; 103:17; 111:3–4; 119:40–41; 141:1; 143:1, 11–12; 145:7; because of his righteousness he shows justice (e.g., Ps 31:1; 35:24) or mercy (Ps 5:8; 51:14; 71:2, 15–16, 19, 24; 88:12) on behalf of his servant. God's "righteousness" would also vindicate or save in 1QS 11.5, 9–14. For Old Testament (and some early Jewish) background to Paul's justification doctrine, see Stuhlmacher, *Justification*, 13–24.

[367] Here the LXX construes the servant as the one vindicated. As in his omission of the pronoun from Hab 2:4 (Rom 1:17; Gal 3:11), Paul presumably knows that the Hebrew can be understood differently (or perhaps reckons the people acquitted in the servant, who has already carried out their suffering).

[368] In Romans, cf. also Rom 12:1–15:7; A. Schlatter, *Romans: The Righteousness of God* (trans. S. S. Schatzmann; Peabody, MA: Hendrickson, 1995), 26–27.

[369] Rightly S. Westerholm, *Justification Reconsidered: Rethinking a Pauline Theme* (Grand Rapids, MI: Eerdmans, 2013), 68.

[370] Perhaps the point, if meant theologically rather than lexically, in N. T. Wright, *Justification: God's Plan & Paul's Vision* (Downers Grove, IL: IVP Academic, 2009), 116, 121; cf. more lexical treatment on 164, 178.

A Closer Look: Christ-Faith (Gal 2:16; 3:22)

The meaning of Christ-faith (Gal 2:16; 3:22; Rom 3:22) is one of the most vigorously debated points in Pauline theology today.[371] Grammatically, a genitive construction such as *pistis Christou* simply means "faith relating to Christ." Thus it could be an objective genitive (*faith in Christ*), the majority view (and the one defended here), a subjective genitive (Christ's faith[fulness]), or could reflect some other relation between the two nouns.

Historically, barely any early church father seems aware that the phrase even *could* be translated as a subjective rather than an objective genitive.[372] It appears significant that the Greek fathers, for most of whom Greek was their native language and who emphasized Christ's obedience, nearly always read this phrase as faith in Christ. Catholics and Protestants alike have historically followed the objective genitive reading,[373] as do the main texts of nearly all translations. Comparatively few interpreters argued for the subjective genitive reading before the 1970s, though some who did so (such as Karl Barth) are very significant figures, as are many today.

On the subjective genitive reading, it is Christ's faithful obedience to the point of death that saves (Rom 5:19; Phil 2:8), although the contexts never or at best extremely rarely expressly designate this obedience as *pistis*. Various arguments may support the subjective genitive, though some of these arguments have some weaknesses:

Before the New Testament, *pistis* often appears with a subjective genitive;[374] but then, trust in a particular object was rarely as important in other circles as it was in early Christianity.[375] Moreover, *pistis*, like other verbal

---

[371] See esp. fully the discussion in M. F. Bird and P. M. Sprinkle, eds., *The Faith of Jesus Christ: Exegetical, Biblical, and Theological Studies* (Milton Keynes: Paternoster; Peabody, MA: Hendrickson, 2009).

[372] R. A. Harrisville, "ΠΙΣΤΙΣ ΧΡΙΣΤΟΥ: Witness of the Fathers," *NovT* 36 (3, 1994): 233–41; R. B. Matlock, "Πίστις in Galatians 3.26: Neglected Evidence for 'Faith in Christ'?" *NTS* 49 (3, 2003): 433–39 (on p⁴⁶ on Gal 3:26). Supposed cases of the subjective genitive interpretation in some early translations may represent simply a wooden rendering of *pistis Christou* rather than interpretation (as also in the KJV).

[373] B. McCormack, "Can We Still Speak of 'Justification by Faith'? An In-House Debate with Apocalyptic Readings of Paul," pages 159–84 in *Galatians and Christian Theology: Justification, the Gospel, and Ethics in Paul's Letter* (ed. M. W. Elliott et al.; Grand Rapids, MI: Baker Academic, 2014), 173.

[374] J. Dunnill, "Saved by Whose Faith? – The Function of πίστις Χριστοῦ in Pauline Theology," *Colloquium* 30 (1, 1998): 3–25.

[375] R. B. Matlock, "Detheologizing the πίστις Χριστοῦ Debate: Cautionary Remarks from a Lexical Semantic Perspective," *NovT* 42 (1, 2000): 1–23.

nouns, does appear with the objective genitive in earlier Greek, contrary to some detractors.[376]

Many advocates of the subjective genitive understanding point out the redundancy of "believing" in Christ in the context if "faith of Christ" means the same thing.[377] On the objective genitive reading, of course, the recurrence is not redundant but emphatic.[378] Moreover, this would hardly be Gal 2:16's only redundancy: Paul three times repeats law-works, with which he contrasts faith in Christ – an idea that also occurs three times if the verb phrase and noun phrase are synonymous.[379] Indeed, some of the repetition may be arranged chiastically: A: not justified by the works of the law; B: but through faith in Christ; B': by faith in Christ; A': not justified by the works of the law.[380]

One of the strongest arguments for the subjective genitive, one that would surely decide the case were there not (in my view) more compelling evidence in the other direction, is Paul's clear use with respect to God's faithfulness in Rom 3:3. The same may be true for the faith of Abraham in Rom 4:16.

Yet, ultimately, Paul's usage in particular contexts must decide the case. Supporters of the subjective genitive argue that contexts support their reading. I believe, however, that the contexts are much more intelligible on an objective genitive reading (see the commentary on the relevant passages).

The arguments for the objective genitive reading that I deem strongest are the cognate verb in the relevant contexts and what I see as the most natural exegesis of those contexts.[381] If Paul meant Christ's faithfulness, we might expect him to explain that somewhere, but against the usual understanding of the subjective genitive reading, Paul *nowhere* depicts Christ as believing or calls Jesus's obedience faithfulness. That is, Jesus is *nowhere* the

[376] R. A. Harrisville III, "Before πίστις Χριστοῦ: The Objective Genitive as Good Greek," *NovT* 41 (2006): 353–58.
[377] M. Barth, "The Faith of the Messiah," *HeyJ* 10 (1969): 363–70. That Paul does this in *every* context where he uses *pistis Christou* would strengthen the argument, but the counterargument is that Paul disambiguates in every case.
[378] With, e.g., T. H. Tobin, *Paul's Rhetoric in Its Contexts: The Argument of Romans* (Peabody, MA: Hendrickson, 2004), 133–34; A. J. Hultgren, *Paul's Letter to the Romans: A Commentary* (Grand Rapids, MI: Eerdmans, 2011), 637–42; Sanders, *Paul*, 510; Barclay, *Gift*, 380.
[379] R. B. Matlock, "The Rhetoric of πίστις in Paul: Galatians 2.16, 3.22, Romans 3.22, and Philippians 3.9," *JSNT* 30 (2, 2007): 173–203, here 193.
[380] Cf. P. Ellingworth, "A note on Galatians 2.16," *BT* 56 (2, 2005): 109–10.
[381] See also J. D. G. Dunn, *The Theology of Paul the Apostle* (Grand Rapids, MI: Eerdmans, 1998), 381–84.

subject of the cognate verb *pisteuô*, although Paul employs this verb a full forty-two times in his undisputed letters.[382] Jesus is, by contrast, sometimes the specific *object* of that faith (e.g., Rom 10:11; Phil 1:29), including explicitly in Gal 2:16 (*we have come to believe in Christ Jesus*).[383] (That tendency continues to constitute also the overwhelming preponderance of data in the other sources from the earliest Christian movement of which Paul was a part.)[384] Indeed, even the adjective *pistos* (normally, *faithful*), though applied four times to God and once each to various other figures, never applies to Christ in Paul's letters.[385]

Granted, cognates do not always share the same range of meaning, but in this case they appear in the same contexts in clearly interdependent ways. For example, Abraham and his descendants believe (3:6–7, 9) and Scripture thus speaks of his gentile heirs being justified by faith (3:8).

When Paul introduces the potentially ambiguous *pistis Christou* in Gal 2:16, he immediately disambiguates it by making Christ the object of the cognate verb.[386] The phrase's first use in Romans is also immediately disambiguated by designating human believers (Rom 3:22); the following chapter expounds on Abraham's faith as *believing* (Rom 4:3, 5, 9, 11–14, 16–20, 24).[387] Paul does not disambiguate in Phil 3:9, perhaps because his audience in Philippi already understands his teaching, but he has already spoken of human faith (1:25, 27, 29; 2:17), including a clearly objective genitive with faith *in* the gospel (1:27); the context also includes a clearly objective genitive for Christ (the knowledge of Christ; in the NRSV, *knowing Christ*, 3:8).[388]

In the final analysis, although the differences in reading change our understanding of the passages in question, they do not require radically different readings of Pauline theology. In either case, Christ's death and resurrection are what bring salvation, and in either case it comes to those who trust in him. Faith in an unreliable object is worthless; trust in Christ

---

[382] Dunn, *Galatians*, 139; Tobin, *Rhetoric in Contexts*, 132–34; Hultgren, *Romans*, 643; Silva, "Galatians," 789–90.

[383] See also Eph 1:12–13; cf. 1 Thess 4:14.

[384] See John 1:12; 2:11; 3:15–16, 18, 36; 4:21, 39; 5:38, 46–47; 6:29–30, 35–36, 40, 69; 7:5, 31, 38–39, 48; 8:30–31, 45–46; 9:35–36; 10:37–38, 42; 11:25–27, 45, 48; 12:11, 36, 37, 42, 44, 46; 13:19; 14:1, 11–12; 16:9, 27; 17:20–21; 20:31; Acts 10:43; 11:17; 14:23; 16:31; 18:8; 19:4; 22:19; 1 Pet 1:8; 2:6; 1 John 3:23; 5:10, 13.

[385] Tobin, *Rhetoric in Contexts*, 132; Hultgren, *Romans*, 643.

[386] Matlock, "Rhetoric," 193–99.

[387] Matlock, "Rhetoric," 184–87; Barclay, *Gift*, 476–77.

[388] For an objective genitive in Phil 3:9, see V. Koperski, "The Meaning of *Pistis Christou* in Philippians 3:9," *Louvain Studies* 18 (1993): 198–216; Matlock, "Rhetoric," 177–84.

for salvation is rightly placed precisely because Christ is reliable, worthy of trust.[389] As E. P. Sanders notes, "no one wishes to exclude either 'faith in Christ' or 'Christ's faithfulness to God' from Paul's thought. The question is the best definition of the meaning of 'faith in/of Christ' in Galatians, where the phrase first appears."[390] Yet he rightly goes on to observe, "Of course the converts relied on Christ's fidelity, but his fidelity alone did not transfer some people and not others into membership in his body."[391]

Likewise, after arguing for a subjective genitive reading, de Boer rightly notes that even if one thinks of faith in Christ (language that he concedes appears in Romans and 1 Thessalonians), it "cannot be construed as an innate or natural human capacity, but only as an apocalyptic-eschatological *novum* ... elicited by the proclamation of the gospel."[392] Precisely because Christ is faithful/trustworthy, faith in Christ is not misplaced; a subjective genitive reading becomes much more plausible if we think in terms of trusting Christ's reliability.[393] That is, on either reading, the honor belongs to Christ alone. ****

A Closer Look: Law-Works (Gal 2:16; 3:2, 5, 10)

Historically, Paul speaks of the Torah, not simply of generic works. Paul's problem with law-works is not that he opposes good works or even the law. He merely rejects these as a means of justification as opposed to faith in Christ, possibly as a rhetorical forced choice that reduces to the absurd any dependence on something other than Christ.

No major figures of mainstream Christian tradition, including the Reformers, dismiss the value of good works. Luther in fact deemed the content of law-works as positive, since God gave the Torah; what was negative was seeking to be justified by them.[394] Calvin contends that "faith alone is

---

[389] Cf. T. Morgan, *Roman Faith and Christian Faith: Pistis and Fides in the Early Roman Empire and Early Churches* (Oxford: Oxford University Press, 2015), 305. For faith as loyalty or allegiance, see, e.g., Dio Chrysostom *Or.* 3.86, 88. For faith's relationship to trustworthiness in a Roman context, see G. Schiemann, "Fides: Law," *Brill's New Pauly* 5: 415–17, here 415; D. A. deSilva, *Honor, Patronage, Kinship, and Purity: Unlocking New Testament Culture* (Downers Grove, IL: InterVarsity, 2000), 115–16.

[390] Sanders, *Paul*, 509, deciding in favor of the objective genitive.

[391] Sanders, *Paul*, 511.

[392] De Boer, *Galatians*, 239.

[393] See A. Vanhoye, "Πίστις Χριστοῦ: Fede in Cristo o affidabilità di Cristo?" *Bib* 80 (1, 1999): 1–21.

[394] Barclay, *Gift*, 103–04; Wengert, "Luther," 101, 109.

sufficient for justification, but true faith cannot be separated from the Spirit of regeneration."[395]

The phrase *works of the law* could include a subjective genitive (works produced or prescribed by the law), but it more likely uses an objective genitive (works done to observe the law). Thus the phrase semantically matches phrases such as *do/obey the law* (Rom 2:14, 25, 27; Gal 3:10; 5:3; 6:13) or *doers of the law* (Rom. 2:13).[396]

The primary debate today is whether Paul meant all works prescribed by the law or focused on particular boundary markers that separated Jew from gentile. The idea of law-works as boundary markers may be an old rather than recent insight. Many historic Christian thinkers, from Jerome to Aquinas to Erasmus, thought that Paul was dismissing only the ceremonial laws.[397] By contrast, Augustine, Luther, and Calvin believed that Paul criticized dependence on any of the God-given law.[398] Earlier, Chrysostom felt that Paul rejected the law even as a guide for ethics.[399] While it may not remain mandatory as a legal code, however, church tradition was probably right to believe that it continues to provide moral instruction. Even Augustine may have thought that Paul's greater concern involved ceremonial laws, addressing more a positive role for moral law in Gal 5–6.[400]

Luther applies the basic principle more broadly: if one could not be justified by God's own law, then neither could one be justified by anything else (cf. 2:21), including rules created by the church.[401] Many scholars, including myself, believe that Paul would appreciate such applications to broader concerns.

The initial exegetical task, however, is to determine, insofar as possible, the issues that Paul was addressing in his context. Thus, as noted earlier,

---

[395] Calvin on Gal 5:6 (trans. Bray, 176). Note similarly Barclay's citations (in *Gift*, 124) of Calvin *Inst*. 3.6.1; 3.8.1; 3.16.1; Calvin's commentary on Rom 6:2.

[396] S. J. Gathercole, *Where Is Boasting? Early Jewish Soteriology and Paul's Response in Romans 1–5* (Grand Rapids, MI: Eerdmans, 2002), 92; Moo, *Galatians*, 158.

[397] Ambrosiaster on Gal 3:12, in K. Pollmann and M. W. Elliott, "Galatians in the Early Church: Five Case Studies," pages 40–61 in *Galatians and Christian Theology: Justification, the Gospel, and Ethics in Paul's Letter* (ed. M. W. Elliott et al.; Grand Rapids, MI: Baker Academic, 2014), 46–47; Haimo of Auxerre on Gal 2:16 (Levy); Barclay, *Gift*, 104; S. Hafemann, "Yaein: Yes and No to Luther's Reading of Galatians 3:6–14," pages 117–31 in *Galatians and Christian Theology*, 119; M. Koehne, "Saint Thomas Aquinas: on 'Works of the Law' and 'Faith of Christ' in Galatians 2:15–16," *ScrB* 32 (1, 2002): 9–20.

[398] Matera, *Galatians*, 93; Barclay, *Gift*, 104, 121, 340; Wengert, "Luther," 100–02.

[399] Chrysostom *Commentary on Galatians* 3.25–26 (Longenecker, *Galatians*, li).

[400] Augustine *Ep. Gal*. 19 (1B.3.1; Edwards).

[401] Barclay, *Gift*, 104.

scholars today particularly debate whether law-works refers specifically to problematic ethnic boundary markers or, with probably still a majority of scholars, to the whole law.

Those who focus here on eating, circumcision, and holy days do so because these are the particular examples highlighted in the text (2:3, 12; 4:10; 5:2–3, 6, 11; 6:12–15). Along with proselytism, these are also the three major points of criticism against Jews found in Roman literature.[402] E. P. Sanders notes that despite Paul's general language, "works of the law," a particular work, namely circumcision, is primarily at issue in Gal 2:16 (cf. 2:3).[403]

At the same time, the phrase itself does not have such a restrictive meaning. Indeed, Jewish teachers averred that disregarding one commandment de facto cast off the entire law.[404] Despite some construals of *works of the law* in 4QMMT, even at Qumran the phrase probably referred to the entire law,[405] though of course as understood via the community's sectarian lens. Elsewhere in Galatians Paul does speak of the need to perform the whole law (Gal 3:10b; 5:3). That is probably also how first-century Jews would have understood the phrase.[406]

Nevertheless, those who emphasize that Paul speaks of the entire law also recognize the relevance of Jewish–gentile boundary markers in Galatians.[407] Likewise, James D. G. Dunn, who emphasized boundary markers, has clarified that though he meant *especially* boundary markers, he never intended to deny that the phrase "works of the law" included the entire law.[408] Thus a consensus seems to be emerging regarding at least the general point: Paul intended any of the law, but the issues at hand were especially those markers that particularly defined one as having become Jewish – in Galatians, most prominently circumcision (Gal 2:3, 12; 5:2–3, 6, 11; 6:12–13, 15). ****

Paul gives here the reason (*because*, Gr. *hoti*) that a person cannot be justified by the works of the law: *because no one will be justified by the works of the law*. At first this reason might sound tautological, but Paul is providing

[402] See, e.g., Juvenal *Sat.* 14.96–106; Whittaker, *Jews and Christians*, 73–80; Sevenster, *Anti-Semitism*, 136–39.

[403] Sanders, *Paul*, 513–14.

[404] Sanders, *Paul*, 514. See comment on Gal 5:3.

[405] See 1QS 6.18 (works *in* the law); 4Q265 f4ii.6.

[406] Cf. Gathercole, *Boasting*, 92–93, 238; F. Watson, *Paul, Judaism, and the Gentiles: Beyond the New Perspective* (rev. edn.; Grand Rapids, MI: Eerdmans, 2007), 19, 128, 212.

[407] Schreiner, *Galatians*, 161n39; Silva, "Galatians," 790.

[408] J. D. G. Dunn, *The New Perspective on Paul* (rev. edn.; Grand Rapids, MI: Eerdmans, 2008), 23–28; Dunn, *Beginning*, 475n264.

an implicit argument for those familiar with Scripture, at least with psalms used in worship; he is evoking biblical language. The psalmist pleaded with God not to judge his servant, because no one living was righteous by his standards (Ps 143:2). Paul evokes the passage in the Greek translation (LXX Ps 142:2) familiar to his hearers, which renders the second line, "because no one living will be justified/found righteous before you," overlapping with Paul in the words *no one will be justified*. The psalmist goes on to plead for God to preserve his life because of *God's* righteousness (143:11) and steadfast love (143:12), and because the psalmist trusts in him (143:8).[409]

Paul makes slight adjustments in the wording, which was common practice when quoting Scripture or other sources in new contexts.[410] "No one living" becomes "no flesh," perhaps because Paul reserves terminology about life mostly for new life in Christ (2:19–20; 3:11–12; 5:25; 6:8; though cf. 2:14), and Paul will use "flesh" mostly negatively in 3:3; 4:29; 5:13, 16–19, 24; 6:8, 12–13. The change, however, also draws on a common LXX expression, including for humanity's mortality or judgment (e.g., Isa 40:6; 66:16).

The other change, of course, is to apply the general principle of no one being justified before God to the specific matter of no one being justified by the *works of the law*. This specific application remains consistent with the point of a psalm whose author depends wholly on God's righteousness. That Paul applies the text the same way with roughly the same adjustments in Rom 3:20 may suggest that it functioned this way, or came to function this way, regularly in his preaching.

As in the case of the more explicit citations in Rom 3:10–19, no one was likely to dispute Paul's exegesis here, primarily because no one would disagree with the uncontroversial premise. Jewish tradition recognized that all people sin,[411] and the thought would not be controversial among gentiles either (though they defined moral error more broadly). Works of the law could not justify anyone because no one was sinless (presupposed also in 3:10, 12, 21–22).

All have sinned (2:16), making the specific association of gentiles with sin (2:15) a superfluous red herring. But Paul pushes this red herring further toward its absurd conclusion in 2:17. There are a variety of interpretations of

---

[409] See R. B. Hays, "Psalm 143 and the Logic of Romans 3," *JBL* 99 (1, March 1980): 107–15, here 114–15.

[410] See Hermogenes *Method* 30.447; C. D. Stanley, *Paul and the Language of Scripture: Citation Technique in the Pauline Epistles and Contemporary Literature* (SNTSMS 69; Cambridge: Cambridge University Press, 1992), 290–91, 305–06, 322–23, 334–37.

[411] E.g., 1 Kgs 8:46; 2 Chron 6:36; 1 Esd 4:37–38; Jub. 21:21; 1QS 11.9–10.

2:17. The likeliest sense in this context, though, is one that flows directly from the incident narrated in 2:11–14; Paul continues to address Peter here. If eating with gentiles is really as sinful as Peter's Judean critics seem to think, and as Peter's withdrawal from them (had it not been hypocritical) would seem to acknowledge, then Peter, Paul, and other Jews who were eating with gentiles sinned through following Christ in welcoming gentile Christians. (As noted earlier, Paul probably knows Peter's experience of Jesus eating with "sinners.") And if that is the case, then it is following Christ that led them into sin – something their non-Christian critics might insist but something that no Christian would concede. Thus Paul protests, *Certainly not!*[412]

Paul is pressing commitment to Christ to its conclusion: everything else must be evaluated relative to the truth of Christ.[413] In Christ, Peter, Paul, and other believers had torn down (2:18) the barrier between Jew and gentile in the law, which separated Jews as an exclusively holy people (cf. Eph 2:14).[414] (Paul might think here also of a fence around the law.[415] The term Paul uses for *torn down* here, *kataluô*, also could apply to annulling or repealing laws.)[416] Building that wall up again by withdrawing from gentiles would imply that their previous eating with gentiles was transgression (2:18).

But Paul *died* with respect *to the law so that* he *might live* with respect *to God* (2:19). Paul experienced this death at his conversion; this passage echoes 1:13–16 at some key points.[417] In this death he has *been crucified with Christ* (2:19). In Christ the law, which separates God's holy people from gentile sinners, is no longer the ultimate norm for ethics; instead, the empowering resurrection life of Christ within (2:19–20), expressed by Paul also as the fruit of the Spirit (5:16–25), causes believers to do God's will.[418]

Paul was crucified with Christ to the law, just as Christ was born under law to redeem those under law (4:4–5) – i.e., Christ identified with his people.[419] Paul's more detailed elaboration of this idea in Romans helps us

---

[412]   In diatribe, note this phrase in, e.g., Epictetus *Diatr.* 1.5.10; 1.8.15; 1.10.7; 1.11.24; 1.19.7; 1.26.6; 1.28.24; 1.29.9; 2.8.2; 3.1.42. Paul normally uses it after a rhetorical question and to deny absurd and typically virtually blasphemous conclusions.

[413]   With Barclay, *Gift*, 384.

[414]   Cf. Dunn, *Galatians*, 142, for texts about Israel "marked off from the other nations by a wall" (Let. Aris. 139; Eph 2:14).

[415]   M. Ab. 1:1; 3:14; Sipre Deut. 48.1.5; Ab. R. Nat. 2; 3 A; the principle in m. Ber. 1:1; Sanh. 11:4.

[416]   See BDAG definition 3a; cf. Matt 5:17.

[417]   De Boer, *Galatians*, 159, noting "in me"; the law or traditions; God's Son and God's grace.

[418]   Cf. Cousar, *Galatians*, 60.

[419]   Marius Victorinus *Ep. Gal.* 1.2.19, on Gal 2:19 (Edwards), believes Paul died to either the old law or the law understood carnally. Not the Torah itself but its demands on

understand the premises of his argument: Christ died to sin (Rom 6:10) so that those identified with him died with him (6:3–8, 11). Believers died to the law through Christ's body (Rom 7:4); the old person (in Adam) thus died (Rom 6:6) and a new person lives in Christ (Gal 2:20). The principle of solidarity with Christ here resembles the solidarity of descent: Paul's opponents envisioned an ethnic solidarity with their ancestor Abraham, whereas Paul envisioned an ancestral solidarity with Adam (Rom 5:12–21) and a supra-ethnic, spiritual solidarity through adherence to Christ and becoming part of his people.[420]

But how did Paul die to the law *through the law* (2:19)? Pauline theology allows us to explain *through the law* here in multiple possible ways.

- Some argue that Paul died to the law *through* the law because the law conflicts with Christ, as in 2:17 and 3:13.
- Perhaps he died to the law *through* the law because the law points to Christ (3:24; Rom 3:21, 31) and to the law's transformation in Christ (as in Gal 6:2; Rom 8:2).
- Perhaps Paul died to the law *through* the law because the law revealed that its own purpose was not salvation (2:21; 3:21).
- Perhaps he died to the law *through* the law because the law showed Paul his sinfulness and thereby revealed that there was no salvation in the law itself; the law brought him death (as in 3:22; Rom 7:5, 10–11, 13).

In this case, the first two or three explanations, which are mutually consistent now that the fulness of time has come, seem most relevant here because of the context. The law retains value (Gal 5:14) but as approached now from the vantage point of its eschatological fulfillment and embodiment in Christ and his approach to the law (6:2).

The expression *live to God* (2:19; Rom 6:10–11; cf. Rom 14:8; 2 Cor 5:15) could echo an expression from the Jewish martyr tradition. The patriarchs and all the righteous live rather than die with respect to God, even if they must die on account of God and his law (4 Macc 7:19; 16:25). Paul, however,

---

believers' lives ceases (Barclay, *Gift*, 385); Paul is not dead to Scripture (B. Roberts Gaventa, "The Singularity of the Gospel Revisited," pages 187–99 in *Galatians and Christian Theology: Justification, the Gospel, and Ethics in Paul's Letter* [ed. M. W. Elliott et al.; Grand Rapids, MI: Baker Academic, 2014], 198).

[420] Thus one from Abraham was part of Abraham; one from Adam was part of Adam; but in a more spiritual and not simply genetic way, those in Christ were his very body; see Rom 12:4–5; 1 Cor 10:17; 12:12–13.

lives to God because Christ (2:20) and the Spirit (5:25; 6:8; cf. 3:11) live in him.

In this context Paul's crucifixion with Christ is especially to the law (2:19; cf. Rom 7:4, 6). Perhaps he died to the law because his death to sin and the world (cf. 5:24; 6:14; Rom 6:2, 10–11; Col 2:20) rendered his traditional approach to the law superfluous (Gal 5:14, 18, 23) or showed its futility (2:16, 21; 3:10–11, 21–22). In this context, the Galatians themselves re-experienced Christ's crucifixion in Paul's life and/or preaching (Gal 3:1).

Now it is *Christ who lives in* Paul (2:20), just as he elsewhere speaks of Christ and the Spirit living in believers (Rom 8:9–10). Paul will go on to speak of the Galatians having received the Spirit (Gal 3:2), and of all believers living by the Spirit (5:25), Christ living in one is clearly associated with the Spirit living in one. The Spirit authors resurrection life (Gal 6:8; Rom 1:4; 8:2, 6, 10–11, 13; 2 Cor 3:6). What Paul means by the phrase *live by faith in the Son of God* will also become clearer when he addresses life by faith in Gal 3:11.

Some philosophers, most typically Stoics, spoke of the supreme deity dwelling in humans, especially in intellectuals,[421] but this was rarely envisioned in terms of a personal relationship with the deity.[422] With a primary background in Ezek 36:27 (cf. 2 Cor 3:3), Pauline literature often speaks of sharing Christ's death and resurrection and Christ's risen life active in believer (or special ministers) through the Spirit.

It is no longer I who live, but Christ lives in me offers an example of two balanced clauses, an attractive rhetorical form.[423] With another sort of balance, the believer lives both in the flesh (*en sarki*, in a neutral sense, that is, in the body) and in or by faith (*en pistei*) in Jesus (2:20). Paul can use expressions such as *no longer I, but* with reference to other powers ruling one's will (Rom 7:17, 20); one needs the rule of the Spirit to combat the rule of sin (Gal 5:16–18). Everyone could tell the difference between Paul's preconversion life, zealous merely for the law (1:13–14), and his new life devoted to Christ; it was Christ in him that made the difference.

---

[421] E.g., Cicero *Leg.* 1.22.58–59; Seneca Y. *Ep. Lucil.* 41.1–2; 73.16; Epictetus *Diatr.* 1.14.13–14; 2.8.10–11, 14; Marcus Aurelius 2.13, 17; 3.5–6, 12; 3.16.2; 5.10.2; Apuleius *De deo Socr.* 157.

[422] An exception might possibly be Socrates's *daimon*, on which see, e.g., Xenophon *Mem.* 1.1.2; Plutarch *Alc.* 17.4; *Sign Soc.* 10, *Mor.* 580C; Socrates *Ep.* 1.

[423] Anderson, *Glossary*, 90–91; Rowe, "Style," 143; Porter, "Paul and Letters," 582. Paul elsewhere uses a similar "not I, but" (here *no longer I … but*) construction to emphasize God's grace (1 Cor 15:10) or superiority (1 Cor 7:10).

Bridging the Horizons: Union with Christ

Sanders rightly objects to Bultmann's purely existential revision of Paul's understanding of union with Christ and being one body with him, noting that modern Western readers tend to lack a category or analogies to articulate Pauline and early Christian experience.[424] Ancient and medieval interpreters, however, engaged this reality more readily, allowing for experience in a less sterile way than modern critics,[425] as did those from the era of the Reformation.[426] It is probably also more intelligible in the growing experientially oriented movements in global Christianity.[427]

What some call union with Christ does not make Paul literally part of Christ's person, but God's Spirit so suffuses Paul's person that God works in and through Paul,[428] transforming him into what he was designed to be in Christ's image (cf. 2 Cor 3:18).[429] This is a step far beyond even a relationship of companionship, an intimacy through a continuous internal presence too complete for the closest possible analogies (such as perhaps marital intimacy; cf. 2 Cor 11:2; Eph 5:30–32) to be adequate.[430] Obviously such a relationship has an experiential component, though various believers may experience it in somewhat different ways.

The Spirit transforms and empowers the self rather than obliterates it; divine activity shapes human agency rather than replaces it.[431] Fluid images of the Spirit (e.g., Isa 44:3; Joel 2:28) also may facilitate an image of how

---

[424] E. P. Sanders, *Paul and Palestinian Judaism: A Comparison of Patterns of Religion* (Philadelphia, PA: Fortress, 1977), 522–23; Sanders, *Paul*, 724–25.

[425] E.g., Origen *De princ.* 4.4.29; Chrysostom *Hom. Gal.* 3.27 (Edwards); Haimo of Auxerre on Gal 2:20; Bruno the Carthusian on Gal 2:20; Lombard *Galatians* on Gal 2:20 (Levy).

[426] E.g., Desiderius Erasmus *Paraphrases* (Bray, on Gal 2:20); Luther *Second Lectures on Galatians* on Gal 2:20; Calvin *Commentary on Galatians* 2:20 (Bray). See also S. Chester, "It Is No Longer I Who Live: Justification by Faith and Participation in Christ in Martin Luther's Exegesis of Galatians," *NTS* 55 (2009): 315–37.

[427] On which, see, e.g., Philip Jenkins, *The Next Christendom: The Coming of Global Christianity* (New York: Oxford University Press, 2002); Todd M. Johnson and Kenneth R. Ross, eds., *Atlas of Global Christianity, 1910–2010* (Edinburgh: Center for the Study of Global Christianity, 2009); Michael Bergunder, A. F. Droogers, Cornelis van der Laan, Cecil M. Robeck, and Allan Anderson, *Studying Global Pentecostalism: Theories and Methods* (Anthropology of Christianity 10; Berkeley: University of California, 2010).

[428] See Keener, *Mind*, 128–32, 197–98.

[429] See Keener, *Mind*, 154, 156, 206, 210–12, 215. See further M. J. Gorman, *Inhabiting the Cruciform God: Kenosis, Justification, and Theosis in Paul's Narrative Soteriology* (Grand Rapids, MI: Eerdmans, 2009).

[430] Cf. Fee, *Galatians*, 92: here in Gal 2:20 Paul "lets us in on his personal life of devotion."

[431] See Barclay, *Gift*, 441–42. Compare and contrast the understanding of self in Stoic thought; cf. Engberg-Pedersen, *Paul and Stoics*, 53–55.

some dry substances may remain in some sense the same and yet are transformed by being soaked or suffused with fluid. ****

God's Son *loved me and gave himself for me*. A few people spoke of particular deities loving or being loved by people, but Greek religion normally tended to stress barter and obligation.[432] Indeed, Platonically inclined philosophers affirmed the passionlessness of deity.[433]

This idea more closely resembles Jewish tradition, where God loves his people corporately,[434] as well as various individuals[435] or the righteous in general.[436] Some even emphasized that God loved each individual Israelite more than the nations.[437] More rarely, some Diaspora Jews recognized that God loved all humanity.[438]

Jewish tradition did not, however, emphasize the Messiah's love, as here; for Paul, of course, Jesus is a real person, not a theoretical Messiah,[439] and Jesus is also divine (cf. again comment on Gal 1:1, 3). Nor did non-Christian traditions highlight divine love the way that we find it here: a divine one sacrificing his own life for us – for sinners (cf. 2:15; Rom 5:6–10).[440]

Against those who depict Paul's theology of atonement through Christ's death as divine child abuse, Gal 2:20 instead shows that not only the Father (Rom 4:25; 8:32) but also Jesus himself chose to give Jesus in death to save sinners (as also in Eph 5:2, 25).[441]

[432] E.g., W. Burkert, *Greek Religion* (trans. Raffan; Cambridge, MA: Harvard University Press, 1985), 74–75; E. Ferguson, *Backgrounds of Early Christianity* (Grand Rapids, MI: Eerdmans, 1987), 118, 147–48.
[433] Apuleius *De deo Socr.* 146–47. Personal devotion to deities became common in fourth-century savior cults and Neoplatonism.
[434] E.g., Deut 7:7, 13; 10:15; 23:5; 33:3; Isa 43:4; 63:9; Hos 11:1; Tobit 13:10 (NRSV; LXX 13:12); Bar 3:36; CD 8.17; Jub. 31:15, 20; Ps. Sol. 9:8; 4 Ezra 5:27; Rom 11:28; Sipre Deut. 344.1.1; 34.3.1; 344.5.1; Ab. R. Nat. 36, §94B.
[435] E.g., Sir 45:1; 46:13; Philo *Abr.* 50; T. Ab. 7:1; 8:11 A; T. Jos. 1:2; 3 En. 1:8.
[436] E.g., Wis 4:10; 7:28; Ps. Sol. 13:9; T. Jos. 11:1.
[437] Sipre Deut. 97.2.
[438] Sib. Or. 1.72.
[439] L. W. Hurtado, "Paul's Messianic Christology," pages 107–31 in *Paul the Jew: Rereading the Apostle as a Figure of Second Temple Judaism* (ed. G. Boccaccinni and C. A. Segovia; Minneapolis, MN: Fortress, 2016), 115–16.
[440] Jesus handing himself over to death is connected to and reveals the love already mentioned in 2:20; see Rom 5:8; 8:32, 25, 39; John 3:16; 1 John 4:9–11; Diogn. 10.2; cf. de Boer, *Galatians*, 163. The closest but very limited analogy is some Jewish traditions that emphasize God suffering in his people's suffering, for which cf. Judg 10:16; Isa 63:9; Hos 11:8; N. J. Cohen, "Shekhinta ba-Galuta: A Midrashic Response to Destruction and Persecution," *JSJ* 13 (1–2, 1982): 147–59.
[441] With Gathercole, *Substitution*, 25. For the idea of righteous sufferers atoning, see, e.g., 2 Macc 7:37; 4 Macc 6:27–29; 9:24; 17:21–22; cf. Mekilta Pisha 1.105–13; A. Büchler, *Studies in Sin and Atonement in the Rabbinic Literature of the First Century* (1927; repr., New York: KTAV, 1967), 178. For ancient ideas of atonement, see further, e.g., M. Hengel,

Paul continues the first-person voice, and apparently thereby under-lines the personal dimension of this experience; as Chrysostom suggests, "Paul speaks in this highly personal voice," just as the prophets often called God "my God"; "He shows that each of us ought to render as much thanks to Christ as though Christ had come for him alone. For God would not have withheld this gift even from one person. He has the same love for every individual as for the whole world."[442] Likewise Calvin: Why "for me"? Because "We each need to apply to ourselves individually ... It is for each one of us as individuals."[443]

Trust is appropriate to the extent that its object is trustworthy; *the Son of God, who loved me and gave himself for me* is a wholly reliable object of trust, so Paul lives *by faith in the Son of God* (2:20).[444] Although Paul remains in the flesh, i.e., embodied with all the needs and passions that embodiedness implies (5:24),[445] it is in faith in God's Son that he lives, i.e., experiences already the promised resurrection life of the coming age (2:19–20; 3:11; 5:25; 6:8; cf. 1:4). Trust is the appropriate response to benefaction,[446] and the infi-nitely valuable character of the gift here merits unlimited trust.[447]

Just as one is put right with God through trusting Christ, it is in faith that one lives this solidarity with Christ.[448] The idea here is similar to Rom 6:11: reckoning oneself dead and raised with Christ.[449] In this age believers remain in the flesh, subject to its challenges (note the sense of *sarx*, "flesh,"

The Atonement: The Origins of the Doctrine in the New Testament (trans. J. Bowden; Philadelphia, PA: Fortress, 1981); J. Kim, "The Concept of Atonement in Hellenistic Thought and 1 John," *JGRChJ* 2 (2001–2005): 100–16; Kim, "The Concept of Atonement in Early Rabbinic Thought and the New Testament Writings," *JGRChJ* 2 (2001–2005): 117–45; C. Thoma, "Frühjüdische Martyrer: Glaube an Auferstehung und Gericht," *Freiburger Rundbrief* 11 (2, 2004): 82–93.

[442] Chrysostom *Hom. Gal.* 2.20 (Edwards).

[443] Calvin on Gal 2:20 (Childress).

[444] Some read this as a subjective genitive (Christ's faithfulness; de Boer, *Galatians*, 150), but most see it as objective (A. J. Hultgren, "The Pistis Christou Formulation in Paul," *NovT* 22 [3, 1980]: 248–63; Tobin, *Rhetoric in Contexts*, 133).

[445] For Augustine *Cont.* 18 (Edwards), both one's spirit and one's flesh are good, provided the former rules and the latter obeys. Erasmus Sarcerius *Annotations on Galatians* on Gal 2:20 (Bray) contrasts life according to the flesh, following its desires, with life *in* the flesh, as here, "a normal life in the body." For the semantic range of flesh, see Keener, *Mind*, 101–03.

[446] deSilva, *Readings*, 133.

[447] Oakes, *Galatians*, 94, suggests that in Gal 2:20 Paul replaces self-reliance with reliance on Christ. Ancient Israelite devotion also valued radical dependence on God; cf. God as the strength of one's life (Ps 18:1; 27:1; 28:7–8; 31:2, 4; 37:39; 73:26; 118:14; 138:3; 140:7).

[448] Cf. H. N. Ridderbos, *Paul: An Outline of His Theology* (trans. J. R. De Witt; Grand Rapids, MI: Eerdmans, 1975), 232.

[449] See discussion in Keener, *Mind*, 44–49.

in Gal 3:3; 5:13, 16–17, 19, 24; 6:8; though this is less clear in the antecedent references of 1:16 and 2:16), but by faith in Christ's victory believers can live the new life by Christ who lives in us.

One reckons oneself as in Christ. This might resemble imaginatively adopting the persona of Christ, "putting on" Christ (3:27) as if walking in his steps. It is, however, more than mere playacting (cf. comment on 2:13); it is embracing divine truth because of what Christ has done. It includes imitating Christ by living as he lived (each within the sphere of one's own calling and gifting; 1 Cor 11:1; Eph 5:1; 1 Thess 1:6; 1 John 2:6). Yet it can also be envisioned as walking in the way we know Christ walked because we affirm that Christ is living in us and his path therefore exemplifies us how to embrace Christ living in us (2 Cor 13:3–5; Eph 5:2; Col 2:6; cf. Gal 5:16–25; 6:2). ****

Paul refuses to *nullify the grace of God* (2:21). The word translated *nullify* can also mean to reject something as invalid or by refusing to recognize it (BDAG). God's gracious gift was Christ's own life offered in death (2:20). To *nullify* or *invalidate* the gift is to reject it. To refuse a gift was to insult and shame the giver and even declare enmity;[450] the ancient expectation was to respond to a gift by honoring and showing fidelity to the benefactor.[451] Despite the diversity of Second Temple Judaism, virtually all Jews identified "the Torah as the definition of virtue or righteousness."[452] Yet if righteousness came by the law, Christ need not have died. But because he died for us, Paul implies, we must either accept the gift or reject it – choosing friendship with or enmity toward God.

More fully than Gal 2:21, 3:21 sheds light on the failure of the law to provide justification: giving life was not the law's purpose. The problem, then, is not with the *law*, but with believing that one's finite obedience to it makes one right with God. And if not God's own law, Paul would insist, then neither anything else (cf. 4:8–9) except Christ; apparently no other way of our salvation was possible in a moral universe.

If righteousness came by the law – in this context including the law as it made Peter separate from eating with gentiles (2:12) – *then Christ died for nothing*. Since this conclusion is as absurd to Peter, as a believer, as the idea that Christ enabled sin (2:17), it concludes Paul's reproof to Peter based on

---

450 See Marshall, *Enmity*, 13–21, 245–46; also, e.g., Dio Chrysostom *Or.* 40.16, 23; Pliny *Ep.* 6.28.2; 8.6.9; Fronto *Epist. Graec.* 4.2.
451 deSilva, *Honor*, 145–46.
452 Barclay, *Gift*, 400.

the gospel. Now that Christ has come, Christ rather than the law brings one into accord with God's will. Thus one must choose between the law's way of separation and Christ's way of table fellowship with all comers. It was common to conclude an argument with a closing summary,[453] and scholars often find such a conclusion in Paul's closing words to Peter here in 2:21.[454]

3:1–5: TRADING GOD'S PRESENCE FOR RULES

3:1 You foolish Galatians! Who has bewitched you? It was before your eyes that Jesus Christ was publicly exhibited as crucified!

3:2 The only thing I want to learn from you is this: Did you receive the Spirit by doing the works of the law or by believing what you heard?

3:3 Are you so foolish? Having started with the Spirit, are you now ending with the flesh?

3:4 Did you experience so much for nothing? – if it really was for nothing.

3:5 Well then, does God supply you with the Spirit and work miracles among you by your doing the works of the law, or by your believing what you heard?

Galatians 3–4 offers Paul's post-narrative "proofs," as would be expected in typical ancient persuasion.[455] A series of rhetorical questions, as in 3:1–5, commonly characterized forensic rhetoric and its imitations, in defenses or accusations,[456] though they were hardly limited to it. A string of rhetorical questions can feel threatening to those addressed, but this is appropriate in a letter of rebuke.[457] Scholars often compare Paul's opening argument in this section, with its barrage of six rhetorical questions, with diatribe, a conventional pedagogic style.[458]

---

[453] E.g., Rhet. Alex. 20, 1433b.29–1434a.17; Cicero *Fin.* 3.9.31; *Quinct.* 28.85–29.90; Musonius Rufus 3, 42.23–29; cf. Rowe, "Style," 148; Anderson, *Glossary*, 85.

[454] Rightly Schreiner, *Galatians*, 173; Oakes, *Galatians*, 26 (viewing it as a closing maxim; on closing maxims, see Anderson, *Glossary*, 55). Buscemi, *Lettera*, 77, treats 2:21 as the *epilogos*, summing up the *narratio*'s essential content.

[455] Betz, *Galatians*, 128; cf., e.g., Cicero *Quinct.* 11.37–27.85.

[456] E.g., Xenophon *Anab.* 5.8.4–5; Lysias *Or.* 24.24–25, §170; Aeschines *Embassy* 160; Cicero *Sest.* 21.47; 52.1; Quintilian *Decl.* 376.5; Dio Chrysostom *Or.* 46.8–9; Lucian *Tyr.* 10; Apuleius *Apol.* 102; Libanius *Topics* 1.10; in letters, Fronto *Ad Am.* 2.7; *Ad M. Caes.* 1.6.4.

[457] Anderson, *Rhetorical Theory*, 162. In Rom 2:3–4, 21–23; 3:1–9 the questions address and/or stem from an imaginary interlocutor; in 1 Cor 9:1–10, they follow a less intense style, though that letter includes rebukes as well.

[458] Hermogenes *Method* 10.425. Chrysostom *Hom. Cor.* 3.5 (on 1 Cor 1:13) opines that Paul employs such questions when he deems the opposing understanding "absurd."

The point of this section is that the Galatians already have all that Paul's opponents claim to offer them through circumcision; having received the Spirit (3:2), the Galatians are already Abraham's heirs (3:14), making the outward covenant sign superfluous. Their reception of the Spirit (3:2–3, 5, 14; 4:6, 29; cf. 5:5) is a major theme in this section, bolstered by "references to promise (3:14, 16, 18, 19, 22, 29), inheritance (3:18, 29; 4:1, 7), and divine sonship (3:26; 4:5–7)."[459] Just as Paul appealed to his own experience in 1:13–2:21, so now, before launching into an argument from Scripture, he appeals to their own incontrovertible experience of the Spirit.[460] Their experience of the Spirit (3:2–5) continues Paul's emphasis on Christ living in a believer (2:20) and foreshadows his teaching on the Spirit as the dynamic principle empowering believers to live the ethical reality of the law (Gal 5:13–25).

Paul's opponents presumably argued from Scripture, and Paul does the same in two different ways, in 3:6–4:7 and, probably engaging his opponents' arguments even more directly, in 4:21–31. In both sections the argument starts from Abraham, with any other texts (as in 3:10–13) being applied midrashically to expound the foundational text (3:6).[461] Paul naturally appeals especially to Abraham because the reason for any Jewish proselytizers urging gentiles to adopt circumcision was to bring them into the people descended from Abraham.

The opening verse of this new section turns from addressing Peter to addressing the Galatians directly. The opening Greek word Ô, translated as *You*, was sometimes, as here in 3:1, used to introduce a rebuke.[462] Because Paul addresses the hearers as Galatians, some scholars argue that the addressees must be ethnic Gauls, thus residents of north Galatia. This conclusion, however, neglects Paul's style elsewhere. Only a provincial title would link together the disparate peoples of south Galatia, and Paul *normally* uses geographic and provincial designations (e.g., 2 Cor 9:2, 4). More important, in direct address he speaks to the Corinthians in 2 Cor 6:11 and Philippians in Phil 4:15 – using geographic designations. If Paul were using his more usual ethnic designations, he would probably call them

---

459   De Boer, *Galatians*, 167.

460   Cf. the similar appeal to the audience's conversion experience in 1 Cor 2:1–5 (D. J. Lull, *The Spirit in Galatia: Paul's Interpretation of Pneuma as Divine Power* [SBLDS 49; Chico, CA: Scholars Press, 1980], 58). On the connection with Paul's preaching, see Lull, *Spirit in Galatians*, 54–56.

461   With, e.g., Wright, *Justification*, 94, 216.

462   BDF §146.2; see similarly 2 Macc 7:34; 4 Macc 10:10; Mark 9:19; Luke 24:25; Acts 13:10; 18:14; Rom 2:1, 3; Jas 2:20; 1 Clem. 23.4; Philo *Alleg.* 2.46; Josephus *War* 6.124, 348.

"Greeks."[463] Whether an ethnic or provincial title, however, *foolish Galatians* could evoke widespread, embarrassing stereotypes of Galatians. That Paul also labels them foolish (3:1, 3; cf. 1 Cor 15:36) makes clear that he is rebuking them, as already in Gal 1:6.

Later interpreters tried to conform Paul's denunciation here to Matt 5:22 by noting that this is a necessary reproof from love;[464] that is probably a correct observation (see Gal 4:12, 19–20), though even in Matthew the warning was hyperbole (Matt 23:17; cf. Luke 11:40; 12:20; 24:25).

Paul appears appalled here (3:1; cf. 1:6): how could his converts who have already experienced the Spirit (3:2) revert to seeking by fleshly means something they already received by trusting the gospel (3:3)?[465] Paul offers a rhetorically ironic explanation: surely they must have been *bewitched*! This was simply a sarcastic way of reiterating their foolishness – how otherwise could they be *this* foolish?[466] Even being so foolish, their witnessing Christ crucified virtually with their "eyes" (3:1) should have been able "to avert or counter any evil spirit"[467] or the "evil eye" against them.

The term translated *bewitched, baskainô*, referred to an evil eye most often in the simple sense of envy, but sometimes more specifically in terms of an envious eye wishing and casting a curse.[468] One might normally prefer the first, wider sense,[469] but since another's mere envy of their spiritual station would not have wrought their current spiritual confusion, most commentators believe that Paul describes the Galatians as *bewitched* by the "evil eye."[470]

Some scholars suggest that the Galatians in the beginning recognized that Paul himself did not have the evil eye, refusing to spit (a possible translation of *despise* in 4:14), the normal way to avert the evil eye's power, when

---

[463] See further argument in the introduction.

[464] Wolfgang Musculus *Commentary on Galatians* on Gal 3:1; cf. Johannes Brenz *Explanation of Galatians* on Gal 3:1 (Bray).

[465] Cf. T. D. Still, "'In the Fullness of Time' (Gal. 4:4): Chronology and Theology in Galatians," pages 239–48 in *Galatians and Christian Theology: Justification, the Gospel, and Ethics in Paul's Letter* (ed. M. W. Elliott et al.; Grand Rapids, MI: Baker Academic, 2014), 248.

[466] In today's English, Neil, *Galatians*, 47, suggests that Paul is remarking "wryly" that surely these false teachers "must have hypnotized you."

[467] Dunn, *Galatians*, 152.

[468] E.g., P. Oxy. 292.11–12 (c. 25 CE); Pliny *Nat.* 7.2.16–18; Aulus Gellius 9.4.8; J. J. Pilch, "The Evil Eye," *BibT* 42 (1, 2004): 49–53.

[469] Cf. Barclay, *Gift*, 389n3.

[470] E.g., Chrysostom on Gal 3:1; Lightfoot, *Galatians*, 133; J. H. Elliott, "Paul, Galatians, and the Evil Eye," *Currents in Theology and Mission* 17 (4, 1990): 262–73.

they saw him.⁴⁷¹ Now, however, they viewed him more suspiciously (4:16–18). It is, however, his envious rivals who have drawn the Galatians' affections away, perhaps by means of such an evil eye! Paul of course has no need of an evil eye; he curses his opponents directly (in Gal 1:8–9).

Although Paul speaks figuratively here, he did recognize that some people practiced harmful magic (5:20; cf. Acts 13:8–11), a very common practice in his day.⁴⁷² Paul believed in a dangerous devil and demons (1 Cor 10:20; 2 Cor 4:4) and believed that some false teachers acted as Satan's servants (2 Cor 11:13–15). Paul might thus genuinely believe that his opponents had persuaded the Galatians by demonic influence (cf. Gal 3:1; 5:20).⁴⁷³

How could the Galatians fall so far, when Christ was crucified *before your eyes*? Orators and storytellers sought to present their accounts so vividly that hearers imagined that they were at the place described or as if the events unfolded before them. Often this vividness is described as presenting the case *before* their hearers' *eyes*.⁴⁷⁴ This technique was so common that it had a title: "ocular demonstration."⁴⁷⁵ One could also speak of imagining other matters so vividly that they could be described as if seeing them,⁴⁷⁶ and one could also lead readers to "see" vivid images through letters.⁴⁷⁷

How then was Christ's crucifixion *publicly exhibited* before their eyes? One could be influenced by what one read, but it was more influential when provided orally with appropriate delivery.⁴⁷⁸ Theatrical effects could make

---

471 E. M. Yamauchi, "Magic or Miracle? Diseases, Demons, and Exorcisms," pages 89–183 in *The Miracles of Jesus* (ed. D. Wenham and C. Blomberg; Sheffield, UK: JSOT Press, 1986), 138; Elliott, "Evil Eye."

472 See R. MacMullen, *Enemies of the Roman Order: Treason, Unrest, and Alienation in the Empire* (Cambridge, MA: Harvard University Press, 1966), 95–127; D. E. Aune, "Magic in Early Christianity," *ANRW* 23.1: 1507–57 (part 2, *Principat*, 23.1; ed. H. Temporini and W. Haase; Berlin: de Gruyter, 1980); L. H. Martin, *Hellenistic Religions: An Introduction* (New York: Oxford University Press, 1987), 27–29; F. Graf, *Magic in the Ancient World* (trans. F. Philip; Cambridge, MA: Harvard University Press, 1997); D. Frankfurter, *Religion in Roman Egypt: Assimilation and Resistance* (Princeton, NJ: Princeton University Press, 1998), 198–237.

473 J. H. Neyrey, "Bewitched in Galatia: Paul and Cultural Anthropology," *CBQ* 50 (1988): 72–100.

474 E.g., Aristotle *Rhet.* 2.8.14, 1386a; 3.11.1–2, 1411b; Cicero *Orator* 40.139; Quintilian *Inst.* 6.1.31; 8.3.65, 81; Longinus *Sublime* 15.2; Hermogenes *Progymn.* 10. On Ecphrasis 22–23; Josephus *Ant.* 20.123; so here Heinrich Bullinger *Commentary on Paul's Epistles* on Gal 3:1 (Bray); Betz, *Galatians*, 131; Anderson, *Rhetorical Theory*, 162.

475 Rhet. Her. 4.55.68; Cicero *de Or.* 3.53.202; Quintilian *Inst.* 9.2.40.

476 Cicero *Fam.* 14.3.2; Silius Italicus 9.40; 10.584–86; 11.114–16; 12.547–49; Pliny *Ep.* 2.1.11–12; 4.16.4; Plutarch *Demosth.* 18.2; Tacitus *Dial.* 16.

477 Pliny *Ep.* 2.18.3; 5.6.44; Fronto *Ad Ant. Imp.* 1.4; Symmachus *Ep.* 1.84.

478 Pliny *Ep.* 2.3.9–10. One who delivered a letter would ideally mimic even the sender's facial expressions (Cicero *Fam.* 12.30.3).

one's delivery more powerful;[479] oral communication was something like "a performing art."[480] True eloquence included "appropriate elocution and suitable bodily movement," charming the eyes as well as the ears.[481]

In Paul's case, the Galatians may have witnessed Christ's crucifixion not only in Paul's preaching but enacted in Paul's own life; Paul has just noted that he was crucified with Christ (2:20). Apostolic sufferings meant sharing Christ's death (2 Cor 1:5; 4:10; Phil 3:10; Col 1:24), and we have reason to believe that many south Galatian believers witnessed Paul's sufferings (Gal 5:11; Acts 13:50; 14:5, 19, 23; 2 Tim 3:11). Speakers sometimes showed their wounds to display their loyalty (see comment on Gal 6:17); Paul may have done so when he first preached to the Galatians (cf. Gal 6:17).[482] Vivid portrayal was meant to arouse emotion, and Paul's suffering apparently did so (cf. Gal 4:13–15). Paul may have described Jesus's passion in detail (cf. 1 Cor 11:23–26) as well as illustrated it in his own experience. In any case, the message is the same that Paul preached elsewhere: Christ crucified (1 Cor 1:23; 2:2).[483]

Paul frames Gal 3:2–14 with the Galatians' reception of the promised Spirit (3:2, 14). God had promised the Spirit to his people for the time of their coming restoration (e.g., Isa 32:15; 42:1; 44:3; 59:21; 61:1; Ezek 36:27; 37:1–14; 39:29; Joel 2:28–29; Zech 12:10). That they had already received the Spirit, then, meant that they had already been welcomed into God's people, purely by trusting the message about Jesus Christ. To seek some other method to receive the Spirit, then, was to deny their own conversion experience and to abandon their trust in Christ.

---

[479] Cicero *Brutus* 55.203; Valerius Maximus 8.11.ext. 1; Philostratus *Vit. soph.* 1.25.537–38. Even some Stoics, when teaching about communication, might appeal to actors' voices (Diogenes Laertius 7.1.20).

[480] J. Hall, "Oratorical Delivery and the Emotions: Theory and Practice," pages 218–34 in *A Companion to Roman Rhetoric* (ed. W. Dominik and J. Hall; Oxford: Blackwell, 2007), 230, 234.

[481] Valerius Maximus 8.10.praef. (trans. D. R. Shackleton Bailey).

[482] Cf. Witherington, *Grace*, 205; B. S. Davis, "The Meaning of προεγράφη in the Context of Galatians 3.1," *NTS* 45 (2, 1999): 194–212; Hays, "*Poiêsis*," 212n28; S. Muir, "Vivid Imagery in Galatians 3:1: Roman Rhetoric, Street Announcing, Graffiti, and Crucifixion," *BTB* 44 (2, 2014): 76–86, 78, 84.

[483] This may be "Paul's shorthand expression" for the entire gospel message (deSilva, *Readings*, 150), at least where suffering was an embarrassment (1 Cor 1:27–29; Gal 6:14, 17). For crucifixion, see discussion in, e.g., M. Hengel, *Crucifixion in the Ancient World and the Folly of the Message of the Cross* (Philadelphia, PA: Fortress, 1977); G. Samuelsson, *Crucifixion in Antiquity: An Inquiry into the Background and Significance of the NT Terminology of Crucifixion* (WUNT 2.310; Tübingen: Mohr Siebeck, 2011); J. G. Cook, *Crucifixion in the Mediterranean World* (WUNT 2.327; Tübingen: Mohr Siebeck, 2014).

The Galatians' own experience of the Spirit (3:2) demonstrates that they have the blessing of Abraham (3:14); why would they regress from that blessing, promised before the law and fulfilled after the law (3:16–25), to the interim curse (3:10–13)? Granted, the full promise included inheriting the land (Gen 13:15–17; 15:7, 18; 17:8), understood by Paul and his contemporaries more globally (Rom 4:13),[484] but the Spirit is believers' foretaste of the coming world (Gal 5:5; Rom 8:23; 2 Cor 1:22; 5:5). Because the Spirit is divine, receiving the Spirit means God dwelling among them (Exod 25:8; 29:45–46; Lev 26:11; Num 35:34; Ezek 37:27; 2 Cor 6:16), a dwelling place even greater than the land by itself.

In 3:2, Paul challenges believers to remember how they received the Spirit, regarding the soteriological corollary of this experience as self-evident. The Spirit is the nonnegotiable mark of true followers of Jesus, as members of God's eschatological people.[485] As in Luke's account of Cornelius in Acts 10–11, so here the gift of the Spirit to gentiles confirms that God has already accepted them (Acts 15:7–9).[486]

Paul's opponents probably envisioned biblical prophecy differently: the Spirit should enable God's people to keep the law, as in Ezek 11:19–20; 36:26–27. Paul might agree, but he envisioned the law in a very different way, by a very different, specifically Christocentric hermeneutic (cf. Gal 5:14, 16–18, 22–23; 6:1–2).[487]

As already noted, the experience of the Spirit was so tangible that Paul expects no dissent from the Galatian believers about their experience.[488] Some scholars thus contend that this experience was associated with ecstatic manifestations, such as tongues, prophecy, and crying, "Abba!"[489] We do

---

[484] Cf., e.g., Sir 44:21; Jub. 17:3; 22:14; 32:19; 1 En. 5:7; L.A.B. 32:3; t. Ber. 1:12; Mekilta Besh. 7.139–40.

[485] With, e.g., G. D. Fee, "Paul's Conversion as Key to His Understanding of the Spirit," pages 166–83 in *The Road from Damascus: The Impact of Paul's Conversion on His Life, Thought, and Ministry* (ed. R. N. Longenecker; Grand Rapids, MI: Eerdmans, 1997) (and Longenecker, *God's Empowering Presence: The Holy Spirit in the Letters of Paul* [Peabody, MA: Hendrickson, 1994], passim); L. A. Jervis, "The Spirit Brings Christ's Life to Life," pages 139–56 in *Reading Paul's Letter to the Romans* (ed. J. L. Sumney; SBLRBS 73; Atlanta, GA: Society of Biblical Literature, 2012), 139–40, 147.

[486] Cf. Sanders, *Paul*, 464–65; Barclay, *Gift*, 390–91.

[487] See Keener, *Spirit Hermeneutics*, 219–36.

[488] As Fee, *Galatians*, 8, notes. Neil, *Galatians*, 49, suggests that conversion experiences are often less dramatic and the contrasts less stark for those "who become confirmed Christians after having been brought up in Christian homes."

[489] Ambrosiaster *Ep. Gal.* 3.3.3 (citing Acts 19:1–7); Chrysostom *Hom. Gal.* 3.3 (Edwards); Lull, *Spirit in Galatians*, 53–95, esp. 72; cf. A. Loisy, *L'Épitre aux Galates* (Paris: Émile Nourry, éditeur, 1916), 142; Neil, *Galatians*, 49–50. Calvin applies Gal 3:2 to regeneration, but 3:5 to "the other gifts of the Spirit" (*Commentary on Galatians* on Gal 3:2, 5; Bray).

not know what specific manifestations followed the Galatians' reception of the Spirit, but at least in Pisidian Antioch they were apparently noteworthy enough for Luke to specify them. There the experience was somehow notably associated with joy (Acts 13:52), although that seems to characterize early Christian experience in general. Paul's interest in Gal 3:5 might be simply the continuing experience of the Spirit delineated in 5:16–25, which includes joy and other expressions of the Spirit in 5:22–23.

One striking feature of the passage is its implication that the Spirit is a gift, conferred by God's grace in Christ rather than by human worth (Rom 5:5; 2 Cor 1:22; 5:5; 1 Thess 4:8). Some Jewish circles recognized that the Spirit, like wisdom, was God's gift.[490] Others, however, associated the Spirit only with great piety.[491] Here, however, the Spirit is *given* – to gentiles whom the strictest Jews would deem "sinners" (Gal 2:15).

Paul here contrasts the message of faith with law-works (on which, see "A Closer Look" on Gal 2:16). They received the Spirit solely through believing the message. Paul's "message[492] of faith" probably means "the message that elicits faith."[493]

The contrast between Spirit and flesh in 3:3 (cf. also 4:29) will play a fuller role in 5:16–23 and 6:8. Philo, whose thinking both reflected and was influential in Diaspora Jewish thought, contrasts people who live by the divine spirit and reason with those who live by the pleasure of the flesh.[494] Philo's usage is informative; although Paul uses the terms differently than Philo,[495] the language could be familiar in a hellenistic Jewish context.

In light of Gal 6:12–13, however, Paul may also hint here about circumcision, the covenant "in the flesh" (Gen 17:11, 14, 23–25; Lev 12:3; Sir 44:20; Jub. 15:26, 33; cf. Rom 2:28; Eph 2:11; Phil 3:3; Col 2:11). In any case, *having started with the Spirit*, Paul expects them to continue by the Spirit, for which God continues to supply them with the Spirit (3:5). Paul's theology of the Spirit is not a one-off experience but a continued welcoming of this connection with the living God.

[490] Wis 8:21; 9:17; cf. 1QHa 8.29; 15.9; 4Q504 f1–2Rv15; eschatologically, Sib. Or. 4.46.
[491] E.g., m. Sot. 9:15; Sipre Deut. 173.1.3; cf. W. D. Davies, "Reflections on the Spirit in the Mekilta: A Suggestion," *JANESCU* 5 (1973): 95–105, here 98.
[492] In view of 1 Thess 2:13, and Isa 53:1 in Rom 10:16, Paul means "message," not hearing; see R. B. Hays, *The Faith of Jesus Christ: An Investigation of the Narrative Substructure of Galatians 3:1–4:11* (SBLDS 56; Chico, CA: Scholars Press, 1983), 146–48.
[493] Martyn, *Galatians*, 288–89; Wright, *Faithfulness*, 920.
[494] *Heir* 57, as noted by deSilva, *Readings*, 264. Cf. also Philo *Immut.* 2.
[495] See Keener, *Mind*, 101–03, 117, 132–35.

Scholars debate whether *paschô*, the Greek term that the NRSV in 3:4 renders *experience*, refers to the same experience of the Spirit indicated in 3:2–3, 5, or speaks of what they have suffered for the gospel. All other Pauline and NT uses of *paschô* imply suffering, and Paul suffered in Galatia (Acts 13:50; 14:5, 19) as, perhaps, did the Galatians (Gal 4:29). The lexical evidence in this case strongly favors the meaning *suffer*. Still, *experience* fits *both* the term's potential semantic range and the immediate context, probably weighting matters in favor of the NRSV's neutral translation here, with a positive reference to their experience of the Spirit. What else would Paul mean by *so much*?

Although Paul rejects here the idea that his converts are already apostate, he recognizes the possibility that some could follow Christ *for nothing* (3:4), or "in vain," and that his labor for them could be in vain, if they failed to persevere (2:2; 4:11; 1 Cor 15:2; 2 Cor 6:1; Phil 2:16; 1 Thess 2:19; 3:5).[496]

In Greek, Galatians 3:5 lacks an indicative verb, but the sense (provided by the NRSV's *does*) is easy enough to reconstruct: God acts in response to their faith, not their law-works. Luke reports miracles through Paul's ministry in what Paul calls Galatia (Acts 14:3, 9–10, 19–20).[497] In Gal 3:5, however, Paul probably speaks of continuing *miracles*, acts of power, among them, as he expected elsewhere (1 Cor 12:10). Paul plays on cognate words here; God works (*energôn*) miracles among them, and does it not by the works (*ergôn*) of the law.

Here God also continues to *supply you with the Spirit*, matching Paul's interest not merely in an initial experience but in a continuing life in the Spirit (as in Gal 5:16–18, 22–23, 25; cf. Phil 1:19).

3:6–14: EITHER ABRAHAM'S BLESSING OR THE LAW'S CURSE

3:6 Just as Abraham "believed God, and it was reckoned to him as righteousness,"

3:7 so, you see, those who believe are the descendants of Abraham.

3:8 And the scripture, foreseeing that God would justify the Gentiles by faith, declared the gospel beforehand to Abraham, saying, "All the Gentiles shall be blessed in you."

---

[496] Dunn, *Galatians*, 157, noting Paul's concern for apostasy in Rom 8:13; 11:20–22; 1 Cor 9:27; 10:12; 15:1–2; 2 Cor 13:5; Col 1:22–23.

[497] For firsthand accounts of miracles in Paul's own ministry, see, e.g., Acts 20:7–12; 28:7–10; Rom 15:19; 2 Cor 12:12; cf. comment by Sanders, *Paul*, 121–23, 177.

3:9 For this reason, those who believe are blessed with Abraham who believed.

3:10 For all who rely on the works of the law are under a curse; for it is written, "Cursed is everyone who does not observe and obey all the things written in the book of the law."

3:11 Now it is evident that no one is justified before God by the law; for "The one who is righteous will live by faith."

3:12 But the law does not rest on faith; on the contrary, "Whoever does the works of the law will live by them."

3:13 Christ redeemed us from the curse of the law by becoming a curse for us – for it is written, "Cursed is everyone who hangs on a tree" –

3:14 in order that in Christ Jesus the blessing of Abraham might come to the Gentiles, so that we might receive the promise of the Spirit through faith.

Although 3:6 starts a new section, it is certainly connected with the preceding section. *Just as* connects the Galatians' faith (3:5) with Abraham's (3:6), and perhaps the message they heard with God's promise that Abram believed (Gen 15:5). Paul is thus equating Abraham being reckoned righteous with believers receiving the Spirit (cf. 4:6–7),[498] since God's promise of the Spirit was for God's righteous eschatological people. Likewise, Paul identifies the blessing for faithful gentiles in faithful Abraham (3:8–9) with being reckoned righteous (3:6) and the blessing of the Spirit (3:14). The promise of the Spirit (3:5, 14) thus frames 3:6–13.[499]

Paul links verses here based on common key terms or elements.[500] (For simplicity's sake I include here only the conspicuous quotations, omitting his secondary allusions.)

- Gen 15:6 (Gal 3:6) with Gen 12:3 (Gal 3:8), linking God's promises of blessing for Abraham (reckoned righteousness being the chief blessing)
- Gen 15:6 (Gal 3:6) with Hab 2:4 (Gal 3:11), linking righteousness with faith
- Gen 12:3 (Gal 3:8) with Deut 27:26 (Gal 3:10), linking Abraham's blessing (and, in an unquoted line of Gen 12:3, the curse for his enemies) with the curse of the law

---

[498] Luther deemed this identification of justification and receiving the Spirit the missing assumption in Paul's syllogism here (Wengert, "Luther," 97).

[499] Cf. also the association of the Spirit with God's promise in Eph 1:13; Acts 2:33, 39.

[500] For this practice in ancient Jewish hermeneutics, see, e.g., CD 7.15–20; Mekilta Pisha 5.103; Nez. 76.26; 77.38; 130.17.

- Deut 27:26 (Gal 3:10) with Lev 18:5 (Gal 3:12), linking those who do not (lit.) "do these things" (works of the law) with those who do "do these things"
- Deut 27:26 (Gal 3:10) with Deut 21:23 (Gal 3:13), linking curses in Deuteronomy (*cursed is everyone who*)
- Hab 2:4 (Gal 3:11) with Lev 18:5 (Gal 3:12), linking, "that one shall live"

Although proposed chiastic structures are typically too asymmetric to convince, a basic chiastic structure may dominate here:

A   Blessed are the Gentiles in Abraham (3:8–9)
B   Cursed are those who disobey the law (3:10)
C   Shall live by faith (3:11)
C' Shall live by works of the law (3:12)
B' Cursed is the one hanged on a tree (3:13)
A' Blessed are the Gentiles in Abraham (3:14)

Although it sacrifices some symmetry, one further level of framing is probable: receiving the Spirit by faith (3:2–5, 14b).

Paul's argument based on Abraham (3:6–9) seems to be on exegetical ground first initiated by his rivals, who would find the association of the covenant with circumcision (Gen 17:9–14) congenial for their purposes. (Indeed, most of Paul's texts in this section, especially Deut 27:26 and Lev 18:5, seem so counterintuitive that most scholars believe that Paul is probably responding to his opponents' use of them.) Isaac rather than Ishmael was heir (Gal 4:30). Paul's opponents doubted, and Paul must demonstrate, that all believers in Jesus are Abraham's children and heirs (Gal 3:29; 4:7).

Five of six quotations Paul offers here are from the Pentateuch, establishing the foundational character of his claim; the other texts, however, are subsidiary to Gen 15:6,[501] which is the first one he quotes and one that is earlier and more foundational in his canon and in salvation history than most of the others.

The context in Genesis at this point simply addresses Abraham trusting God's promise; faith was trust that could grow in the living context of a relationship with the God who reveals himself. Abram's faith was sufficient for this stage though far from perfect. This relationship of trust was more foundational than the later stipulations of the law. That it existed before the

---

[501]   Silva, "Galatians," 792–93.

law and even before circumcision (cf. Rom 4:10) demonstrates that it can exist without those features.[502]

The faith associated with the promise is basic faith, though it becomes deeper faith through testing. Because faith ultimately demands action consistent with it, it is evident that Abram's faith was hardly complete at this stage. The narrative is thus also about a God who is faithful, who accepts Abram's basic faith but patiently cultivates it over the years. Abraham eventually embraces the covenant requirement of circumcision (emphasized by Paul's rivals) and ultimately even offers the fruit of the promise back to God in obedience in Gen 22:1–19 (cf. Heb 11:17–19; Jas 2:21–23). But Paul's focus here is on Abram's early faith.

Nevertheless, Judeans who cited Gen 15:6 often argued, as Paul's rivals probably did, that it referred to Abraham's faithfulness as obedience.[503] Later rabbis considered faith, including that of Abraham, meritorious; they saw it as a work rather than opposing it to works.[504] God rewarded Abraham's meritorious faith with the coming age.[505] Judean texts regularly praise Abraham's faith or faithfulness in enduring testing, but most often well *after* Gen 15:6.[506] Despite its expansiveness, Genesis Rabbah almost entirely overlooks Abraham's faith in Gen 15:6.[507] Diaspora Jews may have made more use of the text; Philo often notes that Abraham believed or trusted God.[508]

For Paul, Abraham's works expressed his faith in and dependence on God's covenant faithfulness; it was not simply a work in which Abraham depended on himself. Paul's opponents may have pushed back, reiterating the association of circumcision with the covenant, so that Paul later made explicit (in Rom 4:10), what he probably here simply takes for granted: Abraham's justifying faith (Gen 15:6) preceded the covenant by at least thirteen years (Gen 16:16; 17:24–25). Abraham, like the Galatians, was in fact a gentile when he was justified by faith (Rom 4:5–8).[509] It is therefore relevant here that Jewish tradition already understood Abraham as the

---

[502] By contrast, the faith does not, for Paul, exist apart from Christ, since Christ is the object of Abraham-like faith at this stage of salvation history; see Gal 3:17–23; cf. Rom 4:19–20; Heb 11:19.

[503] Dunn, *Beginning*, 477 (citing, e.g., 4QMMT C30–31 = 116–17).

[504] A. Marmorstein, *The Doctrine of Merits in Old Rabbinical Literature* (London: Oxford University Press, 1920), 175–76.

[505] Mekilta Besh. 7.135ff.

[506] Gathercole, *Boasting*, 237–38, citing, e.g., Sir 44:19–21; 1 Macc 2:52; Jub. 17:15–18.

[507] Silva, "Galatians," 795, on Gen. Rab. 44:13.

[508] Philo *Alleg.* 3.228; *Immut.* 4; *Migr.* 44, 132; *Heir* 90; *Names* 177, 186.

[509] H. Boers, "We Who Are by Inheritance Jews; Not from the Gentiles, Sinners," *JBL* 111 (1992): 273–81, here 276. He was thus a "sinner" in the terms framed in Gal 2:15.

first and model proselyte to faith in the true God,[510] and contended that he converted many other gentiles.[511] In this sense, gentile believers in *particular* follow in Abraham's steps (cf. Rom 4:12).

A Closer Look: Righteous Abraham in Jewish Tradition[512]

Jewish people regularly spoke of "our father Abraham"[513] and themselves as his children.[514] Scripture itself already recounted God blessing Israel for Abraham's sake,[515] and Moses entreating God on that basis.[516] But God had also warned against depending on that heritage.[517]

Many believed that Abraham kept all of God's law.[518] Abraham often appears as an example in early Jewish literature,[519] including as a model of righteousness,[520] particularly hospitality[521] and, relevantly here, faith or faithfulness.[522]

The Gospels also contest sufficiency of descent from Abraham for salvation (Matt 3:9//Luke 3:8; Matt 8:11–12//Luke 13:28; John 8:33–39). Dependence on ethnic solidarity with Abraham was perhaps less a formal doctrine than a presumed religious legacy similar to that among nominal churchgoers during Christendom. ****

Scholars debate the nature of Abraham's righteousness here. Paul's focus on the Genesis passage's *reckoned* in his later letter to the Romans (Rom 4:3–11, 22–24) suggests that he was probably already interested in this concept in Gal 3:6, which in turn suggests a forensic emphasis. Although the focus

---

[510]   E.g., Mekilta Nez. 18.36–40; b. Suk. 49b; cf. CD 3.1–2.

[511]   E.g., Sipre Deut. 32.2.1; Ab. R. Nat. 12A; 26, §54B; B. J. Bamberger, *Proselytism in the Talmudic Period* (New York: KTAV, 1968), 176–79. See esp. C. Safrai, "Abraham und Sara – Spender des Lebens," *EvT* 62 (5, 2002): 348–62, who contends that their converts are also viewed as their children.

[512]   Adapting much material here from Keener, *John*, 754–56.

[513]   E.g., 4 Macc 16:20; Sipre Deut. 311.1.1; 313.1.3; cf. Josephus *Ant.* 14.255.

[514]   E.g., 3 Macc 6:3; 4 Macc. 6:17, 22; 18:1; Ps. Sol. 18:3.

[515]   Exod 2:24; Lev 26:42; Deut 4:37; 7:8; 9:5; 10:15; 2 Kgs 13:23; Ps 105:8–9, 42–45; Mic 7:18–20.

[516]   Exod 32:13; Deut 9:27.

[517]   Deut 7:7; 10:22; 26:5; cf. Dan 9:18.

[518]   CD 3.2; Philo *Migr.* 130, citing Gen 26:5; later, see E. E. Urbach, *The Sages: Their Concepts and Beliefs* (trans. I. Abrahams; 2 vols.; 2nd edn.; Jerusalem: Magnes, 1979), 1:318.

[519]   E.g., m. Ab. 5:19; even the model Pharisee (y. Sot. 5:5, §2).

[520]   E.g., Jub. 23:10; Sir. 44:19–22; 2 Bar. 57:2; m. Qid. 4:14; Ab. R. Nat. 36, §94B.

[521]   E.g., Gen 18:2–8; Philo *Abr.* 107–114; Josephus *Ant.* 1.200; T. Ab. 1:4–9, 19 A; 2:3–12 B; J. Koenig, *New Testament Hospitality: Partnership with Strangers as Promise and Mission* (OBT 17; Philadelphia, PA: Fortress, 1985), 15–20.

[522]   Esp. "faithfulness" in testing (1 Macc 2:52). See esp. fully Longenecker, *Galatians*, 110–12.

here may be forensic, it is very unlikely that Paul intended his audience to take his message as *exclusively* forensic, since this would have played into his opponents' hands. Even if gentiles were saved by grace, the opponents could argue for completion by law to make them moral. Paul's interest is not in forensic rightness separated from a new life; he links it with the gift of the Spirit in 3:2, 5, and thus with being born from the Spirit (4:29) and a life fruitful from God's Spirit in 5:16–25. That is, whatever one's conclusions on the lexical matters, Paul expects faith to begin to produce transformation.

That all believers are *descendants of Abraham* (3:7) is the thesis of this new section,[523] which concludes on the same point (3:29). *Those who believe* is literally "those who are of faith" (3:7, 9); Abraham's descendants are necessarily "of faith" because it is through Abraham's faith, not in an abstract way, but in God's promise (Gen 15:5–6), that they came to exist (Gal 4:23, 28–29).[524] In the new phase of salvation history in Paul's day, Abraham's descendants must continue to embrace God's promise, now of his ultimate seed in Christ (3:16). Gentile believers are thus grafted into the patriarchal tree to become members of the covenant people (Rom 11:17),[525] though Paul is still able to distinguish them from "natural" branches (Rom 11:17–23).

That *the gospel* preached to Abraham includes blessing for the gentiles in Gal 3:8 is consistent with Paul's commission to preach the gospel among gentiles (1:16; 2:7). Paul personifies Scripture here, as also in Gal 3:22; 4:30; and Rom 9:17; against his law-affirming opponents, Paul thus evidences his own respect for (as well as knowledge of) Scripture.[526]

Normally when Paul speaks of *scripture* in the singular, he refers to a particular passage; here he refers to the promise initially given in Gen 12:3, before Abraham's circumcision, and then reiterated in 18:18, from which Paul derives the Greek word here translated *gentiles*.[527] *All*

---

[523] With Fee, *Galatians*, 115 (on 3:7–4:7).

[524] Dunn, *Galatians*, 162.

[525] With, e.g., Wright, *Faithfulness*, 1446–48. Paul is not limited to a single ecclesial image, however, elsewhere ethnically depicting (gentile?) Christians as a "third race"; in cultural or postcolonial terms, they are hybridized (cf., e.g., L. L. Sechrest, *A Former Jew: Paul and the Dialectics of Race* [London: T&T Clark, 2009]).

[526] Rabbis, known for their love for the Torah or Scripture, sometimes personify it; see, e.g., Mekilta Shir. 6, passim; Sipra A.M. par. 8.193.1.7; pq. 11.191.1.3; t. Sotah 12:2. Technically, Scripture speaking is prosopopoeia, on which see, e.g., Demetrius *Style* 5.265; Hermogenes *Progymn.* 9. On Ethopoeia, 20.

[527] Paul's conflation may be due to memory (Sanders, *Paul*, 73) but could also deliberately blend related versions of the same promise. For conflation in ancient texts, see Stanley, *Language of Scripture*, 290–91, 322, 337, 342, 349.

the gentiles shall be blessed in you is a legitimate way to translate these promises.[528]

Because Jewish interpreters linked related texts and because consistent readers can observe a work's themes, the more biblically literate would recognize that the promised blessing to gentiles in Abraham was also in Abraham's offspring/descendants (see Gen 22:18; cf. 26:4; 28:14).[529] God's promise of offspring in Gen 15:5 is what Abram believes in 15:6, the passage that Paul addresses in Gal 3:6; now in Abraham's offspring the gentiles are blessed in 3:8.[530]

For Paul, Abraham's immediate offspring Isaac might simply prefigure their ultimate offspring, the Messiah, in whom believers are blessed (3:16). Indeed, in a later letter Paul suggests that Abraham's trust regarding the promised seed involved belief in something virtually analogous to Jesus's resurrection from among the dead (Rom 4:17, 19). Using the traditional Jewish technique of linking similar texts, the nations being blessed in Abraham was a short stretch to the narrower prayer that all nations be blessed in David's royal line (Ps 72:17). Paul's mind is probably already thinking forward to the specific, messianic seed in Gal 3:16.

In 3:9, Paul explains that the reason gentiles can be blessed in Abraham (3:8) is because they follow his model of faith; Abraham is blessed by faith, so those who are also of faith are the ones who are blessed with him.

In 3:10, Paul subverts expectations and undoubtedly shocks his audiences. Whereas Jewish people understood from Scripture that they were blessed and those who walked in the ways of gentiles were cursed, Paul argues from Scripture that some gentiles were blessed (Gal 3:8, citing Gen 12:3) and that those under the law (or under the law in the wrong way) are cursed (3:10, citing Deut 27:26).

Paul's apparent antithesis between faith and works is apparently his own innovation, needed to address his rivals' insistence on *works of the law* already suggested in 3:2, 5, and prefigured in 2:16.[531] ("Obeying" or "doing"

---

[528] In Greek, some of the passages speak of "all the tribes of the earth" (Gen 12:3; 28:14) and others of the equivalent phrase (directly behind Paul's term that the NRSV translates as *gentiles*) "all the peoples of the earth" (18:18; 22:18; 26:4).

[529] R. N. Longenecker, *Biblical Exegesis in the Apostolic Period* (Grand Rapids, MI: Eerdmans, 1975), 118.

[530] Sanders, *Paul*, 521, notes that with the addition of gentiles here Paul now has "Abraham," "faith," "righteousness," and gentiles together (we may add blessing). Sanders, *Paul, the Law, and the Jewish People*, 21, notes Abraham as the link between the texts; Dunn, *Galatians*, 166, notes promise.

[531] On the connection with 2:15–21, cf. also N. Bonneau, "The Logic of Paul's Argument on the Curse of the Law in Galatians 3:10–14," *NovT* 39 (1997): 60–80, here 65.

what the law commands in 3:10 and 12 is equated with *the works of the law* in the first clause of 3:10.) Nevertheless, Paul's antithesis between faith and works makes sense if his point is the antithesis between dependence on God (such as Abraham modeled) and dependence on anything else.

The other presumed antithesis, the antithesis between Abraham and his allies being blessed, on one hand, and, on the other, his adversaries being cursed, goes back to Gen 12:3 (with Israel taking the place of Abraham in Gen 27:29; Num 22:6; 24:9). Paul has already cited part of Gen 12:3 in Gal 3:7. Gen 12:3 promises all the families of the earth being blessed in Abraham, suggesting that at least some from all nations will be blessed with him.[532] This passage speaks, however, of curses as well as blessings, inviting Paul to invoke another text to specify to whom such curses apply.

Paul introduces Deut 27:26 with a Scripture citation formula familiar in Paul (*It is written*) and more generally.[533] Paul can introduce Deut 27:26 precisely because he assumes an implicit *gezerah shevah*, an implicit connection with the not-directly-quoted, yet assumed, remainder of Gen 12:3, a well-enough known text right at the beginning of the Abraham account. This verse is, again, the key text from which Paul has just quoted in Gal 3:8; it addresses curses as well as blessings. Jewish interpretive traditions naturally linked the more developed blessings and curses of Deuteronomy with Abraham's blessing.[534] Whereas Paul's opponents may have linked law-works with Deuteronomy's blessings, Paul appeals to the same context for the curses. These curses apply to those under the law (a hermeneutical principle Paul later invokes in Rom 3:19) who fail to keep it.[535] Paul's introduction of curse in 3:10 in contrast with blessing in 3:8 is therefore anything but arbitrary.

That those who believe, like Abraham, are blessed with him makes sense; for those who are of the law to be cursed, however, takes for granted that those who are of the law are *not* of faith. This assumption in turn sheds light on what Paul means by being of the law: not simply trying to keep the law, but trying to keep it without faith. From Paul's perspective, they do not depend on God's grace, now revealed in his saving gift in Christ. Works of law cannot justify (2:16), nor were they meant to (2:21; 3:21); what matters

---

[532] Or, for Paul, blessed in Jesus the seed of Abraham in 3:16; it is Christ through whom the gentiles are encountering Abraham and faith in Abraham's God.
[533] With this or similar wording, e.g., Neh 10:36; 1 Esd 1:11; CD 7.19; 11.18, 20; 1QS 5.15, 17; 8.14.
[534] Note the verbal reminiscences of Deut 28 in Jub. 20:9–10.
[535] Covenants often included curses for those who violated the covenants' stipulations; see, e.g., *ANET* (1955), 199–206.

for being put right with God is *Christ*-faith (2:16). Paul later clarifies that one can approach the law either with faith (rightly) or (wrongly) on the basis of one's (inadequate) works (Rom 3:27; 9:31–32), from God's Spirit or from mere flesh (Rom 8:2).

Although few Jews in Paul's day violated any of the specific prescriptions in Deut 27:15–25, Paul's wording borrows from Deuteronomic passages that are more encompassing. Many Jews presumably violated some of Deuteronomy's most fundamental commandments (e.g., the prohibition of coveting in Deut 5:21; cf. Rom 7:7), even in Deuteronomy's day (5:29). More importantly, this entire section of Deuteronomy warns of Israel's apostasy and its being scattered because of the curses (28:63–65, 68), as well as predicts its ultimate turning back to God (Deut 30:1–10; this is a belief Paul also shares in Rom 11:25–27). Some interpreters contend that Paul's Jewish contemporaries in fact understood themselves as experiencing even the continuing curse of exile.[536] Although this premise is debated, it is difficult to deny that most Jewish thinkers did at least anticipate an eschatological regathering of the scattered tribes,[537] which indicates the belief that *some* tribes remained scattered at this time.[538]

This larger context in Deuteronomy includes another passage or two from which Paul takes the words *written in the book of,* Deut 28:58 and/or 29:20–21 (LXX 29:19–20), both of which refer to curses for disobedience. Paul's quotations in Gal 3:10, 12, highlight adherence to the law's many individual stipulations rather than rejecting appreciation for the law as a whole or what we might call the spirit of the law.

Scholars often suggest, probably rightly, that Paul here reframes his opponents' proof-texts. Scholars argue this especially because the usual face-value reading of Deut 27:26 would support his opponents' emphasis on keeping the law. Paul's rivals may have emphasized "observing" (lit., "doing") the law in Deut 27:26, but Paul emphasizes the word "all": one must do all the works of the law (see 5:3).[539] Although "all" is merely implicit in the Hebrew text of this verse, it is explicit in the standard Greek rendering Paul shared with his audience. More important, "all" appears in some other passages in this section of Deuteronomy, some of the other wording

---

[536]   See in detail Wright, *Faithfulness,* 139–62.
[537]   See, e.g., 2 Macc 2:18; Ps. Sol. 8:28; Sanders, *Jesus and Judaism,* 96–97.
[538]   See, e.g., Josephus *Ant.* 11.133; *Ag. Ap.* 1.33; 4 Ezra 13:40–43.
[539]   Rabbinic schools sometimes differed starkly over which term or phrase to emphasize in a verse; see, e.g., m. Git. 9:10; Sipre Deut. 269.1.1.

of which Paul incorporates into his citation.[540] In Deut 28:58 and its context, curses would come on Israel "If you do not diligently observe all the words of this law."

Although many scholars doubt that Paul's argument here presupposes the impossibility of keeping the law, a probably larger number of scholars maintain, I believe correctly, the more traditional view that Paul presupposes here that no one perfectly keeps the law. The question here is not what most Jews believed – though most Jews did believe that virtually everyone sinned – but whether *Paul* believed that no one kept it adequately (or whether any human action could be adequate of itself) to *merit* God's favor. As for keeping all the law, Paul was well aware that not every prescription of the Torah could be or was kept in the Diaspora; certainly few Diaspora Jews would make a pilgrimage to Jerusalem three times a year (Exod 23:17; 34:23–24; Deut 16:16).

At the very least, those under the law remain under the *threat* of a curse due to nonfulfillment. Whether or not Paul regarded perfect observance as impossible in principle, he at least warns his audience not to place themselves in the position of having to find out (cf. 5:3). Many Jews would have assumed that provisions in the law for atonement resolved the sins they did commit. Paul, however, finds atonement elsewhere (Gal 1:4; Rom 3:25; 8:3). Moreover, and in the ultimate analysis, the law was never intended for justification anyway (2:21; 3:21).

Critics cannot reasonably object that, because such a premise is not explicit, Paul does not assume it. Paul and other ancient writers often used enthymemes, syllogisms with an obvious minor premise suppressed rather than explicitly stated.[541] Rabbis also often compressed their argumentation by simply assuming premises that their biblically literate peers shared.[542] Today, relevance theory amply illustrates that even in ordinary communication many assumptions are taken for granted and therefore not explicitly stated.[543]

[540] Sanders, *Paul*, 73, plausibly attributes this conflation to memory, but Paul might also deliberately evoke the fuller context.
[541] See, e.g., Hermogenes *Inv.* 3.8; 3.9.152; P. A. Holloway, "The Enthymeme as an Element of Style in Paul," *JBL* 120 (2001): 329–39; M. J. Debanné, *Enthymemes in the Letters of Paul* (LNTS 303; London: T&T Clark, 2006); but cf. differently Aune, *Dictionary of Rhetoric*, 150–57.
[542] M. Silva, "Abraham, Faith, and Works: Paul's Use of Scripture in Galatians 3:6–14," *WTJ* 63 (2, 2001): 251–67, here 262; Silva, "Galatians," 798.
[543] For relevance theory, see, e.g., D. Sperber and D. Wilson, *Relevance: Communication and Cognition* (Oxford: Blackwell, 1986); D. Wilson and D. Sperber, "Representation and Relevance," pages 133–53 in *Mental Representations: The Interface between*

Paul here probably thus assumes a premise that he elsewhere clearly states, namely, that no one keeps all the law[544] – or, relevantly here, at least that the people of the law, Israel, *had* not done so. This premise needed little argument (though Paul dutifully supplies argumentation in Rom 1:18–3:21) precisely because Jewish tradition already understood that everyone sinned.[545] Paul can also take for granted that his fellow Jewish believers, including Peter, recognize that there is no justification apart from Christ (Gal 2:16).

Not only so, but Paul may well read even his main specific texts here (Deut 27:26 and Lev 18:5) in light of their development in the prophetic tradition, which regularly charged Israel for its failure to keep the law's precepts. The warning in Jer 11:3 recalls Deut 27:26; Ezek 20 uses Lev 18:5 to show Israel's historic apostasy. In such passages, Israel's apostasy from the law justifies God's judgment on the Israelites.[546] More generally, various Second Temple Jewish texts lamented Israel's continuing failure.[547]

Curses were meant to divinely enforce laws that could not be fully enforced humanly. Paul's opponents probably warned the Galatians that whoever broke the laws would experience the curse; they should therefore keep the law. Paul, however, turns the warning back on the Galatians: by accepting circumcision, they would obligate themselves to the entire law (5:3), which they would not perfectly observe, and they would thereby incur the curse.[548] The law's curse applied only to those under the law,[549] whereas, Paul says, believing gentiles are already blessed in Abraham (3:7–8).[550]

Language and Reality (ed. R. M. Kempson; Cambridge: Cambridge University Press, 1988); in biblical studies, see e.g., G. L. Green, "Relevance Theory and Theological Interpretation: Thoughts on Metarepresentation," *JTInt* 4 (2010): 75–90; J. K. Brown, *Scripture as Communication: Introducing Biblical Hermeneutics* (Grand Rapids, MI: Baker Academic, 2007), 35–38.

[544] With, e.g., Mussner, *Galaterbrief*, 224–26.

[545] E.g., 1 Kgs 8:46; Eccl 7:20; 1 Esd 4:37; 1QS 11.9–10; Jub. 21:21.

[546] S. Grindheim, "Apostate Turned Prophet: Paul's Prophetic Self-Understanding and Prophetic Hermeneutic with Special Reference to Galatians 3.10–12," *NTS* 53 (2007): 545–65, here 561–64.

[547] Barclay, *Gift*, 405.

[548] Cf. C. D. Stanley, "'Under a Curse': A Fresh Reading of Galatians 3.10–14," *NTS* 36 (1990): 481–511.

[549] Cf. N. H. Young, "Who's Cursed – and Why? (Galatians 3:10–14)," *JBL* 117 (1998): 79–92.

[550] Paul believed that his opponents did not keep all the law (Gal 6:13), and some interpreters contend that his words about lawbreakers in this verse apply especially to his opponents (Silva, "Abraham," 263–64; Silva, "Galatians," 799).

Bridging the Horizons: Jesus Alone Is Our Boast

Any Christian who looks down on members of another faith or looks down on anyone for sins those people have committed misses the point of Paul's understanding of Jesus. Paul does not see himself as preaching a new world religion meant as superior to other religions. Paul sees himself as proclaiming God's saving act for humanity. Those who receive this gift do not do so because of any innate intellectual superiority, social status, or moral merit (Rom 3:23; 1 Cor 1:23–29), and certainly not based on ethnic superiority (Gal 3:28). Rather than envisioning themselves as superior to others, those who truly trust in Jesus should welcome others and share with others the astonishingly good news of this unmerited gift that they themselves have experienced.

Truly following Jesus is not about finding ways to establish our status over nonbelievers, still less about establishing it over fellow believers (whether because of our subsequent spiritual experiences, correct doctrine, or cultural values). It is about God's gracious invasion of undeserving humanity with an opportunity to be brought back to right relationship with him, an invitation that cost God the death of his own Son. When we embrace his grace rather than insisting on our own worthiness, we can freely offer others secure hope without regard to their own prior status before God.

In a relativistic context that renders all beliefs equivalent, even such an offer may sound arrogant, as if Christians alone have the truth. This was no less true in Paul's day: a polytheistic world found Jewish monotheism intolerant, and Christian insistence on Jesus as the only way to Jews' one true God (e.g., John 14:6; Acts 4:12; Gal 2:21) more intolerant still. But relativism that makes itself an absolute is philosophically self-defeating, and in effect neuters the claims of not only the Christian faith but of all religious movements that claim any absolutes.

For Paul, faith in Jesus was an intellectual demand as well as the welcome of a gift. It was not additional insurance for the afterlife just in case it was true; genuine faith in Jesus demanded the abandonment of other gods. It invites us to abandon faith in ourselves as well. We stake our lives, both in this age and in the next, completely on God's gift in Jesus Christ.

Although Paul probably borrowed his citation in Gal 3:10 from his opponents, the case is less clear for his citation of Hab 2:4 in Gal 3:11. If Paul's opponents did employ it, however, they presumably would have expected it to support their position. Non-Christian Judean sources generally applied it to human faithfulness to the Torah.[551] Nevertheless, Paul's application to trusting God in the face of judgment may come closer to Habakkuk's meaning (cf. Hab 3:17–18).[552]

Arguing against opponents who valued Jewish traditional interpretations, Paul uses to his advantage the Jewish exegetical techniques he had absorbed in his past training (cf. 1:14; Acts 22:3). In a common method traditionally called *gezerah shevah*, interpreters linked passages, even by different authors, that used shared vocabulary or themes.[553] Paul knew Scripture so well that he readily linked with Gen 15:6 (cited in Gal 3:6) the one other passage that explicitly and relevantly linked righteousness with faith: Hab 2:4. Indeed, some scholars argue plausibly that the lexical connections between the two Old Testament passages may even suggest that Hab 2:4 deliberately echoes Gen 15:6.[554] This passage may supply the template for Paul's language "from faith" (*ek pisteôs*, as in the Greek text of Gal 2:16; 3:2, 5, 7, 8, 9, 11, 12, 22, 24; 5:5).[555]

A number of capable scholars have argued that Paul deploys Hab 2:4 not with reference to Abraham's faith (Gal 3:6, 9) or that of other believers (3:7–9; cf. Rom 1:16) but with reference to Christ's faithfulness.[556] The most common version of the LXX speaks of "my" faith, i.e., of *God's* faithfulness, and Paul often applies texts about YHWH to Christ. Further, some interpret "the righteous one" in Paul's use of Habakkuk as Christ, so that "his faith" refers to Christ's faithfulness. This argument can appeal to corporate personality and Paul's participationist logic later in Gal 3: those in faithful Abraham are compared to those in faithful Christ.[557]

Certainly Paul does argue elsewhere from those in Adam to those in Christ (Rom 5:12–6:11), but does Paul argue for corporate (ethnic) identity in Abraham, or does he precisely *counter* such an argument from his rivals

---

[551]   1QpHab 8.1–3; b. Mak. 24a (reducing the heart of the Torah to fidelity to God).

[552]   See P. Bovati, "La giustizia della fede: A partire da Ab 2,4," pages 207–32 in *poesía: in memoriam P. Luis Alonso Schökel*. Edited by Vicente Collado Bertomeu. Analecta biblica, 151 (Rome: Pontifical Biblical Institute, 2003); L. Verdini, "¿De qué modo el libro de Habacuc resiste a la violencia? Una propuesta hermenéutica," *RevistB* 74 (2012): 31–45; E. R. Clendenen, "Salvation by Faith or by Faithfulness in the Book of Habakkuk," *BBR* 24 (2014): 505–13, esp. 513.

[553]   E.g., CD 7.15–20 (without the title); Mekilta Nez. 10.15–16.

[554]   Silva, "Galatians," 802; B. T. Arnold, *Genesis* (New CBC; Cambridge: Cambridge University Press, 2009), 157.

[555]   Hays, *Faith*, 150–57; D. A. Campbell, "The Meaning of Πίστις and Νόμος in Paul: A Linguistic and Structural Perspective," *JBL* 111 (1992): 91–103, here 101–03, esp. 101n30.

[556]   E.g., D. A. Campbell, "Romans 1:17 – A *Crux Interpretum* for the Πίστις Χριστοῦ Debate," *JBL* 113 (1994): 265–85, esp. 284–85.

[557]   Hays, *Faith*, 213.

by emphasizing those who have faith *like* Abraham? While Paul would certainly agree that Christ's obedience to the point of death saves believers (Rom 5:19; cf. Phil 2:8), it seems very unlikely that he designates Christ's obedience as "faith," especially in Galatians. Both here and in Rom 1:17, Paul omits the pronoun "my" modifying faith in LXX Hab 2:4. Paul undoubtedly recognizes that the original, Hebrew text reads differently: "his faith," that is, the faith of the righteous person.[558] Paul's deletion of the pronoun that appears in the version most familiar to his audience suggests that, although he may not take space to explain it here, he refers not to God's faith but to that of human beings.[559]

Moreover, Christ is not the subject of any verbs in this section until Gal 3:13; he is therefore a quite unlikely subject here.[560] Given the use of both the noun and cognate verb in the context in Galatians, believers' faith seems likely in view.

One syntactical question arises here. Many understand Paul as saying, "The righteous one will live-by-faith," a reading that seems simpler grammatically and perhaps more in keeping with Habakkuk's context. It also fits the structural parallel between Hab 2:4 and Lev 18:5: living through faith versus living through them (the works of the law).

Others prefer "The one righteous-by-faith will live," which seems to better fit Paul's theology. Paul's contrast with justification by the law could mean that he speaks here of being righteous by faith. Paul has been connecting faith with righteousness (Gal 3:6), not with resurrection from the dead; the latter is, however, promised to the righteous (cf. Rom 8:10–13; 1 Cor 6:14; 15:12–54; 2 Cor 4:14; Phil 3:21; 1 Thess 4:14). Still, he does connect living with faith in 2:20, so the decision here remains difficult.

Paul has prepared for his use of Lev 10:5 here with matching texts that make this citation an obvious choice. It contains *poieô* and *auta* (plus *en*) like Deut 27:26 (Gal 3:10), and *zêsetai* like Hab 2:4 (Gal 3:11).

Although biblical promises of living if one obeyed the Torah (Lev 18:5; Deut 30:6, 19) referred to long life on the land (Deut 4:1, 40; 5:33; 8:1; 30:16,

---

[558]   Silva, "Galatians," 801; R. Jewett with R. D. Kotansky, *Romans: A Commentary* (ed. E. J. Epp; Hermeneia; Minneapolis, MN: Fortress, 2007), 145.

[559]   Interestingly, a Judean wilderness sect interpreted "faith" in the Hebrew text of Habakkuk with reference to faithfulness or allegiance to its teacher (1QpHab 7.5–8.3) although the sect's members, unlike Paul, would have connected this faith with obedience to the Torah. Luke reports Paul preaching from Habakkuk in the chief synagogue of the region (Acts 13:41).

[560]   Das, *Galatians*, 319.

19–20), it was natural to extrapolate from them (as some later rabbis did), by means of an a fortiori argument, an application to the world to come,[561] as scholars often note. That is, if life on the promised land depended on obeying the covenant, why should life in the world to come be any different? Qumran's Damascus Document applies Lev 18:5 to eternal life; probably Ps. Sol. 14:1–2, 4 Ezra 7:21, and Luke 10:25, 28 do the same.

Given the failings of human obedience, Paul much prefers – as more practical than this approach to Lev 18:5 – Hab 2:4, already cited in Gal 3:11. For Paul, the life he is discussing here is "eternal life" (see comment at Gal 6:8).

Despite some significant differences between the contexts of Rom 10:5 and Gal 3:12, they offer similar lines of argument. In one case Paul uses Deut 30 to qualify the possible meaning of Lev 10:5 (Rom 10:5–8), whereas here Paul uses Hab 2:4 to qualify it. Laying texts against each other, using the second to qualify the meaning of the first, was a common midrashic method (on which see further comment later).

As one received a curse for breaking the law (Deut 27:26 in Gal 3:10), one would receive life for keeping it (Lev 18:5 in Gal 3:12) – assuming that one could. He might respond to his opponents' misapplication of Lev 18:5 rather than to its actual meaning, but in any case, Paul's antithesis is surely deliberate.

Paul again links (and in this case contrasts) texts by common key words: one could live by faith (Gal 3:11) or one could live by doing the law (3:12). Paul probably continues to assume as common knowledge that no one perfectly observes the law (see comment on Gal 3:10), although, as at Gal 3:10, commentators debate this matter. Although Paul would presumably agree that no one keeps all the law, his main point is that mere adherence to the law in terms of obeying its precepts *does not rest on faith.*

Although the antithesis between faith and law-works may not seem obvious on the surface, Paul can make use of a well-known principle in contemporary forensic rhetoric, that of *leges contrariae*, typically used for playing one law off against another.[562] That *the law does not rest on faith* (3:12a) rules it out as a means of salvation in light of the righteous living by faith (3:11), underlining the reality that justification is not the purpose of the law (2:21; 3:21).[563]

---

561   Sipra A.M. par. 8.193.1.10 (though cf. pq. 13.194.2.16); Sipre Deut. 336.1.1; cf. m. Mak. 3:15; Peah 1:1.

562   Here, J. S. Vos, "Die hermeneutische Antinomie bei Paulus (Galater 3.11–12; Römer 10.5–10)," *NTS* 38 (1992): 254–70, here 258–60.

563   See S. Eastman, "Galatians," pages 825–32 in *The New Interpreter's Bible One Volume Commentary* (ed. B. R. Gaventa and D. Petersen; Nashville, TN: Abingdon, 2010), 828.

Jewish interpreters often cited one text against another, sometimes citing a third text to break the tie.[564] As some second-century rabbis opined, "Two passages which contradict each other [cannot be reconciled] unless a third passage comes and decides between them."[565] Gentiles also sometimes cited one authoritative text against another proposed by someone else, particularly in (as often with the rabbis) legal argumentation.[566]

The context of Lev 18:5 is avoiding the practices of the gentiles (Lev 18:3, 24), keeping God's practices instead (18:4). Yet Lev 18:5 speaks more generally of "my statutes and ordinances," a phrase that ultimately encompasses all the law (Lev 18:4–5, 26; 19:37; 20:22; 25:18; 26:15, 43, 46). Paul is thus presumably applying it to *all the things written in the book of the law* (3:10), hence the NRSV's translation of "these things" as *the works of the law*.

Lev 18:5 continued to have a life in subsequent Scripture and early Judaism.[567] Nehemiah refers to this passage as he confesses Israel's sin (Neh 9:29).[568] As noted earlier, Ezekiel recycles it in the context of Israel's disobedience and consequent impending judgment (Ezek 20:11, 13, 21).[569] The Dead Sea Scrolls also place the promise (CD 3.16) in the context of Israel's disobedience (CD 3.11–12, 14)[570] but offer hope for the righteous priestly community (3.18–4.1); Psalms of Solomon 14 similarly condemns violators of Lev 18:5.[571] As David deSilva notes, "Israel's collective experience down to the time of Paul (and all the more in the decades after!) is a testimony to the Sinaitic covenant essentially ensuring a fairly consistent state of 'curse' for Israel."[572] Subjected to other peoples time and again, Israel rarely experienced the promised blessings of the covenant.

Abraham's descendants should be blessed (3:8–9), but the law has introduced for them the possibility (realized repeatedly in Israel's history) of a curse. Yet the law cannot annul the earlier and more foundational promise to and through Abraham (3:17–18). Thus Christ has endured the curse for

---

[564]   Sanders, *Paul, the Law, and the Jewish People*, 161 (not on this passage), citing, e.g., CD 4.20–21 and rabbis.
[565]   Beraita de Rabbi Ishmael Pereq 1.7 (trans. Neusner, in Sipra 1:63).
[566]   For posing apparently or actually conflicting laws, e.g., Pliny *Ep.* 2.19.8; Hermogenes *Issues* 40.20; 41.1–13; 83.19–88.2 (esp. 87.2–9).
[567]   Cf., e.g., J. Willitts, "Context Matters: Paul's Use of Leviticus 18:5 in Galatians 3:12," *TynBul* 54 (2, 2003): 105–22; esp. P. M. Sprinkle, *Law and Life: The Interpretation of Leviticus 18:5 in Early Judaism and in Paul* (WUNT 2.241; Tübingen: Mohr Siebeck, 2008).
[568]   Gombis, "Arguing," 89.
[569]   Grindheim, "Apostate," 561–62; Gombis, "Arguing," 88–89.
[570]   Cf. Gombis, "Arguing," 89.
[571]   Grindheim, "Apostate," 563.
[572]   deSilva, *Readings*, 175–76.

us (3:13), and Abraham's spiritual descendants are blessed in Abraham and his seed, especially Christ (3:16, 29).

In Gal 3:13, Paul returns to the thought of 3:10. Again linking texts by shared terminology, Paul offers a second "curse" text from Deuteronomy: if the sufferings ascribed to curses in Deuteronomy 27 represent judgments, then the same could be understood of Jesus's suffering of crucifixion, since it is also a cursed state in Deuteronomy.

In Deuteronomy, what was hanged was the corpse, adding posthumous shame to the execution. Later, however, some peoples would hang a person to death on a stake, a custom adopted widely by Rome. Some Jewish interpreters viewed this action in light of Deut 21:23.[573] The Qumran sectarians deemed the biblical punishment appropriate for capital offenses even while the condemned remained alive.[574]

Jews would not think someone necessarily cursed by God simply because he was crucified by Romans. This association may have originated directly from some of Paul's interlocutors in synagogues that emphasized the Sanhedrin's verdict against Jesus (cf. Acts 13:27–28), or possibly from Paul's own preconversion polemic based on the same premise. But good argumentation turned the perceived advantages of opponents to one's own advantage.[575]

Paul indicates that if they want to view matters purely under the law, then they will have to proclaim Jesus accursed (an ungodly declaration, 1 Cor 12:3)! But even though Jesus was innocent (Acts 13:28), there was a sense in which, under the law (cf. Gal 4:4), he did embrace the curse, to free others from it (3:13).

How could Jesus become a "curse"? Christ became a curse presumably the way that he became sin in 2 Cor 5:21: as a *representative* of sin, and therefore a sin offering. God condemned sin in Christ's flesh (Rom 8:3).[576] Under the law, guilt could be transferred to a lamb or a goat (e.g., Lev 4:24; 5:6; 8:14; 9:15; 16:21; Num 8:12); here it is transferred to Christ. Abraham and surely Christ, his ultimate seed, were blessed; Jesus, who did not merit the curse, experienced it in others' place. Many understand being a curse as figurative for being accursed (as in the Deuteronomy text that Paul cites).

---

[573] 4Q169 f3–4i.7–8.
[574] 11QTemple 64.8–11.
[575] See, e.g., Heath, "Invention," 97; Rowe, "Style," 145–46.
[576] Cf. Loisy, *L'Épitre aux Galates*, 149: by condemning sin in him God destroyed with it the curse attached to it.

Perhaps in another sense Jesus could become a curse literally – in the same sense that his enemies could count him accursed (1 Cor 12:3). Making someone "a curse" or "for a curse"[577] meant using their accursed condition as an analogy of wretchedness: "May you be cursed like so-and-so" (cf. Jer 29:22; LXX 36:22). Thus Jesus, who was accursed (by virtue of hanging on the cross), could be said to be for a curse; people could thus curse others by saying, "Let them be accursed like Jesus," who was hanged on a cross.

Paul's term for *redeemed* here (*exagorazô*) can refer to paying off claims and so satisfying someone wronged, to gain something, to "buy back" (the term's etymology), or, as probably here, to secure someone's deliverance.[578] Paul employs this term in this way only here and in Gal 4:5, and in that context liberation from subjection seems fairly clear. If, as thus appears likely, Paul uses the term in a manner similar to the noun *apolutrôsis*, "redemption" (Rom 3:24; 8:23; 1 Cor 1:30; Col 1:14), he draws on a semantic domain rich with connotations.[579]

Jewish people spoke of how God *redeemed* his people from captivity in Egypt.[580] Israel was thus the Lord's redeemed people,[581] different in this respect from other peoples. They also looked for when he would again redeem them in the future time.[582] This semantic domain does not always involve buying a slave's freedom, but the context of Galatians suggests that Paul may use it that way here (cf. Gal 4:1–3, 8–10).[583]

Having addressed the curse in 3:10 and 3:13, Paul in 3:14 returns to Abraham's blessing for the nations (3:8). Paul's rivals insist that circumcision is necessary to join God's people, a position consistent with wider Jewish belief. Paul, by contrast, responds that the Galatian believers' reception of the Spirit demonstrates that they are already God's people, among

---

[577] Isa 64:10 (LXX 64:9); Jer 24:9; 26:6; 44:8 (51:8); 44:12 (51:12); Zech 8.13; cf. Jer 42:18 (49:18).

[578] BDAG.

[579] For ransom redemption, or liberation with a price, see, e.g., Josephus *Ant.* 12.27; L. Morris, *The Apostolic Preaching of the Cross* (3rd edn.; Grand Rapids, MI: Eerdmans, 1965), 11–64.

[580] Using various terminology, see, e.g., Exod 6:6; 15:13; Deut 7:8; 9:26; 13:6; Mic 6:4; 4Q158 f14i.5; 11Q19 54.16–17.

[581] E.g., Isa 35:9; 51:10; 1QM 1.12; 14.10; 17.6; 4Q266 f11.13.

[582] E.g., 1QM 1.12; 15.1–2; 18.1; 4Q176 f3.2; 11Q19 59.12. Cf. the prophets' new exodus, e.g., Isa 48:20; 51:10; Mic 4:10. Cf. coins associated with Judean revolts in E. Carmon, ed., *Inscriptions Reveal: Documents from the Time of the Bible, the Mishna, and the Talmud* (trans. R. Grafman; Jerusalem: Israel Museum, 1973), 80, 97, 179, 211, §§179, 180, 199; the seventh benediction of the Amida in W. O. E. Oesterley, *The Jewish Background of the Christian Liturgy* (Oxford: Clarendon, 1925), 63.

[583] With Dunn, *Theology of Paul*, 228, citing 1 Cor 7:21–23.

whom he dwells. Although Paul has been addressing Abraham's faith in God's promise since 3:6, in verse 14 Paul begins to use the explicit language of *promise* that will dominate much of his following exposition (3:16, 17, 18, 19, 21, 22, 29) and will help connect this biblical argument with his next one (4:23, 28).

Paul's special focus here is one aspect of the promise: the nations blessed in Abraham (3:8). Genesis depicts a dual promise to Abraham of land and seed. Against some, Paul has not abandoned this conception, though the land element is now subsumed under eschatological inheritance (3:18, 29; 5:21). He develops the concept of seed further in this chapter (3:16, 19, 29). The Old Testament narrows the motif of the promised seed from Abraham's seed to David's (2 Sam 7:12; Ps 89:4; 132:11), so for Paul this promise climaxes naturally in the ultimate seed of promise, Jesus the Messiah.[584]

Paul does not develop the land aspect of inheritance here, but elsewhere he agrees with the early Jewish expansion of that promise to embrace the entire world (Rom 4:13; cf. 5:17; 8:21, 32).[585] As Old Testament passages spoke of Israel inheriting the land, Paul speaks of inheriting God's kingdom (1 Cor 6:9–10; 15:50; Gal 5:21; Eph 5:5).[586] As noted earlier, he has just used other passages that speak in context of life on the land and sinners' expulsion from the land (Gal 3:12). Israel's inheritance came from a covenant, not a will, but Paul will speak of a will (3:15) as he plays on the idea that an inheritance is given to sons (3:29).

Why then does Paul equate the promise with the Spirit? For Paul, the Spirit is the foretaste of the future promise (Gal 5:5; 1 Cor 2:9–10; cf. Heb 6:4–5), the first fruits (Rom 8:23) and actual down payment of the future inheritance (2 Cor 1:22; 5:5; Eph 1:3, 13–14). Given Old Testament promises of God pouring out his Spirit when he restored his people and their land, early Christians not surprisingly associated the Spirit with promise (Acts 1:4–5; 2:33, 38–39; Eph 1:13). Because the Spirit was divine, receiving the Spirit was also itself the greatest gift – God dwelling among his people (e.g., Exod 29:45–46).

---

[584]   With, e.g., Hays, "Galatians," 264.

[585]   See, e.g., Rom 4:13; 1 En. 5:7; Jub. 17:3; 22:14; 32:19; 4Q171 frg. 1 2.ii.4, 8; frg. 1 + 3–4.iii.9; 4Q418 frg. 81 + 81a.14; 2 Bar. 51:3; Mekilta Besh. 7.139–40. For the Old Testament notion, see J. D. Hester, *Paul's Concept of Inheritance: A Contribution to the Understanding of Heilsgeschichte* (SJTOP 14; Edinburgh: Oliver & Boyd, 1968), 22–29; in early Jewish sources, see Hester, *Inheritance*, 30–36, 84.

[586]   R. T. George, *Paul's Identity in Galatians: A Postcolonial Appraisal* (New Delhi: Christian World Imprints, 2016), 193, speaks of this as "a trans-geographical terrain."

Paul can readily connect the Spirit with blessing because of his knowledge of Scripture; in parallel lines, Isa 44:3 announces that God will pour out his Spirit and his blessing on the seed/children of Israel. Those gentiles who now receive the Spirit in Christ belong, with Christ, to the promised seed and thus to God's people (cf. Gal 3:16, 29).

The prophets associated God's Spirit among his people with the time of restoration (Isa 32:15; 44:3; 59:21; Ezek 36:27, 37:14, 39:29; Joel 2:28–29), so those who have received the Spirit (including the Galatian gentile believers, Gal 3:2, 5) are the heirs of the full promise. In short, believing gentiles, as spiritual proselytes marked not by the outward symbol of circumcision but by the greater sign of the Spirit, share in the eschatological promise of the coming world centered in the new Jerusalem (Gal 4:26).[587]

3:15–20: STICK WITH THE FIRST AGREEMENT

3:15 Brothers and sisters, I give an example from daily life: once a person's will has been ratified, no one adds to it or annuls it.

3:16 Now the promises were made to Abraham and to his offspring; it does not say, "And to offsprings," as of many; but it says, "And to your offspring," that is, to one person, who is Christ.

3:17 My point is this: the law, which came four hundred thirty years later, does not annul a covenant previously ratified by God, so as to nullify the promise.

3:18 For if the inheritance comes from the law, it no longer comes from the promise; but God granted it to Abraham through the promise.

3:19 Why then the law? It was added because of transgressions, until the offspring would come to whom the promise had been made; and it was ordained through angels by a mediator.

3:20 Now a mediator involves more than one party; but God is one.

---

[587] Jewish people expected to "inherit" the coming world as well as the land; cf. 4Q418 frg. 69.ii.13; 1 En. 40:9; 2 En. 50:2 (cf. 55:2); Ps. Sol. 14:7; Sib. Or. 1.85; Rom 8:17; Eph 1:14; 4 Ezra 6:59; 7:96; 2 Bar. 44:13. For Paul's view of Christians as spiritual proselytes, see also Donaldson, *Gentiles*, 236–47; Donaldson, " 'Riches for the Gentiles' (Rom 11:12): Israel's Rejection and Paul's Gentile Mission," *JBL* 112 (1993): 81–98, here 98; Donaldson, "Israelite, Convert, Apostle to the Gentiles: The Origin of Paul's Gentile Mission," pages 62–84 in *The Road from Damascus: The Impact of Paul's Conversion on His Life, Thought, and Ministry* (ed. R. N. Longenecker; Grand Rapids, MI: Eerdmans, 1997), 81–82; Donaldson, "Paul within Judaism: A Critical Evaluation from a 'New Perspective' Perspective," pages 277–301 in *Paul within Judaism: Restoring the First-Century Context to the Apostle* (ed. M. D. Nanos and M. Zetterholm; Minneapolis, MN: Fortress, 2015), 295–98.

Paul develops a new but related line of thought in 3:15. Where there is an inheritance there is often a will, but God promised his people an inheritance in his covenant with them. Many scholars argue on clear grounds that *diathêkê* here means *will* (so NRSV); many others argue on equally clear grounds that it must mean *covenant*.

The entire context of this passage addresses being children of Abraham and the promised inheritance (Gal 3:6–29), making the meaning "will" here virtually indisputable. This was the normal Greek meaning – the one Paul's usually predominantly gentile audiences would assume unless influenced by the LXX – and the one used by other first-century Jews such as Josephus.[588] Paul's vocabulary in Gal 3:15–17 employs Greek legal terminology not found in typical Jewish discussions of the covenant.[589]

At the same time, *diathêkê* is the LXX term for *covenant*,[590] which is also how Paul uses the term elsewhere. Paul has been addressing God's covenant with Abraham, so this sense also seems indisputable.[591] Undoubtedly, then, Paul intends both senses of the term here, using human wills as analogies for the biblical covenant with Abraham. Much of Paul's Galatian audience may not have known the difference, but even his Torah-educated opponents could not easily object to his method of argument. Ancient writers and speakers often argued from (or cleverly punned with) wordplays.[592] In this case, since Paul argues in Greek, he is not even playing on different words, but simply on a wider sense of the Greek word *diathêkê* than is conveyed by the Hebrew term for *covenant* in the Old Testament (cf. also his argument from senses of a term in the following verse, Gal 3:16). The argument functions a fortiori from a human will to a divine covenant.

One can well understand, however, why Paul prefaces this argument with the warning that he gives *an example from daily life*, lit., "speaks according to human [reasoning]" (3:15; cf. similar expressions to this effect in Rom 3:5; 6:19).[593] He does not, then, place this argument on the same level as his gospel, which is *not* from human origin (Gal 1:1, 12, 16). This approach

---

[588]   See, e.g., *Ant.* 13.349; 17.244; *War* 1.664; 2.38, 98–99; and passim.
[589]   Das, *Stories*, 76–81.
[590]   In the vast majority of cases it translates the Heb. *berith*.
[591]   Although studies of early Judaism often emphasize Jewish teaching about the covenant and Paul's revised understanding of it, early Jewish sources reveal a wide range of understandings of the covenant (Das, *Stories*, 65–92, esp. 73–76, 91).
[592]   E.g., Rhet. Her. 4.21.29–4.22.31; Fronto *Ad M. Caes.* 2.3.3; Diogenes Laertius 6.2.55, 68; CD 8.10–11; Sipre Deut. 306.22.1; 345.2.2; 345.3.1; 1 Cor 11:3–5.
[593]   Ancient persuasion sought to prepare hearers for shocking statements; e.g., Dio Chrysostom *Or.* 38.5–6; Rowe, "Style," 142, 146.

resembles what rhetoricians called an "artificial proof," and supplements the stronger divine proofs Paul has given from their experience in 3:1–5 and from Scripture in 3:6–14.[594] It may also be relevant that one form of Greek *diathêkê* also specified inheritance through *adoption* (4:5).[595]

Paul's play on different senses may run into trouble with *no one adds to it or annuls it.* Wills were changed all the time; Paul here presumably alludes again to the covenant, which could not be changed once sworn by oath.[596] So *this* will, which is in the form of a covenant, cannot be added to or annulled.[597]

The likeliest of other, perhaps supplemental solutions so far proposed are two. First, the death of the testator *ratified* (3:15) the will, making it unchangeable; no one disputed that a testator (or anyone else) could not alter the will after his death![598] (Moreover, despite some exceptions, in testamentary *adoption* the will was ratified and became irrevocable by the heir's official acceptance.)[599] The more common suggestion is that Paul's point is that no one *other* than a testator could change his will.[600] This suggestion requires of Paul's audience little specific legal knowledge but suggests that Paul could have explained his point more clearly.

Wills provide for heirs to receive their inheritance, matters to which Paul quickly turns (Gal 3:18, 29; 4:1, 7, 30; 5:21).[601]

Inheritance became a frequent source of debate in courts, sometimes dividing relatives;[602] even Jesus was approached as a legal authority to rule

---

[594] Witherington, *Grace*, 240–41, noting also Chrysostom on Gal 3:15.

[595] See B. R. Trick, *Abrahamic Descent, Testamentary Adoption, and the Law in Galatians: Differentiating Abraham's Sons, Seed, and Children of Promise* (NovTSup 169; Leiden: Brill, 2016), 151.

[596] With Das, *Galatians*, 348. The oath appears in Gen 22:16–18.

[597] In 3:19, the law appears as added, which cannot affect the covenant here to which no additions were possible; likewise, *annul* evokes the same Greek term in 2:21, suggesting that to annul this covenant would nullify God's grace (Hays, "Galatians," 263–64).

[598] Wills were opened at the testator's death; see, e.g., B.G.U. 326.21; Plutarch *Caes.* 68.1.

[599] Trick, *Descent*, 173–74, citing D. R. Moore-Crispin, "The Sources and Meaning of ΔΙΑΘΗΚΗ and Related Terminology in Galatians III.15 – IV.7" (PhD diss., University of London, 1975), 152–63. Unlike inheriting, adoption did not require a testator's death (Trick, *Descent*, 174). This solution is, however, so specific that it may require Paul and the Galatians to share a particular contextual understanding.

[600] E.g., de Boer, *Galatians*, 219; Soards and Pursiful, *Galatians*, 143. This does not suggest that Paul attributes the addition of the law to someone other than God; Paul sees that as added as a temporary codicil, not a replacement.

[601] Cf. Rom 4:13–14; 8:17; 1 Cor 6:9–10; 15:50. Jewish people often reapplied God's promise of inheritance to language for the coming age; see comment on Gal 3:18; 5:19. For ancient inheritance laws, see also, e.g., Hester, *Inheritance*, 3–21.

[602] E.g., Lysias *Or.* 16.10, §146; 32.10, §506; Isaeus *Cleon.* 6.35; *Menec.* 28–29; Quintilian *Decl.* 336.

on such matters (Luke 12:13). Wills could be changed.[603] Unfortunately, this made the accusation of forged wills a very common issue, with parties contesting which wills were authentic.[604]

Paul's argument in Gal 3:16 from the allegedly singular form of *offspring* is not the way we would normally argue today. *Offspring* (Gk. *sperma*, "seed") can include many offspring as well as one, so even some ancient interpreters suggested that Paul in Gal 3:16 is still offering limited rhetorical arguments rather than arguing from logic (his speaking in merely human terms in 3:15).[605] On the whole, though, it was an intelligible argument for Paul's contemporaries. Rabbis could distinguish between singular and plural meanings as needed for whatever argument they were making at the time.

Indeed, rabbis sometimes made a move quite like Paul's here. Thus, some noted, "It is not said 'its seed,' but 'its seeds.'"[606] Similarly, Judean teachers inferred from the plural of *blood* in the Hebrew text of Gen 4:10 the moral that the blood of the descendants is included.[607] Likewise, the double *yod* in a word in Gen 2:7 offered rabbis an exegetical basis for God creating humans with two contrary impulses.[608] Women were exempt from certain duties because the biblical text said "sons"[609] – even though this was a generic masculine in Hebrew. One later rabbi even concluded that someone might construe a reference to "seed" as pointing to the Messiah.[610]

Nevertheless, there may be a more consistent method in Paul's apparent madness here. Grammar does not itself highlight the singularity of the seed, but the exclusion of Ishmael's line (Gal 4:21–31, esp. 4:30) indicates that the line of promise does not include *all* of Abraham's physical descendants, a point that Paul develops more thoroughly elsewhere (Rom 9:6–13). Paul undoubtedly knows that Gen 22:2, where God commands Abraham to sacrifice his son Isaac, describes Isaac as his "only" (Heb. *yachid*) son (cf. also 22:16). Paul can make a long-range analogy with Christ as the *ultimate* singular seed of promise, who is also God's Son (Gal 4:6).

---

[603] E.g., P. Oxy. 106 (AD 135); Gaius *Inst.* 2.144.
[604] E.g., Isaeus *Nicost.* 9–11; Cicero *Cat.* 2.4.7; Suetonius *Aug.* 33.2; Tacitus *Ann.* 14.40; Pliny *Ep.* 6.22.3; 7.6.8–9.
[605] Jerome *Ep. Gal.* 2.3.15 (Edwards).
[606] M. Shab. 9:2.
[607] Longenecker, *Galatians*, 131–32; Silva, "Galatians," 807.
[608] Gen. Rab. 14; Tg. Ps.-Jon. on Gen 2:7.
[609] Women were exempt from certain duties (e.g., m. Ber. 3:3) because the text said "sons" (b. Erub. 96b, bar.; Qid. 36a; y. Ber. 2:2, §5) – even though Hebrew also used the same term inclusively (cf. b. Sot. on m. Sot. 7:6).
[610] Gen. Rab. 51:8 (trans. p. 448).

In Genesis, God made promises to Abraham and to his seed (generally translated *offspring* in the NRSV). Rightly or wrongly, a number of scholars argue that one or more of these promise texts (esp. Gen 22:18; 24:7) refer in the first place to a singular seed, namely Isaac. Interpretations limiting Abraham's seed were not unique to Paul; some others interpreted the seed at times as a particular individual, especially Isaac,[611] and later rabbis restricted his seed to those who believe in a future age.[612]

It is possible, though by no means certain, that Paul's rivals were emphasizing Isaac as the true seed (cf. Gal 4:21–31).[613] Whereas they may have viewed the genetic/ethnic line of Isaac as the seed, Paul emphasizes that one becomes part of Abraham's family through spiritual solidarity with Christ, his *ultimate* seed (the promise of which is mentioned again in 3:19).

Rather than using an arbitrary approach, Paul probably envisioned a particular connection between Abraham's seed and Christ. Just as in Rom 4:19–20 Abraham had the same kind of faith as Jesus-believers – resurrection faith[614] – so also here, Abraham's faith in God's promise of seed (in the short run, Isaac and the people of Israel) points toward the ultimate promise of Christ. Christ was the ultimate seed through whom gentiles were being blessed (Gal 3:8), as evident in the fruit of Paul's gentile mission in obedience to Christ (cf. Rom 1:5–6; 15:8–12).

For Paul, drawing on the wider scope of the biblical historical narrative, the promise of a specific seed was applied again more specifically to David's descendants (2 Sam 7:12–16; 22:51; Ps 18:50; 89:4, 29, 36; 132:11–12).[615] Although that passage probably refers to David's royal lineage, 4QFlor shows that it was also applied to the expected Davidic ruler par excellence.

Some also see "Christ" in 3:16 as a corporate figure (cf. 1 Cor 12:12), so that those who are in him are also Abraham's seed (Gal 3:27–29), as those in God's Son are God's sons and daughters (4:4–7).

God ratified his covenant with Abraham (Gal 3:15; cf. Gen 22:16–18), confirming it with an oath (22:16); nothing, therefore, could supersede this arrangement (Gal 3:17). If Abraham was justified by faith (Gen 15:6 in Gal

---

[611] D. Daube, *The New Testament and Rabbinic Judaism* (London: University of London, Athlone Press, 1956), 440–44.

[612] Gen. Rab. 53:12. Still, Abraham's seed was normally understood as Israel; see, e.g., Ps. Sol. 9:9; 18:3–4; 3 Macc. 6:3.

[613] Cf. Longenecker, *Exegesis*, 124.

[614] Cf. Heb 11:17–19.

[615] R. B. Hays, *Echoes of Scripture in the Letters of Paul* (New Haven, CT: Yale University Press, 1989), 85; cf. Hays, "Galatians," 264.

3:6), the subsequent law of Moses could not do away with this way of justification (cf. Rom 10:6–10). Indeed, with 430 years between the promise
to Abraham and the law, faith in God's promise clearly remained sufficient
already during a long era.

Insofar as the promise involved all peoples being blessed in Abraham
(the explicit promise cited in Gal 3:8), it revealed God's ideal plan that could
not be fulfilled in the era of Israel's civil law, which separated Israel from
other peoples to restrict pagan influence.

In any case, Paul is not saying that once the law came it was unnecessary
to obey it; he is claiming rather that justification remained by faith even
once the law was initiated. The prelaw models demonstrate that the form
of obedience that faith took under the law was not the only form that God
could prescribe for all eras. Against Jewish tradition, Paul does not regard
the law as already in effect in Abraham's era.

Playing off the law and promise against each other may be more a rhetorical strategy than an exegetical conclusion; as noted at 2:16, rhetoricians
could pose exclusive alternatives that not everyone viewed as genuinely
exclusive.[616] Rhetoricians challenging a law could compare it with older
ones to show that it violated them.[617] But insofar as the law required some
level of separation from gentiles (cf. 2:12; Lev 20:24) and the promise (cited
explicitly in Gal 3:8) involved blessing them, the law would interfere with
the promise.

In this passage, Paul presents the law's function as temporary (Gal 3:19,
23–25; 4:4–5), but he refers here only to the law's function addressed in the
context: as a guide to bring us to Christ and/or to guard Israel until its fulness in Christ. Paul's entire theology of the law cannot be properly extrapo-
lated from a single (polemical) passage.[618] But he does insist that the law, the
purpose of which was never justification to begin with (3:21), does not contradict and thus cannot render inoperative the promise, which does provide
such justification and membership in God's people.

For Paul, the law offers valuable moral instruction (e.g., 1 Cor 9:8),
though even ethics is deepened in Christ toward God's ideal purpose (Gal
5:14, 22–23; 6:2). It provided basic ethical boundaries to limit Israel's sin
until Christ's coming (cf. perhaps Gal 3:23–24), which brings a new way of

---

[616] For reasoning by contraries, see Rhet. Her. 4.18.25.
[617] Pliny *Ep.* 2.19.8.
[618] A caution often noted, e.g., Luther (1535) on Gal 3:19; Calvin on Gal 3:19–20; Longenecker,
       Galatians, 137 (noting that Paul is here addressing issues raised by his challengers); Silva,
       "Galatians," 805.

righteousness by the indwelling of the Spirit (Gal 5:16–23; Ezek 36:25–26). Paul here also emphasizes another divinely given role of the law: its testimony to the coming Christ and the way of faith (Gal 3:6, 11, 21–22; cf. also 1 Cor 10:4).

Yet Paul also reveals another use of the law, which actually contradicts the Christocentric use just mentioned. Paul's detractors in synagogue disputes undoubtedly claimed that they were satisfied with the way of the law apart from Paul's Christ. In Paul's wider theology, including in Galatians, this last use of the law is actually an abuse, leading away from Christ instead of to him. The law was never intended to be a means of justification before God on its own, simply by observance (Gal 2:21; 3:21). The law in fact testifies that all are under sin (Gal 3:22; cf. Rom 3:10–20). Those who use the law to reject the Christ to which the law testifies are thus under its curse (Gal 3:13).

A Closer Look: Paul and the Law

Against Marcion's rejection of the law, many church fathers found in Paul an appreciation for the continued moral value of the law, even while treating its ritual and civil uses as having filled their purpose. Most scholars in more recent times have also seen Paul as embracing some aspects of the law while treating others as fulfilled.[619]

For Paul, the law as Scripture is good (Rom 7:12, 16) and inspired (7:14); as already noted, it can provide moral guidance (1 Cor 9:8–9) and points to the promise in Christ (Rom 3:21, 27, 31; Gal 3:21; 4:21). Nevertheless, it is inadequate as a meritorious marker of achievement or zeal (Rom 2:12; 1 Cor 15:56; Gal 3:11–12; Phil 3:6, 9), because of human failings (Rom 7:25; 8:3, 7; Gal 3:10). The law was never meant to justify (Gal 2:21; 3:21), any more than any other civil law does that. Like other public laws, it restrained sin (Gal 3:23–24), but apart from God's Spirit it could not transform the heart. Using it without trusting God's promised deliverance in Christ is antithetical to depending on God's grace in Christ (Rom 3:27; 8:2; 9:31–32; 10:5–10; Gal 3:11–13, 18; 5:4; Phil 3:9). The law thus can mark transgression (Rom 3:19–20; 4:15; 5:20; 7:7–9; Gal 3:19), but only its giver can forgive.

Fulfilling the promise of Jer 31:31–34 and Ezek 11:19–20; 36:25–27, God's Spirit inscribes the transcultural moral objective of the law in believers' hearts (Rom 8:2–4; 2 Cor 3:3–6; Gal 5:16–18, 22–23; 6:2). The old covenant's

---

[619]   I concisely survey the range of approaches to Paul and the law in Keener, *Acts*, 2084.

stipulations were a means, not an end; the climactic end or goal was found in Christ (Rom 10:4; Gal 3:17, 19, 23–24).

Paul is not against obeying the law (cf. Gal 5:14, 23; 6:2) but against depending on one's obedience for justification or honor. Paul shared his contemporaries' biblical belief in the priority of divine grace, but he develops much further an emphasis on the incongruity of grace.[620]

Because Jewish people grew up following the law, it remained their usual custom; observing it did not thereby entail seeking to be justified by it any more than any culture's observance of honorable customs does. Making it a salvific or ecclesial requirement for gentiles who had already submitted to Christ and the Spirit, however, treated Christ and the Spirit as insufficient for these purposes. Theologically, this was legalism; socially, it was ethnocentrism. ****

As commentators regularly note, Jewish tradition often viewed the law not as ruling a temporary era but as eternal. Indeed, some aspects of the Torah claim to be eternal in some respect.[621] Some aspects of the Torah, however, could be fulfilled only in the land, only in an agrarian society, and so forth; that is, their principles might need to be recontextualized in a new setting.[622] Indeed, some aspects of the law were concessions to human weakness that fellow short of God's ultimate ideals (cf. Mark 10:5).[623]

Far from placing the law 430 years after Abraham, some Jewish thinkers regarded it as God's first creation, formed before the world.[624] In contrast to Genesis' portrayal of patriarchs who sometimes violated prohibitions later articulated in the law, Jewish tradition claimed that the Torah existed before Sinai.[625] Paul obviously disagrees about the preexistence of the law, a tradition not articulated in the law itself.

Paul is undoubtedly more interested in the intervening centuries than in how he calculates the specific figure. Exodus has Israel in Egypt for 430 years (Exod 12:40–41), whereas Genesis offers a rounder 400 years for Israel's oppression (Gen 15:13; Acts 7:6); more literalistic interpreters tried to resolve the discrepancy in various ways.[626] In particular, the LXX of Exod

---

[620] Barclay, *Gift*, 317–20.

[621] E.g., Exod 28:43; 29:28; Lev 7:34, 36; 16:29–31; 23:14, 21, 31; 24:8–9; Num 18:19.

[622] See further discussion in Keener, *Spirit Hermeneutics*, 75, 166, esp. 221, 234–35.

[623] See Daube, "Concessions to Sinfulness."

[624] E.g., L.A.B. 32:7; Sipre Deut. 37.1.3. See Keener, *John*, 379–81.

[625] E.g., Jub. 2:30; 3:8, 10; 6:2, 18–19; 7:3; 14:24; 16:21; 22:1–9; 44:4; L.A.B. 9:8; 2 Bar. 57:2.

[626] R. H. Charles, *The Book of Jubilees, or The Little Genesis* (London: Adam & Charles Black, 1902), lxxxiv; Longenecker, *Galatians*, 133.

12:40, followed by Josephus,[627] includes the time spent not only in Egypt but also in Canaan beforehand.

In 3:18, Paul forces a choice: the inheritance rests either on promise, that is, God's initiative, or on (keeping) the law.[628] That God "gave" (*kecharistai*) the promise (Gal 3:18) underlines again that it is from grace (*charis*, cf. 1:6, 15; 2:21; 5:4), from God's initiative.

Jewish tradition widely reapplied the language of inheritance to eschatology in ways similar to Paul's language of "inheriting" the kingdom (1 Cor 6:9–10; 15:50; Gal 5:21; Eph 5:5). The righteous expected to "inherit" God's "promises"[629] and to "inherit" eternal life.[630] The promise of inheriting the "land" (e.g., Ps 25:13; 37:9, 11, 22, 29, 34) came to be understood as inheriting the "earth" (the same Hebrew term);[631] Paul himself believed that the righteous would inherit all the world to come (Rom 4:13). Jewish tradition most often associated inheriting the world to come with one of two conditions: being Jewish or studying the Torah.[632]

Why then the law? (3:19) uses a form of question often used by Paul: he employs the same Greek expression (*ti oun*, "What then?" or "Why then?") sixteen times (e.g., Rom 3:1, 9; 4:1; 6:1), roughly half the New Testament occurrences. Asking and answering questions that might occur to the reader or that allow one to develop one's argument was part of sound pedagogy, and characterized, but was not limited to, diatribe style.[633]

As noted earlier, Paul views the law as temporary in the sense of its roles depicted in the present context, belonging to a period between the initiation of the promise (the era beginning with Abraham) and the promise's fulfillment in Christ. The law's restraint of sin (3:24–25) was necessary, like any set of civil laws for a society, but it is no longer *needed* for those who live and walk by the Spirit (cf. 5:16, 18, 23).

The NRSV translation about the seed *to whom the promise had been made* (NRSV; cf. KJV; ASV; NASB; ESV; Louis Segond) might not fit the

---

[627] *Ant.* 2.318.
[628] For the latter reflecting more stipulations, see again Arnold, *Genesis*, 101–02.
[629] Ps. Sol. 12:6.
[630] Dunn, *Galatians*, 186, and others cite, e.g., Ps. Sol. 14:10; 1 En. 40:9; 2 Bar. 57:1–3; m. Ab. 2:7; 5:19.
[631] In the Qumran scrolls, see Hester, *Inheritance*, 34–36; elsewhere, e.g., E. Adams, *Constructing the World: A Study in Paul's Cosmological Language* (Edinburgh: Clark, 2000), 167–68; 4 Ezra 6:59; L.A.B. 32:3.
[632] Hester, *Inheritance*, 84, citing Abot 2:7; 6:7.
[633] See, e.g., Musonius Rufus 5, p. 50.21; 16, p. 104.8; Epictetus *Disc.* 1.1.13; 1.8.11, 14; Dio Chrysostom *Or.* 31.55, 60; 45.10; 46.9; 47.14.

context as well as the NIV translation here: "the Seed to whom the promise referred."[634] Still, the former translation may be simpler grammatically.[635]

Paul notes that the law *was added*[636] *because of transgressions*, but his lack of immediate explication of this clause has given rise to a range of interpretations. The word translated *because* can also mean "for the sake of."

Five of the more significant explanations offered are:[637]

1. God gave the law to provide a means of addressing sin by atoning for it.
2. God gave the law to restrain sin.
3. God gave the law to provoke or increase sin.
4. God gave the law to separate Jew from gentile.
5. God gave the law to plainly identify what was sinful, identifying sin as transgression.

Clearly the law was not meant to give life (Gal 3:21). That the law was meant at least partly to address the problem of sin (view 1) is undoubtedly true but not the focus of the present context. That the law was meant to restrain sin (2) would fit the normal use of law, a possible understanding of the pedagogue's role in 3:24–25, and Paul's larger theology. Still, the law by itself was never able to make one right (3:21).[638] That the law was given to provoke or increase sin (3) may fit the law's activity in Rom 4:15; 5:13, 20; and 7:5, 8, but not necessarily its *intention*.[639] That the law was given to separate Jew from gentile (4) fits one Old Testament function of the law and would explain why the law in this sense was temporary (between the promise to Abraham

---

[634]   That is, the dative here specifies not the recipient of the promise (indirect object) but its referent (dative of respect, more common in Koine, on which see BDF §197; D. B. Wallace, *Greek Grammar beyond the Basics: An Exegetical Syntax of the New Testament* [Grand Rapids, MI: Zondervan, 1996], 144–45).

[635]   Paul and other early Christian writers use the dative form of this noun as an indirect object (Luke 1:55; Acts 3:25; 7:5; Rom 4:13, 16). Paul normally uses "Christ" with the dative following the preposition *en* or sometimes *sun* (or particular verbs such as *douloô*).

[636]   The verb for *added* here appears also in Acts 13:36 (a speech in south Galatia), but it is a common Lukan term. Hays, "Galatians," 264; de Boer, *Galatians*, 228; Das, *Galatians*, 358, see it as a virtual synonym for the adding of a codicil, prohibited in Gal 3:15 (though some, e.g., Hays, "Galatians," 267; Das, *Galatians*, 357, also acknowledge that *God* gave the law *through* angels).

[637]   Following esp. the survey of views in Das, *Galatians*, 358–61.

[638]   Luther (1535) on Gal 3:19 noted that God gave the law, like civil authorities, to control sin (citing 1 Tim 1:9), but that Paul in Gal 3:19 addresses a different function of the law, that of revealing sin.

[639]   Witherington, *Grace*, 256, rightly observes the "difference between the purpose of the Law and its effect on fallen human beings."

of blessing the nations and its fulfillment in the good news of Christ). It also fits the Pauline understanding that the law divides Jew from gentile (Eph 2:11–16, esp. 2:15), but it does not so easily account for *because of transgressions*. Fitting the fifth view, divine law virtually by definition does specify sin and so transforms it into transgression (5), fitting Rom 4:15; 5:20.

The last view has much to commend it, if Paul intends to be that specific here. Yet Paul may have had more than one of these particulars in view, speaking more generally. Had there been no sin, there would have been no need for the law. The law, then, does not belong to God's eternal *ideal*, direct purpose in the way that the promise does. God initiated both the promise and the law because of his gracious purpose, but the need to address sin (whether to prevent it, atone for it, or identify it) was what required the law until God would address it more fully in Christ.

Paul argues that, whereas the promise came directly from God to Abraham and to those reckoned with him, God mediated the law through angels and Moses. Building on some limited evidence in Scripture (Deut 33:2, explicitly in the LXX; cf. Exod 3:2; Ps 68:17), Jewish tradition already emphasized that God gave the law through angels.[640] Whereas this tradition was meant to glorify the law, and may have been so used by Paul's rivals, Paul turns it to opposite effect here.[641] Some scholars have read too much into Paul's treatment of the law's mediation and contended that Paul denied that God himself authored the law; but his language (*through* angels) strongly implies that the angels mediated the law rather than authored it.

In addition to Paul, some other Jews may have recognized angelic mediation as potentially subordinating the law; thus one tradition insists that Moses received the Torah "Not from the mouth of an angel and not from the mouth of a Seraph, but from the mouth of the King over the king of kings."[642] Paul's older contemporary Philo of Alexandria emphasizes mediation through powers subordinate to God for most lesser tasks.

Moses appears widely in early Judaism as the mediator of the law,[643] and scholars today nearly always see him as the second mediator here (besides the angels). Although English translations naturally prefer more idiomatic

---

[640]   See esp. Jub. 1:27; 2:1; 4Q216 5.1; Josephus *Ant.* 15.136; Heb 2:2.
[641]   Paul presumably believed the tradition, but persuaders sometimes simply assumed common opinion for the sake of argument (Dio Chrysostom *Or.* 23.9).
[642]   Abot R. Nat. 1, §2 B (trans. p. 25).
[643]   E.g., 1 Esd 9:39; Philo *Dreams* 1.143; *Mos.* 2.166; L.A.B. 11:2; T. Mos. 1:14; 3:12; Sipra Behuq. pq. 8.269.2. 15; Sipre Deut. 305.1.2.

English, Paul more literally speaks of the law given "by the hand of a mediator," which echoes the LXX phrase that could also be rendered "by the hand(s) of Moses."[644] Mediators could be valuable, but God's direct action appears as superior here.

The basic point of 3:20 is clear enough: the law's mediation reduces its claim to authority. The details, however, strike many as obscure. Paul's meaning in 3:20 is either so poorly expressed or so contextually loaded with information no longer available to us that it has generated a plethora of interpretations – according to one count already in the nineteenth century, 250 or 300![645] These views are sometimes classified in three to five main categories:[646]

1. Moses mediates not for one but for many angels (3:19).
2. The one seed of 3:16 applies to the one people of God.
3. The law was given not to one, like the promise (3:16), but to many Israelites (3:20), thus distinguishing law from promise.
4. The law functioned like a contract between two parties, whereas God acted unilaterally in giving the promise.
5. God gave the promise directly and unilaterally (and is thus just one party) but the law is mediated through angels and Moses.

The last two of these are likeliest.[647] The one God (3:20) acts directly for the single progeny (3:16), whereas the law involved God delegating multiple layers of mediation for the people (cf. Rev 1:1).

Jewish people regularly recite the Shema (Deut 6:4), confessing God's oneness. God's oneness was the foundational doctrine of Judaism, and this is not the only time that Paul appeals to it to prove a theological point (cf. 1 Cor 8:5–6). Perhaps more relevantly here, in Rom 3:30, Paul argues from God's oneness for the conclusion that he must be the God of Jew and gentile alike.[648] Others drew conclusions from God's oneness, such as the necessary oneness of God's people.[649]

---

[644] E.g., LXX Lev 26:46; Num 15:23; 36:13; with Moo, *Galatians*, 235.
[645] Lightfoot, *Galatians*, 146.
[646] Moo, *Galatians*, 236–37.
[647] With, e.g., Betz, *Galatians*, 171–72; Matera, *Galatians*, 134; Moo, *Galatians*, 237; Das, *Galatians*, 366.
[648] Cf. also Eph 4:3–6; similarly the conclusion of Josephus *Apion* 2.193 that the one God for humankind means that the temple should be for all humankind; in Sipre Deut. 31.4.1, he is one God for everyone.
[649] Philo *Virt.* 35; Num. Rab. 10:5.

3:21–25: THE FORMAL LAW AS A STOPGAP

3:21 Is the law then opposed to the promises of God? Certainly not! For if a law had been given that could make alive, then righteousness would indeed come through the law.

3:22 But the scripture has imprisoned all things under the power of sin, so that what was promised through faith in Jesus Christ might be given to those who believe.

3:23 Now before faith came, we were imprisoned and guarded under the law until faith would be revealed.

3:24 Therefore the law was our disciplinarian until Christ came, so that we might be justified by faith.

3:25 But now that faith has come, we are no longer subject to a disciplinarian.

The next section (3:21–4:11) shifts the imagery from justification to images of subjection and liberation. Prior mention of inheritance (3:18) and being children of Abraham (3:7) are now developed here. Inheritance (3:29; 4:1, 7; cf. 4:30; 5:21) normally belongs to children rather than to slaves,[650] and believers are Abraham's and God's children rather than slaves (3:26; 4:6–7; cf. 4:28, 31). Paul's previous use of *under* (*under a curse*, 3:10) reinforces the subjugation imagery of this section:[651]

- Under sin (3:22; cf. Rom 3:9; 7:14)
- Under the law (3:23)
- Under a pedagogue (3:25)
- Under guardians (4:2)
- Under elementary things (4:3, 9)
- Under the law (4:4, 5)

Paralleling sin (3:22) and the law (3:23, 25; 4:4–5) does not make the law sin (cf. Rom 7:7), but it does line it up in the sin column (see discussion of *corresponds* at Gal 4:25–26), since the law had to be added to the promise only because of transgressions (3:19).

Paul begins 3:21 with a rhetorical question, which he answers with his standard severe negation, "Certainly not!" (see comment on Gal 2:17).

---

[650] Though the will could free a slave and name him or her heir (Gaius *Inst.* 1.21).

[651] I include here also references to the Greek *hupo* that the NRSV fails to render consistently as *under*. Beyond the section, see also "under the law" in 4:21; 5:18; cf. Rom 6:14–15; 1 Cor 9:20.

Contrary to some modern interpretations of 3:19, Paul did not reject the God-given character of the law. In 3:21, Paul makes clear, despite his agenda, that the law is not against God's promises.[652] If *any* law could have given life or righteousness, it surely would have been the law that God gave his people. But this law simply was not *meant* to give life or righteousness, because it *could* not give them (cf. 2:20–21; cf. Rom 7:10). In principle the law provided both life and righteousness (Deut 6:24–25),[653] but Paul has already argued that in practice it fails to do so because of human sin (Gal 3:10, 13, 22; cf. Rom 8:3). As an ancient Christian writer observed, "Law without grace, then, can expose disease but cannot heal."[654]

Life here evokes Paul's earlier argument: those who do its work will have life (3:12), but they instead come under its curse for violating it (3:10). Life instead comes by faith (3:11), specifically in God's Son (2:20).

In 3:22, Paul contends that *the scripture has imprisoned all things under the power of sin*, so that none would achieve life by their own power and so that the promise then would come instead to those who believe (as in 3:14; cf. Rom 4:14–16). Many scholars contend that *the scripture* here refers to a particular passage, namely Deut 27:26 cited in Gal 3:10. A very persuasive reason for this contention is that Paul elsewhere refers to a particular passage when he cites a definite article with the singular of Scripture (Rom 4:3; 9:17; 10:11; 11:2; Gal 3:8; 4:30). But 3:10 is twelve verses earlier, with three quotations and other allusions intervening, so the connection with that verse is less than obvious.

Even if Paul might think of this verse more than of other potential ones, he might think of it as simply representative of the wider witness of Scripture. By *scripture* Paul might refer to the law (cf. Rom 3:31 with 4:3; Gal 4:21–22), which can bring curses but not life (3:10, 21). In this case, he speaks of *scripture* in a general way, which is also the case if he refers to the testimony of scripture in general to human sinfulness (e.g., 1 Kgs 8:46).

---

[652]   *Promises* here (also 3:16) might be a generalizing plural, since Paul has a specific, central promise in view in this letter (Gal 3:14, 17–18, 22, 29; 4:23, 28); or the singular promise elsewhere in Galatians might encompass the twofold promise of land and seed (Paul emphasizing the latter). More often interpreters suggest here a reference to the multiple times that God reiterated the promise. Paul is, in any case, aware of more than one promise (Rom 9:4; 15:8; 2 Cor 1:20; 7:1), such as nations blessed in Abraham (Gal 3:8) and the promise to Abraham of seed (4:23, 28).

[653]   The NRSV translates *dikaiosunē* as *justification* in 2:21 but as *righteousness* in the parallel text, 3:21.

[654]   Fulgentius *On the Truth of Predestination* 1.41 (Edwards).

In support of this understanding, Paul elsewhere marshals Scripture to show that all have sinned (Rom 3:10–18), and he later speaks of God's similar activity without specifying particular references (Rom 11:32). Those who knew Scripture would know that even God's own people had repeatedly disobeyed his law and warranted judgment rather than blessing.

Paul uses similar language again in Rom 11:32, suggesting that Paul may have preached this way on multiple occasions. Soards and Pursiful observe the parallels:[655]

Gal 3:22	Rom 11:32
Scripture	God
Locked up	Locked up
All things	All people
Under sin	In disobedience
In order that	In order that
"The promise from the faith of Jesus Christ may be given to those who believe"	"he may show mercy to all"

The NRSV is right to translate the neuter plural *panta* in 3:22 as "all things," but this form could also evoke Paul's only other use of this form in Galatians: "all peoples" (NRSV, "all the Gentiles") in 3:8 (cf. Rom 1:5; 15:11; 16:26). Thus 3:22's reference to *what was promised through faith* applies to the promise of blessing to the gentiles who believe in 3:8.

Some view being *imprisoned* wholly positively here, meaning guarded and hemmed in to protect God's people from sin. Protecting them from sin and pagan surroundings is undoubtedly part of Paul's meaning; pedagogues restricted boys, protecting them morally.[656] Nevertheless, the vocabulary that he employs for this puts a negative spin on this positive concept perhaps employed by Paul's rivals. Moreover, imprisoning all *under the power of sin* in 3:22 is hardly a positive image, and this image affects how we hear what follows.

Even though Paul will immediately explain his reference to being under the law (3:23) simply as akin to being under a pedagogue (3:24–25),[657] he

---

[655] Soards and Pursiful, *Galatians*, 156. The parallel between scripture and God in these texts is consistent with the personification of the former here (Silva, "Galatians," 806; Das, *Galatians*, 368); see comment on Gal 3:8.

[656] M. J. Smith, "The Role of the Pedagogue in Galatians," *BSac* 163 (2006): 197–214, here 212–13.

[657] Orators could use epidiorthosis to calm hearers outraged by a shocking statement used to grip their attention; see Dio Chrysostom *Or.* 38.7; Hermogenes *Inv.* 4.12.203.

later compares this situation to being treated as a slave (4:1–3). Jewish sources speak of a fence around the law,[658] but if a fence is envisioned here, it is the law around God's people, separating them from paganism, as in an earlier hellenistic Jewish document.[659]

Yet the law that was designed to keep Israel from sin also reveals sin (3:19) so that all peoples may be condemned and thus recognize the need for Christ (cf. Rom 3:19–20). This particular role of the law ended for God's children when a more adequate means of fulfilling the promise arrived, namely when *faith came* (3:23, 25), i.e., when *Christ came* (3:24).[660] Faith was already part of God's plan before the law (3:6), but now that the promise is fulfilled in Christ, faith has been *revealed* (3:23). Paul's term for *revealed* is the same term he used for God's Son being revealed in him in 1:16, as the revelation of Jesus Christ in 1:12. Paul speaks here not of individuals' experience but of the course of salvation history. *Faith* refers to trusting God for salvation, rather than referring to *the faith* as a title for the Christian message or beliefs per se.[661] Again, this is not novel in salvation history (3:6), but its total sufficiency, because of the completed revelation of its object, Jesus Christ and his salvific work, has supplanted any interim arrangements.

The language of "under the law" is significant here. It might reflect the language of Paul's rivals. One could speak of conversion to Judaism, surmounting ethnic ties, as consenting to live "under [*hupo*] the same laws" as Jews.[662] In a context where Paul also uses *hupo* for unpleasant subordination, however, the phrase takes on negative overtones, as Paul, if he uses his opponents' language, turns their language against them.[663]

As in 2:15–17, "we" in 3:23–25 and 4:1–5 refers to those under the law, whereas in 3:26–29 and 4:6–10, "you" addresses the Galatians.[664]

---

[658] E.g., m. Ab. 1:1; 3:14, 18; Sipre Deut. 48.1.5; Ab. R. Nat. 2; 3 A; b. Ber. 4b; Yeb. 90b; Sanh. 46a; cf. perhaps CD 20.25.

[659] Let. Aris. 139, 142; cf. perhaps CD 1.16; 5.20.

[660] Context (esp. 3:23a, 25) invites us to translate *eis* (3:23–24) primarily temporally, as *until*, even if the law as pedagogue (3:24–25) also leads us to Christ as the true teacher (3:24).

[661] It is articular here and in 3:25 because it refers to the faith noted in 3:22.

[662] Josephus *Ag. Ap.* 2.210; with Longenecker, *Galatians*, 117.

[663] T. A. Wilson, "'Under Law' in Galatians: A Pauline Theological Abbreviation," *JTS* 56 (2005): 362–92, may carry this too far in construing "under the law" as shorthand for "under [the curse of] the law," though theologically this is implied (3:10). In the immediate context, the emphasis might rest more on subjugation (3:25; 4:2–5; cf. 3:22).

[664] Nevertheless, both 3:14 and 4:5–6 suggest that Paul's usage is more complex than simply applying "we" to Jews and "you" to gentiles in all of Galatians.

A Closer Look: Pedagogues

Although the NRSV translates *paidagôgos* as *disciplinarian*, this is not the primary feature of a pedagogue's responsibilities that Paul emphasizes. Pedagogues were sometimes harsh, using corporal punishments to keep their charges in line, but they were often gentle and well loved.[665] The image is not a negative one per se.

More generally, pedagogues were (usually) slaves who escorted boys, especially to school, carrying their bags and keeping them out of trouble along the way.[666] Pederasty was widespread,[667] so pedagogues remained with the children en route to and during school to ward off potential molesters.[668] Pedagogues were guards (*phrouroi*) and protectors of youths,[669] just as Gal 3:23 depicts the law as having guarded (*ephrouroumetha*) God's people in their youth.

Sometimes pedagogues would literally lead (*agô*) younger boys, hence their name.[670] One might contrast Paul's understanding of the law as pedagogue with the Spirit's leading in the current era in Gal 5:18, although Paul ultimately has stronger reasons for his choice of words in 5:18 (see comment there).

A pedagogue ruled the youth, keeping him in check morally.[671] Pedagogues were proud and received compliments when boys did well, and were criticized when boys performed poorly.[672] Just as pedagogues protected boys from sexual predators, one of the law's roles was to protect God's people from pagan practice around them; the mature could discern more critically with less oversight.

---

[665] N. H. Young, "The Figure of the Paidagogos in Art and Literature," *BA* 53 (1990): 80–86, here 80, 83; Young, "PAIDAGOGOS: The Social Setting of a Pauline Metaphor," *NovT* 39 (1987): 150–76, here 165.

[666] E.g., Plato *Lysis* 4, 208C (cited in, e.g., Longenecker, *Galatians*, 146; Matera, *Galatians*, 139).

[667] E.g., Lysias *Or.* 3.5, §96; Aeschines *Tim.* 9–12; Catullus 15.9–19; Virgil *Ecl.* 2.17, 45; 8.80–84; Petronius *Sat.* 8–11, 41, 79–80, 85–86, 92; Dio Chrysostom *Or.* 66.1, 7, 11; 77/78.28, 36; D. F. Greenberg, *The Construction of Homosexuality* (Chicago: University of Chicago, 1988), 144–47; C. A. Williams, *Roman Homosexuality* (2nd edn.; New York: Oxford University Press, 2010), 78–84, 122, 203.

[668] Young, "PAIDAGOGOS: Setting," 158–59.

[669] Young, "PAIDAGOGOS: Setting," 159.

[670] Young, "Figure of Paidagogos," 81. For the association with *agô*, see sources in Young, "PAIDAGOGOS: Setting," 156n76.

[671] See Young, "PAIDAGOGOS: Setting," 159–62.

[672] Libanius *Anecdote* 2.15–17.

Although pedagogues sometimes cared even for babies, usually they took charge of a boy from his nurse around age six.[673] Ancient sources often emphasize that the pedagogue's role was temporary, lasting only until the boy became a young man after puberty. Once reaching maturity, a young man was no longer under the pedagogue's authority. The young man now followed "his own laws."[674] Norman Young's research on ancient pedagogues concludes that Gal 3:24–25 highlights two important aspects of the role of pedagogues, namely that the role was temporary,[675] and that the role included restrictive guarding of the boy.[676]

There may be more. The author who can play on multiple Greek senses of *diathêkê* as both "will" and "covenant" in 3:15 surely can consider multiple roles of a *paidagôgos* here. In view of the parallel with guardians in 4:2, the restrictive role should also include a protective dimension.[677] Moreover, Paul emphasizes in 4:1 that heirs who are youths are no different than slaves, so he undoubtedly also considers the usual slave status of pedagogues.[678]

Pedagogues did sometimes play a role in youths' basic education, at least in Roman circles,[679] and certainly everywhere they influenced children.[680] If Paul envisions anything of that character here, his contrast elsewhere between fathers and pedagogues (1 Cor 4:15) is apropos; Paul probably viewed even his own earlier, "advanced" training in the law (Gal 1:14–15) as merely elementary learning associated with slavery when compared with the advanced and experiential revelation available for those free in Christ (cf. Philo's approach to Hagar and Sarah in my comment on Gal 4:24–25). ****

Like a pedagogue, the law (here personified)[681] was an appropriate master during its proper time; afterward, however, it would hold a different role. For Paul, the coming of Christ (3:24) and the era of faith (3:23, 25) marked

---

[673] Young, "Figure of Paidagogos," 81–82. Cf. Plato *Laws* 7.808DE (Longenecker, *Galatians*, 147).
[674] Xenophon *Lac.* 3.1, in Das, *Galatians*, 374.
[675] Young, "PAIDAGOGOS: Setting," 174–75.
[676] Young, "PAIDAGOGOS: Setting," 170–73.
[677] Moo, *Galatians*, 243. Young, "PAIDAGOGOS: Setting," 171, might downplay too much the protective dimension of such restriction.
[678] Young, "PAIDAGOGOS: Setting," 158, 163, notes that when not slaves, they were ordinarily freedmen; they could be bought or hired.
[679] J. Carcopino, *Daily Life in Ancient Rome: The People and the City at the Height of the Empire* (ed. H. T. Rowell; trans. E. O. Lorimer; New Haven, CT: Yale University Press, 1940), 104.
[680] Plutarch *Educ.* 7, *Mor.* 4A.
[681] On personification, see also comment on Gal 3:8.

the fulfillment of the promise to Abraham of gentiles being blessed (3:8). The pedagogue was therefore no longer necessary to protect God's people from gentile paganism or to restrict their behavior. Modern studies of moral development note children's need for rules, before they develop their own moral reasoning.[682] With Christ's sacrifice, God's people now reached a phase of maturity, doing right because of new hearts by the Spirit rather than because of ancient rules (5:18–23; cf. Jer 31:33; Ezek 36:26–27; 2 Cor 3:3).

In 3:26–29, Paul shifts from "we" (in 3:23–25), which must at least include the Jewish people, to "you," preaching directly to his predominantly gentile audience. Just as "all" peoples were under sin (3:22), so are "all" of the Galatian believers now God's children (3:26). Following are statements about their new identity in Christ:

- God's children (3:26)
- Baptized (initiated) into Christ (3:27a)
- Clothed with Christ (3:27b)
- Corporately one in Christ Jesus, beyond other distinctions (3:28)
- Abraham's offspring (3:29a)
- And thus heirs (of the coming world) according to the promise (3:29b)

In 3:26–29, Paul reinforces the point that gentile believers are full members of God's people, in the following ways:

- Like biblical Israel, they are God's children, through trust (3:26).
- Impure gentiles were cleansed to join Israel through baptism, now applied to all believers (3:27).
- With respect to belonging to God's people, ethnicity no longer makes a difference (3:28a).
- Slaves and women were normally not heirs under biblical law, but now both groups (3:28bc) are heirs (3:29b).
- All believers, not just Jews, are Abraham's offspring (3:29).

In the Greek text of verse 26, the inclusion of gentiles is more conspicuously emphatic than in English translation; "all" (*pantes*) appears first in the sentence, underlining its priority.

Because Paul's language here so closely parallels his language in other passages (1 Cor 12:13; Col 3:9–11), and because only the Jew/Greek part of

---

[682] Cf., e.g., discussions in J. Piaget, *The Moral Judgement of the Child* (trans. M. Gabain; New York: Simon and Schuster, 1997); M. Killen and J. G. Smetana, eds., *Handbook of Moral Development* (2nd edn.; New York: Psychology Press, 2013).

the formula is directly relevant to Paul's case, many think Paul here reflects a preexisting formula. Whether Paul inherited a widely used formula or simply framed himself a teaching that he adapted for different settings, the pattern is clear:

Gal 3:27–28	1 Cor 12:13	Col 3:10–11
Baptized into Christ (3:27a)	Baptized into one body (12:13a)	–
Clothed with Christ (3:27b)	(in the one Spirit, 12:13a)	Clothed with the new person (3:10a)
Jews or Greeks (3:28a)	Jews or Greeks (12:13b)	Greek or Jew, circumcised or uncircumcised (3:11a)
–	–	Barbarian, Scythian (3:11b)
Slave or free (3:28b)	Slaves or free (12:13c)	Slave, free (3:11c)
Male and female (3:28c)	–	–
All of you are one in Christ Jesus (3:28d)	(One body in Christ, 12:12–13; drinking from one Spirit, 12:13d)	Christ is all and in all (3:11d)

3:26–29: YOU ARE ALL HEIRS ALREADY

3:26 for in Christ Jesus you are all children of God through faith.

3:27 As many of you as were baptized into Christ have clothed yourselves with Christ.

3:28 There is no longer Jew or Greek, there is no longer slave or free, there is no longer male and female; for all of you are one in Christ Jesus.

3:29 And if you belong to Christ, then you are Abraham's offspring, heirs according to the promise.

Minor children might be under a *paidagōgos* (3:24), but with the coming of the full revelation of Christ God's children in this phase of salvation history no longer have that restriction (3:25). This is relevant for Paul's audience in Galatia because they are all God's children through faith in that revelation (3:26).

Although Paul explicitly introduces believers' identity as *children of God* in 3:26 for the first time in Galatians, in a sense he has been discussing this matter since 3:7, since Scripture already declared Abraham's descendants to be God's own children (Exod 4:22–23; Deut 14:1; Isa 43:6, 11; Jer 31:20; Hos 1:10; 11:1, 10).[683] That is, gentile believers have become part of God's people.

---

[683] Not that they always acted as such (Deut 32:5, 19–20, 43; Isa 1:2, 4; 30:1, 9; Jer 3:14, 19, 22; 4:22).

The NRSV understandably renders the Greek *huioi* ("sons") in 3:26 more inclusively as *children*, since in Greek a masculine title could be employed if even a single member of the group was male. But Paul has reason to employ the masculine Greek designation here, one that in fact places women and men on the same footing: insofar as sons were the chief heirs, in this context Paul stresses that all believers, regardless of gender or other divisions (3:28), are heirs (3:29b; cf. 1 Pet 3:7). Moreover, *huioi* here invites another connection: we also have the Spirit of God's Son (*huios*) within us; God's Son, Abraham's ultimate son (Gal 3:16), physically identified with our state to transform us inwardly into his state as *huioi* (4:4–7).

Paul uses the formula "in Christ" (Gal 3:26, 28) not only in this letter but frequently (it appears more than eighty times in the Pauline corpus). In this letter, Paul employs the formula "in Christ" for churches (1:22), freedom (2:4), justification (2:17), Abraham's blessing (3:14), being God's "sons" in *the* Son (3:26), and unity (3:28).

Baptism into Christ here (3:27) parallels faith in Christ in 3:26, as distinct but complementary elements of Christian conversion.[684] Many take Paul's language of baptism *into Christ* as signifying movement into the sphere of Christ from outside it (cf. 1 Cor 12:13).[685] Alternatively, it could simply signify baptism "with reference to" Christ,[686] different prepositions in the early Christian formulation simply reflecting different Greek ways to translate the underlying Semitic original.[687]

A Closer Look: Baptism's Meaning in Its Ancient Context[688]

Ritual lustrations were common throughout the ancient world, though first-century Christian sources lack the vocabulary typical of Greek purifications.[689] More relevant, evidence from Josephus, coins, and especially

[684] Longenecker, *Galatians*, 155.
[685] E.g., Moo, *Galatians*, 252; Das, *Galatians*, 381–82. In Koine Greek, *eis* did not necessarily convey movement, but Paul's usage is consistent.
[686] Cf. the possible or likely meaning of baptism *eis* as "with respect to" in Mark 1:4; Acts 2:38; 1 Cor 10:2.
[687] L. Hartman, "'Into the Name of Jesus,'" *NTS* 20 (4, 1974): 432–40, here 439–40; Hurtado, *Lord Jesus Christ*, 201–02. Possibly the phrase echoes one used in proselyte baptism (see I. Abrahams, *Studies in Pharisaism and the Gospels* [1st ser.; Cambridge: Cambridge University Press, 1917], 45). Samaritans allegedly circumcised "in the name of Mount Gerizim" (t. Abod. Zar. 3:13).
[688] Condensed from Keener, *Acts*, 977–82.
[689] Nock, "Vocabulary," 134.

archaeology attests the widespread pre-Christian practice of ritual washings in Judea.[690] Some count more than 300 immersion pools uncovered so far in Judea and Galilee.[691] The initial baptism at Qumran, like most other Jewish washings, was apparently viewed only as the first among many.[692] Among such washings, John's baptism was distinctive by being eschatological, in light of God's coming kingdom, and probably singular rather than repeated.[693]

Whereas such lustrations provide a general context, and John's baptism offers the most immediate antecedent and model, ancient hearers first encountering Christian baptism could understand its initiatory element precisely because immersion was often used for initiation when gentiles converted to Judaism. By definition, the only fully initiatory Jewish baptism – that is, as an act of conversion – was proselyte baptism. Although Christian baptism more closely resembles John's baptism, neither John's nor early Christian baptism arose *sui generis* (which could have rendered its symbolism unintelligible). Jewish initiatory purification of proselytes hardly borrowed the Christian practice, and their independent rise would seem too analogous for coincidence.

The conversion ritual provided a clear, symbolic line of demarcation between a proselyte's gentile past and Jewish present. Although Judaism employed circumcision as the primary sign of entering the covenant, both circumcision and baptism would have normally been required for new converts to Judaism.[694]

Evidence and arguments for pre-Christian proselyte baptism seem compelling:

(1) Most ancient initiations at least included ritual washing; Jewish ritual cleansing was widespread, and idolaters (as most gentiles were) were ritually impure before conversion.[695]

---

[690] See, e.g., Josephus *Ant.* 6.235; 18.19; R. L. Webb, *John the Baptizer and Prophet: A Socio-historical Study* (JSNTSup 62; Sheffield, UK: JSOT Press, 1991), 108–32.

[691] J. L. Reed, "Archaeological Contributions to the Study of Jesus and the Gospels," pages 40–54 in *The Historical Jesus in Context* (ed. A.-J. Levine, D. C. Allison Jr., and J. D. Crossan; Princeton, NJ: Princeton University Press, 2006), 52.

[692] See, e.g., Josephus *War* 2.150. Most commonalities between John and Qumran are also shared with the rest of Second Temple Judaism (J. E. Taylor, *The Immerser: John the Baptist within Second Temple Judaism* [Grand Rapids, MI: Eerdmans, 1997], 15–48).

[693] See Mark 1:4–5; 11:30; John 1:28; 3:23; Josephus *Ant.* 18.117.

[694] See, e.g., t. Abod. Zar. 3:11; b. Yeb. 46a–47b; Bamberger, *Proselytism*, 49–52.

[695] Cf. similarly K. Pusey, "Jewish Proselyte Baptism," *ExpT* 95 (4, 1984): 141–45.

(2) In the late first or early second century, even the gentile sage Epictetus takes for granted knowledge of Jewish proselyte baptism,[696] and other Diaspora sources attest it not long after.[697]

(3) Pharisees in the time of Jesus (the houses of Hillel and Shammai) apparently argued about proselyte baptism already in Jesus's era.[698]

(4) A Diaspora Jewish source possibly from the late first century takes for granted that even gentiles are aware of the Jewish custom of immersion in running water when turning from sins.[699]

(5) Second-century rabbis rarely acknowledged and even less often accepted Christian teachings; they surely would not have borrowed initiatory immersions from Christians, especially once Christians were widely using it.[700] Yale archaeologist Carl Kraeling long ago noted how a "sense of historical proportion" rendered impossible the view that Judaism took proselyte baptism from the Christians.[701]

Innovatively, John's baptism summoned Israelites to turn to God the same way Jewish people expected gentile proselytes to do. Like the Qumran sect, but with a more radical and public symbolism, John deemed only the true remnant of Israel prepared for the Lord (Matt 3:9//Luke 3:8). ****

Paul viewed baptism as not merely a demarcation and conversion but also as entrance into Christ's body, initiation into Christ's experience analogous to ancient Israel's initiation into the experience of redemption and the covenant (1 Cor 10:1–4).

Baptism relates to Paul's argument in Galatians precisely because, as in its antecedent Jewish form, it involves becoming part of God's people. A natural corollary of gentiles being impure was the need for them to be ritually purified when converting to become part of Israel. Gentiles converting to Judaism, thus becoming members of Israel, were circumcised (if male) and baptized. Paul rejects the need to circumcise gentiles, but Jesus's movement retained initiatory washing, an act with intelligible symbolism throughout the empire and especially in Judea. Unlike circumcision, washing posed no

---

[696] Epictetus *Diatr.* 2.9.20.

[697] Possibly Juvenal *Sat.* 14.104; see also Justin *Dial.* 29.1.

[698] See m. Pesah. 8:8; Abrahams, *Studies*¹, 37; Schiffman, "Crossroads," 128–31.

[699] Sib. Or. 4.162–65. The association of turning from sin (4.162–64), repentance (4.168–69) and washing in water (4.165) is significant.

[700] Cf. also H. H. Rowley, "Jewish Proselyte Baptism and the Baptism of John," *HUCA* 15 (1940): 313–34, here 313; R. E. O. White, *The Biblical Doctrine of Initiation* (Grand Rapids, MI: Eerdmans, 1960), 320; Schiffman, "Crossroads," 128; Cohen, *Maccabees to Mishnah*, 53.

[701] C. H. Kraeling, *John the Baptist* (New York: Scribner's, 1951), 99–100.

major physical barrier to conversion, although public identification with an often-despised sect exacted social costs.

Because Jesus's movement practiced it for Jew and gentile alike, it remained an appropriate line of demarcation, a public act of conversion also in Paul's work among gentiles. (By this I do not imply that the water itself saves, but that this was the initiatory rite by which believers demonstrated the crossing of boundaries into the church.) Unlike circumcision, baptism applied to women as well as men, pointing toward the non-differentiation of gender with respect to membership in God's people in Gal 3:28.

Most scholars view the baptism here as water baptism, but because early Christian tradition spoke of Spirit baptism as well (Mark 1:8; Matt 3:11// Luke 3:16; John 1:33; Acts 1:5; 11:16), some prefer that idea here,[702] as in the closest parallel text (1 Cor 12:13; cf. "clothed" in Gal 3:27). The matter is less than certain, but if Paul refers to Spirit baptism here, he is again framing the section with related ideas, alluding to their clear experience of the Spirit in Gal 3:2–5.

What does it mean to be clothed with Christ (3:27b)? Citing Gal 2:20, John Chrysostom explained, "He wants our soul to be a dwelling place for Christ, and Christ to surround us like a garment, so that Christ is all things for us, both inside and outside ourselves."[703] Some scholars associate the image with baptism, but this is the only Pauline passage that explicitly includes baptism in the immediate context of a figurative putting on, meaning that Paul rarely offers this "clue" to his meaning for "putting on."[704] Some note that a Roman boy would mark manhood by donning the *toga virilis*, but again the Pauline texts do not all associate "putting on" with maturation.[705]

More helpfully, a Greek idiom existed; one playing the role of Tarquinius could be said, figuratively, to don Tarquinius,[706] and one could put off the

---

[702] Dunn, *Galatians*, 203; Fee, *Presence*, 861–62; D. Hunn, "The Baptism of Galatians 3:27: A Contextual Approach," *ExpT* 115 (11, 2004): 372–75.

[703] Chrysostom *Homily* 24.1–3, on Rom 13:14 (Burns).

[704] Contrast Rom 13:12, 14; 1 Cor 15:53–54; Eph 4:24; 6:11, 14; Col 3:10, 12; 1 Thess 5:8. The apostolic fathers also speak of figuratively clothing oneself with virtues, and apparently not in a baptismal context (1 Clem. 30.3; Poly. *Phil.* 1.2; Hermas 20.2; 22.8; 26.2; 27.4; 34.8; 39.7, 10; 42.1, 4; 43.4; 44.1; 45.4; 61.2, 4; cf. 65.3; 75.1; 90.2).

[705] Doubting the connection, J. Bligh, *Galatians: A Discussion of St Paul's Epistle* (London: St Paul, 1970), 325. Affirming it, see J. A. Harrill, "Coming of Age and Putting on Christ: The *toga virilis* Ceremony, Its Paraenesis, and Paul's Interpretation of Baptism in Galatians," *NovT* 44 (3, 2002): 252–77; with an insightful anticolonial observation, D. C. Lopez, *Apostle to the Conquered: Reimagining Paul's Mission* (Minneapolis, MN: Fortress, 2008), 168.

[706] Burton, *Galatians*, 204, citing Dionysius of Halicarnassus *Ant. rom.* 11.5.2.

soldier and put on (i.e., act as) a sophist.[707] More importantly, Scripture had already long offered a figurative use of this image (Isa 52:1; 61:10; Zech 3:3–4). "Clothing oneself" with a quality was a Semitic idiom. Other Jewish sources also spoke of being "clothed" with qualities,[708] the Spirit,[709] or eschatological clothing (cf. 1 Cor 15:53).[710] Perhaps most likely here, being clothed with Christ may evoke being clothed with the divine Spirit in LXX Judg 6:34; 1 Chron 12:18; 2 Chron 24:20, again applying a divine image to Christ.

Paul's use of a unity formula is not unique to this passage (Gal 3:28; cf. 1 Cor 12:13; Col 3:11), but the examples in the formula here may be tailored for this passage. One possible reason for highlighting slave status and gender in Gal 3:28 (instead of the list in Col 3:11) is the question of inheritance (cf. Gal 3:29).[711] A slave's testament was not legally binding,[712] and children and friends were much more frequent heirs.[713]

Rules regarding women's inheritance varied geographically and culturally. Roman law generally allowed women to inherit.[714] Biblical law allowed daughters to inherit only if there were no sons (Num 27:8) and if they married within their clan (Num 36:6–9). But in classical Athens, if a man had a daughter but no sons, the daughter's sons inherited.[715] Most important, God promised an "inheritance" in the land to Israel, not to gentiles. Now, in Christ Jesus, all – Jew and Greek, slave and free, male and female – are heirs according to the promise (Gal 3:29). The real heirs are not those born of the flesh but those born according to the Spirit and promise (4:28–29).

More often proposed as a reason for highlighting slaves and gender here is the matter of circumcision.[716] Women could not be circumcised, and slaves had no personal say in being circumcised (Gen 17:12). Jewish teachers

---

[707] Burton, *Galatians*, 204, citing Libanius *Ep.* 968, though this source is considerably later.
[708] E.g., 4 Macc 6:2; Apoc. Mos. 20:1; 4 Ezra 3:26.
[709] L.A.B. 27:9–10; b. Meg. 14b.
[710] Ps. Sol. 11:7; 1 En. 62:15–16; 2 En. 22:8 (cf. 22:9–10).
[711] Special thanks for this insight to Esau McCaulley (Northeastern Seminary).
[712] Pliny *Ep.* 8.16.1. Slaves themselves could be inherited; see, e.g., P.S.I. 903 (AD 47); Quintilian *Decl.* 311.7.
[713] In Judea, see C. Hezser, "The Impact of Household Slaves on the Jewish Family in Roman Palestine," *JSJ* 34 (4, 2003): 375–424, here 412.
[714] A. L. Bean, "Inheritance," 3:33–41 in *Dictionary of Daily Life in Biblical and Post-biblical Antiquity* (4 vols.; ed. E. M. Yamauchi and M. R. Wilson; Peabody, MA: Hendrickson, 2016), 39.
[715] D. M. MacDowell, "Inheritance: Greek," 757–58 in *OCD*[3], 757.
[716] T. W. Martin, "The Covenant of Circumcision (Genesis 17:9–14) and the Situational Antitheses in Galatians 3:28," *JBL* 122 (1, 2003): 111–25; Fee, *Galatians*, 141; Barclay, *Gift*, 396; Das, *Galatians*, 383.

regarded women, slaves, and minors as exempt from many biblical commandments,[717] though Jewish women were superior to gentiles.[718]

Many scholars point to a Jewish benediction attributed to a late second-century rabbi: "A man must recite three benedictions every day: 'Praised [be Thou, O Lord …] who did not make me a gentile'; 'Praised [be Thou, O Lord …] who did not make me a boor' (an ignorant person); 'Praised [be Thou, O Lord …] who did not make me a woman.'" His explanation for the woman is that she is exempted from some of the commandments.[719]

Whether such a Jewish prayer existed in the first century, and how many Galatians (unlike Paul) would have been familiar with it had it existed, is unclear, but this benediction rests on an earlier Greek saying, wherein a famous sage thanked Fortune "that I was born a human being and not one of the brutes; next, that I was born a man and not a woman; thirdly, a Greek and not a barbarian."[720] The setting and application differ,[721] but such sayings at least illustrate the sort of ideas that Paul's claim may address.[722]

Scripture itself could inform Paul's formulation or at least his thinking: Joel 2:28–29 (MT/LXX 3:1–2) announced the Lord pouring out his Spirit on all humanity,[723] on both male and female, on all ages, and on slaves (presumably as well as free). Paul apparently echoes this verse elsewhere (Rom 5:5). If this background informs Paul's thought in Gal 3:28, it recalls his appeal to gentiles' experience of the Spirit (3:2–5, 14). (To whatever extent that passage informed Paul's thinking, however, his audience might not infer it.)

Many philosophers valued the virtue of being a world citizen rather than emphasizing ethnic or civic particularities.[724] Regarding locality of birth as an accidental characteristic, Stoics appealed to Socrates's admonition "never to say 'I am an Athenian,' or 'I am a Corinthian,' but 'I am a citizen of the

717 E.g., m. Ber. 3:3; Hag. 1:1; Suk. 2:8; cf. "men" in Josephus *War* 2.515. In Sipre Num. 39.6.1, they and proselytes did not belong to "Israel" proper. They were likewise excluded from the temple's court of Israel (Josephus *War* 5.198–99).
718 E.g., m. Naz. 9:1.
719 T. Ber. 6:18 (trans. Neusner; 7:18 in other versions).
720 Diogenes Laertius 1.33 (trans. R. D. Hicks, LCL 1:35); cf. Plutarch *Marius* 46.1.
721 G. N. Uzukwu, "The Problem with the Three Expressions of Gratitude Found in Greek Writings and Their Alleged Relationship to Gal 3:28," *CNS* 31 (3, 2010): 927–44.
722 Cf. Philo *Spec. Laws* 1.211.
723 Lit., *all flesh*; in Acts 2:17 Luke (although not Peter within the narrative) applies this to all peoples (cf. Luke 3:6).
724 Seneca Y. *Ep. Lucil.* 28.4; Musonius Rufus 9, p. 68.15–16, 21–22; Epictetus *Diatr.* 2.10.3; Maximus of Tyre 36.3; Marcus Aurelius 10.15; 12.36; Diogenes Laertius 2.99; Philostratus *Ep. Apoll.* 44; Philo *Creation* 142; *Spec. Laws* 2.45; *Cont.* 90.

universe.' "[725] Likewise, social class was a mere accident of birth, with true, heavenly wisdom available to all.[726] Paul's primary motivation, however, is an eschatological vision of unity in Christ (see Isa 2:2–4; 19:24–25; 56:3–8; Zech 2:11). Paul is thus posing not an elimination of ethnic differences but a unity that encompasses diversity, as in his treatment of diverse gifts in the body in Rom 12:4–8 and 1 Cor 12:4–30 (cf. also Rom 14).

Paul joins the first two pairs with *or* but the third pair, *male and female*, with *and* (3:28). Instead of his usual wording for men and women, Paul here uses the precise terminology for *male and female* that appears in the creation narrative. Most commentators thus suspect an allusion to Gen 1:27 here; the three-word phrase together quotes exactly the phrase in Genesis. Paul envisions a restoration of the primeval unity of male and female that flourished before the judgment of Gen 3:16, as part of the new creation (Gal 6:15).[727] He undoubtedly presupposes Christ as the new Adam (1 Cor 15:45), although he does not articulate this premise for his Galatian audience.

Some find here an allusion to primeval androgyny, a prototype of the new creation.[728] Some Jewish thought understood the original Adam as a hermaphrodite before Eve was taken from him.[729] Paul's interest, however, is not a return to the putative androgyny of the old creation, but the transcendent status of a new creation.[730] His allusion to Gen 1:27 does not indicate whether Paul shared the common contemporary understanding of that passage in terms of primal androgyny. What Paul is clearly *not* doing is speaking of women's advancement in terms of them becoming masculine, a familiar idea among some ancient thinkers.[731] Indeed, if anything, believers' unity with Christ depicts us as feminine (cf. 1 Cor 6:16; Eph 5:30–32).

Because the adjective "one" in *all of you are one in Christ Jesus* is masculine, the likeliest assumed predicate nominative is "one person" (*anthrôpos*),[732] as

---

[725]   Epictetus *Diatr.* 1.9.1 (trans. W. A. Oldfather, LCL 1:63).

[726]   Seneca *Ep. Lucil.* 32.11; 44.1–2.

[727]   With K. Giles, *Created Woman: A Fresh Study of the Biblical Teaching* (Canberra: Acorn, 1985), 29; Martyn, *Galatians*, 377, 381; Moo, *Galatians*, 254.

[728]   Hippolytus *Ref.* 5.2 shows the extent to which Naassene gnostics later took this premise.

[729]   See Philo *Creation* 76, 134; D. Daube, "The Gospels and the Rabbis," *Listener* 56 (6, 1956): 342–46, here 343, 346; Daube, *New Testament and Judaism*, 72.

[730]   Paul may shift to neuter to follow the language of Gen 1:27; seventeen of the thirty-four LXX uses of *thêlus* ("female") are neuter; sixteen are feminine; and one (2 Macc 7:21) is masculine; thirty-three of the LXX uses of *arsên* ("male") are neuter; sixteen are masculine; and one is feminine.

[731]   As in Philo *Embassy* 320 (see more extensively R. A. Baer Jr., *Philo's Use of the Categories Male and Female* [ALGHJ 3; Leiden: Brill, 1970]); Gospel of Thomas 114.

[732]   With R. Y. K. Fung, *The Epistle to the Galatians* (NICNT; Grand Rapids, MI: Eerdmans, 1988), 176; de Boer, Galatians, 244; Moo, *Galatians*, 254.

in the "one new humanity" of Eph 2:15. On this line Chrysostom remarks, "you have one form, one character, that of Christ … The former Jew or slave is clothed in the form … of the Lord himself and in himself displays Christ" (cf. Gal 2:20).[733]

Paul's *one in Christ Jesus* here resembles "one body in Christ" in Rom 12:5. Unlike "person" (*anthrôpos*), "body" is neuter. But his body metaphor elsewhere does suggest the level of unity envisioned; although Paul presumably borrows the "body" language from popular political and philosophic discourse,[734] he uses it in a more organic way that may resemble Stoic usage also for the cosmos. Given the probable allusion to the original creation in "male and female," he probably envisions a restoration of God's ideal in terms of being one in the new Adam, Christ (Rom 5:15–21; 1 Cor 15:22, 45–49; cf. Eph 4:22–24; Phil 2:6; esp. Col 3:10–11).

Paul's ideal could challenge Greco-Roman culture, with its emphasis on social classification and stratification. Certainly dismantling division between Jews and Greeks challenged a live issue of his day, one sometimes carried to the point of genocide.[735] The division between slave and free was considered a fundamental division in society.[736] Free persons, for example, did not eat with slaves.[737] Without seeking to overthrow the social order, Paul at times challenged social stratification.

Bridging the Horizons: Unity and/or Equality in Principle Only or Also in Practice?

A declaration such as "neither slave nor free" would have sounded like nonsense to a slave society such as the Roman empire where such divisions lay on the surface.[738] Differences between male and female were even more pronounced, not only in roles but also, conspicuously, in apparel.[739] As no one

733 Chrysostom *Hom. Gal.* 3.28 (Edwards).
734 Hierocles *Siblings* (Stobaeus *Anth.* 4.84.20); Aristotle *Pol.* 1.1.11, 1253a; Dionysius of Halicarnassus *Ant. rom.* 6.83.2–6.86.5; Sallust *Ep. Caes.* 10.6; Cicero *Resp.* 3.25.37; Livy 2.32.9–12; Dio Cassius 4.17.10–13.
735 See, e.g., Josephus *War* 2.305–08, 457, 466–68, 478, 497–98; 7.368.
736 See, e.g., Cicero *Inv.* 1.25.35; Seneca *Ep. Lucil.* 47.2–3; Gaius *Inst.* 1.9–10; Justinian *Inst.* 1.3–4.
737 See, e.g., Seneca *Ep. Lucil.* 47.2–5 (who complains about this separation).
738 J. S. Jeffers, *The Greco-Roman World of the New Testament Era: Exploring the Background of Early Christianity* (Downers Grove, IL: InterVarsity, 1999), 235, noting Christian impetus in abolition (235–36).
739 See, e.g., A. T. Croom, *Roman Clothing and Fashion* (Charleston, SC: Tempus, 2000); B. Cosgrave, *The Complete History of Costume and Fashion from Ancient Egypt to the Present Day* (New York: Checkmark, 2000).

suggests that Paul explicitly advocated a unisex clothing style, it seems clear that Paul was not seeking to eradicate all gender difference in his world. In what sense, then, did he intend "male and female"?

Augustine suggested that "Difference of race or condition or sex is indeed taken away by the unity of faith, but it remains embedded in our mortal interactions ... within the orders of this life they persist. So we walk this path in a way that the name and doctrine of God will not be blasphemed."[740] Citing Gal 3:28, Chrysostom argued that virtue could be the same in either gender.[741] Praising the ministry of other women in Rom 16, he contends that 1 Tim 2 prohibited women not from all teaching, but only a presiding position in the altar area.[742] Chrysostom did not press Gal 3:28 in all spheres, but did use it to urge the freeing of slaves.[743]

Until the Civil War in the United States, interpreters usually applied Gal 3:28 only to salvation in Christ, but in its wake the Holiness movement adopted the text in support of social liberation for women. Continuing the abolitionist hermeneutic, Holiness interpreters pressed the principles of the text against a more traditional proof-texting approach.[744]

Today scholars continue to debate whether Gal 3:28 has, or at least whether Paul intended it to have, implications for Christian life beyond salvation. Paul's primary concerns lie elsewhere; this age is passing (1 Cor 7:31), so such matters are temporary anyway.[745] Some contend that the verse addresses only salvation, making it compatible with Pauline household codes described elsewhere.

Others contend that texts about women ministering (Rom 16:1–7; Phil 4:2–3) and prophesying (1 Cor 11:5) reveal Paul's genuine sentiments and that more restrictive passages in the Pauline corpus must be interpreted in light of their particular situations and this broader egalitarian principle.

From 1 Corinthians, it does appear that Paul was willing to live with some social conventions so long as the gospel was promoted. Paul does not try to

---

[740] Augustine *Ep. Gal.* 28 (1B.3.28–29; Edwards).
[741] Chrysostom *Homily* 30.2–3, on Rom 16:3–5 (Burns; Bray).
[742] Chrysostom *Homily* 31.1–2, on Rom 16:6 (Burns).
[743] Longenecker, *Galatians*, li.
[744] See here S. J. Lennox, "'One in Christ': Galatians 3:28 and the Holiness Agenda," *EvQ* 84 (3, 2012): 195–212. For abolitionists' preference for principles, see G. J. Usry and C. S. Keener, *Black Man's Religion: Can Christianity Be Afrocentric?* (Downers Grove, IL: InterVarsity, 1996), 100–09, 187–88n234.
[745] Das, *Galatians*, 387n276, cites approvingly to this effect S. Briggs, "Slavery and Gender," pages 171–92 in *On the Cutting Edge: The Study of Women in Biblical Worlds: Essays in Honor of Elisabeth Schüssler Fiorenza* (ed. J. Schaberg, A. Bach, and E. Fuchs; New York: Continuum, 2004), 186.

eliminate culturally established marks of gender distinction such as women's head coverings in the relevant spheres. Jew and gentile, slave and free remain distinct socially in this age although one in Christ, and the same may be assumed for men and women.

Still, Paul appreciates the value of manumission (1 Cor 7:21; Phlm 13–14), a frequent practice; like Stoics, he may have recommended being content with one's state but welcoming a more beneficial state if it becomes possible.[746] Paul might feel that the creational distinctives he recognizes in 1 Cor 11:7 entail head coverings in his context (11:2–16). Nevertheless, the new creation has reintroduced a level of mutuality (cf. 1 Cor 11:8–9) that recalls the original creation of male and female together as one, reigning in God's image (Gen 1:26–27). Contexts might limit how this principle would be addressed (e.g., they might invite continuing the conventional cultural practice of head coverings),[747] but the principle did challenge existing prejudices. As one conservative Reformed commentator notes, Paul's approach to gender roles was as controversial in his day as in our own, but "for exactly the opposite reason."[748]

One can hardly say that Gal 3:28 addresses "only" salvation as if salvation itself lacks transformative implications for relationships. One cannot fully isolate Gal 3:28 from relevance to social contexts since social conflict informs the entire letter. The already side of the already/not yet tension of the kingdom did impact social relationships between Jews and gentiles (Gal 2:11–14) and slave and free (Phlm 16), so we can expect it to impact mutual respect within marriage as well.[749]

Paul may have accepted most social norms for their strategic value,[750] yet valued principles that could be expressed in different ways in different

---

[746] Cf. Marcus Aurelius 4.25; 5.27.

[747] For the cultural setting, see, e.g., C. S. Keener, "Head Coverings," *DNTB* 442–47; Keener, *Paul, Women, and Wives: Marriage and Women's Ministry in the Letters of Paul* (Grand Rapids, MI: Baker Academic, 1992), 22–31.

[748] P. G. Ryken, *Galatians* (Reformed Expository Commentary; Phillipsburg, NJ: P&R Publishing, 2005), 152.

[749] Cf. Eph 5:21; 6:9; S. D. Lowe, "Rethinking the Female Status/Function Question: The Jew/Gentile Relationship as Paradigm," *JETS* 34 (1, 1991): 59–75; M. Mikhael, "St. Paul and the Place of Women in the Church," *NETR* 23 (2, 2002): 125–42; B. Roberts Gaventa, "The Singularity of the Gospel Revisited," pages 187–99 in *Galatians and Christian Theology: Justification, the Gospel, and Ethics in Paul's Letter* (ed. M. W. Elliott et al.; Grand Rapids, MI: Baker Academic, 2014), 196.

[750] Cf. 1 Tim 5:14–15; 6:1; Tit 2:5, 8, 10; A. Padgett, "The Pauline Rationale for Submission: Biblical Feminism and the hina Clauses of Titus 2:1–10," *EvQ* 59 (1, 1987): 39–52.

settings. Indeed, more than equality he probably valued humbling oneself and voluntarily serving others (5:13; Rom 12:10, 16; 1 Cor 4:9–13; 2 Cor 4:5), regardless of gender. Some thus see this passage as Paul's transcultural principle in light of which his contextually oriented applications in other passages must be understood.[751]

Even when men affirmed equality in principle, this affirmation did not always translate into egalitarian practice. As early Stoicism became mainstream, for example, it quickly lost its original egalitarian ideals,[752] though some of the ideal remained.[753]

Teachings of equality in principle did not therefore automatically lead to egalitarian practice, although all these sects were more progressive than many of their contemporaries. By itself, Gal 3:28 does not tell us how Paul implemented this principle in particular kinds of situations; for that, we must turn to his other letters (e.g., Rom 16:1–7; Eph 5:21–33; Phil 4:3). Paul stood on the more progressive side of these matters in his era, but wrote in a context that suspected minority cults of undermining conventional family values. Paul accommodated these concerns, but had he been contextualizing instead for the usual Western context today, I have argued elsewhere, he would have supported women's full and equal participation in the Christian community.[754] ****

Gal 3:29 caps off this part of Paul's argument, and with 3:7 provides an *inclusio* that frames the section. Since Christ is Abraham's ultimate seed (3:16), those who are Christ's also belong to Abraham. (The term for offspring here, *sperma*, is the same term used elsewhere in Galatians only at 3:16, 19, in both verses for Christ.) Through Christ, gentile believers become children of Abraham by faith, as in 3:7.

Paul describes converts the way other Jews, and probably his opponents, described proselytes.[755] Gentiles in Christ can become part of Abraham's covenant spiritually without becoming ethnically or culturally Jewish.

---

[751] W. H. Leslie, "The Concept of Woman in the Pauline Corpus in Light of the Social and Religious Environment of the First Century" (PhD diss., Northwestern University, 1976), 28, 49.

[752] A. Erskine, *The Hellenistic Stoa: Political Thought and Action* (Ithaca, NY: Cornell University Press, 1990), 149, 181; Engberg-Pedersen, *Paul and Stoics*, 77; D. L. Balch, *Let Wives Be Submissive: The Domestic Code in 1 Peter* (SBLMS 26; Chico, CA: Scholars Press, 1981), 143–49.

[753] Cf. the tension in Musonius Rufus 3, 38.26–27; 3, 40.6–7; 4, 46.31–48.26.

[754] Keener, *Paul, Women & Wives*, vi–ix, 139–224; for the range of approaches to gender in Paul's era, see discussion in Keener, *Acts*, 605–37.

[755] Cf. Donaldson, "Convert," 81–82.

Paul's inheritance language (3:18, 29; 4:1, 7, 30; 5:12) naturally clusters in the section where his sonship language appears (3:7, 16, 19, 26, 29; 4:4–7, 22, 28, 30–31). Since the Galatian believers *belong to Christ*, they are *heirs according to the promise*. Since the Spirit is the fullest present embodiment of the promise (3:14), and they have received the Spirit (3:2, 5), they already have the benefit that Paul's opponents purport to provide through circumcision. Nothing can be added to Christ's finished work to finish it further; we can only activate by faith and in experience what Christ has already provided.

4:1–7: A MORE MATURE ERA IN CHRIST

4:1 My point is this: heirs, as long as they are minors, are no better than slaves, though they are the owners of all the property;

4:2 but they remain under guardians and trustees until the date set by the father.

4:3 So with us; while we were minors, we were enslaved to the elemental spirits of the world.

4:4 But when the fullness of time had come, God sent his Son, born of a woman, born under the law,

4:5 in order to redeem those who were under the law, so that we might receive adoption as children.

4:6 And because you are children, God has sent the Spirit of his Son into our hearts, crying, "Abba! Father!"

4:7 So you are no longer a slave but a child, and if a child then also an heir, through God.

This new paragraph (4:1–7) continues to develop the thought that precedes. The preceding context explains that before Christ and the way of faith came, the law was a pedagogue to keep its subjects in line (3:23–24). Thus even God's own people, his children, were under the authority of a slave guardian (pedagogues usually being slaves). Now that Christ has come as Abraham's ultimate offspring, however (3:16), whoever is in him is a child of God and an heir (3:26–29), no longer under this slave guardian (3:25).

Paul here reiterates the preceding point more explicitly: insofar as they were under a slave guardian, in practice the heirs were no better off than slaves (4:1). They remained under elementary teachings, the law being merely a pedagogue and not a full teacher (4:3). But the promised offspring Christ (3:16), God's Son, redeemed us from that domain (4:4), to give us adoption as children (4:5). Although Israel was already God's child (e.g., Exod 4:22; Deut 32:43; Jer 31:20), it was a subject, minor child; and under the law, gentiles were normally not God's children at all.

The proof that God adopts even gentile believers (Gal 4:5) is their experience of the Spirit (4:6; cf. 3:1–5, 14). Thus they are, as Paul already emphasized in 3:29, heirs (4:7).

The problem with the metaphor so far, of course, is that the Galatian gentiles had not knowingly been under the law before. The written law excluded them, but it did not rule them. So Paul shows that their pagan past (4:8) was slavery comparable to being under the law (4:9–10; cf. 4:3) – a shocking comparison for those who regarded law observance as far better than paganism! Yet Paul argues that turning to the law was like going back to paganism (4:9), in that they were relinquishing their position as heirs in Christ for something that was designed only for the former era, not the present.

Again, as noted before, Paul's polemical approach here should not be used to neglect what he says elsewhere. The law is holy, just, and good (Rom 7:12), inspired by the Spirit (7:14). It remains useful for moral instruction (13:8–10; 1 Cor 9:8–9; cf. 1 Tim 1:8–10), condemns much of what is wrong (Rom 3:20; 4:15; 7:7; cf. 1 Tim 1:9–10), and remains the valuable possession of the Jewish people (Rom 3:2). But it was meant to point toward Christ and the need for Christ (Rom 3:19, 21, 31) and could never supplant the fuller revelation and ultimate salvation in Christ (Gal 2:21; 3:21–22).

The theme of sons as heirs frames the paragraph (4:1, 7). The minor child is heir and *owner of all* (4:1),[756] yet could not access this owned property until he achieved maturity,[757] which did not precede puberty. Although not all cultures agreed, in economic terms Roman law treated children as their fathers' slaves, with the father owning the property "until the children have obtained their freedom like bought slaves."[758]

Guardians and trustees (4:2) were typically of higher status than *pedagogues*,[759] but the image maintains the youth being under authority in any

---

[756] Cf. "heir of everything" (P. Ryl. 2.153.15, 41, 42; Das, *Galatians*, 142).
[757] Although Paul normally relegates full possession to the future resurrection (Rom 8:32; 1 Cor 15:50; cf. Gal 5:21), he envisions maturity here as the first coming of Christ (Gal 3:24), whereupon the heirs receive the Spirit, the down payment of their future inheritance (Gal 3:14; 5:5; cf. 2 Cor 5:1, 5).
[758] Sextus Empiricus *Pyr.* 3.211 (trans. R. G. Bury, LCL 1:469).
[759] The guardian, often a friend of the father, was often also higher than the trustee, who was often a slave, though some used such terms interchangeably. A child might need both guardians and pedagogues (Philo *Embassy* 26–27).

case. Paul presents nature's divisions of time (4:8–10) and, for Israel, the law (4:3–4), as such guardians; full maturity and freedom would come only in Christ.

Greek and Roman wills (cf. 3:15) often named a guardian or guardians to govern the child in case of the father's decease. *Guardians* here reflects the Greek term *epitropos*; such a guardian would control the estate and from it provide for the child until the child came to maturity.[760]

The term translated *trustees* normally designates household managers, who were sometimes slaves or freedpersons.[761] Such household managers were not normally designated in charge of the youth, but they did run the estate to which the youth was heir.

How do such images relate to the image of the pedagogue (3:24–25)? In at least one case, a pedagogue became a guardian after the father's death.[762] More pervasively, some used *epitropos* mostly interchangeably with *paidagôgos* (treated in 3:24–25).[763] Paul apparently does recognize the difference, given his accurate legal language here, but his point in any case remains that the youth remains subject to others.

Until the date set by the father reflects legal language attested elsewhere. The *date* was most commonly a legal term (*prothesmia*) for an appointed day after which proceedings were disallowed. The laws best known to us from antiquity fixed the time directly rather than the father fixing it, except perhaps for special, temporary guardianships.[764] Here the time appointed by the father, however, may mean simply the time of majority, of being an adult.

What is most important for understanding the passage is the point Paul seeks to make, since in this context God *does* set the time of majority (Gal 4:4). In any case, until the specified time, the child under his father's authority does not inherit: "Someone in our power can have nothing of his own. And so where he is instituted heir he cannot accept the inheritance except when we tell him to do so."[765]

---

[760]   Dio Chrysostom *Or.* 31.73; Young, "PAIDAGOGOS: Setting," 155.
[761]   Note slave stewards in Chariton *Chaer.* 3.7.1; Quintilian *Decl.* 353; 388 intro; Ps.-Lucian *Affairs* 10; freedpersons in Tacitus *Hist.* 1.49; Josephus *Ant.* 18.194; S. Treggiari, "Jobs in the Household of Livia," *PBSR* 43 (1975): 48–77, here 49. See here Trick, *Descent*, 156–57; esp. the abundant sources in J. K. Goodrich, "Guardians, Not Taskmasters: The Cultural Resonances of Paul's Metaphor in Galatians 4.1–2," *JSNT* 32 (3, 2010): 251–84, here 275–78. Galatia was very familiar with estate managers (see Goodrich, "Guardians," 268).
[762]   Young, "PAIDAGOGOS: Setting," 156.
[763]   Young, "PAIDAGOGOS: Setting," 155–56.
[764]   Burton, *Galatians*, 212–14.
[765]   Gaius *Inst.* 2.87 (trans. W. M. Gordon and O. F. Robinson, LCL, 162–63).

Paul varies pronouns less precisely in this context, perhaps to include his gentile audience in the Jewish privilege of God's people, before turning exclusively to his audience in 4:8–10.

A more lively debate concerns the meaning of Paul's term *stoicheia* (4:3, 9), which the NRSV interpretively renders *elemental spirits*.[766] Most scholars agree that Paul compares the law to *stoicheia* in 4:3 as well as paganism in 4:8–10, but they diverge fairly widely on how Paul uses the phrase *elemental spirits of the world*. Following are four major categories of views:

1. Basic components, such as fundamental principles of learning
2. Basic elements of nature/creation, such as earth, air, water, and fire
3. Heavenly bodies
4. Spirit beings worshiped as deities

Despite this basic fourfold division of views, representatives of such positions overlap considerably. Avoiding overlap is difficult, particularly since even Diaspora Jews thought that gentiles worshiped elements and stars (Wis 13:2–3) and many gentiles did regard as divine celestial bodies.

Such a range of interpretive options is not new. Jerome listed views circulating in his day as including "angels that preside over the four elements"; celestial bodies worshiped by the pagans; and such elementary teachings as the law and the prophets.[767]

1 Fundamental Principles of Learning

The term *stoicheia* was used for letters of the alphabet and thus for rudimentary knowledge about a topic. Just as Paul could insult the Galatians as foolish (Gal 3:1), philosophers could criticize others for their lack of basic understanding, expressed in terms of alphabetic letters.[768]

This association with rudimentary knowledge could prefigure Paul's allegorical treatment of Hagar and Sarah, since Philo, the most widely known Diaspora Jewish intellectual of his era, allegorized Hagar as elementary, sensory knowledge but Sarah as advanced education.[769] Some philosophically minded pagans compared deity images to elementary teachers sketching

---

[766] Cf. KJV: "elements"; ASV: "rudiments"; NASB: "elemental things"; ESV: "elementary principles"; NET: "basic forces"; NIV: "elemental spiritual forces."

[767] Jerome *Ep. Gal.* 2.4.3 (Edwards).

[768] Heraclitus *Ep.* 4; Seneca *Ep. Lucil.* 48.11; cf. first rudiments in Epictetus *Diatr.* 3.2.10.

[769] See comment at Gal 4:22–24.

letters so their pupils could trace over them,[770] an approach that would fit Gal 4:8–10.

Many older modern commentators, as well as some contemporary ones, prefer this background for *stoicheia* here. Pagans had merely elementary knowledge about deity from nature, such as seasonal cycles (Gal 4:8–10, esp. verse 10), and the law was elementary compared to the revelation of Christ and the living experience of the Spirit (4:3–6). This image fits the immature minor status of those under the law. Jerome seemed to lean toward this view, the law and prophets being like "the initial and early stages of our studies."[771] It was the law as understood "according to the letter."[772]

This view thus fits perfectly the context of both references in Gal 4 as well as the references in Col 2:8, 20, without the need for further speculation. What it does not fit, by itself, is the usual use of the entire phrase *elemental spirits of the world*. At the least, this position requires an adjustment to say that Paul refers here to something *more* elemental than the alphabet: the basics of the cosmos/life itself. In this case, *the world* can refer to the earthly existence to which Paul has been crucified (Gal 6:14), including material, law matters such as circumcision (6:15a), because Paul's focus is now the new creation (6:15b).

2 Elements of Nature

Surveying a wide range of evidence, recent research demonstrates that while *stoicheia* by itself may fit any of the proposals, the expression found in Paul, *stoicheia tou kosmou*, "elements of the world," virtually always indicates the basic elements of nature. Most Greeks came to envision four basic elements of nature as: air, fire, earth, and water.[773] Commentators today often regard this lexical conclusion as "really the only one possible."[774]

---

[770] Maximus of Tyre *Or.* 2.2.

[771] O. O'Donovan, "Flesh and Spirit," pages 271–84 in *Galatians and Christian Theology: Justification, the Gospel, and Ethics in Paul's Letter* (ed. M. W. Elliott et al.; Grand Rapids, MI: Baker Academic, 2014), 281, who notes that Jerome nevertheless allows for the nature veneration interpretation.

[772] Jerome *Ep. Gal.* 2.4.8–9 (Edwards).

[773] See, e.g., Vitruvius *Arch.* 8. preface 1; Epictetus *Diatr.* 3.13.14; Diogenes Laertius 8.2.76.

[774] M. C. de Boer, "The Meaning of the Phrase τά στοιχεῖα τοῦ κοσμοῦ in Galatians," *NTS* 53 (2007): 204–24, here 207; cf. also de Boer, *Galatians*, 253.

But while de Boer concludes that this is the obvious lexical meaning, he warns that it "is not adequate to the argumentative context in which Paul makes use of the phrase."[775] Most scholars who settle on the view that the term refers to the four elements do allow that these elements are themselves somehow venerated, an often complementary position revisited later in view 4. Augustine thought that Paul referred to gentiles worshiping the physical elements.[776] De Boer himself contends that it refers to a religion based on nature that involved calendrical observances (summarized by the metonymy *stoicheia*, referring to nature's four elements), like those in the law (see Gal 4:10).[777]

3 Heavenly Bodies

These elements are associated with days and seasons and years (Gal 4:10), which in turn can be associated with heavenly lights that determine these (Gen 1:14). Given these associations, some scholars have argued that Paul refers here to heavenly bodies that pagans thought influenced the earth astrologically.

Astrology was widespread, including among Judeans and Galileans. By Paul's day a widely circulated Diaspora Jewish treatise viewed knowledge of the elements, seasons, and so forth as part of having wisdom.[778]

For what it is worth, Paul describes heavenly bodies differently in 1 Cor 15:40–41. More important, the language he uses here is not attested as applied to heavenly bodies until roughly a century after Paul, and could ultimately depend on him.[779] Most important, as noted earlier, "elements of the world" appear to have always referred to the four elements of nature. Still, one could take those four elements as metonymy for calendrical observances dependent on nature (cf. Gal 4:10).[780] Early church fathers often link the *stoicheia* with heavenly bodies.[781] The early commentator Ambrosiaster thought Paul meant new moons and the sabbath.[782] One could also associate them with deities (cf. Gal 4:8).

---

775 De Boer, "Meaning," 208; cf. de Boer, *Galatians*, 253, 256.
776 Lightfoot, *Galatians*, 167.
777 De Boer, "Meaning," 216–17, 220–21; de Boer, *Galatians*, 254.
778 Wis 7:17–21. By the third century some Jewish circles spoke of *stoicheia* as rulers associated with the degrees of the zodiac (T. Sol. 8:2, 4; 18 passim).
779 W. Carr, *Angels and Principalities* (Cambridge: Cambridge University Press, 1981), 74.
780 So again de Boer, "Meaning," 220–21.
781 Lightfoot, *Galatians*, 167.
782 Ambrosiaster *Ep. Gal.* 4.3.

4 Spirits Worshiped as Deities

The *stoicheia* to which the Galatians were *enslaved* (4:3) were or included the non-gods of 4:8, to which the Galatians risk becoming enslaved again (4:9) as their acceptance of Jewish regulations includes special religious days (4:10).

Even though *stoicheia* are attested as astral spirits and other spirits or deities only after the first century, many have found appealing the view that these are personified cosmic powers[783] or deities associated with the elements.[784] Certainly Paul did believe in angelic powers in the heavens, as shown in different terminology in other undisputed (Rom 8:38) and disputed but certainly early (Eph 1:21; 3:10; 6:12; Col 1:16; 2:15) Pauline texts. Paul also describes such gods as demons (1 Cor 10:20), so a case can surely be made for understanding Gal 4:8 thus (see comment there) and for linking *stoicheia* (4:9) with these entities.[785]

Paul may have known the Wisdom of Solomon, a hellenistic Jewish work that claimed that pagans considered fire, wind, and water (three of the four "elements"), as well as stars, to be gods (Wis 13:2). Philo similarly complains about "those who venerate the elements [*stoicheia*]: earth, water, air, and fire," under the names of deities such as Poseidon and Demeter.[786]

Although these are Diaspora Jewish stereotypes of gentiles rather than gentiles' reports of their own beliefs, they were not without foundation. Herodotus claimed that the Persians sacrificed "to the sun and the moon, and to earth, fire, water, and the winds."[787] Some spoke of sun, moon, and stars as the "visible" gods;[788] many gentiles regarded stars as divine beings.[789] People widely worshiped and invoked personified aspects of the cosmos of deities.[790]

---

[783] See, e.g., H. Schlier, *Der Brief an die Galater* (5th edn.; KEK; Göttingen: Vandenhoeck & Ruprecht, 1971), 191; O. Cullmann, *The State in the New Testament* (New York: Scribner's, 1956), 108.

[784] G. C. H. MacGregor, "Principalities and Powers: The Cosmic Background of Paul's Thought," *NTS* 1 (1, September 1954): 17–28, here 21.

[785] Neil, *Galatians*, 63–64; see esp. C. E. Arnold, "Returning to the Domain of the Powers: Stoicheia as Evil Spirits in Galatians 4:3,9," *NovT* 38 (1, 1996): 55–76, here 70.

[786] Philo *Cont.* 3; cf. Diogenes Laertius 7.1.147. Likewise, though without using the terminology of *stoicheia*, "some have deified the four first principles: earth and water and air and fire," while others have done this with the celestial bodies and still others the entire world (*kosmon*; *Decal.* 53, cited by, e.g., deSilva, *Readings*, 199).

[787] Herodotus 1.131 (trans. Waterfield).

[788] Apuleius *De deo Socr.* 116–20, 128.

[789] E.g., Cicero *Nat. d.* 2.15.39–40; *Resp.* 6.15.15; Seneca *Ben.* 4.23.4; Iamblichus *Myst.* 1.17, 19; condemnation of this view in 1 En. 80:7–8.

[790] J. B. Rives, *Religion in the Roman Empire* (Oxford: Blackwell, 2007), 16.

Before their conversion, Galatians would have venerated such elements no less than did others. The interior of Asia Minor was especially known for its worship of the Earth Mother.[791] She was often depicted as a strict guardian of justice.[792] Paul's emphasis on the heavenly mother of believers (Gal 4:26) was not unique to him or to correspondence with Galatians but could be formulated and emphasized here to counter such a belief.

Jewish tradition recognized angels over various features of nature, making the idea of spirits of the elements of nature here quite plausible;[793] angels could also be identified with the host of heaven, the stars.[794] At some point after the first century, language similar to *stoicheia* came to be applied to such angels.[795] Some Jewish circles understood all the world as lying under the power of the evil one.[796]

Which of the four approaches is most relevant to Gal 4? Purely textually, I would favor the first approach; lexically, I would naturally favor the second approach as it has been developed into the third or especially fourth approach. Cumulatively, the textual and lexical evidence currently available both seem strong enough that it is difficult to force a choice here.

It is possible, however, that we are mixing apples and oranges by contrasting all these approaches, and that some or all of these senses may be reconciled by Paul's usage. Under what rubric could the Torah and the world's physical elements be compared? Knowledge about God through nature was very basic; Paul may present the Torah, as understood without its fulfillment in Christ, in the same way (cf. 3:24). Both general and special revelation remained limited until the arrival of the ultimate special revelation that they supported, namely Christ (4:3–4).

Thus Paul means what he says. He uses the language of "elementary matters" deliberately to put both forms of season-observing religions in their place. The particular elementary matters that the Galatians had experienced

---

[791] E.g., I. Eph. 1214–1227, 1269; Lucretius *Nat.* 2.611; Euripides *Bacch.* 58–59, 79; Rhet. Her. 4.59.62; Valerius Maximus 7.5.2; Seneca *Ep. Lucil.* 108.7; Lucian *Gout* 30–32; Ps.-Lucian *Affairs* 42; Apuleius *Metam.* 11.4–5; Diogenes Laertius 6.1.1.

[792] S. M. Elliott, "Choose Your Mother, Choose Your Master: Galatians 4:21–5:1 in the Shadow of the Anatolian Mother of the Gods," *JBL* 118 (1999): 671–76, here 674–75, also noted in George, *Identity*, 201.

[793] E.g., Jub. 2:2; 1 En. 6:7 (with OTP note); 60:12–22; 66:2.

[794] E.g., 1 En. 60:1; 61:10; 100:10; 2 En. 4:2; 23:1; 1QM 10.11–12; 12.1; 11Q10 30.5; 2 Bar. 51:10.

[795] 2 En. 1a.5.

[796] Cf. 1QM 6.6; 14.9; 15.1–2; 1Q27 f1i.9–10; 4Q491 f8–10i.6; Jub. 21:21; Asc. Isa. 2:4; Apoc. Zeph 3:8.

before conversion, however, were the elements of nature that they wrongly venerated as deities.

In contrast to Rom 8:17, Paul's image in 4:4–7 is less about individual heirs than about a corporate heir. At the right stage in history, Christ made it possible for God's people to function without being under the law in its traditional, codified form. But those previously outside the law also can come into this role as freed sons in Christ the ultimate Son.

In 4:1–3, Paul describes both Jews under the law and pagans as in bondage under the elementary matters, like children who had not yet experienced liberation from their pedagogues or (in this paragraph) guardians. Paul returns to that depiction of the shared, lamentable state of humanity in 4:8–11. He interrupts that depiction, however, by reminding them of the glorious new condition they experienced in Christ: God sent his Son to make both Jews and gentiles his sons and heirs (4:4–7; cf. 3:27–29). Why would they want to go back to what they had before (4:8–11; cf. Num 11:5; 14:3–4)?

Both Jews and gentiles remain as minors under authority different from themselves until the right time in salvation history: the coming of Christ (4:4). Christ came to redeem those under the law ("us," in this case the Jewish people), to give them adoption. But though gentiles were under different guardians, Paul hastens to show that "you" gentiles have also been adopted (though perhaps in a way more complicated than restoring disinherited sons; cf. Rom 11:24). The Spirit they have received (3:5) bears witness that they are also God's children and thus heirs (4:5–7; cf. 3:29).

Galatians 4:4 lies at the center of this description, rhetorically underlined with anaphora (repetition of opening elements) in 4:4–5 (*born … born; in order to … so that* [the same Greek term as *in order that*]). Some scholars suggest here a pre-Pauline creed or at least traditional language. This thesis is not implausible, but the passage is consistent with Paul's Christology (e.g., 1 Cor 8:6; Phil 2:5–11).

What is striking is that Paul can refer to such concepts here without explanation, suggesting that his audience already knew these matters and his rivals had not challenged them. Thus whatever the sources of the specific wording, the passage's Christology was apparently a shared belief in the early Jesus movement.[797] The further similarity of Gal 4:4 to Rom 8:3 (God sending his Son to save) and of Gal 4:5–7 to Rom 8:15–17 (liberation from

---

[797]   L. W. Hurtado, "Paul's Christology," pages 185–98 in *The Cambridge Companion to St Paul* (ed. J. D. G. Dunn; Cambridge: Cambridge University Press, 2003), 196.

slavery, adoption, God's children and heirs, the Spirit's assurance and the Abba cry) suggests that Paul was accustomed to using such formulations, wherever they originated.

What does Paul mean by saying that *the fullness of time had come* (4:4)? In the first place, he continues his image of the child reaching maturity, i.e., a new phase in life (4:1–2). This image relates to salvation history rather than to the personal experience of an individual. Jewish expectations of impending deliverance rested on the belief that God controlled history and that all his words would be fulfilled in their appointed time.[798] Oracles such as Dan 9:24–27, which most first-century Jews understood as pointing to a fulfillment in the first century,[799] gave some of Paul's contemporaries confidence that they were on the brink of deliverance.

Jesus's followers were convinced that the promised time was fulfilled (Mark 1:15; Eph 1:10).[800] This was the time of Christ (Gal 3:24), the era of faith (3:22–23, 25). Now had come the fulfillment of the promise (3:17–18) in the promised seed Christ (3:16, 19) and by the Spirit (3:14). God's people were *no longer* under a pedagogue, and were thus *no longer* de facto *a slave* (3:25; 4:7).[801] Christ was *born under the law*, with *under* in this context signifying subjection shared with other mortals (3:23, 25; 4:1–3).

Scholars debate how much to read into the description that *God sent his Son* (4:4). Some note the use of *sent* language for prophets. Paul does not speak here of a mere prophet, however, but of God's *Son*, sent for a unique and cosmic mission (Rom 8:3; John 3:16–17; 1 John 4:9–10). *Son* was a messianic title in at least some Jewish circles, was sometimes divine language in Greco-Roman circles, and in the Jesus tradition indicates a special intimacy with the Father and a unique role for Jesus.[802] Comparisons with divine wisdom,[803] *logos* (divine

---

[798]   E.g., 4 Ezra 7:74; Sib. Or. 3.570–72 (probably second century BCE); L.A.B. 3:10; T. Ab. 7:16 B; b. Sanh. 97–99; cf. 2 Bar. 29:8.

[799]   R. T. Beckwith, "Daniel 9 and the Date of Messiah's Coming in Essene, Hellenistic, Pharisaic, Zealot and Early Christian Computation," *RevQ* 10 (4, 1981): 521–42; Wright, *Faithfulness*, 116–17, 130, 142 (citing Josephus *War* 6.312–15); cf. also *War* 3.400–01.

[800]   With Ridderbos, *Paul: Outline*, 45; F. F. Bruce, *The Time Is Fulfilled* (Grand Rapids, MI: Eerdmans, 1978), 31.

[801]   With de Boer, *Galatians*, 262.

[802]   For discussion, see C. S. Keener, *Historical Jesus of the Gospels* (Grand Rapids, MI: Eerdmans, 2009), 271–76.

[803]   Wis 9:10–17; Sir 1:4; 24:8–9. See E. Schweizer, "Zum religionsgeschichtlichen Hintergrund der 'Sendungsformel' Gal. 4:4f., Rm. 8:3f., Joh. 3:16f., I Joh. 4:9," *ZNW* 57 (1966): 199–211, here esp. 206–08; R. G. Hamerton-Kelly, *Pre-existence, Wisdom, and the Son: A Study of the Idea of Pre-existence in the New Testament* (Cambridge: Cambridge University Press, 1973), 111.

reason),[804] or other exalted figures are thus closer to the point than are mere prophetic figures.[805] As such, and in conjunction with clearer Pauline texts to this effect (Rom 8:3; 1 Cor 1:24, 30; 8:6; 10:4; Phil 2:6–7; Col 1:15–17), the passage supports Jesus's preexistence.[806] God sends the preexistent Son here just as, in a parallel manner, he sends his preexistent Spirit in Gal 4:6.

Yet unlike divine wisdom or any possibly personified *stoicheia*, Christ *was born of a woman*, a historical event within the lifetime of some of Paul's contemporaries. Some earlier interpreters sometimes found here a proof-text for the virgin birth, but *born of a woman* is simply a Semitic and LXX idiom indicating a human being (Job 14:1; 15:14; 25:4). In connection with sending, its focus is not virgin birth but simply incarnation.

Born under the law (4:4) means that Jesus shared others' subjection to the law (4:5) and therefore could redeem them from under the law's curse (4:5; cf. 3:13) by way of exchange, presumably because he had not violated the law (Rom 8:3; 2 Cor 5:21). Jesus was born in the era of subjection to the law (Gal 3:23–24), and brought the new era not simply by birth but by redeeming his people (4:5), which he did on the cross (1:4; 3:13).

God redeemed gentile believers from the law that excluded gentiles from his people,[807] so that now they can be adopted, like Israel, as his children (Gal 4:5). That he has sent the Spirit of his Son into our hearts (Gal 4:6) confirms this adoption; Christ, God's Son, now lives in us, working in and through us (2:20; cf. 2 Cor 13:3–5).

---

[804] E.g., Philo *Agr.* 51.

[805] A range of Jewish circles awaited a climactic figure; see N. T. Wright, "Messiahship in Galatians?" pages 3–23 in *Galatians and Christian Theology: Justification, the Gospel, and Ethics in Paul's Letter* (ed. M. W. Elliott et al.; Grand Rapids, MI: Baker Academic, 2014), 7. On Jesus among exalted figures, see further, e.g., C. S. Keener, "Jesus and Parallel Jewish and Greco-Roman Figures," pages 85–111 in *Christian Origins and Greco-Roman Culture: Social and Literary Contexts for the New Testament* (ed. S. Porter and A. W. Pitts; Leiden: Brill, 2013).

[806] With, e.g., Lightfoot, *Galatians*, 168; Burton, *Galatians*, 217; Matera, *Galatians*, 150; Hays, "Galatians," 283; Fee, *Pauline Christology*, 213–16; Das, *Galatians*, 410–11, 414; R. T. George, "'God Sent His Son, Born of a Woman' (Gal 4:4). The Idea of Incarnation, Its Antecedents, and Significance in Paul's Theology," *Doon Theological Journal* 5 (1, 2008): 65–85; C. Tilling, *Paul's Divine Christology* (Grand Rapids, MI: Eerdmans, 2015).

[807] Or codified a standard that few gentiles could meet; though like other Jews, Paul seems to have had a lower standard for gentiles to begin with (Rom 2:14–15, 26–27; cf. 1 Cor 5:1; 1 Thess 4:5). Many Jews allowed for righteous gentiles so long as they kept the several most important rules (see Jub. 7.20–25; Sib. Or. 3.757–59; Ps.-Phoc. 3, 8–54, 135–36, 147–48, 154; t. Abod. Zar. 8:4–8; Mekilta Bah. 5.90ff (Lauterbach 2:236); Sipre Deut. 343.4.1.

Paul's use of *adoption* here is flexible enough (cf. Rom 8:23) to depict not only gentile adoption but possibly Jewish liberation from slave-like sonship (4:1) to the status of mature, free children and the Spirit-experience of being God's children more fully (4:1–5). Many Judeans anticipated in some sense Israel's eschatological adoption.[808] Further, in Gal 4:4–6 Jesus alone is the natural *Son* (4:4); all others, by comparison, come by adoption.

God's mission for his Son was *to redeem* (4:5). Paul employs this word for *redeem* (4:5) in this way elsewhere in his extant letters only at 3:13, where Christ takes the curse for us, even as here he is *under the law* with us (4:4–5). There is a reversal of status here: the *Son* (*huios*) is *born under the law* (4:4), so that those *under the law* become *children* (a "son," *huios*;[809] 4:5–6) and thus heirs (4:6–7). Thus Christ, though rich, became poor to make us rich (2 Cor 8:9) – that is, sharing his inheritance (Rom 8:17).

In this context, *under the law* (Gal 4:4–5) signifies subjection (3:23, 25) and slavery (4:1–3); to *redeem* here therefore involves freeing a slave, possibly (as in the common commercial use of the term) by paying a price.[810] If paying a price is in view here, there seems little doubt that it involves the substitution or exchange of Christ himself (3:13; cf. use of the cognate verb for purchasing believers with a price in 1 Cor 6:20; 7:23). Manumission of slaves was a common practice in the Greco-Roman world; Jews could recall how God redeemed them from slavery in Egypt (see comment on Gal 3:13).

Adoption made one a legal heir. Though the fullness of the inheritance awaits the resurrection of our bodies (Rom 8:23), the Spirit is our foretaste and first fruits of that promise (Rom 8:15, 23; see comment on Gal 3:14).[811] Theologically, Paul draws on the analogy of Israel as God's children, and elsewhere applies the language of *adoption* (*huiothesia*) explicitly to the Israelites (Rom 9:4). Nevertheless, the *image*, including for Israel, must be informed with the sorts of adoption known to Paul's audience, for which reason scholars examine especially Greek and Roman adoption practices.

---

[808] See T. J. Burke, "Adoption and the Spirit in Romans 8," *EvQ* 70 (4, 1998): 311–24.

[809] The NRSV's inclusive language here rightly notes that Paul's message is gender inclusive, but inadvertently obscures the logic of his wording (contrast here NIV; ESV); cf. G. Vall, "Inclusive Language and the Equal Dignity of Women and Men in Christ," *Thomist* 67 (4, 2003): 579–606.

[810] With, e.g., Hays, "Galatians," 284; Moo, *Galatians*, 218.

[811] Cf. Keener, *Mind*, 153–55, 176–79.

A Closer Look: Adoption

Paul's term (*huiothesia*) clearly applies to adoption.[812] We should also remember that the chief point of the adoption analogy is an alien entering a new family as an heir; Paul used similarities with adoption in his analogy, but it is precarious to press every detail in any analogy.

Scholars debate whether Greek[813] or Roman[814] adoption practice is more relevant to the passage.[815] Because Galatia was in the eastern part of the empire, most Galatians would be more aware of Greek practice[816] (and perhaps local traditions now lost to us). But citizens of Pisidian Antioch and Lystra, two of the three or four named cities where south Galatian churches flourished, may have also been familiar with Roman practice; they were, after all, Roman colonies. Moreover, imperial succession made Roman adoption familiar to most knowledgeable urban dwellers in the empire.[817]

Roman adoption was meant to pass on the family name and property.[818] Roman adoption ended a person's connections with one's prior family, canceled all former debts, transferred all the adoptee's assets to the adopter, and made the adoptee his[819] heir.[820] An adoptee was legally of the same status as a child by birth.[821]

---

[812] J. M. Scott, *Adoption as Sons of God: An Exegetical Investigation into the Background of Huiothesia in the Pauline Corpus* (WUNT 2.48; Tübingen: J. C. B. Mohr, 1992), 2–57, cited by Trick, *Descent*, 151, as decisive.

[813] E.g., Ramsay, *Galatians*, 337–38; Trick, *Descent*.

[814] E.g., F. Lyall, "Roman Law in the Writings of Paul – Adoption," *JBL* 88 (1969): 458–66; Lyall, *Slaves, Citizens, Sons: Legal Metaphors in the Epistles* (Grand Rapids, MI: Zondervan, 1984), 67, 81–88; Hester, *Inheritance*, 59.

[815] For background on Greek adoption, see J. C. Walters, "Paul, Adoption, and Inheritance," pages 42–76 in *Paul in the Greco-Roman World: A Handbook* (ed. J. P. Sampley; Harrisburg, PA: Trinity Press International, 2003), 44–51; on Roman adoption, 51–55; on the two types of Roman adoption, see further W. W. Buckland, *A Text-Book of Roman Law from Augustus to Justinian* (3rd edn.; rev. P. Stein; Cambridge: Cambridge University Press, 1963), 121–27.

[816] Trick, *Descent*, 154. Roman law applied to Romans, and was not intended to supersede local laws or customs on such matters (Trick, *Descent*, 154, 161).

[817] E.g., Suetonius *Aug.* 63.2; *Tib.* 15.2; later, Pliny *Ep.* 10.1.1; 10.3A.1.

[818] Lyall, *Slaves*, 69; S. T. Carroll, "Adoption," 1:11–17 in *Dictionary of Daily Life in Biblical and Post-Biblical Antiquity* (3 vols.; ed. E. M. Yamauchi and M. R. Wilson; Peabody, MA: Hendrickson, 2014), 15.

[819] In Gaius *Inst.* 1.104, only men could adopt.

[820] E. Ferguson, *Backgrounds of Early Christianity* (Grand Rapids, MI: Eerdmans, 1987), 51; C. S. Wansink, "Roman Law and Legal System," *DNTB* 984–91, here 990. One wishing to remain part of the birth family could refuse to be adopted (Seneca *Controv.* 2.1.19; Buckland, *Text-Book of Roman Law*, 127).

[821] Gaius *Inst.* 2.136.

Whereas birth was simply by chance, adoption allowed one to select the best heir.[822]

Roman adoption emulated slave emancipation, an image certainly relevant in this context (Gal 4:1, 3, 5). A Roman father was head of his household, with significant legal authority over sons as well as slaves. He could free his children from his authority in a manner analogous to the freeing of slaves.[823] In the adoption ceremony the original father would fictively "sell" the adoptee three times, thereby legally freeing the son from his household; on the third selling, the adopter could fictively "redeem" the adoptee, making him his own son.[824]

Greeks also frequently practiced adoption.[825] Those who support a Greek legal image here also offer the following reasons:

1. Paul sees God as adopter and provider of the purchase price, whereas in Roman law these may come from two different persons.
2. Romans had just one guardian and one trustee, whereas Greeks allowed for multiple guardians.
3. In Paul's analogy, the youth is freed from both guardians and trustees simultaneously, but Roman custom freed the youth from the *tutor* at fourteen (around puberty) but the *curator* only later, often age twenty-five.
4. There is no thought in Galatians of the Roman practice of the adopter fictively purchasing the child from the genetic father.

To these points one could respond:

1. Analogies for God are always limited; no human roles exhaust the analogy.
2. Romans were not in fact limited to a single guardian;[826] and Paul may need the plural to prepare for the plural *stoicheia* that fill this role in 4:3.
3. Paul's household managers are probably just that – not an analogy for the *curator* from whom a child was liberated at twenty-five.
4. The word translated *redeem* in 4:5 is actually consistent with the idea of purchase, to which Roman law may offer at least a partial albeit not complete analogy.

---

[822] Tacitus *Hist.* 1.16, regarding imperial adoption.
[823] Gaius *Inst.* 1.117. This was an imaginary sale, peculiar to Roman law (1.119).
[824] Dunn, *Galatians*, 217; see Buckland, *Textbook of Roman Law*, 132.
[825] G. A. Deissmann, *Paul: A Study in Social and Religious History* (New York: Harper, 1957), 174–75; Trick, *Descent*, 141–75; esp. D. R. Moore-Crispin, "Galatians 4.1–9: The Use and Abuse of Parallels," *EvQ* 61 (3, 1989): 203–23.
[826] See Goodrich, "Guardians," 271–72; Das, *Galatians*, 142.

Supporters of Roman law point out that Greek adoption also did not sever ties with the family of origin, lacking the stronger emancipatory power of the Roman image (though even Roman adoption did not sever every connection).

Ultimately, a decision between Greek and Roman law does not change the most important point of the text. Paul himself probably did not know the details of such laws any more than most modern Americans who have not adopted a child know the intricacies of modern adoption law, and neither did his audience. What they did know was the connection "between adoption and inheritance."[827] Both Greek law and Roman law made the adopted child an heir, and in both cases one could adopt for this express purpose. Paul's interest is that gentiles are grafted into Abraham's family and so become heirs as ancient Israel was. ****

Paul wants his audience to understand what becoming God's children genuinely required. Why would they resort to circumcision to achieve a status they already possess? Would not any right-thinking person be envious of their status and the Spirit-experience that confirmed it?

Paul shifts to "you" in 4:6 not to imply that what he says is untrue of Jewish believers (cf. 4:5) but to reinforce for his mostly gentile audience that they too are directly included as the children of whom Paul is speaking (4:5) and thus heirs (4:7), as he had affirmed in 3:29.

The image of the father in Gal 4:2 depends on God's Fatherhood of his people (3:29). Paul can presume here a widely understood belief in early Christianity; corporate Jewish prayers already commonly addressed God as Father (see comment on 1:3), though not as Abba.

Yet not only the understanding of God's fatherhood but the early Christian experience of the Abba cry must be earlier than Paul, since Paul expects the church in Rome, where he has not visited, to be aware of it (Rom 8:15). It is understood (albeit with Pauline translation provided) in both Galatia and Rome, even though it is an Aramaic phrase preserved from the earliest phase of the Jesus movement.

Many scholars have assumed that this cry therefore goes back to the Lord's Prayer that Jesus taught his disciples. That *Abba* was used in the Lord's Prayer is possible, but the one location in the gospel tradition where *Abba* is *specifically* preserved for us is Mark 14:36, in Jesus's prayer at Gethsemane. The *Abba* prayer might therefore recall Gethsemane and Jesus's cries of

---

[827] Walters, "Adoption," 43–44.

anguish as he prepared to face the world's hostility,[828] a usage relevant for its recurrence in Rom 8:15 (cf. 8:17–23, 26, 35–39).

It should not be lost on us that the Spirit inspiring the Abba cry here is the Spirit of God's Son, so that we as God's children utter the very term of love and intimacy that Jesus expressed to his Father, including in settings like Gethsemane. It is a prayer in a sense moved by "Christ in us" (Gal 2:20), as we share in Jesus's relationship with his Father (cf. John 10:14–15).

That the inspiring Spirit, normally identified as the Spirit of God, is here the Spirit of God's Son is significant also for Christology, as with the "Spirit of Christ" in Rom 8:9 (cf. also 1 Pet 1:11), the "Spirit of Jesus Christ" in Phil 1:19, and the "Spirit of Jesus" in Acts 16:7. Jewish thought traditionally viewed the Spirit as an aspect of God, so Jesus is here presented as divine in some respect (cf. Gal 1:1, 3).[829]

Some suggest that *Abba* reflects an ecstatic cry.[830] Varying definitions of the meaning of "ecstatic" today make this designation less helpful, though we cannot doubt that an acclamation of "Father!" will normally carry some affectionate emotion. Given early Christian understanding of the Spirit, identifying the cry as "charismatic" may be more apropos.[831]

Technically here the Spirit offers the cry, "Abba" (4:6),[832] whereas in Rom 8:15 *believers* cry, "Abba!" *by* (or in) the Spirit. Because the Spirit was often associated with prophetic inspiration (e.g., Num 11:25–29; 1 Sam 10:10; 19:20; Joel 2:28–29),[833] an association even more dominant in early Judaism

---

[828]   D. C. Allison Jr. *Constructing Jesus: Memory, Imagination, and History* (Grand Rapids, MI: Baker Academic, 2010), 417–18; R. Rodríguez, *If You Call Yourself a Jew: Reappraising Paul's Letter to the Romans* (Eugene, OR: Cascade, 2014), 156–57.

[829]   Fee, *Presence*, 405; Fee, *Pauline Christology: An Exegetical-Theological Study* (Peabody, MA: Hendrickson, 2007), 220, 590–91; cf. M. M. B. Turner, "The Spirit of Christ and Christology," pages 168–90 in *Christ the Lord* (ed. H. H. Rowdon; Leicester, UK: Inter-Varsity, 1982); Turner, "The Spirit of Christ and 'Divine' Christology," pages 413–36 in *Jesus of Nazareth, Lord and Christ: Essays on the Historical Jesus and New Testament Christology* (ed. J. B. Green and M. Turner; Grand Rapids, MI: Eerdmans; Carlisle, UK: Paternoster, 1994); A. K. Grieb, "People of God, Body of Christ, Koinonia of Spirit: The Role of Ethical Ecclesiology in Paul's 'Trinitarian' Language," *AThR* 87 (2, 2005): 225–52.

[830]   E.g., Lull, *Spirit in Galatians*, 109. Others cited to this effect include Käsemann, Kuss, Dodd, Schlier, and Betz.

[831]   With, e.g., Fee, *Presence*, 409; cf. also J. B. Cobb Jr. and D. J. Lull, *Romans* (St. Louis, MO: Chalice Press, 2005), 118.

[832]   The participle translated *crying* in 4:6 is neuter, referring back to *pneuma*, Spirit.

[833]   See further M.-A. Chevallier, *Ancien Testament, Hellénisme et Judaïsme, La tradition synoptique, L'oeuvre de Luc* (vol. 1 in *Souffle de Dieu: le Saint-Esprit dans le Nouveau Testament*; Le Point Théologique 26; Paris: Éditions Beauchesne, 1978), 27–29; C. J. H. Wright, *Knowing the Holy Spirit through the Old Testament* (Downers Grove, IL: IVP Academic, 2006), 63–86.

than in the Old Testament,[834] it appears here that the Spirit inspires God's children to cry, "Abba!"[835]

In 4:7, gentiles who trust Christ are no longer slaves (4:3) and, like those who were already children yet once comparable to slaves under the law (4:1), they are now just children. Given the clear statement to this effect in 4:7a, *If a child then also an heir* in 4:7b may be translated "Since a child …"

Under Roman law, one became an heir by birth or adoption, not by the father's decease.[836] The difference between slaves and children is not that only the former owe obedience; in Paul's world, both owed obedience, and both usually gave it. The difference is that the son is the father's heir, and on maturity will exercise authority (even over slaves). The final *through God* (*dia theou*) implies that God himself has brought about this state of affairs, through the actions narrated in 4:4–6 (sending his Son, redeeming, sending his Spirit).

4:8–11: RETURNING TO EMPTY PRACTICES

4:8 Formerly, when you did not know God, you were enslaved to beings that by nature are not gods.

4:9 Now, however, that you have come to know God, or rather to be known by God, how can you turn back again to the weak and beggarly elemental spirits? How can you want to be enslaved to them again?

4:10 You are observing special days, and months, and seasons, and years.

4:11 I am afraid that my work for you may have been wasted.

Paul's rousing praise of Christ and believers' status in him is cut short with an abrupt but (in the NRSV) untranslated, strong adversative (*alla,*

---

[834]   Sir 48:24; Jub. 31:12; 1 En. 91:1; 1QS 8.16; Philo *Flight* 186; Josephus *Ant.* 6.166; L.A.B. 28:6; 4 Ezra 14:22; Sipre Deut. 22.1.2; t. Pisha 2:15; see further E. Best, "The Use and Non-use of Pneuma by Josephus," *NovT* 3 (3, 1959): 218–25, here 222–25; R. P. Menzies, *Empowered for Witness: The Spirit in Luke-Acts* (London: T&T Clark, 2004), 49–101; Menzies, *The Development of Early Christian Pneumatology with Special Reference to Luke-Acts* (JSNTSup 54; Sheffield, UK: Sheffield Academic, 1991), 53–112; M. M. B. Turner, *Power from on High: The Spirit in Israel's Restoration and Witness in Luke-Acts* (Sheffield, UK: Sheffield Academic, 1996), 86–104 (including inspired wisdom and praise); C. S. Keener, *The Spirit in the Gospels and Acts: Divine Purity and Power* (Grand Rapids, MI: Baker Academic, 2010), 10–13, 31–33.

[835]   With J. D. G. Dunn, "Spirit Speech: Reflections on Romans 8:12–27," pages 82–91 in *Romans and the People of God: Essays in Honor of Gordon D. Fee on the Occasion of His 65th Birthday* (ed. S. K. Soderlund and N. T. Wright; Grand Rapids, MI: Eerdmans, 1999), 82, 85.

[836]   Wansink, "Law," 991.

"but") beginning 4:8. Paul was not the only person to denounce false gods. Although too prudent to critique society's dominant paganism publicly, intra-Jewish ridicule of worshiping images was common.[837] Even some gentiles mocked popular pagan practice.[838] Paul is more circumspect than to specify the Galatians' particular deities in a letter (cf. Acts 19:37), but he is not afraid to criticize, on a generic level, veneration of false deities (cf., e.g., 1 Cor 10:14; 12:2; 2 Cor 6:16; Gal 5:20; 1 Thess 1:9).

What sorts of deities had the Galatians worshiped before their conversion? For the most part, their pantheon coincided with the deities worshiped elsewhere in Greco-Roman Asia Minor; for example, Zeus and Hermes often appear. Certainly the imperial cult was a major element in local worship, especially in Pisidian Antioch where a prominent temple was devoted to the emperor's honor.[839] The imperial temple, probably fairly recently completed,[840] was so large that visitors traveling the *Via Sebaste* would see it long before reaching Antioch.[841]

Despite their prominence, however, emperors represented only a few of the putative divinities that Paul's confrontational message would have urged the Galatians to turn from (Gal 4:8; cf. 1 Cor 8:5–6; 1 Thess 1:9; Acts 14:15; 17:29–30; 19:26). Some other deities were distinctively identified with the interior region of Anatolia. Some of these deities were known as strict enforcers of morality,[842] perhaps contributing to the Galatians' religious zeal.[843]

In Pisidian Antioch, the cult most dominant beside that of the imperial deity was the community's patron deity, Mên Askaênos.[844] One of his two temples lay on a hill, an hour's steep ascent above Antioch, strewn with dedications.[845] But probably no deity was more closely associated with the interior of Asia Minor, and especially Phrygia, than the Great Mother, Cybele, the mother goddess associated with earth.[846]

---

[837] E.g., Wis 13:10–14:7; Bel and Dragon; Ep Jer; Let. Aris. 134–38; Sib. Or. 3.8–35; 4.4–23.
[838] E.g., Dio Chrysostom *Or.* 11; Lucian *Z. Cat.* 2–8; *Lover of Lies* 2–5; Philostratus *Vit. Apoll.* 5.14. See further C. S. Keener, "The Exhortation to Monotheism in Acts 14:15–17," pages 47–70 in *Kingdom Rhetoric: New Testament Explorations in Honor of Ben Witherington III* (ed. T. M. W. Halcomb; Eugene, OR: Wipf & Stock, 2013).
[839] See esp. Hardin, *Imperial Cult.*
[840] Mitchell, *Anatolia*, 2:10.
[841] Hansen, "Galatia," 395.
[842] Mitchell, *Anatolia*, 1:189, 191; 2:25–26; cf. Niang, *Faith*, 51.
[843] See here Arnold, "Astonished," 437–43.
[844] Mitchell, *Anatolia*, 2:9, 24.
[845] Mitchell, *Anatolia*, 2:9–10.
[846] See esp. S. M. Elliott, "Choose Your Mother," 671–76; Elliot, *Cutting Too Close for Comfort: Paul's Letter to the Galatians in Its Anatolian Cultic Context* (LNTS 248;

These are presumably some of the Galatians' former objects of worship that might come to mind when they hear about *beings that by nature are not gods* (4:8). Paul himself may be less acquainted with, and surely less interested in, the specifics. His language evokes earlier biblical and early Jewish denunciations of objects of worship that were truly "no gods," as in 2 Chron 13:9; Isa 37:19; Jer 2:11; 5:7; 16:20.[847] This need not mean, as the language sometimes implied, that Paul regards the non-gods as nonentities altogether. Paul probably means something similar to his reference to *so-called gods* in 1 Cor 8:5 and thus to the alleged gods that are actually *demons* in 1 Cor 10:20.[848] Many other hellenistic Jews regarded pagan deities as demons.[849]

Yet his complete phrase, *by nature are not gods*, also appears to evoke a technical distinction in hellenistic religion between deities that were so only by human custom and those that were so *by nature* (*phusei*, as here).[850] The latter included sun, moon, and stars. A philosophic approach called Euhemerism employed the latter in demythologizing hellenistic religion; hellenistic Jewish apologists exploited this system in its own critique of paganism.[851] This approach in turn took two directions, one that denied the existence of such deities altogether and the other that viewed them as demons; as noted earlier, Paul's language elsewhere indicates that he followed the demonic interpretation.[852]

Thinkers regularly appealed to nature as a standard for evaluating morality and utility; in this case, Paul may allude to their previous veneration of nature, such as the mother goddess associated with earth and fertility, and remind them that *by nature* the *stoicheia*, the world's elements, were just that: lifeless elements. They were no gods. The demonic dimension enters only when they are worshiped (1 Cor 10:25–29); thus Paul's wording differs from Gal 4:3, where they *were enslaved to the elemental spirits of the world*. In 4:8 the Greek verb is active and should not be translated (as in the

New York: T&T Clark, 2003). Against reconstructing too much of Galatians based on this background, see Hardin, *Imperial Cult*, 5–11.

[847] Also, repeatedly, Ep Jer 23, 29, 51–52, 65, 72.

[848] Arnold, "Returning," 70; Moo, *Galatians*, 275.

[849] Deut 32:17; Ps 106:37; Ps 95:5 LXX; Isa 65:3 LXX; Bar 4:7; 4Q385a f3ac.7; Jub. 1:11; 22:16–17; 1 En. 19:1; T. Job 3:3; T. Sol. 5:5; 6:4; Sipre Deut 318.2.1–2; later, cf. Did. 6.3; Justin *Dial.* 55; Athenagoras 26.

[850] Betz, *Galatians*, 214; Dunn, *Galatians*, 224; Das, *Galatians*, 419.

[851] Cf. Let. Aris. 136; Wis 14:15–16; Sib. Or. 3.121–58, 551–54, 588; Klauck, *Context*, 281.

[852] With Betz, *Galatians*, 215.

NRSV) *were enslaved*, but rather "served, acted as slaves to." Their belief, not something in nature itself, made them slaves.[853]

Luke depicts Paul as having earlier urged Galatians to turn from false deities, which God tolerated in an earlier time, to the true creator of realms celestial and terrestrial (Acts 14:15–16). To a Galatian farming community, Paul declared that this God graciously provided fruitful "seasons" (14:17, using the same Greek term as in Gal 4:10).

In 4:9, Paul's tone might begin to shift toward his appeal of *pathos* that is clearer in 4:12–20.[854] How can the Galatian Christians *turn back* now that they *have come to know God*? The idea of knowing God reflects biblical language for God's people maintaining their side of the covenant that he had established with them (e.g., Jer 9:24; 22:16). Someday Israel would know God fully (Jer 31:34; Hos 2:20); some gentiles would also enter this covenant relationship (Isa 19:21).

But Paul corrects himself: perhaps they really do not know God, even though they are known by him (4:9b)! Speakers sometimes deliberately retracted what they had said, replacing it with something more suitable to drive home a point. Here Paul hints at their sorry spiritual state. Nevertheless, even *to be known by God* was a great honor (1 Cor 8:3), especially in a world where people often thought that gods were paying no attention to them despite their offerings. So why would they turn back?

Paul elsewhere uses this term for *turn back* to include conversion from idolatry (1 Thess 1:9) or spiritual blindness under the law (2 Cor 3:16); in Acts 14:15 Luke depicts Paul as summoning people in this region to turn from idols, again employing this term. Here, however, Paul warns the Galatians that they are on the verge of deconverting.[855] Paul's language is emphatic, three times using words for *again* (albeit just twice in the NRSV). Pagan religion was festive and communal, which might offer temptations to turn back, but the religion they served was in fact merely about *stoicheia*, elements, objects in nature or ideas drawn from nature.[856]

---

[853]   de Boer, *Galatians*, 274, also notes this based on the different lexical nuance of the term used here.

[854]   Cf. J. Van W. Cronjé, "The Stratagem of the Rhetorical Question in Galatians 4:9–10 as a Means towards Persuasion," *Neot* 26 (2, 1992): 417–24, emphasizing Paul's emotion-laden question here.

[855]   Deconversion was not uncommon in antiquity; see A. D. Nock, *Conversion: The Old and the New in Religion from Alexander the Great to Augustine of Hippo* (Oxford: Clarendon, 1933), 157–60.

[856]   Nontheistic naturalism today also makes nature autonomous from a creator and designer, but without always generating religious pronouncements based on its approach.

The element of shock here, however, is that it is their new observance of the Jewish calendar (4:10) that represents a turning back that Paul deems equivalent to the practices of their pagan past. So wholly and solely sufficient is Christ that turning back to slavery[857] under anything elementary, whether the law (4:1–3) or *beings that by nature are not gods* (4:8), is deemed apostasy. Having the fuller reality, how can they turn to what was at best preparatory (cf. similarly Heb 2:2–3; 10:26–31)? The *stoicheia* are *weak* (4:9), a fitting term for idols (Wis 13:17–19), which are often even depicted as "dead," i.e., lifeless (Wis 13:10; 14:29; 15:15; Ep Jer 70–71).

Paul may equate the real spirits behind idolatry with demons (1 Cor 10:20), but while they are not absolutely powerless (cf. Job 1:13–19; Rom 8:38; Eph 6:12), they are nothing before God, hence void of value and virtually impotent. They are created entities, dependent on creation, and in early Christian sources often appear to be so weak as to be parasitic on bodily life (e.g., Mark 5:9–12). Insofar as gods depended on mortals to feed them, they could be deemed not only desperately poor (*ptôcha*) but even utterly dependent on mortals for support.

Whether the *stoicheia* here are the non-gods of 4:8 or simply elementary concepts about religion (which include the strictures of both non-gods and Torah) is a matter of much debate; see discussion at 4:3. The language *by nature* in 4:8 may suggest, as noted earlier, that the elements of nature and cosmic lights are in fact the non-gods that the Galatians formerly venerated as deities.

Paul addresses calendrical observances in 4:10. Just as in their former paganism (4:8–9), the Galatians were now placing themselves under calendrical rules, like spiritual slaves instead of God's children ruled by the Spirit of Christ (cf. 4:1–7). Relevant to 4:10, Jewish people recognized from Scripture that God had provided the sun, moon, and stars for *seasons* and *days* and *years* (Gen 1:14);[858] many gentiles thought similarly. Astrology played a prominent role in the Greek form of the calendar[859] dominant in the eastern Mediterranean world, where Paul and the Galatians lived.

---

[857] Romans traditionally allowed a master to re-enslave a misbehaving slave; after the third offense the re-enslavement was permanent (Valerius Maximus 2.6.7a).

[858] Cf. also Jub. 2:8–9; Sir 43:6; Philo *Creation* 55. Besides annual seasons, one might also think of "times and seasons" (Acts 1:7; 1 Thess 5:1) in an apocalyptic sense (4 Ezra 4:37; 14:5; 2 Bar. 20:1; 48:2; 54:1; 83:6).

[859] J. Rüpke, *Religion: Antiquity and Its Legacy* (New York: Oxford University Press, 2013), 115.

Various days were deemed unlucky;[860] later rabbis also prescribed which days were particularly dangerous.[861] Particular times were consecrated to particular deities in the same way that sacred land was.[862] Many of these days were related to celestial indicators, including constellations.[863] Most festivals, however, were local or kept at local times.[864] Each festival was related to a deity.[865]

South Galatia would have its share of festivals. For example, March 24 began the sacred time for wailing for Cybele, mother of the gods.[866] In Pisidian Antioch, as archaeologist Stephen Mitchell observes, "The packed calendar of the ruler cult dragooned the citizens of Antioch into observing the days, months, seasons, and years which it laid down for special recognition and celebration." Christians could not conceal their allegiances in such an environment.[867]

Because they *turn back again* to preconversion practices (4:9), and because they are turning toward circumcision (5:2), it seems clear that Paul is (perhaps hyperbolically) virtually equating the contemporary Jewish festival calendar with their former pagan calendar. This may be because of how the Galatians risk approaching it: not as a commemoration of God's past acts for his people, but as a requirement of the law that they consider adopting.

Paul's term for *observing* the days was also used by other Jews for observing the sabbath[868] and festival days.[869] Under circumstances demanding less polemic, Paul allowed different approaches to festivals (Rom 14:5–6) and may have even observed some himself, for whatever reasons (cf. Acts 20:6, 16). Certainly his churches knew about festivals (1 Cor 5:7; 16:8).

---

[860] Ovid *Fasti* 1.58; Aulus Gellius 5.17; Plutarch *Alc.* 34.1; *Alex.* 14.4; *Cam.* 19.1–8; *Rom. Q., Mor.* 269F; Rüpke, *Religion*, 102–03.

[861] E.g., b. Shab 129b (partly based on the planets).

[862] Rüpke, *Religion*, 19.

[863] Ovid *Fasti*, e.g., 2.79; 3.711–12; 5.417–18; 6.788.

[864] Rüpke, *Religion*, 94–97; R. Haensch, "Inscriptions as Sources of Knowledge for Religions and Cults in the Roman World of Imperial Times," pages 176–87 in *A Companion to Roman Religion* (ed. J. Rüpke; Oxford: Blackwell, 2011) 178.

[865] (Ps.)-Dionysius *Epid.* 1.256; see, e.g., Ovid *Fasti* 3.811–12; Arrian *Alex.* 4.8.1; Socratics *Ep.* 18; Burkert, *Religion*, 226–27, 265.

[866] Suetonius *Otho* 8.3.

[867] Mitchell, *Anatolia*, 2:10. For festivals for the emperor, cf. also Josephus *War* 4.655.

[868] Josephus *Ant.* 3.91; 13.234; 14.264.

[869] Josephus *Ant.* 11.294; cf. fasts in *Ag. Ap.* 2.282. Together these account for roughly half of Josephus's use of the verb; the exceptions are *Ant.* 2.206; 15.154; 16.312; *War* 2.468; 4.268. Diogn. 4.5 probably echoes Gal 4:10.

Most interpreters take "days" as sabbaths, months as "new moons" (Col 2:16), "seasons" as the regular Jewish festivals or fasts, and "years" as the sabbatic (seventh) year and/or the jubilee. The LXX uses the Greek term for *seasons* with respect to the appointed times for festivals.

Like circumcision and eating gentile food, after the Maccabean period breaking the sabbath became a conspicuous marker of violating God's covenant.[870] The Jewish sabbath, known throughout the empire,[871] was sometimes regarded as superstitious,[872] but many gentiles were attracted to Jewish holy days.[873]

Because festal days, both Jewish and pagan, were connected with astral observations, scholars often connect them with the *stoicheia* of 4:9.[874] Indeed, in Judean tradition, angels governed the seasons.[875] Treating calendrical calculations as idolatry would probably be hyperbole, since astronomical observations do not necessarily entail worship; but Scripture offered a long tradition of some inappropriately connecting the two.[876]

But what if one celebrated festivals on the wrong day? While this practice might have been overlooked in the Old Testament (2 Chron 30:2–3, 17–20, 23), it became a matter of life and death in early Judaism. As James D. G. Dunn points out regarding 4:10, "disagreements regarding the proper observance of such [Jewish] festivals was a regular feature of intra-Jewish factional dispute."[877]

Thus, for example, in keeping with ancient Middle Eastern custom, the Pharisaic movement followed a lunar calendar;[878] the Essenes instead insisted on a solar calendar.[879]

So severe was this division that either side regarded the other as unfaithful to Jewish tradition and identity. Thus, for observers of the solar calendar, the lunar calendar was corrupt,[880] and those who observed it were like ignorant *gentiles* or sinners![881] Pharisaism's successors, however, declared that it is the gentiles who reckon by the sun.[882] Feelings about getting the fixed

---

[870] Dunn, *Galatians*, 227, cites Josephus *Ant.* 11.346.
[871] See, e.g., Suetonius *Tib.* 32.2; Gager, *Anti-Semitism*, 57.
[872] Seneca *Ep. Lucil.* 95.47; Tacitus *Hist.* 5.4; Plutarch *Superst.* 8, *Mor.* 169C.
[873] E.g., Barclay, *Jews in Diaspora*, 276, citing, e.g., Philo *Mos.* 2.20–21; Josephus *Ag. Ap.* 2.282; Horace *Sat.* 1.9.71–72; Seneca *Ep.* 95.47.
[874] Again, esp. de Boer, "Meaning"; de Boer, *Galatians*, 257; also Moo, *Galatians*, 277.
[875] 1 En. 72:1; 82:10–20; 2 En. 19:4–5.
[876] Deut 4:19; 2 Kgs 17:16; 21:3, 5; 23:4–5; 2 Chron 33:3, 5; Jer 8:2; 19:13; Zeph 1:5.
[877] Dunn, "Echoes," 470–73, quotation from 470.
[878] See, e.g., m. Rosh hash. 1:3–5.
[879] Jub. 1:10; 6:32–38; 23:19; 49:7–8. Cf. 1QS 10.3–4; 1QM 10.15; 1QpHab 11.6–7; also 1 En. 72:32; 82:6–7.
[880] Jub. 6:36.
[881] 1 En. 82:4–8, esp. 82:4; Jub. 6:35.
[882] Mekilta Pisha 2.35ff (Lauterbach, 1:18).

days of the calendar correct obviously ran high on both sides. Paul's opponents apparently bought into such feelings, but Paul no longer (cf. Gal 1:14) regarded the calendar as a matter of true consequence.

The looming threat of his converts' apostasy (4:8–10; 5:2–4) is now expressed in distress (4:11) that will trigger the letter's heaviest *pathos* section (4:12–20). (Cf. Paul's concern in 2:2 about laboring "in vain.") This is not the only place where Paul warns his converts that if they pursue the wrong path their faith and his work will have been in vain (1 Cor 15:2, 10, 14; 2 Cor 6:1; cf. Phil 2:16) or the only place where he fears the possibility (1 Thess 3:5). Elsewhere he sometimes counters these concerns fairly confidently (1 Cor 15:58; 2 Cor 7:4, 16; 8:22; 1 Thess 3:6); he does so only fairly weakly in Galatians (Gal 5:10).

4:12–20: PLEA TO RETURN TO EARLIER RELATIONSHIP

4:12 Friends, I beg you, become as I am, for I also have become as you are. You have done me no wrong.

4:13 You know that it was because of a physical infirmity that I first announced the gospel to you;

4:14 though my condition put you to the test, you did not scorn or despise me, but welcomed me as an angel of God, as Christ Jesus.

4:15 What has become of the good will you felt? For I testify that, had it been possible, you would have torn out your eyes and given them to me.

4:16 Have I now become your enemy by telling you the truth?

4:17 They make much of you, but for no good purpose; they want to exclude you, so that you may make much of them.

4:18 It is good to be made much of for a good purpose at all times, and not only when I am present with you.

4:19 My little children, for whom I am again in the pain of childbirth until Christ is formed in you,

4:20 I wish I were present with you now and could change my tone, for I am perplexed about you.

There is a clear break in tone between 4:11 and 4:12, with new and more direct deliberative appeal and the letter's first imperative.[883] It is also a section seething with *pathos*.[884]

---

[883] With, e.g., Longenecker, *Galatians*, 184, 186; Oakes, *Galatians*, 26, 144.

[884] See esp. T. W. Martin, "The Voice of Emotion: Paul's Pathetic Persuasion (Gal 4:12–20)," pages 181–202 in *Paul and Pathos* (ed. T. H. Olbricht and J. L. Sumney; SBLSymS 16; Atlanta, GA: SBL, 2001), 181–202.

A Closer Look: *Pathos*

Although Paul writes letters, he does so as one who is normally a preacher. Paul's letters often appeal to *pathos*, or emotion, as well as arguments from character (*êthos*) and from logic.[885] Like Paul, a skilled speaker might alternate between argumentation and emotional appeal.[886] The Roman rhetorician Quintilian focused on particularly negative emotions, presumably as the most effective (as often in news media and politics today). "*Pathos*," he declared, "is almost entirely concerned with anger, dislike, fear, hatred and pity."[887] A "fearful tone" is "wavering, full, halting, and mournful," whereas an angry tone should be "sharp, rapid, with short abrupt clauses."[888]

A speaker would often seek to stir compassion for himself or the defendant,[889] for example by recalling past unjust sufferings.[890] Ideally, one should arouse pity for one's own position but anger for that of one's opponent, shifting emotional gears as needed.[891]

However conventional, letters often revealed affection,[892] including in the conventional protest that a friend should write or visit (cf. Rom 1:11; 15:22).[893] Gal 4:10–20 employs many stock motifs from the conventional ancient theme of friendship.[894] Paul's letters are often warm and affectionate, more so than is usual in the usually brief, business-oriented letters that dominated antiquity.[895] ****

[885] J. L. Sumney, "Alternative Rationalities in Paul: Expanding Our Definition of Argument," *ResQ* 46 (1, 2004): 1–9.
[886] Dionysius of Halicarnassus *Isaeus* 3.
[887] Quintilian *Inst.* 6.2.20 (trans. H. E. Butler, LCL 2:429), cited also by Witherington, *Grace*, 305.
[888] Cicero *De or.* 3.217–18 (trans. E. W. Sutton, H. Rackham); Hall, "Delivery," 222.
[889] E.g., Isaeus *Menec.* 44, 47; Valerius Maximus 8.1. acquittals 2; Seneca *Controv.* 4.pref.6; Plutarch *Cic.* 39.6.
[890] Dio Chrysostom *Or.* 40.12.
[891] Rhet. Alex. 36, 1443b.16–21; Cicero *Brutus* 93.322; Quintilian *Inst.* 4.1.33; *Decl.* 298.10.
[892] E.g., Cicero *Fam.* 1.9.1; 2.2.1; 2.3.2.
[893] E.g., Cicero *Att.* 1.9, 12; 7.10; *Fam.* 2.10.1; 14.10.1; 15.20.2; 16.25.1; 16.26.1–2; Symmachus *Ep.* 1.5.1.
[894] Betz, *Galatians*, 221; A. C. Mitchell, "'Greet the Friends by Name': New Testament Evidence for the Greco-Roman *topos* on Friendship," pages 225–62 in *Greco-Roman Perspectives on Friendship* (ed. J. T. Fitzgerald; SBLRBS 34; Atlanta, GA: Scholars Press, 1997), 227–30; S. J. Kraftchick, "Πάθη in Paul: The Emotional Logic of 'Original Argument,'" pages 39–68 in *Paul and Pathos*, 63.
[895] Sanders, *Paul*, xx, 131–32; Wright, *Faithfulness*, 452.

The request formula (in 4:12, *I beg you*) was common in letters.[896] Paul seeks reconciliation, perhaps surprising the Galatians, who did not realize that their interest in his circumcisionist rivals constituted enmity with him (cf. 4:16).

"Become like me" probably evokes traditional conceptions of friendship. Greeks often claimed that a friend was like a second self.[897] In Scripture, also, one could emphasize one's solidarity with another by declaring, "I am as you are."[898] Such statements of intimacy, solidarity, or sharing of all possessions appear elsewhere as well.[899] Thus, for example, Cicero rhetorically asks his brother, "What has ever given me pleasure without your sharing it, or you without my sharing it?"[900]

In his becoming all things to all people for the sake of winning some (1 Cor 9:20–22), Paul has, like Peter, become like the gentiles outside the law by eating with them (Gal 2:14). Now he urges the Galatian gentiles to imitate his own flexibility: he has become like them, so they should become like him in recognizing that God did not now require adherence to the conventional form of the law for covenant identity or spiritual maturity. To accept his opponents' yoke of the law would make them unlike him.

Paul urging others to become like himself in some way is not unique to Galatians. Paul elsewhere invites his disciples to imitate him or praises them for doing so, because he imitates Christ (1 Cor 4:16; 11:1; Phil 3:17; 1 Thess 1:6; 2:14).[901] Young people regularly imitated not only their parents but also their teachers.[902] Apart from Cynics, philosophers were often reluctant to urge imitation of themselves,[903] but it was considered acceptable to praise oneself for the purpose of inspiring positive imitation.[904]

---

[896]   R. N. Longenecker, *Introducing Romans: Critical Issues in Paul's Most Famous Letter* (Grand Rapids, MI: Eerdmans, 2011), 218. See regularly Cicero's letters of recommendation, e.g., *Fam.* 13.14.2; 13.20.1; 13.24.3; 13.26.2.

[897]   Diodorus Siculus 17.37.6; Valerius Maximus 4.7. ext. 2ab; Cicero *Fam.* 7.5.1; 13.1.5; cf. P. Oxy. 32.5–6; Cicero *Fin.* 1.20.70; Seneca *Ep. Lucil.* 95.63.

[898]   MT and LXX of 2 Kgs 3:7; 2 Chron 18:3.

[899]   E.g., Pliny *Ep.* 6.18.3; 6.26.3; 6.28.3; 6.30.1; 6.32.2.

[900]   Cicero *Quint. frat.* 1.3.3 (trans. W. G. Williams, LCL 4:463).

[901]   B. Fiore, "Paul, Exemplification, and Imitation," pages 228–57 in *Paul in the Greco-Roman World: A Handbook* (ed. J. P. Sampley; Harrisburg, PA: Trinity Press International, 2003), esp. 237–45.

[902]   E.g., Xenophon *Mem.* 1.2.3; Quintilian *Inst.* 1.2.26; Lucian *Peregr.* 24; Fiore, "Exemplification," 233–34.

[903]   A. J. Malherbe, *Paul and the Popular Philosophers* (Philadelphia, PA: Fortress, 1989), 57, 70. For Cynics, see, e.g., Diogenes *Ep.* 14; Epictetus *Diatr.* 4.8.31.

[904]   Plutarch *Praising* 15, *Mor.* 544D; also Marshall, *Enmity*, 354; cf. 4 Macc 9:23; Xenophon *Cyr.* 8.6.10.

The context suggests that Paul's *You have done me no wrong* (Gal 4:12) means, "You did not wrong me" (when I first visited you, 4:13–14), thus implying the question, "So why are we at odds now?" (4:15–16).[905]

In 4:13–14, Paul goes on to elaborate how the Galatians did him no wrong and in fact welcomed him hospitably.[906] Paul begins 4:13 with "you know," an appeal to their own knowledge of him. Paul often offers such appeals in letters to those he knows personally (e.g., 1 Thess 1:5; 2:2, 5, 11; 4:2). Paul appeals here to *êthos*, to his character that they know.[907]

In 4:13–14, Paul speaks of how the Galatians received him on his first visit. Scholars debate the meaning of "first" visit here. In classical Greek, the term translated *first* originally meant the former of two, but by this period it could also mean simply "formerly" or "earlier." Yet even on the earliest possible date of Galatians, if the letter's destination is southern Galatia Paul had come through their cities at least twice before writing Galatians, since he visited them again (Acts 14:21–23). Given the two visits of Acts 14 as well as the possible meaning of simply "earlier," the only insight that Gal 4:13 contributes to the date of Galatians is an elementary one: Paul wrote to churches of Galatia only after he had founded them.

Paul's point is simply that when he visited them, they received him well, implying (and eventually demanding more explicitly, 4:15a, 16), "What has changed?" One arguing in a court could protest an opponent now raising a new charge that they should have raised earlier if it were really based on genuine misdeeds.[908]

Although some have suggested other forms of weakness,[909] Paul speaks specifically of a *physical* weakness. Although bodily weakness could have other senses, normally interpreters think here of sickness or injury. Letters frequently included mention of current health issues.[910] Scholars have

---

[905] One could note the inconsistency of a charge; see, e.g., Plutarch *Cic.* 25.2.
[906] On hospitality as a central value in antiquity, see, e.g., Homer *Il.* 6.212–31; 9.199–220; Pindar *Ol.* 4.12–15; Cicero *Fam.* 13.36.1; 13.73.2; Ps.-Phoc. 24; m. Ab. 1:5, 15; 3:12; Koenig, *Hospitality*, esp. 15–20.
[907] Common in persuasion, e.g., Xenophon *Apol.* 3; Aeschines *Tim.* 181; Lysias *Or.* 16.10, §146; 19.24, §154; Cicero *Sull.* 24.68–28.77; *Vat.* 10.25–26; Hermogenes *Inv.* 2.5.118–19.
[908] Hermogenes *Inv.* 3.5.148; Quintilian *Decl.* 301.19.
[909] E.g., Jerome *Ep. Gal.* 2.4.14 on Gal 4:13 (Edwards).
[910] E.g., Fronto *Ad M. Caes.* 5.18–19 (33–34); 5.30–31 (65–66); 5.54–56 (69–71); 5.59; *Ad Am.* 2.2; still more common in the papyri, e.g., BGU 27; P. Cairo Zen. 59060.1; 59251.1; P. Lond. 42.2–5; P. Oxy. 292.11–12; P. Giess. 17.4; G. A. Deissmann, *Light from the Ancient East* (Grand Rapids, MI: Baker, 1978), 151, 154, 179–80, 180n4, 184, 188, 192–94, 201–02; Weima, *Endings*, 34–39. Also some speeches, e.g., Dio Chrysostom *Or.* 39.7–8.

speculated extensively about the particular issue to which Paul alludes here, which the Galatians knew but the particularity of which probably does not affect Paul's point.

Somehow Paul's physical infirmity became an opportunity to share the gospel with them (Gal 4:13), though one may suspect that Paul would in any case seize on even the smallest opening as an opportunity for the gospel.[911] Most often commentators envision some sickness here, though suggestions become increasingly speculative as they become more specific. Many have appealed to a supposed parallel with Paul's thorn in the flesh (2 Cor 12:7); but the thorn may have been the persecutions mentioned in the surrounding context.[912]

Some suggest malaria near the coastal lowlands, which could have driven Paul to the Galatian hill country of the Anatolian interior.[913] There may, however, have been other factors leading Paul to south Galatia.[914] Others have suggested epilepsy, because *despise* in 4:14 can mean "spit," and people sometimes spat to avert the evil eye or a hostile demon.[915] (People sometimes associated epilepsy with spirit possession because of its sometimes similar bodily effects.) The evidence is thin, however.

Still others suggest that Paul had an eye problem, based especially on Gal 4:15 but also some additional factors such as the "large letters" of 6:11. The primary support for this thesis in 4:15, however, turns out to have been simply a figure of speech, and stronger explanations exist for 6:11 (see comments on these passages).

The suggestion that provides the most fruitful connections with other material in Galatians, although it remains uncertain, is that Paul refers here to wounds from his experiences of persecution.[916] One could generate sympathy by alluding to one's losses or wounds in battle[917] and so presumably

[911]   With Mussner, *Galaterbrief*, 307, whose worthy line on the subject is quoted directly in Longenecker, *Galatians*, 191.
[912]   The wording there probably reapplies to this adversity the figurative thorn of Num 33:55; Josh 23:13.
[913]   W. M. Ramsay, *St. Paul the Traveller and the Roman Citizen* (3rd edn.; London: Hodder & Stoughton, 1897), 94–97. On the prevalence and character of malaria in Paul's era, see further Keener, "Fever," 395–97, 399.
[914]   See Keener, *Acts*, 2037–38; information in Mitchell, *Anatolia*, 1:151–52; 2:6–7.
[915]   See W. Wrede, *Paul* (trans. E. Lummis; London: Philip Green, 1907), 22–23.
[916]   Allowed by Jerome; advocated by Chrysostom *Hom. Gal.* 4.14; Theodore of Mopsuestia; Augustine; Aquinas; Luther *First Lectures* on Gal 4:13, citing 2 Cor 11–12 (though also noting inner temptations); A. J. Goddard and S. A. Cummins, "Ill or Ill-Treated? Conflict and Persecution as the Context of Paul's Original Ministry in Galatia (Galatians 4.12–20)," *JSNT* 52 (1993): 93–126.
[917]   E.g., Seneca *Controv.* 1.4.2; see comment on Gal 6:17.

also in ministry. When Paul preached to them, he may have shown them his *scars* (6:17), a sign of Christ crucified in him (2:20; 3:1).

Those skeptical of the persecution view often note that Paul's ailment drove him to Galatia rather than, as in the case of persecution, occurred to him after he reached there.[918] But we have no record of what Paul may have experienced in Perga before traveling further inland (Acts 13:13). Paul was beaten in synagogues and elsewhere more often than Luke can narrate (2 Cor 11:24–25). Further, Paul faced hostility in south Galatia well before his stoning in Lystra (Acts 13:50; 14:5, 19). While the persecution thesis remains speculative, it is therefore no more so than competing proposals.

The question on any view is whether all or only some of the Galatian churches knew of Paul's infirmity (4:13) and witnessed his condition. Many cities in both north and south Galatia were more than fifty miles apart.[919] Perhaps only the house congregations of one city saw him. Or perhaps his ailment was chronic or recurrent and persisted during his evangelization of the region; this description would also fit serious wounds, which would normally take time to heal. Whatever Paul's physical weakness, far from hindering his ministry to them, as one might expect for a person of lesser determination,[920] it invited it.

Paul highlights their past affection in 4:14. In the ancient Near East, other people would withdraw from a suffering person, considering such suffering a curse from deities that one would not want to offend.[921] Unpleasant appearance and especially physical deformity invited ridicule, just as did weakness in rhetorical gestures.[922] Although there were exceptions, many associated disability and other physical afflictions with divine judgment or poor character, including in Phrygia.[923] Paul's "weakness" here thus could also affect perception of his status[924] and reception of his persuasion.[925] Paul's physical imperfection by Galatian standards could grant credibility

918 Buscemi, *Lettera*, 430; Das, *Galatians*, 460.
919 See J. Murphy-O'Connor, "Gal 4:13–14 and the Recipients of Galatians," *RB* 105 (2, 1998): 202–07; Sanders, *Paul*, 776–77.
920 Cf. M. Dibelius and W. G. Kümmel, *Paul* (Philadelphia, PA: Westminster, 1953), 42–43.
921 J. H. Walton, *Ancient Near Eastern Thought and the Old Testament: Introducing the Conceptual World of the Hebrew Bible* (Grand Rapids, MI: Baker Academic, 2006), 146.
922 See Marshall, *Enmity*, 62, 64–65; Suetonius *Jul.* 45.2. For a widely known example, note Thersites in Homer *Il.* 2.212–77.
923 Cf. R. L. Gordon, "Raising a Sceptre: Confession-Narratives from Lydia and Phrygia," *JRA* 17 (2004): 177–96.
924 With Marshall, *Enmity*, 153.
925 See, e.g., Pliny *Ep.* 2.3.9; 6.11.2; Suetonius *Claud.* 30; Lucian *Prof. P. S.* 20; Philostratus *Vit. soph.* 1.24.529; 2.5.572.

to his opponents' claim "that it is really *he* and not they who stands under God's curse."⁹²⁶

An infirm stranger might be suspected of association with the evil eye, a suspicion that could undercut normal conventions of hospitality.⁹²⁷ Paul's term translated *despise* (NRSV; my trans., *reject*) in 4:14 originally meant "spit," and many scholars argue that it retains that meaning (rather than its more common figurative sense) here. People sought to ward off the evil eye and its demonic power by spitting. If the Galatians recognized that Paul was not bewitched and hence they did not spit when he preached to them, Paul might well ask who has now bewitched them to produce such a different response to his ministry now (a common understanding of Gal 3:1). (Nevertheless, it remains possible that simple Greek alliteration dictated Paul's word choice here.)⁹²⁸

If Paul's apparently repulsive appearance involved wounds, the evil eye interpretation here would probably falter.⁹²⁹ But it would not be less reason to be repulsed by Paul, especially if the wounds or bruises were inflicted by authorities respected by the Galatian gentiles, such as civic authorities in Perga, or by Galatian Jews, such as those from a synagogue in Perga.

In any case, Paul's appearance was a *test* for the Galatians (4:14a). His appearance made it potentially more difficult for them to receive Paul's message, but they passed the test.⁹³⁰ Instead of viewing Paul negatively, as his potentially preternatural affliction could have invited, they embraced him superlatively. Far from associating him with the evil eye or anything demonic, they received him as an *angel of God* (4:14).⁹³¹ This is a highly honorable association. Some Jewish sources, for example, claimed that God spoke through Moses or Aaron as if they were his angels.⁹³²

An angel of God probably evokes the biblical "angel of the Lord," the likeliest background if Paul draws on the Old Testament in his description. In the Old Testament, God's angel spoke for him, and some passages identify the two.⁹³³ The leading Diaspora Jewish intellectual, Philo, spoke of God's

⁹²⁶ Das, *Galatians*, 461.
⁹²⁷ Longenecker, *Remember the Poor*, 213n5.
⁹²⁸ Aune, *Dictionary of Rhetoric*, 33.
⁹²⁹ Witherington, *Grace*, 309, thus counts the evil eye interpretation of 4:14 against the persecution interpretation of 4:13.
⁹³⁰ Evil can provide an opportunity to prove one's character (Eccl. Rab. 12:1, §1).
⁹³¹ Dunn, *Galatians*, 234.
⁹³² 4Q377 f2ii.11; possibly 4Q545 f1ai.8, 17.
⁹³³ Gen 48:15–16.

logos, or reason, as the Lord's angel;[934] the highest angel is the Lord himself;[935] those who cannot see God directly see his angel/*logos* as his image.[936]

The likeliest specific background to supply his language would be texts where a person respectfully addresses another as like "an angel of God." Thus some speakers address David as like "an angel of God."[937] After wrestling with an angel, Jacob tells Esau that he sees his face like one seeing God's face (Gen 33:10).[938]

Commentators often suggest that the Galatians' early reception of Paul as a divine or angelic figure may correspond to the incident in Lystra when Paul was initially mistaken for a deity, which in Diaspora Jewish terms might be more positively understood as an angel. We lack enough details to be sure of the nature of the connection, but both deities and angels were believed to visit mortals at times in disguise.[939]

Does the next phrase, *as Christ Jesus,* equate Jesus with an angel or progress to an even higher level of honor?[940] Grammatically and rhetorically, either is possible. If the "angel" here is the divine angel of the Lord, however, Paul might not envision a significant difference. In a passage that would be understood as messianic, David's house would be regarded "like God, like the angel of the LORD" (Zech 12:8).[941] Presumably, Christ is being presented in a divine role here, in keeping with Paul's Christological assumptions that surface also in Gal 1:1, 3; 4:6.

For Paul to be identified with Christ (here figuratively; 4:14) is not surprising. Paul is an agent of Christ (Gal 1:1; 2:20; 3:1; 6:17), and whoever welcomed Jesus's agent welcomed Jesus himself (2 Cor 5:20–21), as Jesus himself taught (Matt 10:40//Luke 10:16//John 13:20). In Scripture, God counted the treatment of some individuals or groups as treatment toward himself (Exod 16:8; 1 Sam 8:7; Prov 19:17; Zech 2:8).

[934] Philo *Alleg.* 3.177; *Cher.* 3; *Immut.* 182; *Conf.* 146; *Flight* 5; *Names* 87.
[935] *Dreams* 1.157. The highest angel is the *logos* in Philo *Heir* 205.
[936] *Dreams* 1.239.
[937] See LXX 2 Sam 14:17, 20; 19:27; cf. Esth 15:13.
[938] From the second century, mainstream Christians identified Jesus with the angel of the Lord until potential Arian associations in the fourth century forced the image's discontinuation.
[939] See, e.g., Homer *Il.* 4.86–87, 121–24; Virgil *Aen.* 1.314–15, 657–60; Ovid *Metam.* 1.212–13, 220, 676; Gen 18:1–16; Heb 13:2.
[940] Fee, *Galatians,* 166, sees *as Christ Jesus* as a higher progression than even Old Testament "angelic theophanies."
[941] Philo believed that God sometimes presents himself as an angel (*Dreams* 1.238–39).

In 4:15, Paul contrasts their present alienation with their past affection. One way of arguing was to point out that in the past the hearer would have granted one's request, so they should be all the more ready to do so now.[942] Chrysostom insightfully explains, "Do you see the absurdity of receiving him as an angel of God when pursued and persecuted but not receiving him when he commands what is necessary?"[943]

Appeals to others' love for one were common,[944] and Paul, depending on his relationship with his churches or the members' with one another, elsewhere appeals to this (2 Cor 6:13; 8:24; Phil 2:1). When Paul asks *What has become of the good will you felt?* (4:15), the Greek term translated *good will* in the NRSV is *makarismos*, or blessedness/happiness, and probably refers to them counting it a blessing to receive this great messenger of God (4:14).[945] Paul now elaborates rhetorically on the blessing they had once counted it to receive him.

There is no thought that the Galatians would have actually extracted their eyeballs literally, but it succeeds as a grotesque and therefore gripping image.[946] Given the proximity of Paul's mention of a physical problem (4:13–14), modern interpreters sometimes argue that the mention of eyes reflects the Galatians' past sympathy for Paul's putative eye condition. The mention of eyes says nothing about Paul's infirmity, however. A person could speak of loving another person as one's own eyes;[947] sacrificing one's eyes was thus idiomatic for self-sacrificial love.[948] An analogous idiom in English today would be "You would have given your right arm for me."[949]

Rhetorical questions (4:16) are often a means to protest one's innocence. Paul elsewhere can ask ironically, "How have I wronged you?" (2 Cor 12:13, 17–18). "If I love you more," Paul the wounded lover pleads, "am I to be loved less?" (12:15). This sort of questioning was also relevant for responding to charges of enmity.[950] For example, one demands

---

[942] Hermogenes *Inv.* 3.11.159.
[943] Chrysostom *Hom. Gal.* 4.14 (Edwards).
[944] See, e.g., Fronto *Ad M. Caes.* 3.2; 5.1–2; 5.52 (67). For requests to prove one's love, see, e.g., Cicero *Fam.* 7.14.2; *Att.* 12.18; Plutarch *Alex.* 39.4; Symmachus *Ep.* 1.27.
[945] Reading the Greek genitive here as subjective, with Matera, *Galatians*, 160.
[946] Cf., e.g., Seneca the Elder *Controv.* 1.4.10 (tearing out eyes rather than seeing the horrible crime); Silius Italicus 10.637 (mothers of his slain troops must wish to rip out his eyes).
[947] Callimachus *Hymn* 3 (to Artemis), lines 210–11; Catullus 3.5; 14.1–3; 82.1–4.
[948] With Betz, *Galatians*, 227–28; C. S. Keener, "Three Notes on Figurative Language: Inverted Guilt in Acts 7:55–60, Paul's Figurative Vote in Acts 26:10, Figurative Eyes in Galatians 4:15," *JGRChJ* 5 (2008): 41–49, here 47–49; Petronius *Sat.* 1; Sipre Deut. 313.1.4.
[949] Hays, "Galatians," 294.
[950] E.g., Aeschines *Embassy* 23; Cicero *Sest.* 52.111.

in protest to know why they are treating him like an enemy when he has loved them so much.[951]

Many scholars doubt that Paul is asking a question here (as in most translations, e.g., NRSV, KJV, NASB, NET, WEB, NIV, ESV), contending that instead he is offering a statement of protest regarding their current attitude toward him. Either way, 4:16 presumes that the relationship is no longer what it should be and protests that the fault does not lie with Paul.

Probably some Galatian believers assumed that they could merely supplement Paul's teaching with the new message brought by his rivals. Paul, however, declares that the options are mutually exclusive. As in ancient partisan politics, friendship with one's enemy made one an enemy; one had to choose one side or the other.[952] If enemies maligned one, one's friends were obligated to come to one's aid.[953]

Some later Jewish-oriented but sectarian adherents of Jesus's teaching, probably influenced by the circles that spawned Paul's opponents in Galatia, did indeed call him "the enemy."[954] Those Jews who saw "living like a gentile" by eating with gentiles as betraying their people (see Gal 2:14–15; comment on 4:10) could think of Paul as an apostate.[955]

Moralists often remarked that true friends would tell the truth even when it was painful to hear, whereas flatterers (cf. 1 Thess 2:5) were really enemies rather than friends (Prov 27:6).[956] This principle was especially true in friendships[957] (where such boldness often proved safer than in politics). Paul refuses to be such an unfaithful friend; he speaks for his hearers' good.

"The truth" Paul is telling them here is the truth mentioned earlier in Galatians – the "truth of the gospel" (2:5, 14). Paul here was seeking the Galatians' good;[958] how did this make him their enemy? The real enemies were Paul's opponents, to whom the Galatians ought not to be listening.[959]

---

[951] Sallust *Pomp.* 1.
[952] See, e.g., (Ps.)-Lysias *Or.* 9.13, §115; Aeschines *Tim.* 54–57, 193–95; Cicero *Scaur.* 17.38; further Marshall, *Enmity*, 67–69.
[953] Demosthenes *Ep.* 2, §26.
[954] Longenecker, *Galatians*, 26–27, 193, and others cite Kerygmata Petrou (probably late second century); Ps.-Clem. Hom., Ep. Pet. 2.3; Ps.-Clem. Recogn. 1.70.
[955] For one nuanced discussion of the charge, see Barclay, "Paul among Jews."
[956] See, e.g., Dionysius of Halicarnassus *Ant. rom.* 11.9.1; Tacitus *Hist.* 1.15; Plutarch *Aem. Paul.* 11.3; *Flatt.* 1–37, *Mor.* 48E–74E; Dio Chrysostom *Or.* 4.15.
[957] Plutarch *Profit by Enemies* 6, *Mor.* 89B; *Flatt.* 17–37, *Mor.* 59A–74E.
[958] Arguing that one acted for others' good defended against charges of wrongdoing; see Rhet. Alex. 4, 1427a.24–30, esp. 26–27; Dio Chrysostom *Or.* 45.10.
[959] Hermogenes *Inv.* 3.11.159 (trans. G. A. Kennedy, p. 115) regards it as obvious that "One ought not to obey the orders of an enemy."

Probably the Galatians do not in fact consider Paul an enemy. Paul is simply making the necessity of the choice clear to them. Loyalty was one of the virtues expected from true friends.[960]

Paul shifts focus somewhat in 4:17–18. As in 2 Corinthians, once Paul is in the mode of *pathos* he can shift quickly from a personal plea of deep affection (2 Cor 6:11–13) to warning against rivals (6:14–7:1). It was important, when possible, to show that one's opponents did not have one's best interests in mind.[961]

The NRSV's *They make much of you* is an attempt to capture the range of meaning in the Greek phrase *zēlousin humas*. The term *zēloô* here surely holds its usual meaning with a personal object, "have deep interest in, court the favor of";[962] this is the sense it must carry in 4:18 (*good to be made much of*) and presumably carries the same meaning in 4:17.

But some argue that Paul plays on additional nuances of the term. Because of its cognate term in 1:14, some believe that it retains associations of zeal for the law, which would in any case be true of the interests of Paul's opponents. Moreover, the term can mean "be jealous of," which could be fitting in the possible context of amatory rivalry (4:17–18) and possible reference to the evil eye (3:1).

Many see Paul's language here as portraying his rivals *courting* the Galatians, as in a rivalry for their affection. This would explain why, instead of telling the hard truth as Paul does (Gal 4:16), the rivals simply engage in a seducer's flattery.

The rivals are zealous for the Galatians, *but for no good purpose* (4:17b). This contrasts with Paul's *good purpose* in 4:18, a contrast enabled by Paul's choice of a term (*zēloô*) with potentially either positive or negative connotations.[963] That *they want to exclude you* to make you zealous for them might evoke the motif of the "excluded lover," which appears frequently in ancient literature and speech. Ancient sources were full of laments of unrequited love, and the image of locking a lover out often occurred in contexts of insincere love or emotional manipulation.[964] If Paul plays on such a theme

---

[960] Rhet. Alex. 36, 1442a.13–14; Valerius Maximus 3.8.ext. 5–6; 4.7.pref; Chariton *Chaer.* 3.3.1; Dio Chrysostom *Or.* 66.28; Prov 18:24; 27:10; Sir 6:7–16; 12:8; 22:25; 37:1–2.

[961] E.g., Cicero *Verr.* 2.3.96.223.

[962] Lightfoot, *Galatians*, 176; Matera, *Galatians*, 161; Moo, *Galatians*, 287.

[963] Cf. Josephus *War* 4.161: the "Zealots" claimed to be zealous for good things, but were really zealous for evil.

[964] See the abundant evidence in Smith, "*Ekkleisai.*" See further Fredrickson, "Motifs."

here, this is not the only passage in which he is ready to expose the exploitive character of opponents (2 Cor 11:20). Someone deeply concerned for his letter's recipient might charge that another lover might pretend greater love simply because his passion is greater, but in reality he is simply more shameless.[965]

What do the rivals *want to exclude* them from? By treating the Galatian believers as not yet members of God's people, Paul's rivals are excluding them from the people of God until they become circumcised. In practice this probably means refusal of table fellowship until the gentile believers are circumcised (see Gal 2:11–14). Paul's language of exclusion here (using *ekkleiô*) probably also evokes his earlier image of being imprisoned or locked up under the law (3:23, using *sugkleiô*).

Many view 4:18a as a familiar aphorism that Paul bends to his purpose.[966] A TLG search for examples prior to the third century unfortunately suggests otherwise,[967] though this does not bring into question the idea's intelligibility. Many read the passage as Paul himself having courted them for their good before, yet now they unfaithfully welcome someone to court them with dishonorable motives. Courting does not suit the parental image explicit in 4:19, but Paul can readily shift metaphors (cf. 1 Cor 3:6–10). If Paul intends the image of "courting" in Gal 4:17–18, it is only because he portrays his rivals as sexual predators; Paul is normally the concerned parent who is responsible for a daughter's continued virginity and proper betrothal (cf. 2 Cor 11:2).

A majority of interpreters today believe that the Galatians are objects of Paul's zeal in a good way in 4:18; he is the one who has told them the truth (4:16) and he struggles again in birth pangs for them (4:19). Paul might intend a double application: the Galatians might well think he speaks of his zealous love for them when first hearing 4:18a, but the last part of the verse might highlight instead the faithful love they ought to be showing Paul. If Paul does not invite their love directly, he does so at least indirectly, if the final part of the verse refers instead to his own faithfulness in loving them even when apart. Reciprocity was essential,[968] and ancient ethics deemed fickleness (which they have shown, 4:14–16) a vice.[969]

---

965 Fronto *Ep. Graecae* 8.5, though not sexually pursuing his imperial pupil, in a letter sets himself up as a rival against one who would sexually exploit him.

966 Burton, *Galatians*, 247 (in form); Witherington, *Grace*, 314; deSilva, *Readings*, 215.

967 Courtesy of PhD student Donald Murray Vasser.

968 See comment on Gal 6:6.

969 E.g., Cicero *Pro Flacco* 11.24; *Quint. fratr.* 1.2.2.4; see further discussion in comment on Gal 2:11–14.

The *pathos* of this section (4:12–20) reaches its apex in 4:19, as Paul shares the pain that his children's waywardness is putting him through. Ideally, a letter was supposed to share the author's heart and character;[970] Paul speaks as one willing to suffer for his dear children, though they are creating this suffering needlessly.

Paul has been addressing them especially with the endearing title of siblings (rendered inconsistently in the NRSV; 1:11; 3:15; 4:12, 28, 31; 5:11, 13; 6:1, 18); they are elsewhere here Abraham's (3:7; 4:28, 31), Sarah's (4:27–28, 31), and God's (3:26; 4:6–7) children, but as Abraham is their long-range ancestor, Paul is their short-range parent.

Paul's *again* might allude in part to the physical pain, whether sickness or persecution, that originally brought him to them (4:13); in any case, it surely alludes to the struggles he underwent to bring their churches to birth (cf. Acts 13:50–51; 14:2, 5, 19). The image is, however, more pervasive in Jewish sources. As a metaphor for suffering, the image of "birth pangs" was applied to men as well as women,[971] although in the metaphor they are being compared to women.[972]

The image of birth pangs was suitable to any terrible affliction,[973] but often stands for the promised pangs that would usher in the new world or its ruler.[974] For Paul, eschatological tribulation was a present experience (Rom 8:22); birthing new believers as a foretaste of the new creation (Gal 6:15; 2 Cor 5:17) was part of that tribulation (cf. Rom 8:17–23; Col 1:24; 2 Thess 1:4–5).[975]

The birthing is their being *born according to the Spirit* (4:29), as those who share in Jesus's filial relationship to God not through the law but through the Spirit (4:4–6). The Galatians, if converted at all, were converted when they received the Spirit (3:2), and this not by law-works but through believing Paul's preaching of Christ (3:1–2).

That the Galatians need to be birthed again suggests how far they have fallen. Other features of Galatians may suggest that they have not yet fallen away fully (5:1–2; the frequent label of "siblings," e.g., 1:11; 3:15), but Paul

---

[970] Demetrius *Style* 4.227; Seneca *Ep. Lucil.* 75.1–3; cf. 2 Cor 6:11.

[971] E.g., Jer 30:6; 50:43 (LXX 27:43); Hos 13:13; 4Q429 f3.3.

[972] E.g., Sir 19:11; 48:19; Isa 45:10; Jer 6:24; 13:21; 22:23; 50:43 (LXX 27:43); Hos 13:13; 1QHa 11.8.

[973] E.g., Ps 48:6; Isa 21:3; 42:14; Jer 4:31; 31:8; 48:41; 49:22, 24; Mic 4:10.

[974] Isa 66:7–8; Mic 5:2–4; 1QHa 11.8–11; 1 En. 62:4; 4 Ezra 4:40–43; Mark 13:8//Matt 24:8.

[975] Luke summarizes Paul's teaching in Galatia as tribulation ushering in the kingdom (Acts 14:22).

presents them here as if they have (cf. similarly his rhetorical pleas to the Corinthians in 2 Cor 5:20; 6:1–2). Christ is in believers (Gal 2:20), and if he is not yet in the Galatians, they are not yet converted (2 Cor 13:5). Through embracing Christ's truth, the process of formation into his image may be progressive (Rom 12:2; 2 Cor 3:18)[976] and its consummation future (Rom 8:29; cf. 1 Cor 15:48–52; Phil 3:21). If the process has not yet begun, however, they are not in Christ. Though the current image may be hyperbolic, the imminent danger of falling away against which the hyperbole warns is real (see comment at 5:4).

The image here is of Paul as the Galatians' mother, as most commentators recognize.[977] God is all believers' ultimate Father (Gal 1:3–4; 4:6), but divine and human paternity were not always incompatible; some Jews compared those who converted gentiles with those who had begotten them.[978] Abraham's and Sarah's promised descendants were also God's children (Gal 3:7, 26; 4:6–7, 27–31); Paul is a more proximate Sarah sort of figure in this spiritual lineage. The pangs already prefigure those of Sarah in Isa 51:2, alluded to in Gal 4:27, and Isa 54:1, quoted in the same Pauline verse.

What is most intriguing is that Paul uses birth pangs language in two adjacent paragraphs, in Gal 4:19 and in 4:27. Given that Paul uses cognates of this language elsewhere only rarely (1 Thess 5:3; Rom 8:22), the proximity of these references is likely no coincidence. As a messianic Jew, part of Israel's righteous remnant, and perhaps as part of Jesus's movement more generally, Paul is part of Zion travailing to bring forth. The delivered remnant gives birth to the fully restored people of God (Isa 66:7–13).

Gal 4:20 revisits the question of Paul's absence, raised in 4:18. Unlike Paul, Paul's opponents retain direct access to the Galatians. Paul often must remind churches of his presence in heart (1 Cor 5:3; Col 2:5).[979] In any case, Paul wishes that he could speak directly to the Galatians. Longing to see another was a common theme in letters (cf. Rom 1:11; 2 Tim 1:4).[980]

---

[976]   Cf. Keener, *Mind*, 152, 156–58, 206–15, esp. 215.

[977]   Jerome *Ep. Gal.* 2.4.19 (Edwards); J. Cherian, "Paul: A Mother to His Churches – A Brief Examination of Parental Imagery in 1 Thess. 2:1–12 and Gal. 4:19–20," *DhDeep* 5 (1, 2001): 35–47; see esp. B. Roberts Gaventa, *Our Mother Saint Paul* (Louisville, KY: Westminster John Knox, 2007).

[978]   Sipre Deut. 32.2.1; Ab. R. Nat. 12A; 26, §54B; citations in W. D. Davies, *Paul and Rabbinic Judaism: Some Rabbinic Elements in Pauline Theology* (4th edn.; Philadelphia, PA: Fortress, 1980), 119.

[979]   In a figurative, not metaphysical way; see, e.g., P. Oxy. 32; Cicero *Fam.* 1.7.1; further discussion at Gal 3:1 (X-refs).

[980]   See, e.g., P. Oxy. 528.6–9; Cicero *Fam.* 8.15.2; 16.1.1; Pliny *Ep.* 6.1.1–2; 6.4.1–5; 6.7.1–3; 6.14.1; 7.5.1–2; Fronto *Ad M. Caes.* 2.4; 2.10.3; 2.14; 3.9.2; 3.19; 4.5.3; 4.7; 6.6.1.

Letters were supposed to be substitutes for presence,[981] but face to face conversation was normally deemed preferable to pen and ink (cf. 2 John 12; 3 John 13).[982]

Paul wanted to be present so he could change his tone. Good speakers could vary tones as needed,[983] sometimes even within a single speech.[984] Questions, answers, and exaggeration to heighten intensity cannot properly "be delivered in the same pitch and tone of voice."[985] But in a letter Paul could only depend on the reader to try to convey his heart in a way that he would rather deliver in person.

Now Paul laments that he is *perplexed* (4:20). Some communicators used claims of such perplexity to convey the intensity of their emotion. An orator might feign or arouse such feeling for dramatic purposes,[986] but it could also be authentic,[987] including in letters.[988] One could profess to be at a loss as to what to say.[989] It was often most effective in the end of a speech;[990] Paul uses it here to conclude the main *pathos* section of his letter.

4:21–5:1: ABRAHAM'S FREE HEIRS VERSUS HIS SLAVE CHILDREN

4:21 Tell me, you who desire to be subject to the law, will you not listen to the law?

4:22 For it is written that Abraham had two sons, one by a slave woman and the other by a free woman.

4:23 One, the child of the slave, was born according to the flesh; the other, the child of the free woman, was born through the promise.

4:24 Now this is an allegory: these women are two covenants. One woman, in fact, is Hagar, from Mount Sinai, bearing children for slavery.

---

[981] See Achilles Tatius 5.20.5; A. J. Malherbe, "Ancient Epistolary Theorists," *OJRS* 5.2 (1977): 3–77, here 15; Stowers, *Letter Writing*, 39, 62, 157.

[982] E.g., Socrates *Ep.* 6; Cicero *Fam.* 2.3.2; 4.6.1; 4.10.1; 13.47.1; *Att.* 13.19; Pliny *Ep.* 6.2.9.

[983] E.g., Cicero *Fam.* 9.21.1; Dionysius of Halicarnassus *Demosthenes* 15.

[984] E.g., Pliny *Ep.* 3.13.4; 6.33.7–10. Sudden variations, however, could be problematic (Cicero *Brutus* 43.158).

[985] Dionysius of Halicarnassus *Demosthenes* 54 (trans. S. Usher, LCL 1:445).

[986] Probably Isocrates *Antid.* 140, 310, 320; Cicero *Verr.* 2.5.1.2 (in light of 2.5.2.5); Dio Chrysostom *Or.* 37.9 (probably from Favorinus); Dio Chrysostom *Or.* 47.12–20, esp. 18; Apuleius *Apol.* 84; in a rhetorical letter, Fronto *Ad M. Caes.* 4.7.

[987] See, e.g., Dio Cassius 8.36.5; Plutarch *Cic.* 20.1.

[988] E.g., Cicero *Fam.* 2.4.1; 2.11.1; *Att.* 3.5.

[989] E.g., Cicero *Verr.* 2.5.66.170; *Orator* 40.137.

[990] Anderson, *Glossary*, 24, citing *Inst.* 6.1.3.

4:25 Now Hagar is Mount Sinai in Arabia and corresponds to the present Jerusalem, for she is in slavery with her children.

4:26 But the other woman corresponds to the Jerusalem above; she is free, and she is our mother.

4:27 For it is written,

> "Rejoice, you childless one, you who bear no children,
>   burst into song and shout, you who endure no birth pangs;
> for the children of the desolate woman are more numerous
>   than the children of the one who is married."

4:28 Now you, my friends, are children of the promise, like Isaac.

4:29 But just as at that time the child who was born according to the flesh persecuted the child who was born according to the Spirit, so it is now also.

4:30 But what does the scripture say? "Drive out the slave and her child; for the child of the slave will not share the inheritance with the child of the free woman."

4:31 So then, friends, we are children, not of the slave but of the free woman.

5:1 For freedom Christ has set us free. Stand firm, therefore, and do not submit again to a yoke of slavery.

Paul has been engaging and elaborating the Abraham material of Genesis since 3:6, except for his digression to develop *pathos* in 4:12–20. Since argumentation required a different tone than *pathos*, there clearly is a shift in tone at 4:21, possibly in keeping with the shift Paul proposes in 4:20. Paul's contrast between slave and free is not meant to denigrate slaves (cf. 3:28) but to appeal to his audience's reason: freedom is a more desirable state than being enslaved.

Much of Paul's appropriation of the Old Testament Hagar narrative is counterintuitive. Hagar, a gentile to whom the Lord reveals himself, is the first biblical figure to explicitly meet the angel of the Lord (Gen 16:7–13); in other circumstances, one might have expected Paul to use Hagar as a model. In this instance, however, his rivals have probably unfortunately appropriated her first.

Persuaders liked to be able to turn opponents' advantages against them in debate.[991] For many centuries some scholars have suggested that the curious character of Paul's argument here stems from him opposing an argument by his rivals.[992] After all, Paul nowhere else uses allegory in this form, or

---

[991] See Rhet. Her. 3.3.6; Heath, "Invention," 93–94; Rowe, "Style," 145–46.
[992] E.g., Theodore of Mopsuestia *Commentary* (Edwards); Ramsay, *Galatians*, 431–32; C. K. Barrett, *Essays on Paul* (Philadelphia, PA: Westminster, 1982), 162.

the term anywhere else, even where it would have been convenient.[993] Paul assumes that his largely gentile audience is also familiar with this story; it may be that they heard it from his rivals. It is not difficult to guess how his rivals could have used the story had they wished. When Judeans at Qumran allegorize, they emphasize obedience to the Torah.[994]

As is evident elsewhere in Galatians, Paul's opponents insist that gentiles cannot become true descendants of Abraham without accepting the covenant obligations of Abraham's children, such as circumcision. As noted earlier, they probably depended on circumcision as a covenant obligation in Gen 17:9–14.

Considering Paul's gentile converts only partially converted to Judaism, the opponents may have considered them something like Ishmaelites, somehow related to Abraham but outside the covenant.[995] Even Ishmael was circumcised (Gen 17:25), but his descendants were gentiles, and some Judean traditions were emphatic about this point.[996] Most important for Paul's point, Isaac, not Ishmael, was the heir (Gal 4:30); Paul reaffirms that gentile believers are, along with Jewish believers, *heirs* (3:29; 4:7), that is, the spiritual line of Isaac.

Paul must now reverse his opponents' line of interpretation. Because his opponents neglect the promise, the way of the Spirit, it is they who are Abrahamites outside the covenant. They are spiritual Ishmaelites, circumcised yet missing the very fulfillment that the law had promised. Paul has connected the law with slavery (3:22–25; 4:1–5); this offers a fitting point of connection with the slave line of descent (4:24–25, 30–31).

The allegorical correspondences appear especially in 4:24–26; by contrast, 4:28–31 can function typologically, based on principles and analogies. Martyn charts out the "antithetical correspondences" between two covenants in 4:22–27 and then the more typological correspondences between two sons in 4:28–30.[997]

(Earlier covenant, 4:24)	(Eschatological covenant, 4:24)
Slave woman (4:22–23)	Free woman (4:22–23)
Gives birth according to the flesh (4:23)	Gives birth through promise (4:23)

[993] E.g., with circumcision and food laws (Hays, *Echoes*, 166), as among some of his contemporaries.
[994] See CD 6.3–11, which Bruce, *Galatians*, 218, parallels with the thinking of Paul's rivals.
[995] Hays, *Echoes*, 111; Longenecker, *Galatians*, 199.
[996] Jub. 16:17–18, cited by Hays, *Echoes*, 113–14.
[997] The following chart is taken, with minor modifications, from Dunn, *Galatians*, 244, who follows Martyn, "Antinomies," 418–19. For an earlier version of such a chart, see Lightfoot, *Galatians*, 179.

Mount Sinai (4:24–25)	(Mount Zion, not named)[998]
Bears children for slavery (4:24)	Our mother (4:26)
Hagar (4:24–25)	"The other woman" (Sarah; 4:26)
Present Jerusalem (4:25)	Jerusalem above (4:26)
In slavery (4:25)	Free (4:26)
Wife with fewer children (4:27)	Desolate woman with many children (4:27)

First son	Second son
Born according to the flesh (4:29)	Born according to the Spirit (4:29)
Persecutes (4:29)	Child of promise (cf. 4:28)
Drive out; must not share inheritance (4:30)	Inherits all (4:30)
Born of slave woman (4:30–31)	Born of free woman (4:30–31)

Antithesis was a standard rhetorical device, designed to hold attention, like other forms of parallelism.[999] Comparison was also a standard rhetorical exercise (see comment at Gal 2:7–9), one that Paul sometimes develops at some length (see esp. Rom 5:12–21; 1 Cor 15:42–49; 2 Cor 3:6–18; 11:21–23; Gal 5:16–17).[1000]

A Closer Look: Paul's Allegory in Gal 4:21–31

Paul's use of the verb *allêgoreô* in Gal 4:24 (NRSV: *an allegory*) has generated no small concern from commentators.

Allegorization was natural in a Greek philosophic milieu, especially in Alexandria.[1001] Philosophers, including early Stoics and especially later Platonists and Pythagoreans, regularly allegorized offensive elements of myths.[1002]

Christian interpreters have approached Paul's exposition here in various ways. Origen used Paul's words here to support his own approach to texts.[1003] By contrast, Theodore of Mopsuestia, far from denying the literal sense, warned that Paul is here countering errorists who abuse Genesis and

---

[998] Dunn has here "promise."

[999] For antitheses in rhetoric, see Rhet. Alex. 26, 1435b.25–39; Dionysius of Halicarnassus *Lysias* 14; Anderson, *Glossary*, 21–22; Rowe, "Style," 142.

[1000] See C. Forbes, "Paul and Rhetorical Comparison," pages 134–71 in *Paul in the Greco-Roman World: A Handbook* (ed. J. P. Sampley; Harrisburg, PA: Trinity Press International, 2003); he treats Gal 4:21–31 on 158–59.

[1001] See esp. Philo, e.g., *Plant.* 36, 129 (using Greek myth); *Post.* 7; *Free* 80; *Dreams* 1.102; H. A. Wolfson, *Philo: Foundations of Religious Philosophy in Judaism, Christianity, and Islam* (2 vols.; 4th rev. edn.; Cambridge, MA: Harvard University Press, 1968), 1:87–163.

[1002] See numerous samples in Keener, *Acts*, 1260–61.

[1003] Esp. in *Cels.* 4.44. See Longenecker, *Galatians*, xlvii–xlviii.

deny the actual historical sense.[1004] Already the Old Testament prophets used figures of their own time as signs or symbols of what was coming, in addition to (rather than instead of) those figures' historical experience (Isa 8:18; 20:3; Ezek 12:11; Zech 3:8).

Yet Augustine argued that the letter – merely literal interpretation – of the law kills.[1005] Noting Paul's appeal to "allegory," ninth-century interpreter Haimo of Auxerre inferred the necessity of a spiritual significance beyond the literal words.[1006] After experiencing allegory's medieval abuses, on the other hand, Luther and subsequently Calvin rejected this approach.[1007]

In some respects Paul's exegesis in Gal 4:21–31 is comparable to Judean midrash: an initial text developed by means of an additional citation, with links to both texts via keywords,[1008] and a closing text and application, referring to the initial text (cf. Gen 21:10).[1009] Gentiles in Galatia would not, however, be as familiar with this approach as with his use of homiletical allegory, which public speakers in Roman colonies such as Pisidian Antioch and Lystra would have sometimes probably used.[1010] It is not the sequence of his exposition (plausibly related to Paul's Judean background) but the allegorical links in Gal 4:24–26 that confound most readers today.

How much of Paul's exegesis is allegorical and how much is typological? To some extent that decision depends on how we define the terms. One contemporary distinction between typology and allegory is that typology connects type and antitype by means of an analogous situation, whereas allegory lacks such concern.[1011] Many scholars find some or much allegory here; others see Paul's argument as wholly typological, extrapolating the biblical "narrative of divine promise."[1012] Ancient thinkers often did parallel figures or events they deemed analogous,[1013] as did Paul (1 Cor 10:11).

[1004] Theodore of Mopsuestia *Commentary* (TEM 1:73–74; Edwards).

[1005] Augustine *Letter to Paulinus* 186; *Easter Sermon* 251.7 (Bray).

[1006] Haimo on Gal 4:24 (Levy), comparing the sacraments.

[1007] C. G. Bartholomew, *Introducing Biblical Hermeneutics: A Comprehensive Framework for Hearing God in Scripture* (Grand Rapids, MI: Baker Academic, 2015), 197–98; Luther's *Second Lectures on Galatians* on 4:24; Calvin *Commentary on Galatians* 4:24 (Bray).

[1008] Freedom (4:22, 23, 26, 30), slave (4:22, 23, 30, 31) and child/children (4:22, 25, 27, 28, 30, 31).

[1009] E. E. Ellis, "How the New Testament Uses the Old," pages 199–219 in *New Testament Interpretation: Essays on Principles and Methods* (ed. I. H. Marshall; Grand Rapids, MI: Eerdmans, 1977), 204–05.

[1010] Witherington, *Grace*, 322, citing Quintilian *Inst.* 8.6.47.

[1011] R. P. C. Hanson, *Allegory and Event* (London, SCM, 1959), 7, as cited in Hansen, *Galatians*, 141.

[1012] Hays, *Echoes*, 57.

[1013] Plutarch *Thes.* 1.2; *Sert.* 1.1; *Demosth.* 3.2; Appian *Bell. civ.* 2.21.149; Keener, *Acts*, 557–62, 569–74, 1363.

Luther and Calvin were certainly fond of Paul theology, but not so much of Paul's argument here. "Allegories are not the basis for theology," Luther warned, "but they may be used to illustrate particular points that were originally made on a different basis," as Paul has already done.[1014]

That is, Paul is making a homiletical/rhetorical/polemical move at this point (probably directed against use of the same text by the agitators), not offering a hermeneutical model. This suggestion is consistent with the ancient semantic range of *allêgoreô*. Paul is speaking to Galatians on his authority, reinterpreting a story they have heard, offering not the sort of exegesis he more typically engages in (cf. 3:6–14), but exhortation.

A Different Kind of Allegory

The term *allegory* has more than one sense, as Chrysostom warns on this passage.[1015] Besides a method used to extract desired morals from problematic mythic narratives, in rhetoric (persuasion) "allegory" also included any "of a group of figures which say one thing but hint at another."[1016] Figures could include something like an extended metonymy; in metonymy, something is called by a name of something else associated with it.[1017] The form of allegory used here is meant not to teach truth about persons within the narrative world, but about those within the audience's world; one can speak allegorically from a story that was not originally intended as allegory.[1018]

Such allegorization gave stories a secondary level of meaning rather than implying that the new exposition reflects their original meaning.[1019] "An ancient allegory," Witherington explains, "was not like Bunyan's *Pilgrim's Progress* or Spenser's *Faerie Queene* where detailed point by point 'this is that' sort of referents were the norm."[1020]

[1014] Luther *Second Lectures on Galatians* on 4:24 (Bray). See similarly Calvin *Commentary on Galatians* on 4:21 (Bray).

[1015] Chrysostom *Commentary on Galatians* 4.22; also cited by Calvin *Commentary on Galatians* on 4:24 (Bray).

[1016] Anderson, *Glossary*, 14–16; Rhet. Her. 4.34.46.

[1017] Rhet. Her. 4.32.43; Rowe, "Style," 126. A. Davis, "Allegorically Speaking in Galatians 4:21–5:1," *BBR* 14 (2, 2004): 161–74, here 166–67, notes here another kind of allegorical device used to startle the reader: a metaphor whose interpretation is not apparent, using a word to mean another word (citing Quintilian).

[1018] Quintilian *Inst.* 5.11.21; 8.6.48, explained by Witherington, *Grace*, 323.

[1019] Witherington, *Grace*, 330.

[1020] Witherington, *Grace*, 327; cf. de Boer, *Galatians*, 296. Even when speakers genuinely allegorized some details (e.g., Maximus of Tyre *Or.* 26.8), they drew principles or analogies based on figures' character where possible (e.g., 26.5–6; cf. Dionysius of Halicarnassus *Comp.* 4).

The question then is whether Paul meant that the Hagar narratives were *composed* as allegory or that he was *reading* them as allegory – corresponding to the difference between the authorial intention of Genesis and Paul's rhetorical/homiletical use of Genesis. Some exegetes of Galatians have long noted this distinction.[1021] If Paul is responding to arguments of opponents, the latter – Paul referring to his rhetorical use – seems more likely.

Paul's language of alignment or correspondence (4:25–26) may suggest that he refers to his own analogy, rather than the Genesis author's intention.[1022] More important, Paul elsewhere uses a midrashic "this-is-that" in which a figure in the text *corresponds* to (rather than is simply a symbol for) a figure in his own world (2 Cor 3:17). It may thus be better to understand *allêgoreô* in 4:24 as "figuratively" rather than to import subsequent, loaded senses of "allegorize."

What justifies Paul's correspondences in this case is his understanding of his soon-to-be-cited cotext, Isa 54:1. This passage was the haftarah reading that was read together with Gen 16:1 (Gal 4:27;[1023] see comment at Gal 4:27).

His Opponents' Allegory?

Noting that Paul nowhere else uses allegory in this manner, most interpreters contend that Paul's unusual use of allegory here responds to an allegorical approach by his opponents. But where did they get it? They were probably Judeans (cf. 4:25), but, like Paul, they were teaching in the Diaspora. Could they have drawn on some prior Diaspora Jewish outreach to gentiles the way that Paul often drew on prior hellenistic Jewish apologetic?

Philo, master Jewish allegorist, regularly allegorized Hagar as merely elementary learning, whereas Sarah represented advanced learning and

---

[1021] E.g., Chrysostom, Severianus, and Theodore of Mopsuestia, in Lightfoot, *Galatians*, 180; Calvin *Commentary on Galatians* on 4:24, in Bray.

[1022] Hays, "Galatians," 301.

[1023] See K. H. Jobes, "Jerusalem, Our Mother: Metalepsis and Intertextuality in Galatians 4:21–31," *WTJ* 55 (2, 1993): 299–320; J. Willitts, "Isa 54,1 in Gal 4,24b–27: Reading Genesis in Light of Isaiah," *ZNW* 96 (3–4, 2005): 188–210; H. Le Cornu with J. Shulam, *A Commentary on the Jewish Roots of Galatians* (Jerusalem: Academon, 2005), 299; S. Di Mattei, "Paul's Allegory of the Two Covenants (Gal 4.21–31) in Light of First-Century Hellenistic Rhetoric and Jewish Hermeneutics," *NTS* 52 (1, 2006): 102–22; Moo, *Galatians*, 306; M. S. Harmon, "Allegory, Typology, or Something Else? Revisiting Galatians 4:21–5:1," pages 144–58 in *Studies in the Pauline Epistles: Essays in Honor of Douglas J. Moo* (ed. M. S. Harmon and J. E. Smith; Grand Rapids, MI: Zondervan, 2014), 156.

appropriation of virtue.[1024] Paul's opponents presumably believe that their deep teaching on the Torah is advanced learning; it was such teaching that freed one from passion and enabled one to live virtuously.[1025] Paul would be inverting such an idea when he represents the Torah, like the elements venerated by gentiles, as mere elementals (4:3, 9–10).[1026] Elementals are not bad, just incomplete.[1027] Ultimately virtue is found by the Spirit, by Christ living in and through believers as children walking close to God (2:20; 4:6; 5:16–23). ****

Paul begins with a call to attention: *Tell me*! (4:21) Didactic exhortation sometimes used this phrase, on occasion when preparing to quote a respected source.[1028] Paul now seeks to show his gentile converts who want to be under the law that they do not really understand what the law teaches. The term translated *law* included the Genesis and Exodus narratives as a sort of prologue,[1029] and it is back to these, from which Paul drew his crucial text in Gal 3:6, that Paul turns.

Paul's *it is written* usually precedes a quotation of Scripture, but in 4:22 it precedes a summary. This apparent anomaly may be an additional clue that Paul is here responding to opponents rather than simply appealing to Scripture on his own ground.

Paul's rivals were teaching the Galatians to become descendants of Abraham through circumcision, whereas Paul taught that they did so by faith like Abraham's (3:6–7; Rom 4:16). Being Abraham's physical descendant does not automatically confer the promise that came through faith; after all, only one of Abraham's two sons came through promise (cf. Rom 9:7). The true line through Sarah was the line of promise; it is those who (like Abraham) trust God's promise in Christ who are heirs (4:27–31).

In Genesis, God blessed *the child of the slave* because he was Abraham's son (Gen 21:13; cf. 16:10). The issue is not that *the child of the slave* was bad (although cf. Gal 4:29), but that he could not be allowed to inherit and so

---

[1024] *Post.* 130, 137; *Sacr.* 43–44, 59; *Worse* 59; *Cher.* 3, 6–10; *Drunk* 59; *Alleg.* 3.218, 244; *Names* 255; *Heir* 61, 258; *Prelim. St.* 2, 6, 12, 14, 20, 23–24, 63, 69, 72–73, 156, 180; *Flight* 2, 128; *Abr.* 99, 206; *Dreams* 1.240; *QG* 3.19, 22–23, 60.

[1025] On this ideal in Diaspora Judaism, see S. K. Stowers, "Paul and Self-Mastery" pages 524–50 in *Paul in the Greco-Roman World: A Handbook* (ed. J. P. Sampley; Harrisburg, PA: Trinity Press International, 2003), here 531–34; Rodríguez, *Call*, 129, 155.

[1026] See here Witherington, *Grace*, 324–25.

[1027] Cf. Philo *Prelim. St.* 9, 11, 121–22.

[1028] Epictetus *Diatr.* 2.19.12. Cf. similarly "Hear" (Epictetus *Diatr.* 3.24.68).

[1029] See Rom 3:31 in light of 4:1–3; 4 Macc 18:10 in light of 18:11–18; Jub. 30:12; Philo *Worse* 6, 159; *Post.* 80, 96; *Abr.* 1; *Migr.* 177; *Flight* 167; *Jos.* 28.

reduce the inheritance to the child God had promised, Isaac (21:10–12; Gal 4:30). Throughout Genesis, the chosen line is repeatedly narrowed down, to Shem, to Abram, to Isaac, and to Jacob.

Being *born according to the flesh* simply refers to birth in the natural manner. Being *born through the promise*, however, refers to the special circumstances of Isaac's birth: he could be born only because of God's promise, by extraordinary divine agency.[1030] Isaac thus was the promised seed who prefigured the ultimate promised seed of Abraham, Christ (Gal 3:16), and ultimately all believers (3:29; 4:28).

The expected contrast between birth *according to the flesh* and birth according to the Spirit awaits the application in 4:29; in 4:23, Paul is still expounding the Genesis text, where it is promise that is more explicit. But anyone who has followed Paul's argument so far already understands that Paul also links promise with the Spirit (3:14).

Abraham had some descendants according to the flesh (such as Ishmael) and others according to the promise (through Isaac). In Paul's day, those according to the flesh were those dependent only on the flesh for their relationship with Abraham: ethnic descent and circumcision. Those who trust God's promise, ultimately fulfilled in Christ, are Abraham's children supernaturally, who have faith like Abraham had. They have the reality of the Spirit (3:2–5). All this reiterates what Paul already emphasized in 3:6–9, 14, 29.

It is thus straightforward for Paul to parallel Hagar[1031] and her line with the covenant that depended on the flesh, the Sinai covenant that he has already associated with slavery (4:1–3).[1032] While Paul's nemeses would bristle at the language of enslavement to the law, they would not simply dismiss the notion that present Jerusalem experienced enslavement. One could speak of a conquered people as being in slavery, and no one questioned that earthly Jerusalem remained under Roman rule.

As the "Lord" of Exod 33–34 corresponds to the Spirit today in 2 Cor 3:17, so here the non-inheriting line stands for those who, not recognizing

---

[1030] "Natural processes did not produce his conception," Chrysostom notes in *Hom. Gal.* 4.23 (Edwards).

[1031] But for omitting "Hagar" in Gal 4:25, see Lightfoot, *Galatians*, 192–93.

[1032] Cf. Nicholas of Lyra on Gal 4:25 (Levy); Hansen, *Galatians*, 144; Fee, *Galatians*, 180; de Boer, *Galatians*, 299. The opponents probably noted the necessity of circumcision both in the Abrahamic and Sinai covenants, blending those covenants (see discussion in what follows).

the time of fulfillment, still keep the law without the Spirit, the children of Sinai, whose center is in earthly Jerusalem (Gal 4:25).

For those wanting to emphasize the importance of Jerusalem and Judea, Sinai was literally and conspicuously in the sphere of Nabatean Arabia. (Paul had already reminded the Galatians that he knew Nabatea; Gal 1:17.) Sinai thus links the law with Arabia, and some first-century Jews counted Arabs as conspicuous descendants of Hagar and Ishmael.[1033] In any case, it is the covenant that Hagar represents, rather than Hagar herself, that connects with Sinai directly.[1034]

Mount Sinai contrasts with the heavenly Jerusalem (4:26–27), the eschatological Zion, a mountain giving forth a Torah greater than Mount Sinai (Isa 2:2–3; cf. 51:1–4; 65:17–18; 66:8). Yet it is the prophetic haftarah of Isa 54:1, Paul's cotext in this passage that he will cite in Gal 4:27 (see comment there), that allows Paul to apply the text as he does, clarifying what for several verses appear somewhat muddied waters. When Paul elsewhere uses this term for *bearing* or *born* (*gennaô*) figuratively, he uses it for his role in bringing others to spiritual birth (1 Cor 4:15; Phlm 10; cf. Gal 4:19; 3 John 4). Hagar's *children for slavery* thus probably refer to Paul's opponents and their converts (cf. Rev 2:23).[1035]

Paul's opponents probably emphasized to the Galatians the explicit, mandatory sign of circumcision in the Abrahamic covenant (Gen 17:10–14), requiring Paul to gain the upper hand by reclaiming the Abrahamic covenant for believers aside from circumcision. In terms of textual exegesis alone Paul's opponents were more faithful to the biblical text; what they were not taking into account was the hermeneutical role of fulfillment in Christ, as guaranteed by the Spirit. That is, their application was for the wrong era; they were not reckoning with the arrival of an entirely new age in Christ.

Paul's opponents probably blended the covenant with Abraham with the covenant at Sinai; but Paul has already argued that the law cannot supersede the covenant with Abraham (3:15–18), and that it is thus itself superseded by the coming of Christ, who fulfills the promise to (and thus the covenant with) Abraham (Gal 3:14, 16, 23–25; 4:1–5). Because the Abrahamic promise is fulfilled in Christ, the new covenant (1 Cor 11:25; 2 Cor 3:6) is of a piece with that promise.[1036]

[1033] Jub. 20:13; Josephus *Ant.* 1.214; 2.32.
[1034] Di Mattei, "Allegory," 110.
[1035] Martyn, *Galatians*, 437, 451, 453; Matera, *Galatians*, 173.
[1036] Das, *Stories*, 65–92, rightly points out that covenant structures do not dominate Paul's thought the way some scholars have argued. Particularly important here is his distinction

Philo applies the title "mother city" to heavenly citizenship,[1037] to the *logos*,[1038] and, like some other Jews,[1039] to Jerusalem.[1040] The image of Zion here is the image of the eschatological, heavenly Jerusalem of Isa 54:1, 11–13; 65:18–20; 66:8 11.

The term translated *corresponds to* (*sustoicheô*) in 4:25, which sets up the line of contrasts, appears in tables of categories, a function that fits the correspondences noted here (LSJ, BDAG). Thus the sense is, with the NRSV (also e.g., NASB, NIV, ESV), *corresponds to*, not "represents." Paul links Hagar, the slave woman, with the Sinai covenant, which he has already associated with slavery (4:1–3); he thereby also links Hagar with present Jerusalem, where (given the presence of the temple) the Sinai covenant is most fully observed. The popular link between Hagar and Arabs also facilitates Paul's homiletical move here.

Paul's adversaries undoubtedly knew and perhaps reported biblical assurances that Jerusalem/Mount Zion would be a new Sinai, with God's law going forth to the nations (Isa 2:3). For Paul, however, that prophecy addresses a new, eschatological Jerusalem (Isa 65:17–18), to which he turns in Gal 4:26.

A Closer Look: Heavenly Jerusalem

In Scripture the title *Jerusalem* included the people (Jerusalemites) as well as the place, so the contested imagery for God's people in Gal 4:25–26 seems clear. As an educated Pharisee (Phil 3:5), Paul had surely spent time in Jerusalem himself, but he is ready to cede the title of earthly Jerusalemites to his opponents, since he looks to a greater city.

The context of the new creation in Isa 65:17 and 66:22 includes a new Jerusalem (Isa 65:18).[1041] Jewish people expected that God would prepare this city for his people,[1042] and even rebuild the temple, and perhaps the city, himself.[1043] Paul contrasts the present and future/heavenly Jerusalem

between the continuing covenant with Israel as a people and the covenant in which gentiles are included (89, 91).

[1037] *Conf.* 78; *Dreams* 1.181; QG 4.178.
[1038] *Flight* 94.
[1039] In Josephus, see *Ant.* 11.160; *War* 2.400, 421, 517, 626; 4.181, 228, 234.
[1040] Esp. in his more political essays: *Flacc.* 46; *Embassy* 203, 281, 294, 334.
[1041] The same is true for works taking their cue from Isaiah (Jub. 1:29; Rev 21:1–2).
[1042] 4 Ezra 8:52. For its restoration, see also Tob 13:16/17; Ps. Sol. 11:2–8.
[1043] 1 En. 90:29; probably 4 Ezra 8:52; 10:27; 13:36; the temple in Jub. 1:29. On restoration eschatology, see Sanders, *Jesus and Judaism*, 77–90.

(4:25–26), as well as the older covenant law with the new way of Christ (3:17–23; 4:1–5).

Although in many sources the city was future, in many texts it was also heavenly.[1044] Some sources view it as a currently hidden city that will be revealed at the end.[1045] Apocalyptic imagery sometimes conflated the future world and the current heavenly one.[1046] "In both apocalyptic writings and Qumran the heavenly Jerusalem could be conceived of as already present," Andrew Lincoln points out, and from Paul's early Christian, already/not yet eschatology Paul could argue that believers already experience a foretaste of this citizenship.[1047] ★★★★

Although only in Gal 4:27 does Paul cite Isa 54:1, it informs how he applies the Sarah/Hagar story in Genesis throughout Gal 4:21–31.[1048] Isa 54 is the haftarah reading for Gen 16 in later liturgy, and the linkage occurs in various later texts. This shared linkage suggests an early tradition of linking the two texts, surfacing also here in Gal 4. Other Jews also applied Isa 54 to the future time of restoration.[1049]

The verse Paul cites immediately follows the suffering servant making God's people right with him (Isa 52:13–53:12). Paul elsewhere showed his belief that Isa 53 was fulfilled and that now was the time to proclaim the good news (Isa 52:7).[1050] The promised eschatological restoration to God has come; Jesus's followers in Galatia have entered that restoration, whereas Jerusalemites who reject it continue to live as in the pre-restoration judgment.

Jerusalem is desolate in Isa 54:1 because of Israel's sins (cf. the mother in Isa 50:1). The Greek term translated *desolate* here also means "desert" or "deserted," and is so used of the ruins of Jerusalem that the Lord will restore (Isa 51:3; 52:9; 58:12).

[1044] Cf. Heb 11:16; 12:22 (cf. 11:10); 4 Ezra 8:52; 4 Bar. 5:35; Hamerton-Kelly, *Pre-existence*, 109–10; more fully, see Lincoln, *Paradise*, 18–22.

[1045] 4 Ezra 7:26; 10:27, 54; 13:36; 2 Bar. 4:2–6.

[1046] See A. T. Lincoln, *Paradise Now and Not Yet: Studies in the Role of the Heavenly Dimension in Paul's Thought with Special Reference to His Eschatology* (SNTSMS 43; Cambridge: Cambridge University Press, 1981), e.g., 149.

[1047] Lincoln, *Paradise*, 29; cf. 22.

[1048] With Jobes, "Mother"; Willitts, "Isa 54,1"; Harmon, "Allegory," 156.

[1049] Isa 54:1–2 is quoted in 4Q265 f1.6; other parts of Isa 54 appear in CD 6.8; 4Q176 f8–11.12; cf. perhaps 4 Ezra 9:43–45; 10:47–48. The precious stones of Isa 54:11–12 figure heavily in subsequent traditions; see Tob 13:16; 4Q164 fr1.1–6; Pesiq. Rab Kah. 18:4–6; b. B. Bat. 75a; J. M. Baumgarten, "The Duodecimal Courts of Qumran, Revelation, and the Sanhedrin," *JBL* 95 [1976]: 59–78, here 77).

[1050] See Isa 52:7 in Rom 10:15; Isa 52:15 in Rom 15:21; Isa 53:1 in Rom 10:16 (all noted in Hays, *Conversion*, 46–47).

In the wider context of this section of Isaiah, the mother who bore God's people is Sarah (Isa 51:2b),[1051] who was once barren but ended up with "many" descendants (51:2d). (Given the term *ôdinô*, "suffer birth pangs," in the LXX of both Isa 51:2 and 54:1, midrashic interpreters were bound to link the passages, though in 54:1 the mother has *not* suffered birth pangs.) Likewise in this context, when God would restore his people, he would spread his word to the nations (51:4–5). In a closely parallel passage, the desolate land would become crowded with children born during Israel's bereavement in exile (Isa 49:19–20), as the nations would bring Israel's scattered children (49:22–23).

Like the barren mother Sarah's birth of God's people (Isa 51:2), the birth of Isa 54:1 would be a miraculous birth. The barren mother here has neither born nor labored (unlike Sarah in Isa 51:2 and Paul in Gal 4:19!), yet has many children (Isa 54:1).

Isaiah may think of just one woman, Jerusalem, first desolate because of exile and then restored in splendor. Without necessarily denying continuity between the figures, Paul might regard them as chronologically and spatially separate. Some ancient hearers might have even been ready to consider Isaac (4:26–31) and Ishmael (4:24–25, 29–30) eschatologically; some, for example, read Esau as representing the present evil age, with Jacob representing the imminent age to come.[1052]

Some other biblical texts may also envision gentile inclusion in the future Zion,[1053] not least one that, in the LXX, speaks of "Mother Zion" (Ps 86:5 LXX; ET 87:5).[1054] In any case, Paul sees the influx of gentiles as children of Abraham and Isaac as fulfilling Isaiah's promise.[1055] The noncircumcising gentile mission was winning far more converts than were those circumcising the flesh in converts to other versions of the Christian movement or Judaism.

[1051] The only Old Testament reference to Sarah outside Genesis; see Hays, *Echoes*, 118–19; Silva, "Galatians," 809, citing the esp. relevant M. C. Callaway, *Sing, O Barren One: A Study in Comparative Midrash* (SBLDS 91; Atlanta, GA: Scholars Press, 1986), 63.

[1052] 4 Ezra 6:7–10; cf. Gen. Rab. 6:3. In later rabbis, Esau represented the present dominion of Rome.

[1053] Lincoln, *Paradise*, 24, cites Isa 44:5; 45:22; 49:6; 56:6, 7; 60; 66:18–21.

[1054] See C. M. Maier, "Psalm 87 as a Reappraisal of the Zion Tradition and Its Reception in Galatians 4:26," *CBQ* 69 (3, 2007): 473–86; Das, *Galatians*, 505.

[1055] Cf. A. D. Myers, "'For It Has Been Written': Paul's Use of Isa 54:1 in Gal 4:27 in Light of Gal 3:1–5:1," *PRSt* 37 (3, 2010): 295–308; K. M. Schmidt, "Die Wehen des Völkerapostels: Gal 4,19 und die topographische Verankerung des Heidenapostolats innerhalb von Gal 1,13–2,14 und Gal 4,21–31," *SNTU* 36 (2011): 111–56.

When Paul wrote Galatians, earthly Jerusalem was flourishing and the sometimes persecuted Christian movement was, by comparison, more like a deserted woman. Yet Paul, who had labored over the Galatians for birth (4:19) and believed that the present sufferings were the messianic birth pangs of the new age (Rom 8:22), anticipated a different future. In that day gentiles would rejoice with God's people (Rom 15:10, citing LXX Deut 32:43).[1056]

Whatever one makes of some elements of Paul's connections in 4:24–26, Paul draws a simpler analogy in 4:28–29. In Abraham's day, the child born according to normal, fleshly means (4:23) was not the child or line that God had promised. The child God had promised (4:23) came supernaturally. In the same way, converts made according to the flesh (ethnically and/or by circumcising their flesh, Gen 17:11, 13–14, 23–25) do not represent the promised line; that belongs to those converted by the supernatural/divine act of the Spirit (Gal 4:29), as Paul's converts were (3:2–3, 14; cf. 1 Cor 2:4–5; 2 Cor 3:3, 6; 1 Thess 1:5–6).

Born according to the flesh presumably refers here to those born *only* according to the flesh, as opposed to those also born from the Spirit; cf. parallel language in John 3:5–8, esp. 3:6.[1057] God's Son was *born of a woman, born under the law* (4:4) so God could make believers his children as well through *the Spirit of his Son* (4:5–6). Believers are thus *born according to the Spirit* (4:29).

Paul's claim that *the child who was born according to the flesh persecuted the child who was born according to the Spirit* (4:29) may be figurative, simply to allow the comparison for present conflict. Nevertheless, Paul probably was aware of tradition to the effect that Ishmael did oppress Isaac. (Ishmael's seed also sometimes opposed that of Isaac; Judg 8:24; Ps 83:4–6.)[1058]

Josephus reports that Sarah loved Ishmael until her own son Isaac was born, but then she feared that, being much older than Isaac, Ishmael might mistreat him once Abraham died.[1059] In later Jewish tradition, the brothers disputed about the birthright.[1060] More important is how ancient interpreters read Gen 21:9 (the verse that immediately precedes the verse quoted

[1056] The LXX diverges here from the MT. Paul's citation of that text, which comes from a section of Scripture that he often mines, employs the plural form of the same verb for rejoicing as in Isa 54:1 here in Gal 4:27.
[1057] See also John 1:12–13, in the context of God's people (1:11); cf. 1 John 3:9; 4:7; 5:1, 4, 18.
[1058] Noted by Lightfoot, *Galatians*, 184; Bruce, *Galatians*, 223. Within Genesis, cf. Gen 37:28.
[1059] Josephus *Ant.* 1.215.
[1060] Tg. Neof. 1 on Gen 25:34.

in Gal 4:30), which says something to the effect that Sarah saw Ishmael "playing with her son Isaac." The word that can be translated "playing" is ambiguous, with a range of meanings from innocent to sinister. Philo says that Ishmael, though illegitimate, played with Isaac, the genuine heir, as if he was his equal.[1061] Later interpreters connected his jesting with idolatry and various other offenses.[1062] Jewish tradition often viewed Ishmael as wicked.[1063]

There may have been some basis in the biblical text for believing that Ishmael did something negative to Isaac (cf. Gen 16:12). It is hard to imagine that Ishmael would not be affected by himself, as presumed heir, being displaced in the eyes of the community, as he would be, by Isaac's birth. Moreover, the text of Genesis seems to presume that what Sarah saw Ishmael doing (Gen 21:9) was what precipitated her demand that Hagar and Ishmael be sent away (Gen 21:10).

In Hebrew, the verb can mean "laugh," "jest," or "play," an important motif in Genesis about God's ways being surprising (Gen 21:6). But if the verb has anything to do with Sarah's reaction (that is, if Sarah is not simply reacting to *seeing* Ishmael at the feast for Isaac's weaning), it may suggest something more malevolent. Maybe instead of laughing with Sarah he was laughing at Isaac.

It can refer to disbelief in God's promise (Gen 17:17; 18:12–15), to mocking a warning from God (Gen 19:14); to sexual activity (26:8), including molestation (39:14, 17) or other abuse (Judg 16:25) or misbehavior (Exod 32:6). Historically some interpreters have inferred a negative sense, equating it with persecution because this ridicule opposed God's promise.[1064]

While Ishmael may have been thought to do something that could be an analogy for "persecuting," the question arises as to who was persecuting Spirit-born persons in Paul's day (*so it is now also*, 4:29). In Galatians, each of the other four uses of the verb here translated "persecute" probably refers to non-Christian Jews persecuting Jewish followers of Jesus (Gal 1:13, 23; 5:11; 6:12). That also fits the experiences of Paul in Galatia that Galatian believers would have witnessed (Acts 13:50–51; 14:2, 19). While the vast majority of persecution between Jews and Christians over the centuries has come from the latter side,

---

[1061] Philo *Sobr.* 8. At least under Roman law, children of concubines and anyone born in slavery was deemed illegitimate (J. F. Gardner, *Women in Roman Law and Society* [Bloomington: Indiana University Press, 1986], 143).

[1062] T. Sot. 6:6; Tg. Neof. 1 on Gen 21:9; Gen. Rab. 53:11.

[1063] Jub. 15:30; Sipre Deut. 312.1.1; 329.3.1; 343.5.2.

[1064] Calvin, *Commentary on Galatians* on 4:29 (Bray).

early Jewish sources report many intra-Jewish conflicts that grew violent,[1065] and the direct testimony of one of the former persecutors (Gal 1:13) can leave little doubt that some of this intra-Jewish persecution was directed against Jewish followers of Jesus.[1066]

A Closer Look: Rebirth, Conversion, Inheritance

That Paul employs the image of rebirth for conversion here is no accident. Rebirth from God's Spirit or word was a familiar early Christian image (John 1:12–13; 3:3–6; 1 Pet 1:23; 1 John 3:9), but also plays on an image of conversion probably already circulating in first-century Judaism. In the Diaspora, Justin also testifies independently to the mid-second century Jewish belief, apparently widespread, that the proselyte is "like one who is native born."[1067] It was, in fact, a commonplace that a proselyte's status was that of a newborn child.[1068] A convert was no longer the person he had been as a Gentile, before God, the law, or Israel; his legal standing was that of an Israelite.[1069]

In the halakah, a proselyte had lost all previous connections; the convert had begun a new life.[1070] Thus, in terms of legal status, a proselyte had no relatives.[1071] It may not be surprising that gentiles accused converts to Judaism of disowning their families of origin.[1072] This condition naturally raised debates about the propriety of postconversion inheritance.[1073]

Conversion to Judaism was in a sense adoption into a new ethnic community. In Gal 4, God adopts gentiles as his children without their adopting a new ethnicity – though as children of Abraham they should see themselves as grafted into the heritage and story of ancient Israel.[1074] ****

[1065] Addressed in Keener, *Acts*, 462–64.

[1066] See also 1 Thess 2:14–16, which most scholars today accept as authentic.

[1067] *Dial.* 123.1; see L. W. Barnard, "The Old Testament and Judaism in the Writings of Justin Martyr," *VT* 14 (4, 1964): 395–406, here 403.

[1068] Often noted: e.g., S. B. Hoenig, "Conversion during the Talmudic Period," pages 33–66 in *Conversion to Judaism: A History and Analysis* (ed. D. M. Eichhorn; New York: KTAV, 1965), 54; G. F. Moore, *Judaism in the First Centuries of the Christian Era* (3 vols.; Cambridge, MA: Harvard University Press, 1927–1930), 1:335.

[1069] Mekilta Nez. 1:47ff (Lauterbach, 3:5); b. Yeb. 47b; Hoenig, "Conversion," 48, 54; Bamberger, *Proselytism*, 60.

[1070] Bamberger, *Proselytism*, 63–64

[1071] B. Yeb. 98a; Gen. Rab. 18:5; cf. b. Sanh. 58a; Yeb. 22a; see further Bamberger, *Proselytism*, 86.

[1072] Tacitus *Hist.* 5.5.

[1073] M. Dem. 6:1; t. Dem. 6:13; b. Bek. 47a; Yeb. 62a.

[1074] Paul emphasizes only the Abrahamic/promise part of the heritage here, but exodus allusions in Rom 8 and more explicit but negative wilderness references in 1 Cor 10:1–12 (esp.

Paul rhetorically asking his audience what the Scripture says matches him asking rhetorically whether they would heed the law in 4:21, questions strategically placed toward the beginning and end of 4:21–31. As *pathos* was most appropriate at the end of a speech, Paul invokes a passionate text before the rousing affirmation and probably concluding exhortation of this section (4:31–5:1).

Paul here quotes Sarah's words to Abraham in Gen 21:10, but God confirms these words as his own counsel in 21:12, a passage that Paul quotes elsewhere (Rom 9:7; cf. Heb 11:18). Thus Paul cites these words not as spoken by Sarah, but as spoken by "Scripture."

In Gal 4:30, Paul probably wants his audience to apply the demand of Gen 21:10, cited here, to their persecutors from the previous verse, which cites Gen 21:9. The Galatian believers are to cast out the rival teachers, as Paul may further urge in another way in Gal 5:9–10 (see comment there).

Whatever Ishmael's offense in Gen 21:9, if any, Sarah's motive in seeking Hagar's and Ishmael's expulsion is explicit: to prevent Isaac having to share the inheritance with Ishmael (Gen 21:10). A way to protect the full inheritance for Isaac was to free Hagar and Ishmael now and to send them away before Abraham's decease.[1075]

The moral of 4:30–31, ultimately, is: Do not let anyone take your inheritance. You are already *true* children and have the firstfruits of the blessing of Abraham (3:14, 29). Those trying to get you circumcised in order to be children of Abraham are from the fleshly (Hagar) line of Abraham, not the spiritual line to which you belong.

Gal 5:1 summarizes what Paul has argued so far and introduces what follows (esp. in 5:13, after his additional digression with *pathos* in 5:2–12). Rhetorically, the Greek sentence commands attention, especially by doubling "freedom" language. Paul emphasizes *freedom*, highlighting it by placing it first in his Greek sentence.[1076]

Indicatively, we are children of the free woman (4:31) and therefore free in Christ. But imperatively, we must stand firm to maintain that freedom (5:1); in Paul's theology, a past conversion remains effective only so long as the person does not deconvert (cf. 4:19; see comment on 5:4). Tension between indicative and imperative is a significant theme in discussions of

"our ancestors" in 10:1; cf. 5:7, 13) suggest that Paul envisioned a fuller grafting (cf. Rom 2:26–29; 1 Cor 5:1; Gal 6:16; 1 Thess 4:5).

[1075] Cf. Hammurabi 171; Lipit-Ishtar 25.

[1076] Martyn, *Galatians*, 446–47.

Pauline ethics (e.g., Rom 6:4; 1 Cor 5:7; Gal 5:1, 13; Phil 2:12–13).[1077] In practice, it might resemble God telling Israel, "The promised land is yours: Go
in and take it" (cf. Num 33:53). That is, it is already a reality in terms of God's
perspective, but this promise and guarantee still must be implemented on
the human level.

Paul often uses this verb for standing (*stêkô*), especially in the imperative
(see esp. Rom 14:4; 1 Thess 3:8), urging perseverance, which is also important in the context of Gal 5:1 (see 5:4). Such "standing" contrasts with "falling" (Rom 14:4; cf. 1 Cor 10:12) or "stumbling" (cf. Rom 14:13), an expression
that Jewish people already used as a metaphor for apostasy.[1078] We "stand,"
rather than commit apostasy, by faith (Rom 11:20) as well as in faith (1 Cor
16:13; 2 Cor 1:24). That is, we persevere by continuing as believers in Jesus;
the Galatians risked apostasy by forfeiting their dependence on Jesus for
dependence on something else.

Paul warned the Galatians not to submit *again* to slavery not because
they had observed the law itself before but because they were returning to
elementary matters appropriate at most (in the case of the law) for an earlier
stage of salvation history (Gal 4:3, 8–10).

Scholars debate the precise sense of the expression translated *For freedom* (5:1a). It may represent the place to which Christ has brought them,
the realm of freedom, or possibly the purpose or goal for which Christ
has freed them. Many scholars emphasize that *for freedom* appears in pre-
Christian Greek inscriptions in which a slave is manumitted "for freedom,"
being formally sold to a deity but, aside from some cultic obligations, now
free with respect to people.[1079] Although the idea would fit here, the expression usually does not carry such a narrow sense.[1080]

[1077] See R. Bultmann, *Theology of the New Testament* (trans. K. Grobel; 2 vols.;
New York: Scribner's, 1951), 1:332; W. G. Kümmel, *The Theology of the New Testament
according to Its Major Witnesses – Jesus, Paul, John* (trans. J. E. Steely; Nashville,
TN: Abingdon, 1973), 224–28; Barclay, *Obeying*, 225–27; Fung, *Galatians*, 278–83;
Dunn, *Theology of Paul*, 626–31; Engberg-Pedersen, *Paul and Stoics*, 224, 233, 238–39;
A. Saldanha, "Rediscovering Paul – The Indicative and the Imperative," *ITS* 45 (4,
2008): 381–419; F. J. Matera, *Romans* (Grand Rapids, MI: Baker Academic, 2010), 161–
63; V. Rabens, "'Indicative and Imperative' as the Substructure of Paul's Theology-and-
Ethics in Galatians: A Discussion of Divine and Human Agency in Paul," pages 285–305
in *Galatians and Christian Theology: Justification, the Gospel, and Ethics in Paul's Letter*
(ed. M. W. Elliott et al.; Grand Rapids, MI: Baker Academic, 2014), esp. 302. See, however, challenges in F. W. Horn and R. Zimmermann, *Jenseits von Indikativ und Imperativ*
(Tübingen: Mohr Siebeck, 2009).

[1078] See, e.g., Ezek 14:3–7; Sir 9:5; comment on Gal 5:4.

[1079] Deissmann, *Light*, 323–28.

[1080] TLG search by my PhD student Donald Murray Vasser.

Paul's language would be intelligible to gentiles; a freed slave who proved difficult could be re-enslaved under some circumstances (see Gal 4:9).[1081] For Paul, Christ liberates us from sin and from the need for external rules; yet this was not by self-discipline but because of the indwelling righteousness of God's Spirit (5:22–23; Rom 14:17).

The image of the *yoke* often indicates corporate subjugation when applied to people.[1082] But there were also positive yokes; thus when God will convert the nations they will serve under his yoke (LXX Zeph 3:9).[1083] One should place one's neck "under the yoke" of wisdom to learn instruction.[1084] Here Paul probably evokes the traditional Jewish figure of the privilege of the yoke of Torah.[1085] One accepts the yoke of the kingdom of heaven by keeping commandments[1086] such as reciting the Shema.[1087] For Paul to praise freedom from the "yoke" of the Torah (Gal 5:1, playing on a familiar expression) thus subverts Jewish expectations.[1088]

5:2–6: CIRCUMCISION CANNOT SUPPLEMENT CHRIST BEFORE GOD

5:2 Listen! I, Paul, am telling you that if you let yourselves be circumcised, Christ will be of no benefit to you.

5:3 Once again I testify to every man who lets himself be circumcised that he is obliged to obey the entire law.

5:4 You who want to be justified by the law have cut yourselves off from Christ; you have fallen away from grace.

5:5 For through the Spirit, by faith, we eagerly wait for the hope of righteousness.

5:6 For in Christ Jesus neither circumcision nor uncircumcision counts for anything; the only thing that counts is faith working through love.

[1081] See Valerius Maximus 2.6.6; 2.6.7a; Suetonius *Claud.* 25.1; for limits on such revocation, see Tacitus *Ann.* 13.26–27.

[1082] E.g., Gen 27:40; Lev 26:13; 2 Chron 10:4; Jer 2:18, 20; 1 Macc 8:18, 31; 13:41; 1 En. 103:11; Sib. Or. 3.391–92; Josephus *Ant.* 8.213.

[1083] For being under God's yoke, cf. further Ps. Sol. 7:9; 17:30; cf. Jesus's "yoke" in Matt 11:29–30.

[1084] Sir 51:26. Wisdom can be equated with Torah in Sir 24:23; Bar 4:1.

[1085] E.g., Jer 5:5; 2 Bar. 41:3; m. Ber. 2:2, 5; Sipre Deut. 344.4.2.

[1086] Sipra Sh. pq. 12.121.2.5; Sipra Behar par. 5.255.1.9 (avoiding usury).

[1087] E.g., y. Ber. 2:2, §2.

[1088] See de Boer, *Galatians*, 309; deSilva, *Readings*, 245; Das, *Galatians*, 520. By contrast, "freedom" in James is always associated with the law or a law (Jas 1:25; 2:12; cf. 2:9–12).

As Gal 4:12–20 interrupted Paul's argumentation from Scripture, dividing two expositions, so does 5:2–12 interrupt the continuity of his language of freedom in 5:1 and 5:13. Whereas the *pathos* Paul evoked in 4:12–20 was primarily sympathy for him, here, by contrast, Paul rhetorically invokes the emotion of anger toward the opponents.[1089] Some also see this section as recapitulating major points from Paul's argumentation in 4:21–31 or even the entire letter; such recapitulation was a common practice.

Although Paul does not explicitly address the question of circumcision in Galatia until Gal 5:2, he has already been preparing for it (2:3; cf. 2:7–9, 12), like a good persuader building rapport before addressing the most controversial matter.[1090] Circumcision was often the final step in conversion, after accepting other Jewish customs (Gal 4:10).[1091] It usually took some time to prepare converts, who would, among other things, have to relearn even "shopping and cooking practices."[1092]

That *Christ will be of no benefit to you* may evoke the common ancient valuation based on whether an action was profitable.[1093] For Christ not to benefit them, however, would prove not simply inconvenient but eternally disastrous. Although Paul could have used a different Greek word for this same point, Paul selects *ôpheleô*, which offers a wordplay with *opheiletês*, "debtor" (NRSV, *obliged*) in 5:3. "Christ will not benefit them (*ôphêlesei*), but, instead, they will be in debt (*opheiletês*) to the law."[1094]

A Closer Look: Circumcision[1095]

In the Maccabean period Jews had risked their lives to circumcise their children,[1096] and those who refused would be "children of Beliar" and like gentiles.[1097] Even many gentiles saw this as a distinguishing boundary marker of Jewish ethnicity.[1098]

[1089] Appeal to pity, fear, and anger was considered particularly effective (Quintilian *Inst.* 6.2.20).
[1090] See Kennedy, *Interpretation*, 36, 146, citing Rhet. Her. 1.9–11.
[1091] Dunn, *Galatians*, 264, citing Josephus *War* 2.454; *Ant.* 20.41–45; Juvenal *Sat.* 14.96–104.
[1092] Sanders, *Paul*, 549.
[1093] See, e.g., Aristotle *Rhet.* 1.7.1, 1363b; Theon *Progymn.* 8.45; Seneca *Dial.* 7.8.2; *Ben.* 4.21.6; Musonius Rufus 1, 36.9–12; 4, 46.36–37.
[1094] Dunn, *Galatians*, 265; cf. also de Boer, *Galatians*, 312.
[1095] Condensing Keener, *Acts*, 2215–19.
[1096] 1 Macc 1:60–61; 2 Macc 6:10; 4 Macc 4:25; Josephus *Ant.* 12.256.
[1097] Jub. 15:33–34.
[1098] See, e.g., Petronius *Sat.* 102.14; Tacitus *Hist.* 5.5.1–2; Whittaker, *Jews and Christians*, 80–85; Sevenster, *Anti-Semitism*, 132–36.

Slaves bought from foreigners needed to be circumcised to become part of the covenant people (Gen 17:12–13), as did any foreigners in the land who wanted to join the Passover festival (Exod 12:48). Thus Jewish practice normally treated circumcision as necessary for becoming part of the covenant people.[1099] A minority of Judeans treated it as necessary even for a place in the world to come,[1100] the radical Judean view articulated in Acts 15:1. Some were apparently prepared to impose it even by force on gentiles wishing to remain in the land promised to God's people.[1101] Diaspora Jews, who constituted an easily identifiable minority and who often interacted with gentiles, were more circumspect, avoiding alienating gentile sympathizers who did not wish to become Jews fully.[1102]

Paul's opponents may have resembled the Galilean named Eleazar in Josephus *Ant.* 20.34–45. King Izates had become a Jewish sympathizer through the persuasion of one Ananias, a Jewish merchant, but Ananias tried to prevent him from being circumcised, fearing an anti-Jewish backlash. Eleazar, by contrast, insisted that failure to be circumcised made a mockery of his profession of Jewish faith, and so persuaded the king to act.

If Paul's opponents were something like a Christian version of Eleazar, however, Paul was nevertheless much more radical than Ananias. Ananias opposed circumcision out of "necessity,"[1103] a recognized category of ethical argument that reduced culpability.[1104] But Paul as a matter of principle prohibited imposing any external demand such as circumcision, since those who had received the eschatological Spirit already belonged to God's people, making them already part of the eschatological new creation.[1105] If God granted that promised eschatological covenant blessing – God's *own* Spirit (Gal 3:14) – without the old sign of the covenant, the traditional sign was acceptable but not necessary (1 Cor 7:19; Gal 5:6; 6:15). Outward signs were nothing compared to God himself, and a symbol of relationship with God was nothing compared to its eschatological fulfillment.

[1099] See Esth 8:17 LXX; Jdt 14:10; t. Abod. Zar. 3:12; Ber. 6:13, *ed. princ.*

[1100] See Donaldson, *Paul and Gentiles*, 275, and discussion there.

[1101] Josephus *Ant.* 13.318; *Life* 113, 149–50 (noting his own objections); see also Harrison, "Refuse to Circumcise."

[1102] See Hengel and Schwemer, *Between Damascus and Antioch*, 71–73.

[1103] *Ant.* 20.42.

[1104] Quintilian *Inst.* 3.8.22–25; Ps.-Quintilian *Decl.* 262.5; Dio Chrysostom *Or.* 3.91; Hermogenes *Issues* 77.6–7.

[1105] Cf. Isa 32:15; 42:1; 44:3; 59:21; Ezek 36:27; 37:14; 39:29; Joel 2:28–29. On the centrality of the Spirit to Paul's argument in Galatians, see also, e.g., G. D. Fee, *Paul, the Spirit, and the People of God* (Peabody, MA: Hendrickson, 1996), 102–03.

The early Christian consensus was that God accepted gentiles who committed their allegiance to Jesus; most likely saw them as God-fearers who would share the world to come, but not as members of God's people descended from Abraham.[1106] Where Paul was radical was in not requiring them to become proselytes by physical circumcision,[1107] or, to put it somewhat differently, Paul welcomed gentiles who received the Spirit as proselytes without requiring circumcision.

Circumcision posed a deterrent to conversion for many gentiles. As de Boer notes, it was "no small step for an adult man especially in antiquity (no anesthesia, the high risk of infection, social derision)."[1108] Gentiles often ridiculed circumcision,[1109] subjecting converts to shame, perhaps especially from family and other close associates. ****

Paul's *testify* (cf. 4:15; Rom 10:2; 2 Cor 8:3; 1 Thess 2:12) probably suggests a solemn affirmation of what he knows firsthand; *again* probably recalls Gal 5:2.[1110] If one was going to keep the law, one should go all the way; Paul knew better than most others what that lifestyle would look like (Gal 1:14; Phil 3:5).

Literally, *to obey the entire law* is "to do the entire law," evoking the wording of Paul's biblical argument about doing all the things written in the book of the law in 3:10 (cf. also 3:12). In light of these connections, *every man* in 5:3 probably also evokes "everyone" in 3:10. Paul's phrase "Do all the words of Torah" is common in Deuteronomy,[1111] and these passages appear to deal with the Torah "*in its entirety*."[1112]

As noted earlier, a Galilean "skillful in the law" – language Josephus sometimes associated with Pharisees[1113] – insisted that circumcision was necessary for conversion.[1114] Shammaites, the leading Pharisaic school in this period, were probably particularly rigorous and probably influenced Paul's rivals (cf. Acts 15:5). But even the later sages, who followed the school of Hillel, declared that "If a heathen is prepared to accept the Torah except one religious law, we must not receive him [as an Israelite]."[1115]

[1106] Dunn, *New Perspective*, 38; Keener, *Acts*, 2205, 2218, 2228, 2259, 2262, 2269.
[1107] Sanders, *Jesus and Judaism*, 229, 276; Sanders, *Paul*, 462.
[1108] De Boer, *Galatians*, 61.
[1109] E.g., Philo *Spec. Laws* 1.1–3; Josephus *Ag. Ap.* 2.137.
[1110] Unless it refers to where Paul previously stated the requirement *to obey the entire law*, i.e., in 3:10 (so Schreiner, *Galatians*, 314).
[1111] Deut 28:58; 29:28(29); 32:46; also see Josh 1:7–8; cf. 22:5; 23:6.
[1112] Gathercole, *Boasting*, 92.
[1113] Josephus *War* 1.110; 2.162; *Life* 191; cf. *Ant.* 20.201.
[1114] Josephus *Ant.* 20.43–44.
[1115] B. Bek. 30b, bar. (Soncino trans.).

The NRSV's *obliged* reflects a Greek term that can mean "debtor" or one under moral obligation.[1116] Paul elsewhere refers to the law, when approached by human works, as a matter of debt (Rom 4:4), whereas our only debt should be the love that fulfills the law (13:8).[1117] But whereas full proselytes had to obey all the law's stipulations (5:3), Paul declares that the full righteousness to which the law points ("the whole law") can be fulfilled (or at least summarized) simply by consistent love (5:14; see comment there).[1118]

Jewish teachers emphasized that one should be as "careful concerning a light commandment as with a heavy one, since you do not know how God will assign reward."[1119] Speaking hyperbolically, they ruled that whoever keeps a single commandment keeps their life, but whoever neglects it neglects their life.[1120] Their point was that whoever cast off any commandment or principle of the law was discarding the authority of the law as a whole.[1121] Likewise, accepting some commandments implied recognizing the validity of them all.[1122]

Nor would Diaspora Jews overlook biblical commandments. "To transgress the law in matters either small or great is of equal seriousness," 4 Maccabees warns, "for in either case the law is equally despised" (4 Macc 5:20–21, NRSV). This way of putting the matter comported with the widely known Stoic doctrine to roughly the same effect: all wrong acts are equally wrong.[1123]

Paul has already warned against seeking to be justified by works of the law (2:16; 3:11). Now he warns that if they pursue this course they will be *cut off from Christ*, and will have *fallen away from grace*. *Cut off* (from *katargeô*) is the language of annulling something (as in 3:17) or rendering it ineffective

[1116] Obligation was a major Greco-Roman social concept, conspicuous in the need for reciprocity; see, e.g., Dio Chrysostom *Or.* 44.4; Pliny *Ep.* 2.13.1–2; cf. 4 Macc 16:18–19; for sin as a debt, see Sipre Deut. 349.1.1.
[1117] But C. F. D. Moule, "Obligation in the Ethic of Paul," pages 389–406 in *Christian History and Interpretation: Studies Presented to John Knox* (ed. W. R. Farmer, C. F. D. Moule, and R. R. Niebuhr; Cambridge: Cambridge University Press, 1967), contends that Paul retains moral obligation.
[1118] Matera, *Galatians*, 181, and others, note the contrast.
[1119] M. Ab. 2:1; cf. Sipre Deut. 96.3.2; 115.1.2; Matt 5:19; Matt 5:18//Luke 16:17.
[1120] Ab. R. Nat. 35, §77 B; Sipre Deut. 48.1.3.
[1121] E.g., m. Hor. 1:3; Sipre Deut. 54.3.2; cf. Jas 2:10; T. Ash. 2.2–8.
[1122] Sipra Qed. pq. 8.205.2.6; Behuq. par. 5.255.1.10.
[1123] See, e.g., Arius Didymus 2.7.11k, p. 84.15–17; 2.7.11L, pp. 85.34–87.7; 87.13–20; known among outsiders, e.g., Cicero *Fin.* 4.27.74–75; Pliny *Ep.* 8.2.3.

(as in 5:11). It follows naturally from the idea of Christ no longer being of benefit to them (5:2).

"Falling" or "stumbling" can designate apostasy (Rom 11:11, 22; 14:4, 13; 1 Cor 8:9, 13; 10:12).[1124] As in Gal 4:19 or 2 Cor 5:20; 6:1–2, Paul's depiction of them as unconverted is probably hyperbole. Nevertheless, Paul's warnings of apostasy envision a real possibility (cf. Rom 8:13; 11:22; 1 Cor 9:27; 2 Cor 13:5–6; Col 1:23; 1 Thess 3:5). Ancient sources do reveal that many who had become Christians reconverted back to paganism afterward.

Already in Scripture, if the righteous turn to the way of sin, their righteousness will be forgotten (Ezek 18:24, 26; 33:12–13, 18), but if the wicked turn to righteousness they will live (33:14–16, 19). Jewish people lamented apostasy;[1125] some expected apostasy as one of the tragic signs of the end time,[1126] a view that Paul may well have shared (cf. Mark 13:12–13; Matt 24:12; 2 Thess 2:3).[1127] Paul certainly did not teach the popular doctrine today of "once-saved-always-saved";[1128] a convert does not regularly move in and out of the saved community, but a convert who deconverts is again a nonbeliever.

The Spirit is the foretaste of the coming world (Rom 8:23; 1 Cor 2:9–10; 2 Cor 1:22; 5:5). In the present, faith working through love (Gal 5:6) may be a foretaste of the new creation (compare Gal 5:6 with 6:15).

The question of the meaning of *faith* arises again in this verse (see discussion at Gal 2:16). Since Paul is calling for perseverance (5:1–4) and the faith working through love for which he calls (5:6) is presumably believers' love (5:13–14), believers' rather than Christ's faith is likely in view here.[1129] Ultimately what is decisive in the matter is how we construe saving faith earlier in the letter (1:23; 2:16, 20; 3:2, 5–8, 11–12, 14, 22–26), which in my opinion again supports believers' faith here (see especially discussion at 2:16). For Paul, this means depending on Jesus.

[1124] For general figurative use, see, e.g., Plutarch *Cat. Min.* 30.2; Marcus Aurelius 7.22; Babr. 103.20; specifically with regard to apostasy or falling under righteous judgment, Ezek 14:3, 4, 7; 18:30; 33:12; 44:12; Sir 9:5; 25:21; 34:7, 17; 35:15; 39:24; Matt 5:29–30; 11:6; 13:41; 16:23; 18:6–9; Mark 9:42–47; Luke 7:23; 17:1–2; 1QS 2.12; 3.24; 1QpHab 11.7–8; 4Q174, 3.7–9; b. Sot. 22a; John 6:61; 16:1; Jas 2:10; 3:2; 1 Pet 2:8; 2 Pet 1:10; T. Reub. 4:7.

[1125] 1 Macc 1:41–51; see data in I. H. Marshall, *Kept by the Power of God: A Study in Perseverance and Falling Away* (London: Epworth, 1969), 29–50.

[1126] E.g., 1 En. 91:7; T. Iss. 6:1; Naph. 4:1; 3 En. 48A:5–6; m. Sot. 9:15.

[1127] Depending on the meaning of *apostasia*; cf. also 1 Tim 4:1–2; 2 Tim 3:1–5; 2 Pet 3:3; 1 John 2:18–19; Jude 4–8, 12.

[1128] As Das, *Galatians*, 105, 622, rightly observes.

[1129] With D. Hunn, "Πίστις in Galatians 5.5–6: Neglected Evidence for 'Faith in Christ,'" *NTS* 62 (2016): 477–83, here 480–82, esp. 482.

Does the *hope of righteousness* mean "the future hope guaranteed by present righteousness/justification," or "the hope that *is* righteousness," i.e., the verdict of justification at the final judgment? Paul may have been content to leave the grammar open to both readings, perhaps because he envisioned *righteousness*/justification as already/not yet; the present foretaste nurtures our expectation for the consummation.

Hope here includes many conventional Jewish eschatological expectations that Paul elsewhere shares.[1130] But the English word *hope* does not fully communicate Paul's thought, since it might convey merely a wish; Paul's expressions of hope are secured in present reality, so the term *expectation* or *expectancy* better conveys the idea in English.[1131]

After Paul's polemic against the Galatians embracing the law and especially his harsh words against circumcision in 5:2–4, we come to Paul's more nuanced approach to circumcision – that is, what he thought when circumcision was not being used to challenge the sufficiency of Christ (cf. 1 Cor 7:19). *Neither circumcision nor uncircumcision counts for anything* (Gal 5:6), a thesis that he repeats in 6:15, almost at the letter's end. What counts is only *faith working through love*, the equivalent in 6:15 of "a new creation," which in Christ has begun to dawn.

This change does not mean that our various cultures are meaningless. Paul's concern about circumcision was only about it being imposed on gentiles as a spiritual demand.[1132] Paul was not opposed to Jewish people circumcising their children, a nuance that was lost on some critics in his own day (Acts 21:21) as well as afterward. Instead, in the new creation, the old outward sign became a matter of indifference, just as complexion or nose shape would be when choosing athletes.[1133] Paul's sayings about indifferents such as circumcision (Gal 5:6; 6:15; 1 Cor 7:19) are similar to Stoic *adiaphora*,[1134] that is, matters that are themselves neither good nor bad inherently, but that may be used for good or bad depending on the situation.[1135]

[1130] E.g., God's glory (Rom 5:2); the restoration of creation (8:20, 24); the resurrection of the righteous (1 Thess 4:13); the consummation of salvation (5:8).

[1131] I owe this insight to discussion with Jürgen Moltmann.

[1132] With even Augustine *Ep. Gal.* 41 (1B.5.1–3; Edwards); Luther *First Lectures on Galatians* on 2:3 and 5:6; *Second Lectures on Galatians* on 2:3 (Bray).

[1133] Chrysostom *Hom. Gal.* 5.6 (Edwards).

[1134] With W. Deming, "Paul and Indifferent Things," pages 384–403 in *Paul in the Greco-Roman World: A Handbook* (ed. J. P. Sampley; Harrisburg, PA: Trinity Press International, 2003), 395; R. A. Ramsaran, "Paul and Maxims," pages 429–56 in *Paul in the Greco-Roman World*, 437.

[1135] On the adiaphora, see Gal 2:6.

One could read the term translated *working* in 5:6 (*energeô*) as "being activated" (if it is understood as in the passive voice, with many patristic and medieval commentators) or "expressing itself" (if it is understood as in the Greek middle voice, with the vast majority of modern commentators). Although either reading is grammatically possible, the context decisively favors the middle reading: faith expressing itself in love. Paul has spoken about faith throughout the letter so far; now, in this ethical section, he will show that genuine faith expresses itself in love (5:14, 22).

5:7–12: BEWARE OF YOUR DECEIVERS

5:7 You were running well; who prevented you from obeying the truth?

5:8 Such persuasion does not come from the one who calls you.

5:9 A little yeast leavens the whole batch of dough.

5:10 I am confident about you in the Lord that you will not think otherwise. But whoever it is that is confusing you will pay the penalty.

5:11 But my friends, why am I still being persecuted if I am still preaching circumcision? In that case the offense of the cross has been removed.

5:12 I wish those who unsettle you would castrate themselves!

Paul earlier showed that he himself had not run his race in vain (2:2), but now the Galatians were at risk of falling (5:4) instead of running well (5:7). (For comment on Paul's athletic metaphors, see Gal 2:2.) Paul laments that though the Galatians were previously *running well*, someone had now *prevented* them. The term translated *prevented* (*egkoptô*) typically means "slowed progress" or "hindered," but etymologically is "cut in" (*en* + *koptô*).

In the context of *running*, one could obviously slow someone down by cutting in front of them, an action that most commentators infer here.[1136] Such an action could trip or break the stride of a fellow competitor, an action that violated the rules of Greek races.[1137] Commentators less frequently note a concomitant image: if cutting in front of the Galatians risks

---

[1136] See esp. C. E. De Vries, "Paul's 'Cutting' Remarks about a Race: Galatians 5:1–12," pages 115–20 in *Current Issues in Biblical and Patristic Interpretation: Studies in Honor of Merrill C. Tenney Presented by His Former Students* (ed. G. F. Hawthorne; Grand Rapids, MI: Eerdmans, 1975), 118–19.

[1137] E. N. Gardiner, *Greek Athletic Sports and Festivals* (Oxford: Clarendon Press, 1955), 146, cited by Longenecker, *Galatians*, 230.

tripping them, it might cause them to stumble – risking their apostasy (note the term translated *fallen* in Gal 5:4 and comment there).

Most commentators also note Paul's wordplay here. The Greek term *egkoptô* ("cut in") may play on circumcision as a "cutting" of the flesh.[1138] Etymologically, the Greek term for *circumcise* means "to cut around."[1139] Although the LXX obscures the wordplay, the Hebrew text of Gen 17:14 also may play on refusal of circumcision and being "cut off."[1140] After this mention of cutting, Paul applies the cognate verb *apokoptô* for an even more gruesome "cutting" in Gal 5:12. So Paul hopes that those wanting to "cut around" the Galatians' foreskins, who "cut in" to make them stumble, will instead "cut themselves off" in a manner discussed in 5:12. Ancient writers often displayed their rhetorical skill or even made arguments based on wordplays; see comment on Gal 3:15.

In addition to the wordplay about "cutting," Paul may include another in Gal 5:7–8. *Obeying* in 5:7 is the Greek verb *peithô*, which also means "persuaded." A cognate noun appears in 5:8 (*persuasion, peismonê*), with the verb again in 5:10. Whoever has hindered them from their persuaded obedience to the truth, this new persuasion is not from the one who called them; but Paul himself is persuaded that whoever is confusing them will be judged by the one who called them. "The truth" in 5:7 is the truth mentioned earlier in Galatians – the "truth of the gospel" (2:5, 14).

Leaven, or *yeast*, is a fermenting agent that makes dough rise; unless one wanted to start from scratch each time one baked bread, one needed to retain some from a previous batch for a new batch of dough.[1141] Yeast, though small in itself, can spread throughout the dough and thus affect the entire loaf. *The whole batch of dough* thus refers to the Galatian congregations.

Many scholars suggest that Paul was using a common proverb in 5:9, because he quotes the same saying in 1 Cor 5:6 and appeals to the Corinthians' knowledge of the principle. The proverb would be something

---

[1138] In the short run, circumcision would certainly hinder running (Gen 34:24–25), and it had embarrassed hellenized Jews wishing to compete in Greek games (1 Macc 1:14–15), but Paul probably plays on the word for cutting rather than the image of circumcision per se in this verse.

[1139] *Peritemnô* prefixes the verb *temnô* with *peri* ("around"). *Temnô* often means "cut" (in the LXX), sometimes even for cutting off limbs (4 Macc 9:17; 10:19).

[1140] "Cut" also being covenant language in Hebrew (God or mortals would "cut covenants," as in, e.g., Gen 9:11; 15:18; 21:27, 32; 26:28; 31:44; Exod 24:8; 34:10, 12, 15, 27), the "covenant" also being mentioned in the verse.

[1141] M. L. Bailey, "The Parable of the Leavening Process," *BSac* 156 (1999): 61–71, here 63.

like our proverb in English today, "One bad apple spoils the bunch." The
proverb, however, was probably coined by Paul or other early Christians.[1142]

Other writers used leaven in various figurative ways, and commentators cite examples of the image being used negatively. Because leaven could
spread, it provided a useful metaphor for corruption. The context of the
similar use in 1 Cor 5:6 might shed light on Paul's thinking here. In context there, the removal specifically involves the excommunication of the
incestuous man (5:3–5, 13). Whether or not Paul specifies excommunication
here, the idea would not necessarily be foreign to his audience, and would
certainly be familiar to Paul's rivals. Jewish circles already practiced various
forms of excommunication.[1143]

In view of similar language in 1 Cor 5:6–7, Paul probably refers to the
cancerous influence of the relatively small number of persons who have
diverted the believers from obeying the truth (5:7). If the Galatians heed
Paul's warning, they should "Drive out the slave and her child" (4:30); that
is, they should stop welcoming these purveyors of a false gospel.

As noted at 5:7, Paul's use of *confident* here ("persuaded," using the verb
peithô) plays on wording he has used in 5:7–8. Expressions of confidence
were common, and were often meant to inspire compliance with an implicit
request.[1144] Paul uses the expression "persuaded in the Lord" elsewhere as
well (Rom 14:14; Phil 2:24; 2 Thess 3:4; cf. Phil 1:14) in contexts that suggest
Paul's prayerful trust that the Lord will bring the favorable outcome.

Whoever it is that is confusing you is singular in form in Greek; probably, however, Paul simply continues speaking generically as he did in the
question in 5:7. He refers to the same ones "who are confusing you" in 1:7,
the only other use of the verb in Paul's extant letters. Paul is confident that
they will bear their judgment (NRSV: *pay the penalty*), using a term that he
normally uses for divine judgment (Rom 3:8; 5:16).

Most scholars think that in 5:11 Paul answers the charge that he himself
is *still preaching circumcision*.[1145] The charge seems to imply two components: first, that he used to preach circumcision, which Paul does not appear
to dispute; and second, that he is still doing so. Since he obviously had not

---

[1142] A TLG search (by my PhD student Donald Murray Vasser) attests it widely, but initially
only among sources influenced by Paul.

[1143] See Ezra 10:8; 1QS 6.24–7.25; m. Taan. 3:8; M.Q. 3:1–2.

[1144] E.g., Cicero *Fam.* 2.4.2; 13.44.1; Phlm 21; S. N. Olson, "Pauline Expressions of Confidence
in His Addressees," *CBQ* 47 (2, 1985): 282–95.

[1145] E.g., Tyson, "Opponents," 249. Clearly Paul was sometimes the object of charges that he
and his supporters deemed false (Rom 3:8; 2 Cor 6:8; Acts 21:21).

preached it in Galatia, perhaps he is being accused of watering down his gospel for the Galatians to make their conversion simpler yet incomplete, or of hypocrisy (cf. 2:13), or at least inconsistency (cf. 1 Cor 9:19–23), making him a people-pleaser (Gal 1:10).

When had Paul preached circumcision in the past? Many scholars argue that he insisted on circumcising gentiles before his conversion, when he was a zealot for the traditions (Gal 1:13–14). Others contend that Paul's past preaching of circumcision was in his first ministry to gentiles after his conversion, since we know of no direct ministry to gentiles before his conversion; Paul, after all, need not have changed all his views overnight. If we must choose, however, on the whole we have more evidence for his pre-conversion stance (concerning gentiles, not to them) than for his preaching circumcision after his conversion.

Since Paul is accused of "still" preaching circumcision, when would Paul have "preached circumcision" after his conversion more recently? Paul obviously had no problem allowing Jews to circumcise their children. Also, as many commentators note, Luke, whom I take to be a sometime companion of Paul,[1146] offers a report (from apparently shortly before Luke joined Paul; cf. Acts 16:10) of Paul circumcising someone who was (partly) Jewish (16:3). Assuming the south Galatia view, the Galatians themselves would know that Paul had circumcised Timothy, since the incident occurred with one of their own and in their own region (16:1–3).[1147] Luke uses this account to qualify Paul's opposition to circumcision being imposed on gentile converts in the preceding chapter (Acts 15:1–2); Timothy's circumcision is specifically for the sake of mission. Such a nuance, however, could easily be lost on Paul's detractors.

Paul is persecuted, however, because, whenever he may have demanded gentile circumcision in the past, he no longer preaches it for *gentiles*. For Paul, this is intimately related to *the offense of the cross*. In Greek the term for *offense* here is *skandalon*, stumbling stone, a stone over which people trip. It is offensive not in a mild sense such as someone's breath after consuming tuna or garlic but in the much more serious sense of an obstacle or stumbling block for faith. This terminology continues the likely image of falling in 5:4 and being tripped in 5:7.

Paul used the phrase *offense of the cross* in other churches as well (1 Cor 1:23). The *offense*, i.e., the stumbling stone, may go back to Jesus's

[1146] See Keener, *Acts*, 407–14, 2350–74.
[1147] For discussion, see Keener, *Acts*, 2311–22.

identification of himself as a rejected stone, using Ps 118:22–23 (Mark 12:10–11), which he or some of his early followers linked with the stumbling stone of Isa 8:14–15 (Matt 21:42–44, probably including also Dan 2:34). One of the stone texts, Isa 8:14–15, is used by both Paul (Rom 9:33, where it is combined with Isa 28:16) and 1 Pet 2:8 in almost identical wording. Paul inherited the recognition that people would stumble over Christ (Matt 11:6//Luke 7:23); he understood that this stumbling applied most directly to Jesus's execution by Rome, hanged on a cursed tree.

The cross's nature as an offensive stumbling block or obstacle shows why its proclaimers could be *persecuted* (Gal 5:11). Paul's commitment to face *persecution* rather than preach *circumcision* suggests that his rivals were preaching circumcision to avoid persecution (a thesis consistent with 6:12).[1148] There could be pressures on the rivals from local Jewish communities (Acts 13:45, 50; 14:2, 4, 19). Some also suggest concerns that only those who were identifiably Jewish would be exempt from the imperial cult. But such an exemption may not have mattered very much in many cities. The imperial cult was popular and Roman authorities did not hunt down absentees to persecute (although civic authorities might respond to neighbors' complaints). More likely, Paul's rivals were from Judea (cf. Gal 4:25–26) and were responding to pressures there.[1149]

As noted in the introduction, nationalism was on the rise in Judea in the 40s and 50s of the first century, probably generating an increase of nationalism among Jesus's Judean followers as well (cf. Acts 21:20–21). When less nationalist Jewish believers welcomed gentiles without circumcision, they appeared to water down a heritage for which Jews had suffered and died. Jews had also vigorously defended the exemptions from military service and for sabbath celebrations granted them by various authorities; an influx of uncircumcised gentiles could make Rome suspect that others were now exploiting these privileges.[1150]

The history of Christian missions provides subsequent analogies where the sending churches imposed their cultures' values on their mission fields, with some missionaries more concerned about pressures back home than about the needs of their converts. Like some of his subsequent followers

---

[1148] With Eastman, "Galatians," 831.
[1149] Barclay, *Obeying*, 51–52.
[1150] Sanders, *Paul*, 494.

in mission, Paul provides a different, more culturally sensitive model for mission.[1151]

Paul's anger-arousing *pathos* hits a vituperative climax in 5:12. Here Paul wishes that such troublemakers *would castrate themselves*, thus making themselves unfit for the community of God's people (Deut 23:1 [MT 23:2]) just as they claimed the uncircumcised were. In Greek, Paul merely wishes that they would "cut themselves off," but the meaning of the euphemism is transparent enough, as most modern translations and commentators make clear. As Chrysostom put it: "If they will, let them be not only circumcised but emasculated."[1152]

Some pagans associated circumcision with castration; the further wide-spread association of castration with the Galli (see discussion in what follows) would seal Paul's warning that by accepting circumcision they would be returning to the form of ritual religion they had followed before (Gal 4:8–10).[1153] Despite some eunuchs being courtiers and officials, castration or being a eunuch carried a severe stigma.[1154] Castration supposedly deprived one of manhood, often inviting ridicule.[1155]

Paul addresses here not simply castration, but self-castration, an act that most viewed as senseless and that Jews deemed wicked.[1156] Most scholars think that Paul's allusion to castration plays on an image that would resonate particularly well in Galatia: the Galli. (For specifically Phrygian-Galatian connections for the mother goddess Cybele, see discussion at Gal 4:8–10.)

During Cybele's seasonal rites, her lower-level priests would enter a mad frenzy and would castrate themselves.[1157] As G. Walter Hansen suggests, if the opponents desired "to put on a sensational show," available models already existed: "The priests of Cybele, the mother goddess of the

---

[1151] Cf. C. S. Keener, "Scripture and Context: An Evangelical Exploration," *AsJ* 70 (1, 2015): 17–62; Keener, *Spirit Hermeneutics*, 67–76.

[1152] Chrysostom *Hom. Gal.* 5.11–12 (Edwards). One should note, however, that in view of Deut 23 the meaning here should be slicing off the penis, not the testicles.

[1153] With de Boer, *Galatians*, 334.

[1154] E.g., Xenophon *Cyr.* 7.5.61; Seneca *Ep. Lucil.* 114.6; Dio Chrysostom *Or.* 33.39; Lucian *Critic* 17; Philostratus *Vit. soph.* 1.25.541; 2.4.569.

[1155] Xenophon *Cyr.* 5.2.29; Caesar *Alex. W.* 1.70; Virgil *Aen.* 12.99; Lucan *C.W.* 10.133–34; Epictetus *Diatr.* 3.1.31; Lucian *Eunuch* 6, 9; Josephus *Ant.* 4.290–91; y. Shab. 19:3, §3.

[1156] E.g., Josephus *Ant.* 4.290. A eunuch made such by Fortune (cf. Matt 19:12) might be less prone to condemnation (Phaedrus 3.11.6–7).

[1157] See, e.g., Ovid *Fasti* 4.237–44; Pliny *N.H.* 11.109.261; Epictetus *Diatr.* 2.20.17; cf. G. S. Gasparro, *Soteriology and Mystic Aspects in the Cult of Cybele and Attis* (ÉPROER 103; Leiden: Brill, 1985), 26–28, 53.

earth, castrated themselves with ritual pincers and placed their testicles in a box."[1158] People regularly ridiculed the Galli,[1159] especially with regard to their self-castration.[1160]

Paul and his rivals may know that Jesus spoke hyperbolically of cutting off (using the same verb) any organ that causes its possessor to stumble (Mark 9:43, 45). This verb is not used in the LXX for cutting off a person from the community, but is used for cutting off an organ (Deut 25:12; Judg 1:6–7). Paul (or, on some other views, the Paulinist) probably plays on this image figuratively in Col 3:5. In the context of priests of Cybele, the Stoic philosopher Epictetus complains that cutting off (using the same verb, *apokoptô*) organs cannot cut off men's sexual desires.[1161]

Many scholars rightly point out the ironic consequences of such self-mutilation. With one extra slice, Paul's rivals would exclude themselves from the covenant people from which they excluded all uncircumcised persons! They would "cut themselves off" in more ways than one! The Hebrew text of Deut 23:1 (23:2 in Heb.) prohibits from entering God's community those with crushed testicles and those whose male organ has been cut off. The LXX (23:2) prefers a euphemism for the latter: it prohibits those with crushed testicles and those who have been "cut off" (using the verb *apokoptô*, the same verb as in Gal 5:12) from God's *ekklêsia* ("community"). Jewish people took this matter very seriously;[1162] one who eunuched himself (Josephus calls them *Galli*) was counted as if he had murdered his own children.[1163]

Paul is not explicit, but others sometimes alluded to the Galli implicitly to make their point.[1164] "Insinuation was often a more effective way to communicate a point,"[1165] and especially if the point would seem crude if stated more explicitly: "I wish their knives would slip and they'd sever their own dicks." Epictetus offers a similar euphemism: If you want to

[1158] Hansen, *Galatians*, 161 (noting one of these boxes on display at Cambridge).
[1159] E.g., Seneca *Ep. Lucil.* 108.7; Martial *Epig.* 7.95.15; Lucian *Alex.* 13.
[1160] E.g., Seneca *Dial.* 7.26.8; Juvenal *Sat.* 2.110–16 (cf. 6.514–16); Lucian *Syr. G.* 51; cf. Lucretius *Nat.* 2.614–15; Martial *Epig.* 1.35.15; 3.24.13; 3.91; 9.2; 13.64.
[1161] Epictetus *Diatr.* 2.20.19.
[1162] Cf. 1QSa 2.5–6; 4QMMT B.39–44; Josephus *Ant.* 4.290–91; Philo *Spec. Laws* 1.325; *m. Yeb.* 8:2; Gen. Rab. 34:8.
[1163] Josephus *Ant.* 4.290.
[1164] Horace *Sat.* 1.2.120–21.
[1165] On *insinuatio*, see E. W. Bower, "Ephodos and insinuatio in Greek and Latin Rhetoric," *CQ* 8 (1958): 224–30; for examples, see Cicero *Pis.* 2.3; *Vat.* 5.13; Keener, *Acts*, 3415–16, 3743. Note "emphasis" in Anderson, *Glossary*, 41–42.

pluck out your hairs to look like a woman, then "Make a clean sweep of the whole matter; eradicate your – what shall I call it? – the cause of your hairiness."[1166]

The image might seem particularly striking to those gentiles who already associated circumcision with castration. Thus one poet opines that whoever cut off the eunuch's genitals ought to have the same done to him.[1167] It was customary to denounce one's opponents in court or debate as viciously as possible. Cicero emphasized that ridiculing opponents in a way that generated laughter gained the audience's goodwill, so long as the humor rested on wit rather than buffoonery.[1168]

Paul has a similar wordplay in Phil 3:2–3, where he calls advocates of physical gentile circumcision (*peritomê*, which sounds like "cutting around") instead "the mutilation" (using *katatomê*, which sounds like "cutting against").[1169] A wordplay is hardly surprising here; advocates of cutting the Galatians' organs have cut in on them (Gal 5:7, using *egkoptô*). Paul wishes they would instead cut themselves off (*apokoptô*), mutilating themselves in a manner that would disqualify them as they have disqualified others.[1170]

Subsequent readers have evaluated differently the propriety of Paul's remarks. Since Jesus urged followers to bless those who cursed them, Jerome regards Paul's outburst here as a mark of human frailty.[1171] By contrast, Luther, a polemicist hardly averse to crude language himself, deems such language acceptable in defense of the gospel.[1172] We may wish to consider that this curse, although more crude, is actually less harsh than the implied pronouncement of eternal damnation in 5:10 or Paul's explicit curse in 1:8–9. From Paul's perspective, only such punishments can begin to match their crime of damning others with their false gospel (1:7; 5:7).

[1166] Epictetus *Diatr.* 3.1.31 (trans. W. A. Oldfather, LCL 2:17).

[1167] Ovid *Am.* 2.3.3–4; cf. Martial *Epig.* 3.91; 9.2.13–14.

[1168] Cicero *De or.* 2.58.236; 2.61.251; *Brutus* 43.158; 93.322; *Orator* 26.88–90; 40.138.

[1169] With G. F. Hawthorne, *Philippians* (WBC 43; Waco, TX: Word, 1983), 123; F. B. Craddock, *Philippians* (IBC; Atlanta, GA: John Knox, 1985), 56; deSilva, *Readings*, 255; Porter, "Paul and Letters," 580. The cognate verb *katatemnô* appears in the LXX for prohibited mutilations (LXX Lev 21:5, 1 Kgs 18:28).

[1170] With, e.g., De Vries, "Paul's 'Cutting' Remarks," 120.

[1171] Jerome *Ep. Gal.* 3.5.12 (Edwards).

[1172] Luther *Second Lectures on Galatians* on 5:12 (Bray). See also William Perkins *Commentary on Galatians* on 5:12 (Bray).

5:13–15: SERVING ONE ANOTHER

> **5:13 For you were called to freedom, brothers and sisters; only do not use your freedom as an opportunity for self-indulgence, but through love become slaves to one another.**
>
> **5:14 For the whole law is summed up in a single commandment, "You shall love your neighbor as yourself."**
>
> **5:15 If, however, you bite and devour one another, take care that you are not consumed by one another.**

Scholars debate where the final section of the body of Galatians begins. Most likely, it runs from 5:13 to 6:10. Although commentators understandably sometimes concisely summarize the section as chapters 5–6 and provide comment at 5:1 or 5:2, I have, with a majority of commentators, arranged comments on the body's closing section here.

John Barclay surveys the major lines of interpretation for Gal 5:13–6:10:[1173]

1. Viewing the passage as unrelated to the rest of Galatians
2. Approaches that integrate the section within Galatians as a whole
3. Barclay's own view, undoubtedly the dominant approach today, largely followed here: this section is integral to Paul's larger argument: not the law, but faith in Christ, counters sin.[1174] The *Spirit* produces the true righteousness that others sought by the law.[1175]

Acknowledging that a righteous status is a free gift in Christ does not lead to immorality, at least not for those *truly* born from God's Spirit. Far from it! Rather, this gift of righteousness also includes or is accompanied by (depending on the interpreter's lexical evaluation of *dikaiosunê*) divine empowerment to live righteously.

This section thus qualifies Paul's emphasis on the era of the law having ended; the fuller righteousness to which the law always pointed is now fulfilled for those who live by Christ (5:14, 18, 23; 6:2). Paul's words about the passing of the law (3:17–23; 4:1–6) do not refer to the righteousness of the law. Paul expects good "works" (6:4, 10), but as the fruit of Christ's righteousness rather than its cause.

[1173] Barclay, *Obeying*, 9–26.
[1174] Barclay, *Obeying*, 108.
[1175] Augustine *Nature* 67 (Edwards).

Concluding exhortations do characterize many of Paul's letters, including Galatians.[1176] Yet 5:13–6:10 is not exclusively hortatory; indeed, the focus of 5:13–24 is indicative, on what believers already are in Christ.[1177] The tension between indicative and imperative – the summons to "be" (act in accord with) "what you already are" (your identity in Christ) is a significant theme in Pauline discussions of ethics.[1178] Gal 5:13–6:10 is the climax of Paul's argument so far; one expert in ancient rhetoric even contends that "the exhortation of chapters 5–6 … is the point of the letter."[1179]

Writers sometimes concisely outlined what they would cover before covering it.[1180] Paul treats the opposition of the Spirit and the flesh in 5:16–18, then treats in detail (but in reverse order) flesh (5:19–21) and Spirit (5:22–23). Although some interpreters are overly creative in identifying chiastic (inverted parallel) structures, some chiastic structures do appear to emerge from the text. In the following structure, my suggested potential parallels in A/A' and B/B' may well be purely imaginative, but other elements do seem to reflect a pattern.

A (?) 5:1–12: Crucifixion (5:11) rather than circumcision; reject circumcisionists; persevere to eternal life

B (?) 5:13a: avoid self-indulgence
  C 5:13b: become slaves to one another + 5:14
  C 5:14: (Christ's) law: love one another
    D 5:15: stop competing against each other lest you harm each other
      E 5:16: Walk by the Spirit
        F 5:17: the Spirit supplants the flesh
          G 5:18: those led by the Spirit are not under the law
            H 5:19–21: the works of the flesh
            H' 5:22–23: the fruit of the Spirit
          G' 5:23b: against the Spirit's fruit is no law
        F' 5:24: the flesh has been crucified

[1176] Aune, *Dictionary of Rhetoric*, 272; cf. Fronto *Ad M. Caes.* 3.16.2; Rom 16:17–20; 1 Cor 16:13–14; 2 Cor 13:11–12.

[1177] Martyn, *Galatians*, 481–83.

[1178] See, e.g., Dunn, *Theology of Paul*, 626–31; further comment at Gal 5:1.

[1179] Kennedy, *Interpretation*, 146.

[1180] See, e.g., Gorgias *Hel.* 6–8; Pliny *Nat.* 33.21.66; Dio Chrysostom *Or.* 38.8; Arius Didymus 2.7.5a, p. 10.6–7; Tacitus *Ann.* 16.21–32; Pliny *Ep.* 6.29.1–2; Soranus *Gynec.* 1.intro.2; 1.1.3.

E' 5:25: walk by the Spirit
   D' 5:26–6:1: stop competing against each other; use gentleness
     C' 6:2: Christ's law: bear other's burdens (as slaves would)
B' (?) 6:3–5: Do not seek for others to benefit you

A' (?) 6:6–12: Support good teachers; crucifixion rather than circumcision; reject circumcisionists; persevere to eternal life

Having established that God has called the Galatian believers to spiritual freedom (Gal 4:8–9; 4:31–5:1, esp. 5:1), Paul in 5:13 exhorts them to use this freedom to serve one another (5:13). Everyone understood that people sometimes twisted liberty into license.[1181] Some, not least Paul's opponents, might have wished to depict license as the result of Paul's course (cf. Rom 3:8). Yet as in the case of "free" cities, for example, freedom ideally meant a high degree of self-governance rather than external constraint;[1182] it did not entail license.

Self-indulgence here is *sarx*, or "flesh," the realm of which includes whatever has not been transformed by the eschatological Spirit; a mere mark in the "flesh," circumcision (Gal 6:12–13; cf. Gen 17:9–14), was not sufficient to bring the flesh under divine rule.[1183]

Greek culture in particular demeaned slavery (*douleia*, as in 5:1) as the antithesis of freedom. A call to serve (*douleuô*) one another (cf. also 6:2) would therefore sound paradoxical, especially given Paul's emphasis on liberation from slavery earlier in the letter. (The NRSV's *become slaves* probably lays too much emphasis on initial enslavement; the point is rather to regularly *act* as slaves to one another, so serving one another's interests.) As Luther puts it here, "The freedom of the Christian is a slavery to love."[1184]

In 5:14, Paul's summary of the law in the love commandment undoubtedly evokes Jesus's teaching. Although one rabbi after Paul's time named love as the chief commandment,[1185] that was one rabbinic view about the greatest commandment among many.[1186] Others valued love of neighbor,[1187] but did not specifically rank this as the greatest or second greatest commandment. Love remains the supreme virtue pervasively in various strands of the early Christian movement (e.g., Rom 13:8–10; 1 Cor 13:1–13; Gal 5:14, 22; Col 3:14; 1 Thess 4:9; Heb 10:24; 1 John 2:10; 3:14; 4:7–9). Such unanimity

---

[1181] E.g., Livy 5.6.17; 27.31.6.
[1182] See A. J. S. Spawforth, "Free cities," *OCD*³ 609.
[1183] Barclay, *Gift*, 426.
[1184] Luther *First Lectures on Galatians* on 5:13 (Bray).
[1185] Sipra Qed. pq. 4.200.3.7; Gen. Rab. 24:7.
[1186] For the debates, see, e.g., Sipra VDDeho. par. 1.34.1.3; 12.65.1.3.
[1187] E.g., Jub. 36:4, 8; m. Ab. 1:12, attributed to Hillel.

on the topic is nowhere else attested in antiquity. This observation suggests that Jesus's teaching (Mark 12:30–31) strongly shaped early Christian ethics.

Matthew adds that Jesus treated commandments to love as not only the greatest, but a sort of epitome of the commandments (Matt 22:40; cf. also 7:12). This follows a practice familiar from some other Jewish sages: finding commandments that epitomized the Torah as a whole.[1188] Given this tradition, it is reasonable to understand Paul as epitomizing the law here, although Paul's other statements show that he, unlike the rabbis, would not have required literal observance of all the law's stipulations besides the demands of love.[1189] For Paul, it is the spirit of the law that counts; gentile believers are spiritual children of Abraham, but they are not ethnic Israelites living in the holy land before the coming of Christ. As will become clearer in Paul's discussion in 5:16–25 (esp. 5:18b, 23), Paul views this law less as a moralistic prescription than as a *description* of how the moral intention of the law is fulfilled when believers love their neighbors.[1190]

Who is the neighbor one is commanded to love (cf. Luke 10:29)? Jews sometimes applied it to fellow Jews; some sectarians applied it especially to members of their own sects.[1191] The context of Lev 19:18 applies it to foreigners as well as Israelites (Lev 19:33–34), a principle sometimes recognized in antiquity.[1192] Paul applies the principle here especially to their treatment of others in their Christian community, in the context of serving one another (*allêlôn*, 5:13) rather than harming one another (*allêlôn*, 5:15). Still, Leviticus extends the principle beyond one's closest kin (again, as noted, to foreigners), and Paul elsewhere applies the text in a context addressing treatment not only of believers but also nonbelievers (Rom 12:14–13:10).

Galatians 5:15 offers the antithesis to serving one another in 5:13: devouring one another. The strife against which Paul warns in 5:15 is ruled out by love of neighbor in 5:14; in fact, the immediate context of 5:14's quotation of Lev 19:18 warns against bearing a grudge against fellow members of God's people. That Paul specifically raises the warning here, and that social vices

[1188] Philo *Decal.* 154; 4 Macc 2:7–9; Ab. R. Nat. 27 A; 24, §49 B; b. Shab. 31a; E. P. Sanders, *Judaism: Practice and Belief, 63 BCE–66 CE* (London: SCM; Philadelphia, PA: Trinity Press International, 1992), 257–60; cf. Rom 13:9.

[1189] A significant difference, noted by Barclay, *Obeying*, 136. On what at least Paul's fellow Jews may have seen as his selective application of commandments to gentiles, see Barclay, *Obeying*, 124; Sanders, *Paul*, 314, 642–43, 697, 704.

[1190] Barclay, *Gift*, 431 (cf. 473); Betz, *Galatians*, 275; de Boer, *Galatians*, 346.

[1191] CD 6.20–21; 9.2–3; Josephus *War* 2.119.

[1192] Cf. Lk 10:27; T. Iss. 7:6; perhaps Jub. 7:20; 20:2; 36:4; m. Ab. 1:12.

figure so heavily in 5:20–21, suggests that Paul knows about strife in one or more of the churches of Galatia.

One first-century sage declared that biting back one's biter – returning harm for harm – is the action not of a human but of a beast.[1193] Comparisons with beasts, as presumably here, were common in ancient moral literature, usually for people subject to their own passions rather than reason.[1194] Paul uses such images in 1 Cor 15:32 and Phil 3:2. The more specific image of devouring one another also here evokes the ancient horror of cannibalism.

Biting one another was applied figuratively to various forms of hostile behavior.[1195] Israel's exploitive leaders could be depicted as devouring the flesh of the people (Mic 3:2–3). Jesus spoke of religious leaders devouring widows' houses (Mark 12:40), and Paul speaks of his opponents "preying" (the same Greek term) on the Corinthians (2 Cor 11:20). An early Jewish tradition declared that only fear of the Roman government restrains people from "swallowing one another alive."[1196] Those preoccupied with competition – including meritorious spiritual achievement (as, a different way, in Corinth) or going beyond what Christ has provided – are not so free to serve others' needs.

5:16–25: FOLLOWING THE SPIRIT'S STEPS

5:16 Live by the Spirit, I say, and do not gratify the desires of the flesh.

5:17 For what the flesh desires is opposed to the Spirit, and what the Spirit desires is opposed to the flesh; for these are opposed to each other, to prevent you from doing what you want.

5:18 But if you are led by the Spirit, you are not subject to the law.

5:19 Now the works of the flesh are obvious: fornication, impurity, licentiousness,

5:20 idolatry, sorcery, enmities, strife, jealousy, anger, quarrels, dissensions, factions,

5:21 envy, drunkenness, carousing, and things like these. I am warning you, as I warned you before: those who do such things will not inherit the kingdom of God.

[1193] Musonius Rufus 10, 78.27–28.
[1194] See, e.g., Xenophon *Mem.* 1.2.30; Seneca Y. *Ep. Lucil.* 103.2; Musonius Rufus 10, 78.27–28; Epictetus *Diatr.* 4.1.127; 4.5.21; Dio Chrysostom *Or.* 8.14, 21; 32.26; Diogenes *Ep.* 28.
[1195] See, e.g., Seneca *Controv.* 1.8.16; Diogenes Laertius 6.1.4–5; 1 En. 103:11, 15; T. Gad 2:2.
[1196] M. Ab. 3:2, my translation.

5:22 By contrast, the fruit of the Spirit is love, joy, peace, patience, kindness, generosity, faithfulness,

5:23 gentleness, and self-control. There is no law against such things.

5:24 And those who belong to Christ Jesus have crucified the flesh with its passions and desires.

5:25 If we live by the Spirit, let us also be guided by the Spirit.

If we are ruled by the Spirit of God's Son, who fulfilled the law (4:4–6), we do not depend on the formal law (5:18, 23), because we live as God's sons and daughters, and thus in intimate, direct relationship with him rather than under a pedagogue (3:24–25).

In 5:16–25, Paul emphasizes here that the solution to the passions of the flesh is not more laws, but the Spirit who transforms from within. Paul has biblical grounds for affirming that, to the extent that we follow the eschatological Spirit, we follow God's commands (Ezek 36:26–27);[1197] Paul alludes to this text as part of the new covenant reality in 2 Cor 3:3,[1198] and probably alludes to it here as well: the Hebrew text of Ezek 36:27 speaks of the Spirit enabling God's eschatological people to "walk" in his commands and do them.

The contrast between Spirit and flesh unites 5:16–25, with 5:16 introducing this key issue and the image of walking by the Spirit framing the section (5:16, 25).

The NRSV's *live by*[1199] *the Spirit* here is literally "walk by the Spirit," allowing the connection with 5:25. Although Paul is not always consistent with his metaphors even in the same paragraph, walking in the Spirit might continue the imagery of locomotion and the danger of tripping in Gal 5:7 and falling in 5:4.

Although the LXX often changed the Hebrew verb *halak* to a less colorful term for movement (essentially, "go"),[1200] the Hebrew verb meant both "walk" and "conduct one's life."[1201] One should thus "walk in" righteousness,[1202] in God's commandments,[1203] and in his

---

[1197] This passage played a role in the Qumran sectarians' pneumatology; see 1QS 4.21.

[1198] "New" could be a term linking Ezek 36:26 with Jer 31:31.

[1199] The dative probably functions especially instrumentally here, hence "by means of"; with C. F. D. Moule, *An Idiom Book of New Testament Greek* (2nd edn.; Cambridge: Cambridge University Press, 1959), 44; Wallace, *Grammar*, 165–66 (cf. 158).

[1200] E.g., LXX Deut 8:6; 10:12; 11:22; 19:9; 26:17; 28:9; 30:16; Lev 26:3; Mic 4:2.

[1201] Longenecker, *Galatians*, 244; de Boer, *Galatians*, 351.

[1202] E.g., Prov 8:20 LXX; 1 En. 91:19; 94:1; Jub. 21:2; 25:10; 4Q416 f2iii.10.

[1203] E.g., Lev 26:3; 1 Kgs 6:12; 2 Kgs 10:31; Neh 10:29; Ps 78:10; Ezek 20:19; CD 7.6–7; 11Q19 54.17; 11Q19 59.16.

"ways."[1204] Later rabbis spoke of legal and moral discourse as halakah, "walking."[1205] This idea is relevant to the Spirit's alternative here to formal adherence to the Torah (Gal 5:18, 22–23). Paul might even evoke Ezekiel here; God promised to put a new heart and his Spirit in his people so they would walk according to his commandments (Ezek 11:19–20; 36:27; 37:24).

In the Dead Sea Scrolls, consistent with their moral, vertical, and apocalyptic dualism, God set two spirits, one good and one bad, in whose ways people would walk.[1206] This antithesis between "walking" by the Spirit and fulfilling the desires of the flesh may evoke the familiar ancient image of the choice between the two "ways."

Judean and Mesopotamian Jewish sources treat the Torah as the remedy or antidote for the evil impulse.[1207] Diaspora Jews also believed that the law would enable them to overcome passions.[1208] For Paul, by contrast, God's own Spirit is the antidote, enabling one to fulfill the righteousness of the law (cf. Rom 7:5–8:4).[1209]

The struggle between the human mind or spirit and bodily passion was familiar in philosophers, but Paul deliberately reframes that formula by substituting God's Spirit, while recognizing the continuing, valid role of reason provided that it is divinely renewed and empowered.[1210]

The contrast between Spirit and flesh that dominates 5:16–17 is a contrast between flesh and God's Spirit. The Diaspora Jewish thinker Philo at least once uses such language, contrasting the sort of people who live by the divine Spirit and reason, stamped in the divine image, with those who live for the pleasure of the flesh.[1211]

[1204] E.g., Deut 26:17; 30:16; Josh 22:5; 1 Kgs 2:3; 1QS 2.2; 3.20; 4.15; CD 2.15–16; 1QpHab 12.22, 25; 4Q266 f2i.4.
[1205] E.g., Urbach, *Sages* 1:3.
[1206] 1QS 3.18; cf. 4.6, 12; cf. J. Duhaime, "Les voies des deux esprits (*1QS* iv 2–14). Une analyse structurelle," *RevQ* 19 (75, 2000): 349–67. On the two spirits, the spirit of truth and the spirit of error (cf. 1 John 4:6; T. Jud. 20:1–2), see also 4Q544 f1.10–12, f2.13–14; E. J. C. Tigchelaar, "'These are the names of the spirits of …': A Preliminary Edition of *4Q Catalogue of Spirits (4Q230)* and New Manuscript Evidence for the *Two Spirits Treatise* (*4Q257* and *1Q29a*)," *RevQ* 21 (84, 2004): 529–47.
[1207] E.g., m. Ab. 4:2; Qid. 1:10; Sipre Deut. 43.4.1; 45.1.2; Ab. R. Nat. 16A.
[1208] 4 Macc 2:23; Stowers, "Self-Mastery," 531–34.
[1209] See Keener, *Mind*, 117–20.
[1210] See in some detail Keener, *Mind*; Keener, "'Fleshly' versus Spirit Perspectives in Romans 8:5–8," pages 211–29 in *Paul: Jew, Greek and Roman* (ed. S. Porter; Leiden: Brill, 2008).
[1211] Philo *Heir* 57, from deSilva, *Readings*, 264.

A Closer Look: The "Flesh"[1212]

Some Greek thinkers disparaged or relativized the flesh or the body because of its mere materiality or sometimes its association with passion rather than reason.[1213] But Paul's specific verbal contrast between "flesh" and "Spirit" (Rom 8:4–6, 9, 13; Gal 3:3; 4:29; 5:16–17; 6:8; Phil 3:3) appears in Gen 6:3, contrasting mortals as "flesh" with God's Spirit.[1214] Such background may inform Ezek 11:19 and 36:26, where God puts a new Spirit and a new heart in his people's flesh: people cannot be what God created us to be without his Spirit.

In the Old Testament, "flesh" merely connoted mortality and weakness, but the Dead Sea Scrolls, which also contrast flesh and Spirit,[1215] sometimes emphasize also the moral aspect of this weakness, i.e., vulnerability to sin.[1216] As in the Old Testament, Paul can use "flesh" merely to designate human finiteness; but he can also apply it to susceptibility to sin. With the exceptions of 2 Cor 7:1 and Col 2:5, Paul's contrasts between flesh and the Spirit normally involve God's Spirit, as the full context shows (cf. Rom 1:3–4; 7:6; 1 Cor 5:5; Gal 3:3; 4:29; 5:17; 6:8).

Greek thought often connected passions with the body[1217] and viewed them as in opposition to reason.[1218] Educated Mediterranean Diaspora Jews also often associated the body with passions.[1219] Like most Judeans, Paul values the body, anticipating its resurrection (Rom 8:11, 13, 23; 1 Cor 6:13–14; 15:44; Phil 3:21; cf. 2 Cor 4:14; 1 Thess 4:14), though he avoids associating the resurrection with "flesh" because of its connotations of mortality and vulnerability (1 Cor 15:50; cf. Gal 6:8). Bodily passions, neutral if controlled for their legitimate purposes, were dangerous if allowed to overpower the moral discipline of the mind (Rom 1:28; 7:23).

Paul associates "desire" especially with the flesh (Gal 5:16–17; cf. 5:24; Rom 6:12; 13:14; Eph 2:3), though in Gal 5:17 the Spirit asserts desire against

---

[1212] Condensing Keener, Mind, 100–08.
[1213] Epictetus Diatr. 2.8.2; 2.23.30; 3.7.2–3; cf. Plutarch R. Col. 27, Mor. 1122D.
[1214] Cf. similarly Isa 31:3, though here the mortals are horses.
[1215] See J. Frey, "Die paulinische Antithese von 'Fleisch' und 'Geist' und die palästinisch-jüdische Weisheitstradition," ZNW 90 (1–2, 1999): 45–77.
[1216] D. Flusser, Judaism and the Origins of Christianity (Jerusalem: Magnes, 1988), 62–65. See 1QS 3.8; 4.20–21; 9.9; 11.7, 12; 1QM 4.3; 12.12.
[1217] E.g., Xenophon Apol. 16; Plato Phaedo 66CD, 83CD; Cicero Resp. 6.26.29; Seneca Dial. 2.16.1; Dio Chrysostom Or. 4.115; 13.13; Socratics Ep. 14.
[1218] Maximus of Tyre Or. 33.7; Epictetus Diatr. 1.3.3; Diogenes Laertius 10.145–20.
[1219] E.g., Philo Alleg. 2.28; Sacr. 48; Post. 96, 155; Immut. 111; Agr. 64; Plant. 43; Abr. 164; Mos. 2.24; T. Jud. 14:3; 19:4.

the flesh. Although in principle believers' desires are dead (Gal 5:24) as one is in principle dead to sin (2:20; Rom 6:2–10), in practice one must continue to address these desires when they arise (cf. Rom 6:2–13; Gal 5:13–16; 6:1; Col 3:5), perhaps by reckoning them dead and continuing to embrace one's new identity in and with Christ (Rom 6:11).[1220] So long as one lives in the flesh (Gal 2:20), one has amoral impulses that, if unrestrained, would violate God's law. In Christ, however, believers have a new identity, no longer subject to reckoning their identity by their passions; moreover, they now have divine empowerment to be able to choose rightly (Rom 8:1–9).[1221] Insofar as the believer follows the Spirit, the believer will not be dominated by fleshly impulses.

Paul associates the flesh both with religion by limited human strength (Gal 3:2–3) and with sinful behavior (5:16–21, 24). Well-informed religion might distinguish right from wrong, but only God's Spirit transforms a person, and that is God's gift in the new era ushered in by Christ. ****

The verb here translated *gratify* is *teleô*. It usually refers to completing or carrying out something, here probably with reference to *carrying out* the desire of the flesh (i.e., referring to acting on temptation, in thought or outwardly, rather than to the temptation itself).[1222] The NRSV takes the subjunctive negation here as a prohibition: *and do not gratify the desires of the flesh.* More often scholars translate as a consequence: "and thus you will not gratify …" (cf. NASB, NIV).[1223] The other examples in Paul of the aorist subjunctive following a double negation are all negative assertions rather than commands.[1224]

Because the Spirit's desire is contrary to that of the flesh (5:17), those who walk by the Spirit will not fulfill the desire of the flesh (5:16). That is, the way to overcome undisciplined fleshly passion is not to focus on the passion in hopes of mastering or suppressing it, but to live a life dominated by trusting in God, recognizing one's new master in place of one's old one.

The particular sense of Paul's ambiguous grammar in 5:17 may be exegetically insoluble, or at least continue to be heavily debated. What should be clear, however, is the verse's function in the context: it explains why 5:16 is

---

[1220]   This sentence is directly from my *Mind*, 107.
[1221]   See Keener, *Mind*, passim.
[1222]   Cf. Calvin *Commentary on Galatians* on 5:16 (Bray).
[1223]   E.g., J. Lambrecht, "The Right Things You Want to Do: A Note on Galatians 5,17d," *Bib* 79 (1998): 515–24, here 520; Hays, "Galatians," 325; Buscemi, *Lettera*, 549.
[1224]   Rom 4:8; 1 Cor 8:13; 1 Thess 4:15; 5:3.

the case: i.e., the desires of the flesh and those[1225] of the Spirit are incompatible.[1226] This is a moral dualism as exclusive as that found anywhere in antiquity.[1227]

The Galatians therefore cannot have it both ways: i.e., trying to follow both Paul and his rivals – trying to follow both the powerful gift of the Spirit through faith (3:2–5; 4:6) and the way of flesh through circumcision (3:3; 6:8, 12–13) – will not work.[1228] Their incompatible character is delineated in the description of the way of the flesh in 5:19–21 and the way of the Spirit in 5:22–23.[1229]

Turning to details, the final clause of 5:17 can be translated as in the NRSV ("for the purpose of preventing you") or as "so as *to prevent you*, with the result that it prevents you" (not implying intentionality). That is, something (the conflict or the Spirit or the flesh) may seek to *prevent you* from *doing what you want*, or it may simply *prevent you from doing what you want*. A probably larger conundrum is the content of *what you want*, which is related to the question of what prevents you from doing it.

Following are several major views on 5:17:[1230]

(1) The flesh and Spirit each frustrate the other's dominance, producing a stalemate. The problem with this view is the assumption that the flesh could overpower the Spirit, in contrast with what Paul has just stated in 5:16.

(2) The flesh defeats the believer's good wishes (cf. Paul's similar wording in Rom 7:18–19, 21), perhaps including those that come from the Spirit. The problem here is the same as in the first view.

[1225] Cf. Fee, *Galatians*, 210: the Spirit will generate the right desires. In Greek, the verb is only implicit with the Spirit; Paul might be less explicit here because of the negative connotations of the cognate noun "desires" in 5:16, 24 (cf. Rom 1:24; 6:12; 7:7–8; 13:14; 1 Thess 4:5; though not in Phil 1:23; 1 Thess 2:17); he employs the verb negatively in his other undisputed uses, including reference to Exod 20:17//Deut 5:21 in Rom 7:7; 13:9; and perhaps to Num 11:4 in 1 Cor 10:6 (cf. Fee, *Galatians*, 210n13).

[1226] Barclay, *Obeying*, 112; Matera, *Galatians*, 200, 207; Schreiner, *Galatians*, 343; cf. Dunn, *Galatians*, 298.

[1227] E.g., 1QS 4.17–18; T. Jud. 20:1–2.

[1228] Martyn, *Galatians*, 495; Oakes, *Galatians*, 174.

[1229] With Matera, *Galatians*, 199; S. Zahl, "The Drama of Agency: Affective Augustinianism and Galatians," pages 335–52 in *Galatians and Christian Theology: Justification, the Gospel, and Ethics in Paul's Letter* (ed. M. W. Elliott et al.; Grand Rapids, MI: Baker Academic, 2014), 335.

[1230] See more detailed summaries in Barclay, *Obeying*, 112–15; Lambrecht, "Right Things," 517–20; and esp. J. N. Aletti, "Paul's Exhortations in Galatians 5:16–25: From the Apostle's Techniques to His Theology," pages 318–34 in *Galatians and Christian Theology: Justification, the Gospel, and Ethics in Paul's Letter*, 323–30.

(3) The flesh defeats the believer's own good wishes (5:17ad), but Paul parenthetically explains that the Spirit combats the flesh to give the believer victory (5:17bc).

(4) The Spirit defeats the believer's bad fleshly wishes. The problem here is that this view assumes that all the believer's wishes are evil (which is not true even of the apparently unregenerate person in Rom 7:15–21).[1231]

(5) Believers themselves can will either good or evil but the Spirit overcomes the flesh and so empowers believers to choose good. Thus they are not left morally aimless as in Gal 5:13b, doing simply "whatever" they might want.[1232] The prevailing of choosing good here of course assumes that believers avail themselves of the Spirit's power by walking in the Spirit, as noted in 5:16.

Given the Spirit's exclusion of the flesh's triumph in 5:16, a majority of commentators today see the exclusion also in 5:17 (as in views 3–5). As in the final view, most also envision the self as willing but the Spirit empowering the self, when it walks in the Spirit, to will rightly. The believer may will, but cannot do whatever one wants, but ultimately only what the Spirit or the flesh want; one must choose.[1233]

As noted on 5:16, the issue here is not an anthropological dualism, but humanity on its own versus God's Spirit. When believers struggle, it is not the sort of internal division envisioned in Rom 7:7–25. That passage envisions not merely conflict but defeat, and does not mention the role of the Spirit, probably because it depicts life wholly under the law (cf. 7:5).[1234]

Again, in context what matters most is that Paul lays before them a choice between the two ways: the Spirit way of the gospel and the flesh way of circumcision. There is no middle way for them to take, or they will continually

---

[1231] Note here, e.g., Lambrecht, "Right Things," 522.

[1232] Barclay, *Obeying*, 115; Barclay, *Gift*, 428.

[1233] Moo, *Galatians*, 356 (attributing this approach to Barclay, Dunn, Engberg-Pedersen, Mussner, R. Longenecker, and himself).

[1234] The majority view; see, e.g., Ambrosiaster *Comm. Paul's Epistles* (Rom 7:14; CSEL 81:233–35; Bray, *Romans*, 190); Ps.-Constantius *Holy Letter of St. Paul to the Romans* on 7:14, 25 (ENPK 49, 52; Bray, *Romans*, 191, 199); Das, *Debate*, 204–14; Deissmann, *Paul*, 178–79; W. G. Kümmel, *Römer 7 und die Bekehrung des Paulus* (Leipzig: J. G. Hinrichs'sche Buchhandlung, 1929); Ridderbos, *Paul: Outline*, 126–28; Sanders, *Paul and Judaism*, 443; P. J. Achtemeier, "'Some Things in Them Hard to Understand': Reflections on an Approach to Paul," *Int* 38 (1984): 254–67; Achtemeier, *Romans* (IBC; Atlanta, GA: John Knox, 1985), 120–26; Fee, *Paul, Spirit, People of God*, 134–35; C. H. Talbert, *Romans* (SHBC; Macon, GA: Smyth & Helwys, 2002), 188–91; J.-N. Aletti, "Rm 7.7–25 encore une fois: enjeux et propositions," *NTS* 48 (2002): 358–76; Lamp, "Rhetoric"; discussion in Keener, *Mind*, 55–112.

be pulled in either direction. Only the Spirit, not the law, can enable them to overcome the passions of the flesh; they must therefore choose the Spirit.[1235]

Those "led" by the Spirit are not under the law (5:18; cf. 4:5–6). "Under the law" recalls Paul's argument in 3:6–4:31, most explicitly the language of 4:23; 4:4–5, 21. "Leading" is normally language appropriate for a personal actor, fitting some other depictions of God's Spirit in Paul (cf. Rom 8:16, 26; 1 Cor 12:4–6; 2 Cor 13:13; Eph 4:4–6).[1236] It also comports well with the image of the believer "walking" (Gal 5:18); since most movement transpired on foot, one could be led while walking.[1237]

In both contexts where Paul mentions the Spirit's leading (5:18; Rom 8:14), his emphasis is moral (cf. also Eph 5:18–21; 1 Thess 4:9). Some envision this overwhelming experience as a sort of ecstasy; although this depiction may depend to some extent on one's definition of ecstasy, Paul probably envisions the Spirit integrated into human experience in more "normal" ways much of the time, both through the mind (Rom 8:5–7) and through the affective dimension of the believer (1 Cor 14:14–15).[1238]

While Paul in this context is not referring to daily personal guidance, his moral emphasis here belongs to a wider range of early Christian Spirit experience. For Paul, the Spirit inspires intimacy with God (Rom 8:15, 26; Gal 4:6), including in his own life on a daily level (1 Cor 14:18). Both Gentiles and Jews could speak generally of God's leading in terms of God being with them in life and watching over them. More directly, those who prayed the psalms naturally prayed for God to "lead" them.[1239] In Ps 143 [LXX 142]:10, the Psalmist prayed for God's Spirit to lead him, a passage that some interpreters have even found echoed here.[1240]

Probably the primary Old Testament background for the wider early Christian use of the phrase, though, is God leading his people in the wilderness, an image directly informing the early Christian usage in Matt 4:1 and

---

[1235] Cf. Matera, *Galatians*, 207.

[1236] See, e.g., G. D. Fee, "Christology and Pneumatology in Romans 8:9–11 – and Elsewhere: Some Reflections on Paul as a Trinitarian," pages 312–31 in *Jesus of Nazareth: Lord and Christ. Essays on the Historical Jesus and New Testament Christology* (ed. J. B. Green and M. Turner; Grand Rapid, MI: Eerdmans, 1994); Fee, *God's Empowering Presence: The Holy Spirit in the Letters of Paul* (Peabody, MA: Hendrickson, 1994), 839–42; F. Watson, "The Triune Divine Identity: Reflections on Pauline God-language, in Disagreement with J. D. G. Dunn," *JSNT* 80 (2000): 99–124.

[1237] E.g., in Exod 3:1; Isa 11:6; 63:12–14; Acts 9:8; 22:11.

[1238] Cf. God "putting" something in one's heart (Neh 2:12, 7:5), although this is not called "led."

[1239] Ps 5:8 (LXX 9); 25:5 (LXX 24:5); 27:11 (LXX 26:11); 31:3 (LXX 30:4); 43:3 (LXX 42:3, in this instance using the same term as in Gal 5:18).

[1240] Thomas Aquinas (Lecture 3) on Rom 8:14 (Levy, Krey, and Ryan).

Luke 4:1. God's "leading" was often mentioned in connection with the exodus,[1241] and is also sometimes associated with the promised new exodus.[1242] God's Spirit was also connected with the leading in the wilderness (Neh 9:19–20), most explicitly in the prophetic interpretation of the exodus in Isa 63:11–14, where the Spirit represents God's presence among his people.[1243]

In the present moral context, one who is "led by the Spirit" inevitably produces the fruit of the Spirit, against which there is no law (Gal 5:22–23). Against his opponents, who hold that embracing the Torah's stipulations produces righteousness, Paul concludes that the Spirit active within believers produces a righteousness formed by love (5:22) that makes those formal stipulations superfluous (5:18). As with "walking" and the Spirit in Gal 5:16, Paul's primary background for connecting the law and the Spirit is Ezek 36–37, especially 36:27: God would cause his people to walk in his commands by putting his Spirit in them.[1244]

Paul's depiction of the depravity of "works of the flesh" (5:19–21) fits his larger argument here. The law's stipulations do warn against behaviors such as appear in 5:19–21; but they do not produce the fruit of righteousness found in 5:22–23. Paul associates his opponents' emphasis on circumcision and outward compliance with the *flesh* (3:3; 4:29; 6:12–13) and has so far consistently associated *works* with the law (2:16; 3:2, 5, 10; though this association is qualified in 6:4, 10). Paul now shows why the *flesh* on its own cannot fulfill God's law (cf. Rom 8:3, 7–8): left to itself, its character leads to sin.

Virtue and vice lists often appear together, as here (5:19–23).[1245] Their proximity invites an overall contrast between *the works of the flesh* and *the*

[1241]   Exod 13:18, 21; 15:13, 22; Deut 8:2; Neh 9:12; Ps 77:20; 78:14, 52; 106:9; 136:16; Isa 48:21; Jer 2:6, 17; 23:8; Hos 11:2–4; Amos 2:10; Acts 13:17; Wis 10:17–18; Bar 2:11; 1 Enoch 89:22, 24; 4 Ezra 14:4; Sib. Or. 3.255. For the Spirit's presence and the exodus, see Isa 63:10–11, 14; Hag 2:5; Mekilta Shir. 7.17–18; Ruth Rab. 2:1.

[1242]   Ps. Sol. 17:40–41; Pesiq. Rab. 30:2.

[1243]   See W. N. Wilder, *Echoes of the Exodus Narrative in the Context and Background of Galatians 5:18* (StBibLit 23; New York: Peter Lang, 2001). Although I usually agree with Das's critiques, I believe that his critique here (Das, *Stories*, 154–61), although rightly noting lack of verbal precision in the linkages and challenging some overambitious connections, dismisses too much evidence, given the interlocking of exodus motifs in Rom 8:14–17. On 177, Das does allow the possibility of a Pauline echo of Isa 63:14 LXX in Gal 5:18, so long as it is not understood to "entail a 'second exodus' or Exodus/wilderness cloud motif."

[1244]   See Fee, *Galatians*, 124; cf. 2 Cor 3:3, 6.

[1245]   E.g., Aristotle *N.E.* 2.8.1–8, 1108b–1109a; *E.E.* 2.3.4, 1220b–1221a; *V.V.* 1249a–1251b; Rhet. Alex. 36, 1442a.11–14; Cicero *Scaur.* 16.37; *Phil.* 3.6.15; 3.11.28; *Cael.* 22.55; Dio Chrysostom *Or.* 32.27–29; Arius Didymus 2.7.11e, 68.12–20; 1QS 4.3–11; occasionally in letters, Fronto *Nep. Am.* 2.8.

fruit of the Spirit (5:22–23). At the end of both lists is a final statement that includes *such things* (5:21, 23), binding the two lists together. (This summarizing term or a synonym is also appropriate to the form; it appears also in other moral lists.)[1246]

Jewish sources include vice lists, though they became especially prevalent among philosophers and rhetoricians. Some lists include only four elements, but Philo once lists more than 100.[1247] Paul employs them frequently elsewhere (Rom 1:29–31; 1 Cor 6:9–10; Gal 5:19–21; Eph 5:3–5; Col 3:5, 8). He often uses them for homiletical damnation,[1248] although sometimes qualifying this damnation in the context (1 Cor 6:11). Against Stoic ideology, not all offenses were necessarily equal (cf. 1 Cor 5:1), but listing them together reinforced the heinousness of the vices more often excused.[1249]

Vice lists[1250] were usually only loosely connected with the audience's setting.[1251] Moreover, Paul offers only samples of *the works of the flesh*, as *such things* (5:21) makes explicit. Nevertheless, Paul's arrangement is suggestive: sexual sins (5:19); *idolatry and sorcery* (5:20); then eight relational sins (5:20–21a), and then *drunkenness and carousing* (5:21). Under the law, sexual sins (Lev 20:10–16; Deut 22:21–26), idolatry (Deut 13:5–11), and sorcery (Exod 22:18) were all capital offenses, as was regular and incorrigible drunkenness (Deut 21:20). Jewish people often associated idolatry and sexual immorality with gentiles, including when listing vices,[1252] and with some good reason.

Yet in the midst of such heinous offenses Paul includes *enmities, strife, jealousy, anger, quarrels, dissensions, factions, envy* (5:20–21a). These sins were not unknown among Jewish people as well. Such relational sins – together over half the list – appear at a greater proportion than in most of his other vice lists (Rom 1:29–30; 1 Cor 5:11; 6:9–10; Col 3:5; but cf. Col 3:8), although many of his other lists do include strife, jealousy, anger, and the

---

[1246] E.g., Theon. *Progymn.* 9.21–24; Arius Didymus 2.7.5a, p. 10.14–15; 2.7.5f, 30.23, 33; 2.7.10b, 60.1–2; 2.7.10e, 62.16; 2.7.11e, 68.12.

[1247] Philo *Sacr.* 32.

[1248] With Sanders, *Law and People*, 109; Sanders, *Paul*, 558–59.

[1249] See discussion in Sanders, *Paul*, 338–41.

[1250] I borrow this material on vice lists from Keener, *Acts*, 2269–70.

[1251] See more fully Aune, *Dictionary of Rhetoric*, 89–91; Deissmann, *Light*, 316; A. D. Nock, *Early Gentile Christianity and Its Hellenistic Background* (New York: Harper & Row, 1964), 100; T. Engberg-Pedersen, "Paul, Virtues, and Vices," pages 608–33 in *Paul in the Greco-Roman World: A Handbook* (ed. J. P. Sampley; Harrisburg, PA: Trinity Press International, 2003).

[1252] Cf. Let. Aris. 152; Sib. Or. 3.594–600, 757–66; Wis 14:12–31; T. Naph. 3:3; CD 12.9; 1QpHab 4.9–14; 12.13; 1Q22 f1i.7; m. Abod. Zar. 2:1; Sipra A.M. par. 8.193.1.7.

like. Much of the positive fruit listed in 5:22–23 also addresses relationships. It seems likely that Paul knew of strife as a problem in the Galatian congregations (Gal 5:13, 15, 26), though of course it was not limited to them (e.g., 1 Cor 1:12–13; Phil 4:2–3). Social vices do appear in Jewish and Christian lists more frequently than in typical gentile ones.

Rhetorically, Paul's first five offenses end in Greek with –*ia* or –*eia*; after one plural noun (*enmities*) ending in –*ai* he includes two nouns (*strife, jealousy*) ending in –*s*; the rest are plural nouns ending in either –*oi* or –*ai*, with the exception of *envy* (also plural in Greek here, but ending in –*eis*). Greek listeners found such consistencies of sound appealing. This euphony also provides some balance for the list of the fruit of the Spirit in 5:22–23; each of the nine nouns there is feminine and they end in the following pattern: -*ê*, -*a*, -*ê*, -*ia*, -*ês*, -*ê*, -*is*, -*ês*, -*eia* (three instances of –*s*, three of –*ê*, and three of -*a*).

Turning to a few of this list's particulars: Paul's vice lists usually include and sometimes highlight sexual sin. This is probably partly because it was common among gentile men and partly because, unlike some other sins (cf. Col 3:8 in light of 3:5), it was toward the top of his (like other Jewish people's) list of particularly *severe* sins (cf. Lev 18:1–30; 20:10–21; 1 Cor 6:18–19). Such acts of exploitation of others' sexuality are far from true love (cf. Gal 5:14, 22).

Paul uses *porneia* (5:19) generally for sexual sin, including voluntary incest (1 Cor 5:1), prostitution (1 Cor 6:13, 18; 7:2), adultery (1 Thess 4:3), and probably any sort of sexual offense (2 Cor 12:21; Eph 5:3; Col 3:5).

For the nature of local *idolatry* (5:20) in Galatia, see comment on Gal 4:8. "Idolatry" obviously would not appear on gentile vice lists; it was a particularly Jewish way of framing the veneration of deity-statues (e.g., Exod 20:4; Lev 19:4) and by this period specifically characterized gentiles. Paul's term translated *sorcery* here (Gr. *pharmakeia*) is also associated with paganism, such as Pharaoh's magicians (Exod 7:11, 22; 8:3, 14). (Cf. also comment on the evil eye at Gal 3:1).[1253] Usually sorcerers conducted such behavior in private; it was punishable by the state.

[1253] As in Matt 12:24–28; so Dunn, *Galatians*, 304; see Keener, *Spirit in the Gospels and Acts*, 104–09. Since sorcery often manipulated spirits, some Reformers highlighted its demonic aspect (see Luther *Second Lectures on Galatians* on Gal 3:1; Rudolf Gwalther *Sermons on Galatians* on 3:1; Bray); given Paul's harsh condemnation, they also believed it could harm (Luther *First Lectures on Galatians* on 5:20; Johannes Brenz *Explanation of Galatians* on 5:20; John Prime *Exposition of Galatians* on 5:20; Bray).

Moralists deemed it honorable to control one's *anger*;[1254] Diaspora Jews sometimes proposed reason's self-control as the antidote for it.[1255] Philosophers and moralists also often addressed the issue of *envy* (5:21), even in entire essays.[1256] Drunken banquets (5:21) were common in Greek and Roman cities, often to the dismay of Diaspora Jews.[1257] Some philosophers opposed drunkenness,[1258] and Jewish teachers condemned it frequently.[1259]

That Paul had told the Galatians these matters before (5:21) indicates that, despite his dependence on the Spirit to teach them (5:16, 18, 22; 1 Thess 4:9), Paul also gave them ethical instructions during his time with them, as in other congregations. Some of this may reflect traditions concerning Jesus's own teachings (cf. Rom 8:14; 12:14, 17–18; 13:2, 7–10; 1 Cor 7:10–11; 9:13; 11:23–26; 1 Thess 2:16; 4:2, 15–17).[1260] Luke reports that Paul had previously exhorted his converts in this region to persevere (Acts 13:43; 14:22), and such exhortation would probably include some moral instruction.

Noting that Paul warned them before also allows him to prepare for the severe statement that follows: *those who do such things will not inherit the kingdom of God.*[1261] They cannot straddle for long both the ways of the Spirit and the flesh (5:16); the way of the flesh, whether manifest in these particularly detested outward vices or not, will inevitably lead them to spiritual death (cf. Rom 8:13).

[1254] E.g., Cicero *Phil.* 8.5.16; *Prov. cons.* 1.2; Seneca *Ep. Lucil.* 123.1–2; *Dial.* 3–5; Musonius Rufus 3, 40.21; 16, 104.18; Plutarch *Contr. A., Mor.* 452F–464D.

[1255] See, e.g., 4 Macc 1:24; 2:16–17, 20; 3:3.

[1256] E.g., Dio Chrysostom *Or.* 77–78; Plutarch *Envy, Mor.* 536E–538E (hate was worse, since it desired the other's destruction).

[1257] Philo *Cher.* 92.

[1258] E.g., Seneca *Ep. Lucil.* 58:33; 83; *Dial.* 1.3.2; 7.12.3.

[1259] E.g., Sir 31:29–30; 1QpHab 11.13–14; 4QpNah 4.4–5; Josephus *Ag. Ap.* 2.195, 204; Philo *Flacc.* 4, 136; *Mos.* 2.162; T. Jud. 16:1; Sipra Sh. par. 1.100.1.2–3.

[1260] See, e.g., J. Sauer, "Traditionsgeschichtliche Erwägungen zu den synoptischen und paulinischen Aussagen über Feindesliebe und Wiedervergeltungsverzicht," *ZNW* 76 (1985): 1–28; M. Thompson, *Clothed with Christ: The Example and Teaching of Jesus in Romans 12.1–15.13* (JSNTSup 59; Sheffield, UK: JSOT Press, 1991); J. D. G. Dunn, "Jesus Tradition and Paul," pages 155–78 in *Studying the Historical Jesus: Evaluations of the State of Current Research* (NTTS 19; ed. B. Chilton and C. A. Evans; Leiden: Brill, 1994); Kim, *New Perspective*, 259–90; N. H. Taylor, "Paul and the Historical Jesus Quest," *Neot* 37 (1, 2003): 105–26; Allison, *Constructing Jesus*, 346–48; C. L. Blomberg, "Quotations, Allusions, and Echoes of Jesus in Paul," pages 129–43 in *Studies in the Pauline Epistles: Essays in Honor of Douglas J. Moo* (ed. M. S. Harmon and J. E. Smith; Grand Rapids, MI: Zondervan, 2014).

[1261] Ancient persuaders understood the value of preparing an audience for a potentially offensive statement; see Rowe, "Style," 142; Porter, "Paul and Letters," 581.

For the language of "inheriting" the future kingdom and related blessings, see comment on Gal 3:18; this language continues the theme of Abraham's true children being heirs of the promise (3:18, 29; 4:7, 30). Paul sometimes speaks of the kingdom as present (Rom 14:17; 1 Cor 4:20; Col 1:13; 4:11; cf. 1 Cor 15:25) but somewhat more often of the kingdom as future (1 Cor 15:24; 2 Thess 1:5; cf. Rom 5:17), usually in sayings about who will not inherit God's kingdom (1 Cor 6:9–10; 15:50; Gal 5:21; Eph 5:15).[1262] Because talk about a "kingdom" was easily misrepresented (cf. Acts 17:7), Paul for the present speaks more often about the Spirit and power (cf. Rom 14:17; 1 Cor 4:20).

Paul now turns to the fruit of the Spirit in Gal 5:22–23. Virtue lists were quite common in antiquity.[1263] Against the communal strife noted in 5:15, 20–21, most of the virtues here are communal.[1264] Paul designs his list of virtues in an aesthetically pleasing way. Matching the euphony in his vice list (and as noted there), in Greek the virtues in Paul's list have the following endings: *-ê, -a, -ê, -ia, -ês, -ê, -is, -ês, -eia* (three instances of *–s*, three of *–ê*, and three of *-a*).

The fruit of the Spirit is the character of the Spirit of God's Son living in us (4:6), God's image in his children. In what appears to be a wider early Christian understanding, the fruit (related here to the image of sowing, 6:7–9) stems from divine *seed* implanted (1 Pet 1:23; 1 John 3:9).[1265] Those born from the Spirit (Gal 4:29) will share the divine nature (morally) just as any offspring bears the genetic character of its parent (cf. John 3:5–6; 2 Pet 1:4). Other Pauline texts employ "fruit" in ways similar to this passage, albeit with less elaboration (Eph 5:9; Phil 1:11; Col 1:10). This image may stem from traditions of Jesus's sayings (e.g., Matt 7:16–20//Luke 6:43–44).

Paul's choice of the title "fruit" in Gal 5:22 contrasts with his reference to "works" in 5:19: fruit proceeds naturally from an organism's character

[1262] Cf. 1 Thess 2:12; 2 Tim 4:1, 18. K. P. Donfried, *Paul, Thessalonica, and Early Christianity* (Grand Rapids, MI: Eerdmans; London: T&T Clark, 2002), 247–48, adds 1 Thess 2:12 to the "present" context, but this is debatable. For the kingdom in Paul, see Donfried, *Thessalonica*, 233–52.

[1263] E.g., Cicero *Mur.* 14.30; 29.60; Theon *Prog.* 9.15–24; Seneca *Ep. Lucil.* 95.55; Dio Chrysostom *Or.* 32.37; Philo *Sacr.* 27. In Gal 5:22–23, I draw on C. S. Keener, "A Comparison of the Fruit of the Spirit in Galatians 5:22–23 with Ancient Thought on Ethics and Emotion," pages 574–98 in *The Language and Literature of the New Testament: Essays in Honor of Stanley E. Porter's 60th Birthday* (ed. L. K. Fuller Dow, C. A. Evans, and A. W. Pitts; Leiden: Brill, 2016).

[1264] See here J. A. Adewuya, *Holiness in the Letters of Paul: The Necessary Response to the Gospel* (Eugene, OR: Cascade, 2016), 94.

[1265] Cf. Seneca *Ep. Lucil.* 73.16; Musonius Rufus 2, 38.12–14; Epictetus *Diatr.* 1.9.4–6; Philo *Alleg.* 3.40; *Post.* 171; 4 Ezra 3:20.

(cf. Matt 7:17–19//Luke 6:43–44).[1266] In a similar way, Seneca contends that "good does not spring from evil, any more than figs grow from olive-trees. Things which grow correspond to their seed."[1267] Of course, the Spirit's fruit in believers does not imply passivity; a believer should cooperate with what the Spirit births, as in Phil 2:12–13. We do not birth it ourselves, but the fruit grows as believers respond to the Spirit's moral direction (Gal 5:16–18).

Not surprisingly, *love* appears first in Paul's list (5:22). Love is the key and probably foundational virtue here,[1268] as the context demonstrates (see comments there). There is no law against love (5:23), since love fulfills the law (5:14). Saving faith is expressed through love (5:6), which includes serving one another (5:13).[1269]

Joy would not appear in most ancient virtue lists, but Paul mentions joy or rejoicing more than forty times in his letters. That the Spirit produces joy (e.g., Rom 14:17; 15:13), right from conversion (1 Thess 1:6), fits Paul's thinking elsewhere. Luke reports that *joy* accompanied the experience of the Spirit in this region, perhaps in a special way (Acts 13:52). For Paul, this joy depends not on circumstances but on the Spirit, so may coexist with other feelings at times.[1270] Like self-control, celebration in the Spirit may contrast with the sort of worldly partying noted in the preceding vice list (5:19, 21; cf. Eph 5:18–20).

The fruit of the Spirit also includes *peace*.[1271] Some interpreters understand this to mean or include inner tranquility,[1272] which could oppose the sort of conflict that some find in Gal 5:17.

Elsewhere in his letters, however, Paul most often uses *peace* to designate non-hostility or reconciliation and unity.[1273] This understanding better fits the usual semantic range of Paul's term translated *peace*, as well as the context: *peace* naturally contrasts with "biting and devouring" each other (Gal 5:15) and with eight of the works of the flesh in 5:20–21.[1274]

[1266] With, e.g., Chrysostom *Hom. Gal.* 5.22 (Edwards). Note also the contrast between positive fruit and "unfruitful works" in Eph 5:9–11.
[1267] *Ep. Lucil.* 87.25 (trans. R. M. Gummere, LCL 2:337); cf. 4 Ezra 4:31.
[1268] With, e.g., Jerome *Gal.* 3.5.22 (Edwards); de Boer, *Galatians*, 362.
[1269] Love for one another is associated with God's Spirit also in Rom 15:30; Col 1:8 (cf. 2 Cor 6:6; Phil 2:1; 2 Tim 1:7).
[1270] See discussion in Keener, *Mind*, 220–23.
[1271] Here I particularly follow Keener, "Perspectives," 222–25; Keener, *Mind*, 135–38, 140.
[1272] Jerome *Gal.* 3.5.22; Haimo of Auxerre on Gal 5:22.
[1273] E.g., with humans, Rom 3:17; 12:18; 14:19; 1 Cor 7:15; 14:33; 16:11; 2 Cor 13:11; with God, Rom 5:1.
[1274] Augustine, therefore, understood the term here relationally (*Epistle to the Galatians* 51; Edwards).

Patience here (NRSV, NASB, ESV; "forbearance" in NIV) is the Gr. *makrothumia*, which involves patient, calm endurance, whether tested through waiting or through others' provocation. This virtue often appears in Pauline literature, both for God or for Christ (Rom 2:4; 9:22; 1 Tim 1:16) and ordinary humans (Col 1:11; 2 Tim 4:2), especially in virtue lists (2 Cor 6:6; Eph 4:2; Col 3:12; 2 Tim 3:10).

The Greek term translated *kindness* is a fairly generic term for goodness, often including kindness or generosity. It applies in Pauline literature to God (Rom 2:4; 11:22; Eph 2:7; Tit 3:4) and humans (negatively, Rom 3:12), especially in virtue lists as here (2 Cor 6:6; Col 3:12).[1275] The Greek term translated *generosity* is an even more generic term for goodness, displaying especially interest in others' welfare. Paul occasionally uses it elsewhere (Rom 15:14; 2 Thess 1:11); it is the one element of Paul's list of fruit here that recurs in the list of fruit in Eph 5:9.

Faithfulness here is the same Greek term translated as *faith* elsewhere in Galatians. The Greek term can mean either, since faithfulness, as trustworthiness, is often the flip side of faith, trust. Most commentators concur with the translation *faithfulness* here. This is partly because these are expressions of the divine character within us, by the Spirit; God's character is faithful. Some also note that the characteristics in the list are primarily directed toward other human beings, although it should be pointed out that some of them, such as *love* and *joy*, are also appropriate toward God (cf. Rom 8:28; 1 Cor 2:9; 8:3; Phil 3:1; 4:4, 10). Still, given the use of this same Greek word elsewhere in Galatians, one wonders whether it might not involve growing trust in God, responding to the continuing supply of the Spirit that in turn responds to saving faith (Gal 3:2, 5).[1276]

Paul's list continues in 5:23. The Spirit also produces *gentleness* (also translatable as *meekness* or *humility*) in the Dead Sea Scrolls.[1277] In ancient sources, it applied even to leaders, understood not as weakness but as mercy or compassion.[1278] The climax (or at least conclusion) of *the fruit of the Spirit* is "self-control" (Gr. *egkrateia*), which challenges most of the vices listed in 5:19–21. The Greek term denotes restraining the passions. Of all the virtues

---

[1275] Hellenistic Judaism emphasized this virtue; it appears twenty-six times in the LXX (the cognate adjective thirty-eight times), twenty-two times in Josephus (the adjective fifty-two times), and nine times in Philo (the adjective seventy-seven times).

[1276] Fee, *Paul, Spirit, and People*, 98, sees it as further faith, but defines it as "faithful walking in God's ways."

[1277] 1QS 4.3, as often noted.

[1278] See esp. D. J. Good, *Jesus the Meek King* (Harrisburg, PA: Trinity Press International, 1999).

in the list, this was probably the one most often emphasized as a virtue in the Galatians' hellenistic environment, including among hellenistic Jews.[1279]

It is self-evident that, at least among those who shared the values of Paul's milieu (and in general ours), that *there is no law against such things* (Gal 5:23). The issue of how to support biblical ethics without subjecting gentiles to the law, already hinted at earlier (2:16–21), is a major focus in 5:13–6:10, and 5:23 reiterates this emphasis.

Ezekiel promised that God's people would walk in his commandments when he put his Spirit in them; Paul emphasizes that those who walk by the Spirit, following the Spirit's leading, do not need to be under the law (5:18), because the Spirit combats the lusts that the law was intended to constrain (5:16–24). Serving one another in love (5:13–14, following Jesus's teaching) thus fulfills the law of Christ (6:2).[1280]

Although gentiles thought of laws other than the law of Moses, Paul's language would be intelligible to them. Unwritten laws are more immutable than written ones, some said;[1281] those with the law within achieve virtue without written laws;[1282] philosophy persuades people to follow virtue and so is superior to law that must compel virtue.[1283]

Paul highlights again the incompatibility of being ruled by the flesh and ruled by Christ or the Spirit in 5:24. Those who walk by Christ's Spirit will not fulfill the desires of the flesh (5:16), because in Christ the flesh as our identity is already crucified (2:20). When Paul speaks of passions and desires crucified with Christ (Gal 5:24; cf. 2:20; 6:14; Rom 6:3–7), the evil "desire" that he has in mind is not negative emotion per se (in contrast to Stoic concern with "passion"), but the desire already specified as forbidden in the Torah, namely, desiring what belongs to someone else (cf. Rom 7:7, citing Exod 20:17). Such desire is incompatible with the law of love (Gal 5:13–15).

In 5:25–6:10, Paul's discourse becomes more hortatory. In 5:25, Paul begins such exhortations by building on an indicative. *Live by the Spirit* means having eternal life by the Spirit (6:8). This life echoes Paul's

---

[1279] See S. K. Stowers, *A Rereading of Romans: Justice, Jews, and Gentiles* (New Haven, CT: Yale University Press, 1994), 42–82 (mentioning this passage, 79–80); C. S. Keener, "Paul's Positive Madness in Acts 26:24–25," pages 311–20 in *Goldene Anfänge und Aufbrüche: Johann Jakob Wettstein und die Apostelgeschichte* (ABIG; ed. Manfred Lang and Joseph Verheyden; Lepizig: Evangelische Verlagsanstalt, 2016).

[1280] See more fully here Keener, "Fruit," 590–93.

[1281] Seneca the Elder *Controv.* 1.1.14.

[1282] Philo *Abr.* 16; cf. Lucian *Dem.* 59; Diogenes Laertius 2.68.

[1283] Crates *Ep.* 5.

discussion in Gal 3:11–12: this life is by trusting God (Hab 2:4; Gal 3:11) rather than by doing the law (Lev 18:5; Gal 3:12). Living *by the Spirit* is equivalent to Christ living in and through believers (2:20) and thus living to God (2:19). The exhortation is needed, however, precisely because it is not automatic. Even people of the Spirit must beware of stumbling, as becomes explicit in Gal 6:1.

In 5:16 Paul spoke of "walking" by the Spirit; here he extends the metaphor further with a less common term. The NRSV's *guided* (5:25) translates the verb *stoichêo*, which has to do with walking in order. Most scholars think that the verb *stoichêo* means more than "walk" in a generic way since it originally meant "stand in line" or "be aligned with," relevant for a standard of conduct (as perhaps in Gal 6:16).[1284] Paul uses the phrase in this way in Rom 4:12, for walking in the footprints of (translated more idiomatically in the NRSV as "follow the example of") Abraham. In 2 Cor 12:18 and 1 Pet 2:21, one follows in Paul's or Christ's steps; here, one follows in those of the Spirit. *Stoichêo* here may thus mean something like putting our steps in the footprints of the Spirit. Thus we not only "walk" by the Spirit, but we are "led" by the Spirit by walking in the Spirit's path.[1285]

5:26–6:10: THE WAYS OF CHRIST'S LAW

5:26 Let us not become conceited, competing against one another, envying one another.

6:1 My friends, if anyone is detected in a transgression, you who have received the Spirit should restore such a one in a spirit of gentleness. Take care that you yourselves are not tempted.

6:2 Bear one another's burdens, and in this way you will fulfill the law of Christ.

6:3 For if those who are nothing think they are something, they deceive themselves.

6:4 All must test their own work; then that work, rather than their neighbor's work, will become a cause for pride.

6:5 For all must carry their own loads.

[1284] Walking consistently with a standard could fit a different walking metaphor in 2:14, where some were not walking uprightly in line with (*orthopodeô*; NRSV: "acting consistently") the gospel.

[1285] One might compare the Spirit guiding in Jesus's way in John 16:13 (cf. Keener, *John*, 1036–37), and perhaps the Israelites following the cloud of glory. Cf. also Jesus doing whatever he saw the Father do (John 5:19).

>**6:6** Those who are taught the word must share in all good things with their teacher.
>
>**6:7** Do not be deceived; God is not mocked, for you reap whatever you sow.
>
>**6:8** If you sow to your own flesh, you will reap corruption from the flesh; but if you sow to the Spirit, you will reap eternal life from the Spirit.
>
>**6:9** So let us not grow weary in doing what is right, for we will reap at harvest-time, if we do not give up.
>
>**6:10** So then, whenever we have an opportunity, let us work for the good of all, and especially for those of the family of faith.

Commentators usually treat 5:26 as part of 5:24–26 rather than as part of 6:1–10. Nevertheless, 5:26 is, like what follows, hortatory material more specific in application than the general idea of 5:14, 16–25. Gal 5:26, like 6:1–6, is an example of the Spirit-filled life. Gal 5:26–6:10 illustrates somewhat more concretely the behavior that the preceding paragraph (5:16–25) summarizes more abstractly. What do love, patience, kindness, and so forth look like in practice? Interestingly, such behavior does not look like those adhering to, boasting in, and judging others by a rigid code (6:1–3).

Paul now gives examples of righteous, "spiritual" (6:1) behavior that are not covered by the written law, but expresses ultimate righteousness (6:2). Sowing to the flesh in 6:8 thus refers to behavior such as the works of the flesh listed in 5:19–21, whereas sowing to the Spirit refers to behavior such as the Spirit's fruit in 5:22–23 and 6:1–6. (Paul presumably designed the images of fruit and sowing to cohere; the ultimate fruit in 6:8 is eternal life, as in the Greek text of Rom 6:22.) Paul then calls for perseverance (6:9) and summarizes ethics in terms of doing what is good (6:9–10).

Pride, competition, and envy (5:26) fit the urban Mediterranean honor system,[1286] as well as present a potential danger of the Spirit-filled life: namely, looking down on others who fail (6:1).[1287] Whether one boasts because of one's supposed superiority or envies another's supposed superiority, one follows worldly criteria of evaluation. In Christ, believers must all be servants (5:13; 6:2).

[1286] J. M. G. Barclay, "Grace and the Countercultural Reckoning of Worth: Community Construction in Galatians 5–6," pages 306–17 in *Galatians and Christian Theology: Justification, the Gospel, and Ethics in Paul's Letter* (ed. M. W. Elliott et al.; Grand Rapids, MI: Baker Academic, 2014), argues that Paul's instructions in 6:1–10 are to protect the Galatians from the values of (307) "their contest-culture."

[1287] Cf. Dunn, *Galatians*, 318.

Instead of looking down on those who have failed, people of the Spirit bear their burdens by helping them back up (6:1–2). We do not become secure in our identity by comparing ourselves with others who fall; we become secure by walking with the Lord for ourselves (6:3–4). The law of Christ does not do away with the need for church discipline (4:30; 5:9; cf. 1 Cor 4:21; 5:5–7; 2 Cor 12:20–13:2), but we must restore the fallen by the Spirit whose fruit is gentleness (cf. 5:22).[1288]

The NRSV rightly interprets "you who are spiritual" as *you who have received the Spirit* (6:1). Some think Paul addresses the more spiritually mature members, but given the rest of the letter, clearly Paul addresses the Galatian believing community as a whole, as most commentators concur. They have been born from the Spirit (4:29), have received the Spirit (3:2, 5), and insofar as they walk after the Spirit's direction (5:16, 18, 25) they will bear the Spirit's fruit. After all this emphasis on them receiving the Spirit versus the law, Paul would hardly exalt one Christian group above another at the very point of urging them by the Spirit not to look down on other believers! "You who are Spirit-people," then, refers to the same group that Paul here and elsewhere addresses as "brothers and sisters."

As people of the Spirit labor to restore someone, they should do so *in a spirit of gentleness*, which in this context surely means "by the Spirit whose fruit includes gentleness" (cf. 5:22). While it is true that the Greek term translated *spirit* can mean an attitude, "gentleness" here evokes the same term in 5:22, where it is clearly the work of God's Spirit, which also dominates the context (5:16, 18, 25). The Spirit of God could be described in various ways, such as the "Spirit of wisdom" or "Spirit of understanding,"[1289] so it makes sense here to interpret *spirit of gentleness* as the divine Spirit that inspires gentleness.

When *anyone is detected in a transgression* can refer to any of the sorts of sins listed in 5:19–21, but the word *transgression* is significant. *Transgression* may imply violation of God's law; to the extent that believers walk in the Spirit they will fulfill the law's purposes (5:18, 23), but sometimes someone in the believing community will fail. This must be firmly addressed, both for the sake of the transgressor (cf. 1 Cor 5:5b) and for the sake of the church's public testimony (cf. 1 Cor 5:1b; 6:1, 6).

[1288] The combination of firmness and regret at needing to be firm in 2 Cor 12:20–13:3 may be instructive here.

[1289] E.g., Deut 34:9; Isa 11:2; Wis 1:5–7; 7:7; 1 En. 61:11; 1QS 4.3; L.A.B. 27:10.

The word translated *detected* in 6:1 may mean "overtaken by surprise." That is, it might refer to a sin that was not premeditated, one committed, perhaps, in the passion of the moment before the opportunity to reflect. It was thus inadvertent on the part of one who on the whole is devoted to the new life in Christ.[1290] One might compare the difference between inadvertent and deliberate sins in OT (Num 15:22–31). This was not then sin as premeditated rebellion against God. Continuous sins might require more firmness; more public sins would be addressed more publicly *if* prior warnings failed (cf. 1 Cor 5:4–7; 2 Cor 12:20–13:2; 1 Tim 5:20). The purpose, in any case, is ensuring the welfare of the person being corrected; believers should *restore such a one.*[1291]

One who corrects another must avoid the danger of becoming "conceited" (5:26). Temptation itself does not guarantee that sin will result, but it is foolish to pridefully welcome temptation (1 Cor 10:12; cf. Matt 6:13// Luke 11:4). Paul viewed Satan as an active tempter (1 Cor 7:5; 1 Thess 3:5) but believed that God provided ways to persevere in it (1 Cor 10:13).

Paul was not the only moralist to recognize that those who criticize others should also look to themselves (cf. Rom 2:1; 2:1; 14:1, 10, 13).[1292] "There is no surer test of the spiritual person," commented Augustine on Gal 6:1, "than his treatment of another's sin."[1293] All who recognize their own need of grace must show grace to others.[1294]

Greek moral discourse valued giving and receiving reproof appropriately. Even more consistently, Jewish tradition emphasized the importance of giving and receiving correction.[1295] As in Matt 18:15–17, the sequence of reproof among Qumran sectarians was first supposed to be private, then in front of witnesses, and only afterward, if still needed, before the assembly.[1296]

[1290] With Chrysostom *Hom. Gal.* 6.1 (Edwards); Luther *Second Lectures on Galatians* on 6:1 (Bray).

[1291] Restoration was an important practice in ancient moral philosophy; see Betz, *Galatians,* 297.

[1292] See, e.g., Matt 7:1–5; Jas 5:9; Demosthenes *Olynth.* 2.27; Publilius Syrus 52; Longinus *Sublime* 4.1; Seneca *Dial.* 4.28.6–8.

[1293] Augustine *Ep. Gal.* 56 (1B.6.1) (on Gal 6:1; Edwards).

[1294] Cf. Matt 6:12//Luke 11:4; Matt 18:21–22 amplifying or reflecting tradition coherent with Luke 17:4; Sir 28:1–5.

[1295] Prov 1:23, 25, 30; 6:23; 10:10, 17; 13:1, 18; 15:10; 17:10; 19:25; 24:25; 25:12; 27:5; 28:23; 29:15; Sir 20:2; 21:6; 32:17; Philo *Alleg.* 3.193; Jas 5:19–20; Sipra Qed. pq. 4.200.3.3; Sipre Deut. 1.3.2. The Dead Sea Scrolls emphasize reproof (e.g., CD 7.2–3; 9.8; 1QS 5.24–25; 9.17) and apparently include records of rebukes for offenses such as anger and pride (4Q477; Eshel, "Rebukes").

[1296] 1QS 6.1. Disrespect for fellow members of the community warranted punishment (e.g., 1QS 6.26–7.9; 7.15–16).

Such reproof must be humble and without anger.[1297] Public admonition, such as appears in Gal 2:11–14, was appropriate only in the most dramatic situations.[1298]

Bearing one another's burdens (6:2) may continue the slavery image dominant earlier in Galatians. Through love we serve one another (5:13); since we are no longer slaves, we should no longer treat one another as such. If practiced fully, this principle would have dramatic social implications (cf. Eph 6:9). Certainly the ideal of bearing others' burdens would not appeal to persons of status.

In this particular context, bearing *one another's burdens* especially means helping to restore those who are tempted or fallen (6:1),[1299] rather than boasting in one's superiority, since anyone may be tempted (6:1) and none of us is anything in ourselves (6:3). We will each be judged for our own work, rather than by comparison with our neighbor (6:4–5). It is never safe, then, to assume that we are righteous because we are "doing better" than some or many others.

Because Paul appeals to *the law of Christ* here, his specific application of bearing *one another's burdens* to help those who have fallen is surely only one application of what he accepts as a much wider principle. *The law of Christ* may suggest that this behavior was exemplified by Jesus (cf. Mark 10:45).[1300]

Paul may cite a familiar maxim,[1301] and certainly cites a familiar (though not widely practiced) ethic. Thus, for example, one told of a horse that refused to help while an ass carried all the burdens; finally the ass dropped over dead and the horse had to carry the full load.[1302] One would perceive a loved one not as a burden but as one who might lighten one's burden.[1303] As

---

[1297] E.g., 1QS 5.25–26.

[1298] E.g., t. Kip. 4:12.

[1299] With Matera, *Galatians*, 214 (citing Rom 15:1: bearing others' weaknesses); Hansen, *Galatians*, 186; Das, *Galatians*, 607; pace Dunn, *Galatians*, 321–22; cf. perhaps Jerome *Ep. Gal.* 3.6.2 (Edwards). Cf. Cicero *Verr.* 2.3.2.4: prosecuting others' wrongs, he carries a special *oneris*, burden, not to fail in the same areas himself.

[1300] See discussion that follows on *the law of Christ*. Witherington, *Grace*, 425–26, compares the burden-bearing with Jesus's command to take up the cross (Mark 8:34).

[1301] Betz, *Galatians*, 298–99; followed by de Boer, *Galatians*, 376; Das, *Galatians*, 607; see further J. C. Thom, "'Don't Walk on the Highways': The Pythagorean *akousmata* and Early Christian Literature," *JBL* 113 (1994): 93–112, here 107. But cf. the questions raised by R. B. Hays, "Christology and Ethics in Galatians: The Law of Christ," *CBQ* 49 (1987): 268–90, here 287–88.

[1302] Babr. 7.

[1303] Hierocles *On Marriage* (Stobaeus *Anth.* 4.67.24), of a wife, denying that she is either a *baros* or *phortion*, the roughly synonymous nouns used in 6:2, 5.

suggested earlier, some scholars find a slave image here. Although the poor lacked slaves and thus carried their own burdens, this image makes sense insofar as we think of regularly bearing *another's* burdens (5:13c).

The *law of Christ* (6:2) involves living by Christ who lives in us (2:20), thus by the Spirit of God's Son (4:6). This means a life consistent with *his* character (5:22–23), walking in the steps of the Spirit (5:16, 18, 25), which more than fulfills the moral demands of the law (5:18, 23). But what else might the phrase mean in relation to the law of Moses, to the law of love (5:14), and to Christ's earthly ministry more generally?

A Closer Look: The Law of Christ

This phrase, *the law of Christ*, is one of the most debated in Galatians, not because we lack clues but because the surfeit of clues leads to various, divergent suggestions. Following are some of the major views, although many representatives of these views overlap substantially:[1304]

1. The term translated *law*, *nomos*, also means "principle" or "norm," and could carry that meaning here as a wordplay. This view, however, probably does not allow sufficient consistency with the use of *law* in the rest of Galatians.
2. Paul might evoke the expected messianic Torah in Judaism. Unfortunately, any early evidence for this tradition in Judaism is thin.[1305]
3. The law as Scripture, its promises fulfilled by Christ's coming. It is difficult to see, however, how carrying one another's burdens fulfills biblical promises about Jesus in a direct manner.
4. The law of Christ refers to the heart of the law (loving God and neighbor) as summarized by Jesus (Lev 19:18 in Mark 12:30–31) and partially repeated by Paul in this context (Gal 5:14). I comment on this and the following proposals further in what follows.

[1304] See fuller summaries in Barclay, *Obeying*, 126–35; Matera, *Galatians*, 219–21; de Boer, *Galatians*, 378–80; C. Pigeon, "'La loi du christ' en Galates 6,2," *SR* 29 (4, 2000): 425–38; F. Adeyemi, "The New Covenant Law and the Law of Christ," *BSac* 163 (652, 2006): 438–52, here 444–52.

[1305] W. D. Davies, *Torah in the Messianic Age and/or the Age to Come* (JBLMS 7; Philadelphia, PA: SBL, 1952), 70–74 details only late and/or irrelevant evidence. See P. Schäfer, "Die Torah der messianischen Zeit," *ZNW* 65 (1–2, 1974): 27–42; Urbach, *Sages*, 1:297–302, 309.

5. Whether or not Paul envisioned a messianic Torah, he viewed Jesus's teaching, and not only the love commandment, as the law of Christ.[1306]
6. Jesus's example of love by dying for others (2:20; cf. 1:4).[1307]
7. The law of Moses as redefined, reinterpreted, or revised by Christ (5:14).[1308]
8. The Spirit as described in Gal 5:16–25.[1309]
9. A combination of some of these elements.

The law of Moses reflected God's heart as exemplified in ancient Israel's context, and its stipulations addressed an ancient Near Eastern context. Yet God's desire was always for hearts that gladly fulfilled the principles behind those laws (e.g., Deut 4:29; 5:29; 6:5–6; 10:12; 11:13, 18; 26:16; 30:2, 6, 10, 14).[1310] Some thus see *the law of Christ* here as applying the law of Moses in some way.[1311]

Most importantly, Scripture already promised the law written within the hearts of God's people (Jer 31:33), accomplished through the Spirit (Ezek 36:27). Paul elsewhere relates the new covenant experience to these promises (2 Cor 3:3, 6). This understanding obviously comports with the Spirit against whose fruit there is no law (Gal 5:16, 18, 22–23). Paul often modifies "law" with genitive nouns, such as "law of my mind" (Rom 7:23), "law of sin" (7:23, 25; 8:2), or "law of the Spirit" (8:2). The law taught what was right, but its effects on human beings depends on what forces take hold of it.[1312]

But if it is in some way the law of Moses (and I am inclined to think that it is), how is this reframed in Christ? What form does it take? Traditions about Jesus's teachings emphasize the heart of the law (e.g., Matt 5:21–48; 9:13; 23:23; Mark 10:5; Luke 11:42),[1313] especially the love commandment

---

[1306] Davies, *Paul*, 143–45, esp. 144; C. H. Dodd, *More New Testament Studies* (Manchester: University of Manchester Press; Grand Rapids, MI: Eerdmans, 1968), 134–48, esp. 147–48.
[1307] Hays, "Christology and Ethics," esp. 287.
[1308] E.g., Barclay, *Obeying*, 132–34; a growing trend, as noted in T. A. Wilson, "The Law of Christ and the Law of Moses: Reflections on a Recent Trend in Interpretation," *CurBR* 5 (1, 2006): 123–44.
[1309] M. Winger, "The Law of Christ," *NTS* 46 (4, 2000): 537–46.
[1310] Keener, *Spirit Hermeneutics*, 219–36.
[1311] The Qumran sect may offer an analogy of a movement that saw itself as not only continuing the Torah and prophets but experiencing a further stage of revelation; see A. P. Jassen, "The Presentation of the Ancient Prophets as Lawgivers at Qumran," *JBL* 127 (2008): 307–37.
[1312] With Das, *Galatians*, 610–11, rightly bringing together some of the best insights from various positions often posed as alternatives.
[1313] Keener, *Spirit Hermeneutics*, 207–18.

(Mark 12:31) that Paul has already noted in Gal 5:14. Although Paul does not specify that it comes from Jesus, this was one of Jesus's most fundamental and widely influential teachings, probably known to both Paul and the Galatians (see comment on Gal 5:14).

Many interpreters have articulated this view.[1314] This view, like views regarding the law of Moses, is compatible with some other views, such as that Jesus also exemplified this law of love by dying for sinners. Some who agree that the law of Christ includes love believe that it also includes his other ethical teachings, some of which may also be evoked here and in this context (esp. 5:14; 6:6); examples elsewhere include Rom 12:14; 14:13–14; 16:19; 1 Cor 7:10; 9:14; 11:23–25; 1 Thess 5:2, 5, 13.[1315] Some of Jesus's other ethical sayings may be echoed in this context:

- correction (Gal 6:1; Matt 18:15–17; Luke 17:3) without looking down on another (Gal 6:1; Matt 7:1//Luke 6:37)
- carrying burdens (Gal 6:2; Matt 5:41)
- providing for one's teacher (Gal 6:6; Matt 10:10; Luke 10:7; cf. 1 Tim 5:18; Did. 13.2), a practice that Paul knew to be Jesus's teaching (1 Cor 9:14)

Moreover, fairly soon after citing the love command elsewhere (Rom 13:8–10), Paul appeals to Jesus's example (Rom 15:1–2, 5), as he may do here.[1316] If *the law of Christ* includes Jesus's teaching, then it could also include his example, to which Paul clearly appeals in a similar context.[1317] Jesus appeals to his own example in his teaching about serving one another (Mark 10:43–45), by which Paul might illustrate what he means by the law of love (Gal 5:13–14). Certainly Paul's greatest example of love in Galatians is God's Son giving himself in death (2:20). Many scholars thus see *the law of Christ* as an appeal to Jesus's teaching *and* example.

Some combine almost all these views: *the law of Christ* refers to "law as interpreted by the love command in the light of the Jesus-tradition and the

---

[1314] Augustine *Ep. Gal.* 58 (1B.6.2); Theodoret *Ep. Gal.* 6.2 (Edwards); Heinrich Bullinger *Commentary on Paul's Epistles* on Gal 6:2; Erasmus Sarcerius *Annotations on Galatians* on 6:2; Calvin *Commentary on Galatians* on 6:2 (Bray).

[1315] E.g., A. M. Hunter, *The Gospel according to St. Paul* (Philadelphia, PA: Westminster, 1966), 46; Dunn, "Jesus Tradition."

[1316] Dunn, *Galatians*, 322–23. On the preservation of Jesus tradition in this period, see, e.g., C. S. Keener, *Historical Jesus of the Gospels* (Grand Rapids, MI: Eerdmans, 2009); C. S. Keener and E. T. Wright, eds., *Biographies and Jesus: What Does It Mean for the Gospels to be Biographies?* (Lexington, KY: Emeth Press, 2016).

[1317] Hays, "Christology and Ethics," 287, and Barclay, *Obeying*, 133, note that Rom 15:1–3 parallels Gal 6:2 and appeals to Christ's example.

Christ-event."[1318] The Spirit's role in fulfilling the law dominates the preceding context (see comment on 5:16, 18, 23), so it seems logical that Paul meant by *the law of Christ* also what he meant by "the law of the Spirit of life in Christ Jesus" (Rom 8:2). ****

In 6:3, Paul continues the preceding thought: avoiding being conceited (5:26), we should not look down on those we must restore, since we too may be tempted (6:1); we therefore cannot boast by comparing ourselves favorably with another (6:4). In short, the good news of Christ's grace reminds us that none of us is anything by ourselves.

In Greek, Paul earlier uses similar wording with respect to the pillars: "those who were supposed to be" (*tôn dokountôn einai ti*; 2:6); here he speaks of *those who ... think they are something* (*dokei tis einai ti*, 6:3).[1319] The key difference is that in 2:6, others attribute this value to the pillars; here, the arrogant person attributes it to himself or herself. Paul often warns against the dangers of thinking more highly of oneself than one should think (see, e.g., Rom 11:20, 25; 12:3, 16; Phil 2:3), the most analogous passage being 1 Cor 8:2: "If anyone thinks they know something, they don't yet know what's really necessary to know" (my translation).

The idea on which Paul draws was in wide circulation. Ancient philosophy also emphasized self-examination, a matter of interest also to Paul elsewhere (1 Cor 2:15; 11:28; 2 Cor 13:5). Commentators sometimes also cite a Greek proverb about self-evaluation at Gal 6:1. It seems no less apt in Gal 6:3, however, since 6:3 continues the warning of 6:1 against looking down on another who fails. One must know one's own limits so one will not boast about others' failings of which one is capable oneself. The Stoic philosopher Epictetus warned that one who does not know what one is or one's purpose or one's world "will go about deaf and blind, thinking that he is somebody, when he really is nobody."[1320]

Socrates reportedly averred that those who thought themselves great thereby showed themselves fools.[1321] Paul's Stoic contemporary Seneca opined that our finiteness and mortality remind us that we are *nothing*.[1322]

[1318]　Dunn, *Galatians*, 323; H. Schürmann, "'Das Gesetz des Christus' (Gal. vi.2): Jesu Verhalten und Wort als letztgültige sittliche Norm nach Paulus," pages 282–300 in *Neues Testament und Kirche: für Rudolf Schnackenburg zum 60. Geburtstag am 5 Januar 1974 von Freunden und Kollegen gewidmet* (ed. J. Gnilka; Freiburg: Herder, 1974), 289.
[1319]　Sanders, *Paul*, 483, notes the connection.
[1320]　Epictetus *Diatr.* 2.24.19; cf. quite similarly, Marcus Aurelius 8.52.
[1321]　Diogenes Laertius 2.38.
[1322]　Seneca *Ep. Lucil.* 101.1.

Later the Stoic Epictetus warned, "If you think you are somebody ... do not believe yourself."[1323] Or compare the Jewish Wisdom of Solomon: even someone perfect by human standards will be reckoned as nothing without the wisdom that comes from God.[1324]

Since the terms for *burdens* in 6:2 and *loads* in 6:5 are essentially synonymous, many scholars here find a tension that needs to be resolved. Writers did sometimes use paradox to force consideration of a point (see, e.g., 1 John 1:8–2:2). Often the possible paradox here is resolved by saying that the community must judge which kind of burdens need the community's help and which should be carried on one's own. Others suggest that we should be ready to carry another's load but not eager to dump our load on others.

Paul may have agreed with the latter idea (cf. Acts 20:35), but the context suggests a more specific sense here. We cannot justify ourselves by comparing ourselves with others (6:4), as Paul had done under the law (1:14; cf. 2 Cor 10:12).[1325] Paul's primary concern in the immediate context seems to be boasting (6:3) because of competition (5:26) and looking down on others who do not measure up to the righteous standard as well (6:1). Instead of self-deceptively boasting in ourselves (6:3), we should examine our work and come to a realistic self-appraisal (6:4; cf. Rom 12:3).

If we want to evaluate ourselves (6:4), we must do it by our own work rather than by comparing it with someone else's (6:1, 4), since in *this* sense – of answering for our work alone – each of us must carry our own load (6:5). Many scholars thus find here a reference to each of us answering for ourselves at the future judgment (cf. 6:7–9; Rom 14:12). On this view, the difference between 6:2 and 6:5 is one of timing: now we *bear one another's burdens* (6:2), including by helping those who are tempted (6:1). In the day of judgment, however, we will answer for ourselves, not by comparison with these others (6:5).

Relevant to 6:6, reciprocity was expected as part of the ancient Mediterranean honor code,[1326] but it is also part of Paul's theology of being members with one another in the same body (Rom 12:5; cf. 1 Cor 12:12). As

---

[1323] Epictetus *Ench.* 13, in Betz, *Galatians*, 301, who also cites *Diatr.* 4.8.39, and Epictetus's anecdote on Socrates, *Diatr.* 2.8.24–25; 4.6.24; *Ench.* 33.12; 48.2–3.
[1324] Wis 9:6.
[1325] For Gal 6:1–5 contrasting with Paul's approach under the law, cf. also D. B. Garlington, "Burden Bearing and the Recovery of Offending Christians (Galatians 6:1–5)," *TJ* 12 (2, 1991): 151–83, here 153.
[1326] See, e.g., Libanius *Anecdote* 1.20; Symmachus *Ep.* 1.104; Harrison, *Grace*, 1, 15, 50–53, 196, 348, especially here 40–43; comment on Gal 2:9.

suggested earlier, it also probably reflects Jesus's saying about those who receive workers supplying the workers' needs (Matt 10:10; Luke 10:7), a teaching familiar to Paul and other early Christians (1 Cor 9:14; 1 Tim 5:18; Did. 13.2).[1327]

Those who receive ministry in spiritual matters should contribute in material matters (Rom 15:27),[1328] because sowing to the Spirit reaps eternal dividends (Gal 6:8–9). In this way, caring for teachers (6:6) and other believers (6:10) is another way to "bear one another's burdens" (6:2), in addition to teachers and others helping those in spiritual need (6:1).

Paul did receive support on multiple occasions (2 Cor 11:8–9; Phil 4:10, 14–16), but in a more rural context the saying of Jesus (Matt 10:10; Luke 10:7) cited in 1 Cor 9:14 and 1 Tim 5:17–18 refers to provisions such as food and shelter, not to money per se. Probably a generation or two after Paul, this was also most of what congregations would give to prophets, although money could be included.[1329]

Because wandering mendicant preachers developed reputations for seeking money, Paul countered potential accusations of greed (cf. 2 Cor 2:17; 7:2; 11:7–13; 1 Thess 2:5) by refusing pay from churches that might view him as a dependent (1 Cor 9; 2 Cor 12:13–15). Some other popular preachers likewise sought to distinguish themselves from disreputable preachers.[1330] Those careful about accepting money elicited praise.[1331]

Probably most house congregations were too small to afford a full-time teacher, unless a wealthier patron sponsored one. Insofar as time spent preparing teaching (or preparing knowledge they could eventually use for teaching) might reduce time spent earning income, contributions to offset this would benefit the teacher's household.[1332]

Who were the teachers to whom Paul refers here? This role probably appears elsewhere in Paul with reference to the spiritual gift of teachers (Rom 12:7; 1 Cor 14:6), a gift that Paul ranks next to apostles and prophets (1 Cor 12:28–29; cf. Eph 4:11). Some of these teachers might include leaders

---

[1327] With J. G. Strelan, "Burden-Bearing and the Law of Christ: A Re-examination of Galatians 6:2," *JBL* 94 (1975): 266–76, here 276.

[1328] With Jerome *Ep. Gal.* 3.6.6; Schreiner, *Galatians*, 368.

[1329] See Did. 13.1–7.

[1330] See, e.g., Dio Chrysostom *Or.* 35.4, 8, 15; W. L. Liefeld, "The Wandering Preacher as a Social Figure in the Roman Empire" (PhD diss., Columbia University, 1967), 285–87; A. J. Malherbe, "'Gentle as a Nurse': The Cynic Background to I Thess ii," *NovT* 12 (2, 1970): 203–17, here 214.

[1331] E.g., Dio Chrysostom *Or.* 54.3; Plutarch *Arist.* 25.3–5; Philostratus *Vit. soph.* 2.29.621.

[1332] Oakes, *Galatians*, 182.

Paul had appointed earlier (Acts 14:23); then again, given the relative new-ness of such elders to faith in Christ, most of them probably would have proved no match for the "special" Judean teachers from Jerusalem who were Paul's rivals (cf. Acts 20:29; 1 Tim 3:6, 10). Strangely, Paul does not name any teachers here. Paul's silence about leaders in this letter outside this gener-alizing statement does not prove their unfaithfulness (cf. 1 Thess 5:12–13), but it does contrast with Paul's apparent practice in some other letters (cf. Rom 16:1–7; 1 Cor 16:10–11, 15; Phil 4:2–3). In any case, the Galatians would naturally infer from the rest of the letter that their support should go only to those who were teaching in accordance with the gospel they had received from the start, not the message that they had from Paul's adversaries.

The warning not to be deceived (6:7) was common hortatory language, appearing also elsewhere in Paul (1 Cor 15:33), including in warnings of damnation (1 Cor 6:9). In the long run, those who mock God (6:7) suffer the consequences of their folly. The Greek term used here for mockery was not always employed in a technical rhetorical sense, but that definition may communicate the image: "a sneering remark" accompanied by "a certain movement and drawing together of the nostrils."[1333]

"Sowing" was normally an image of hard work. In view of Paul's use of sowing and reaping language elsewhere (1 Cor 9:11; 2 Cor 9:6), "sowing" here includes providing material blessing to sound teachers, from whom one has profited spiritually (Gal 6:6). At the same time, 6:7–10 also cap off the section, with working for the good of all (6:10) covering the entire sec-tion.[1334] Thus the "fruit of the Spirit"[1335] in the present (5:22–23) is a foretaste of the eschatological fruit, the full harvest, in the Spirit (6:7–9).

Agrarian images were naturally pervasive; even cities were not far from the countryside. The present saying *you reap whatever you sow* was such a familiar image in various cultures, commonly worded in similar ways, that we may readily call it a truism or maxim (cf. 1 Cor 9:11; 2 Cor 9:6).[1336] In an

---

[1333] Anderson, *Glossary*, 78. Lightfoot, *Galatians*, 218, renders idiomatically, "to turn up the nose at."

[1334] For 6:7–10 revisiting themes for the whole of 5:13–6:6, see, e.g., A. H. Snyman, "Modes of Persuasion in Galatians 6:7–10," *Neot* 26 (2, 1992): 475–84.

[1335] Paul does use the image of "fruit" elsewhere in financial contexts; see Rom 15:28; 1 Cor 9:7; Phil 4:17; cf. 2 Tim 2:6. It fits naturally with the image of sowing, sometimes synon-ymous with harvest; e.g., Lev 25:3; Ps 107:37 [LXX 106:37]; Isa 37:30; figuratively, Sir 6:19; Philo *Embassy* 293; John 4:36; Jas 3:18; 1 Clem. 24.5.

[1336] Commentators cite, e.g., Job 4:8; Ps 126:5; Prov 22:8; Hos 8:7; Luke 19:21–22; T. Levi 13:6; 4 Ezra 4:28–32; Plato *Phaedrus* 260D; Demosthenes *Cor.* 159; Plautus *Mer.* 71. For further and often closer parallels, see J. L. North, "Sowing and Reaping (Galatians 6:7B): More Examples of a Classical Maxim," *JTS* 43 (2, 1992): 523–27.

old Greek verse, it is just if people treat an evildoer as he has treated others, for if one sows evil, he will reap evil.[1337] So also a pre-Christian Jewish sage: "My child, do not sow in furrows of injustice, and you will not reap these things sevenfold."[1338] Philo often speaks of sowing evil and reaping the same, and offers other, similar formulations.[1339] Some used such proverbs to insist on the certainty of divine retribution,[1340] others simply to insist that one will experience what one causes others to experience.[1341] Paul, of course, envisions direct divine involvement.

The background for the image of Gal 6:8 may include Hos 10:12 LXX: sow for yourselves righteousness, gather the fruit of life; enlighten yourselves with the light of knowledge (cf. Eph 5:9: the fruit of the light): if we want the fruit of the Spirit, we must sow to the Spirit (cf. Gal 5:22–23), which brings life, rather than to the flesh, which brings destruction (5:19–21; cf. Isa 3:10 MT; Prov 1:31).

In view of 6:6, "sowing to the flesh" presumably would include supporting teachers who promote circumcision of Christian gentiles.[1342] Sowing *to your own flesh* must also include accepting their policy of circumcision, by which Paul's opponents would boast in their flesh (6:12–13).[1343] In view of 5:13–24, however, *sow to your flesh* cannot be limited to circumcision; it includes any works such as those in 5:19–21.[1344] A person of the Spirit, secure in their future with God, is free to focus not on self but on serving others (6:9–10).

God's Spirit is naturally associated with resurrection (Rom 1:4; 8:10–11; 1 Cor 15:44; cf. Ezek 37:1–14; Rev 11:11).[1345] The harvest here is eschatological, a familiar image.[1346] "Life" language in Galatians (2:19–20; 3:11; 5:25) is usually shorthand for the longer Jewish expression "eternal life," the life of the

---

[1337] Hesiod *The Great Works* 1.
[1338] Sir 7:3.
[1339] Philo *Embassy* 293; *Conf.* 21, 152; *Immut.* 166; *Names* 268–69; *Dreams* 2.76.
[1340] For reward in Jewish sources, see, e.g., Wis 5:15; m. Ab. 2:2; Sipra A.M. par. 8.193.1.11; Sipra Behuq. pq. 2.262.1.9; cf. Mark 9:41; Matt 5:12//Luke 6:23; Matt 5:11, 46; 6:1; 10:41–42; Rev 22:12.
[1341] Cf., e.g., Prov 26:27//Eccl 10:8a; the "proverb" in Ps.-Callisthenes *Alex.* 1.19 (trans. Ken Dowden): "Whoever makes trouble for another, makes trouble for himself." In Sipre Deut. 238.3.1, getting what one deserves is drinking from one's own urine.
[1342] Davis, "Severianus," esp. 298–99, on Severianus's interpretation, and 300–01.
[1343] Marius Victorinus *Ep. Gal.* 2.6.8 (also including other Jewish customs).
[1344] With Moo, *Galatians*, 386.
[1345] Cf. T. Ab. 18:11 A, although envisioning the breath of life; m. Sotah 9:15; y. Sheq. 3:3; Sanh. 10:3, §1; Gen. Rab. 26:6; Exod. Rab. 48:4; perhaps 1 En. 71:10–11; Sib. Or. 4.46, 189–90.
[1346] 4 Ezra 4:30–32; 2 Bar. 70:2; Gen. Rab. 83:5; cf. Matt 3:12//Luke 3:17; Matt 13:39; Rev 14:15; 16:16.

resurrection (Dan 12:2), a phrase often appearing in early Jewish sources[1347] and in early Christianity, including in Paul (Rom 2:7; 5:21; 6:22–23).

Some Greek and Roman thinkers associated *corruption* (*phthora*) with all earthly, material substances; unlike the pure and eternal heavens, everything earthly was changeable, hence subject to decay and mortality. From this perspective, mortality entails the corruptibility of flesh. Thus, for Paul, the present creation experiences corruption/decay until the new creation (Rom 8:21); the current body is perishable in contrast to resurrection body (1 Cor 15:42, 50); rudimentary human rules (*stoicheia*) about touching, tasting, and the like will perish (Col 2:22). For Paul, believers now live – have eternal life through Christ and the Spirit living in them – even though they live in the flesh (Gal 2:20). But one who has only flesh is fully perishable; only those in whose lives the Spirit plays a part have the promise of imperishable, incorruptible, unending life with their creator.

In exhorting the Galatian believers not to grow weary (6:9), Paul is warning them not to turn away, back to their old life (5:4). For Paul, *doing what is right* follows not from the law but from grace (cf. Rom 7:19, 21). Paul's opposition to "works of the law" (Gal 2:16; 3:2, 5, 10, 12) – works undertaken in order to fulfill the demand of the law – does not mean opposition to good works, which are praised in the Pauline corpus here and elsewhere (e.g., Rom 2:7; 13:3; 2 Cor 9:8; Eph 2:10; Col 1:10; 2 Thess 2:17).

Writers and speakers often concluded a section with a summary statement;[1348] insofar as Gal 6:10 is a concluding summary (thus beginning with *so then*), it shows that we may express love and fruitfully follow the Spirit (5:13–25) not by mere subjective feelings but by our acts of service to others (5:26–6:6).

Whenever we have an opportunity (6:10) could also be translated "as we have time." Paul uses the noun translated *opportunity* (*kairos*) in various significant ways,[1349] among them a reminder of the eschatological character of the present time, requiring us to awaken and value what matters (Rom 13:11; 1 Cor 7:29).[1350] What suggests such a sense here is not the word itself

[1347] 2 Macc 7:9; 4 Macc 15:3; CD 3.20; 1QS 4.7; 4Q181 f1.4; 4Q418 f69ii.13; Ps. Sol. 3:12; 13:11; 1 En. 37:4; T. Ash. 5:2; Philo *Flight* 78; m. Ab. 2:7; Sipre Deut. 305.3.2–3; *CIJ* 1:422, §569; 1:474, §661; 2:443, §1536.

[1348] E.g., Rhet. Alex. 20, 1433b.30–31; 22, 1434b.5–8; 36, 1444b.21–35; examples in Cicero *Fin.* 3.9.31; *Quinct.* 28.85–29.90; Quintilian *Inst.* 4.2.50–51; Ps.-Quintilian *Decl.* 249.14; Musonius Rufus 3, 42.23–29; Lev 11:44–47; 18:24–30; 20:22–23; 1 Cor 14:40.

[1349] It can refer to a key time, as in Rom 5:6; 2 Cor 6:2; 2 Thess 2:6; to the time of the Lord's return, 1 Cor 4:5; to this present age, Rom 3:26; 8:18; 11:5.

[1350] The meaning in Eph 5:16a/Col 4:5b could refer to "opportunity" or to the character of the time, as I suggest here in Gal 6:10.

but its recurrence from 6:9. Because 6:9 refers to the "time" of the eschatological harvest, Paul may play on that "time": in light of that coming day of judgment, let us do what is good in the present time while opportunity remains.[1351] Here, as in many other passages, Paul in a sense summons Christ's followers to an eternal perspective, to make decisions in light of what counts for Christ forever (Rom 12:2; 1 Cor 2:6–10; 4:5; 2 Cor 4:16–5:9; 1 Thess 5:6–8).

To *work* for the good of all includes each one's "work" for the Lord in 6:4; *the good* may recall providing good things to teachers (6:6), but is clearly broader (*the good of all*; cf. Rom 12:14–21; 13:10; 1 Cor 14:23; Phil 4:5; Col 4:5a; 1 Thess 5:15). In succeeding centuries Christians became known for helping not only their own who were in need but also those among the pagans.[1352]

Yet just as the first priority was normally members of one's physical household (cf. 1 Tim 5:8), believers' first priority was the needs of their spiritual household. Love of neighbor (Gal 5:14) included outsiders, but love for members of the family would come first (cf. Rom 13:8a; 1 Thess 4:9; 1 Pet 1:22; John 13:34; 15:12, 17; 1 John 2:10; 3:10–11, 16–17, 23; 4:7, 11–12, 20–21; 2 John 5). To some degree, the image can evoke the household character of the church, which normally met in homes (e.g., Acts 2:46; 12:12–13; 20:20; Rom 16:5; 1 Cor 16:19; Col 4:15; Phlm 2). In particular, the image affirms that God has welcomed gentile believers.

6:11–18: CLOSING APPEAL

6:11 See what large letters I make when I am writing in my own hand!

6:12 It is those who want to make a good showing in the flesh that try to compel you to be circumcised – only that they may not be persecuted for the cross of Christ.

6:13 Even the circumcised do not themselves obey the law, but they want you to be circumcised so that they may boast about your flesh.

6:14 May I never boast of anything except the cross of our Lord Jesus Christ, by which the world has been crucified to me, and I to the world.

6:15 For neither circumcision nor uncircumcision is anything; but a new creation is everything!

[1351] With Marius Victorinus *Ep. Gal.* 2.6.10 (on Gal 6:10; Edwards); Lohse, *Colossians*, 168n31.
[1352] Chrysostom *Hom. Gal.* 6.9–10 (Edwards); Julian the Apostate *Ep.* 22, to Arsacius.

6:16 As for those who will follow this rule – peace be upon them, and mercy, and upon the Israel of God.

6:17 From now on, let no one make trouble for me; for I carry the marks of Jesus branded on my body.

6:18 May the grace of our Lord Jesus Christ be with your spirit, brothers and sisters. Amen.

Paul finally closes this agonizing letter in 6:11–18. In closing perorations, persuaders would often summarize key themes, try to rouse passionate emotions, and emphasize their own character (*êthos*) in contrast to that of their opponents.[1353] Many scholars do find Paul revisiting some themes from earlier in the letter here,[1354] including circumcision (2:3, 7; 5:2–3, 6; 6:12–13, 15), the cross (3:1; 5:11, 24; 6:12, 14), persecution (1:13, 23; 4:29; 5:11; 6:12), and Paul's relationship with the Galatians (cf. esp. 4:12–20). Letter postscripts also sometimes included summaries, though not all agree that 6:11–18 does function as such a summary.[1355]

More clearly, Paul does passionately drive home key points that contrast his character with that of with his rivals. They want to look good in the flesh and boast in the Galatians' flesh (Gal 6:12–13), whereas Paul boasts only in Jesus's cross (6:14). They are trying to avoid being persecuted for the cross (Gal 6:12), whereas Paul shares Christ's wounds likely inflicted on him when he was persecuted (6:17; cf. 2 Cor 4:9–11). They want to impose circumcision and a law they themselves do not keep (Gal 6:12–13), whereas Paul proclaims the new creation (6:15).[1356]

When Paul refers to an epistolary sort of letter, he normally uses an *epistolê* (Rom 16:22; 1 Cor 5:9; 2 Cor 3:2; 1 Th 5:27); here, instead, he uses *gramma* in the plural, which makes more sense when applied to alphabetical letters (e.g., Rom 7:6; 2 Cor 3:6). Therefore nearly all scholars today construe Paul's *letters* here as alphabetic letters. They argue therefore not that Paul wrote by his own hand the entire letter, but rather that he begins in his own handwriting here.[1357]

[1353] Betz, *Galatians*, 313; deSilva, *Readings*, 295.
[1354] Engberg-Pedersen, "Vices," 616; G. D. Fee, "Freedom and the Life of Obedience (Galatians 5:1–6:18)," *RevExp* 91 (2, 1994): 201–17; also some Reformers, including Luther *Second Lectures on Galatians* on 6:18 (Bray).
[1355] Richards, *Letter Writing*, 172. Witherington, *Grace*, 440, offers P. Oxy. 264 as an example, but rightly notes that summaries in letter closings were rare.
[1356] See esp. J. A. D. Weima, "Gal. 6:11–18: A Hermeneutical Key to the Galatian Letter," *CTJ* 28 (1, 1993): 90–107.
[1357] The aorist here is presumably epistolary as in 1 Cor 5:11; 9:15; Phlm 19, 21; and possibly Rom 15:15.

Paul often used an amanuensis; this is explicit in Rom 16:22, but also seems clear whenever Paul signs a letter in a way that is identifiably different from the rest of the letter (1 Cor 16:21; Gal 6:11; Col 4:18; 2 Th 3:17; Phlm 19). This was common practice, including among the literate elite.[1358] Many ancient business documents include closing greetings in a handwriting style distinct from that of the rest of the letter.[1359]

That Paul writes in his own hand communicates several possible points. First, it reminds the Galatians that Paul was among the minority of people literate enough to do so (cf. Gal 1:14). Second, writing this section in his own hand might help authenticate the letter, although Paul's distinctive voice is clear enough in Galatians to leave little doubt of its authenticity.[1360] Paul settled for a signature in his other letters, but a closing summary in an author's handwriting offered a higher level of authentication.[1361]

Third, Paul may augment *pathos* by showing that the matter is so important to him as to warrant his extra effort on their behalf. Fourth, even aside from *pathos*, he is revealing the importance of this matter. Normally he signs only his name or a little more; here he apparently starts writing in his own hand from 6:11 forward. Writing with one's own hand revealed personal commitment and often affection,[1362] and/or the importance of the person being addressed.[1363] This observation remains relevant on *any* of the proposed explanations for Paul's large letters, discussed later.

Scholars have proposed various reasons for Paul's mention of his writing in *large letters*. On any of these views, the action shows a special effort and interest on Paul's part, so the most important element of meaning is not affected by which view is deemed likeliest. Also on any of these views, most people in the congregations would not be able to read the letter itself, both due to literacy levels and the unavailability of extra copies of the letter;[1364] someone would read the copy of the letter to the congregation. So Paul needs to remark about the large letters in his comments themselves.

[1358] E.g., Aune, *Dictionary of Rhetoric*, 270.
[1359] Deissmann, *Light*, 154–55; Aune, *Dictionary of Rhetoric*, 70, 270.
[1360] For charges or suspicions of forged letters, see Livy 40.55.1; Quintilian *Inst.* 5.5.1; Josephus *Life* 356; Arrian *Alex.* 6.12.3; Chariton *Chaer.* 4.6.1–2.
[1361] Richards, *Letter Writing*, 171.
[1362] Cicero *Att.* 5.19; Plutarch *M. Cato* 20.5 (to one's son); Fronto *Ad M. Caes.* 3.3, end; Chariton *Chaer.* 8.4.6.
[1363] Seneca *Ep Lucil.* 83.15. In Plutarch *Cic.* 37.3, Cicero was *offended* that Caesar had not authored the letter to him himself.
[1364] Richards, *Letter Writing*, 169, estimates that, given the cost of papyrus and copying, the cost of a letter the length of Galatians in early twenty-first-century U.S. currency would be about $722, more than 500 pounds.

(1) One view is that Paul's eyesight was poor. Someone suffering from eye inflammation might indeed dictate a letter and keep it brief.[1365] Nevertheless, the actual evidence cited for this position (Gal 4:15) is not compelling.[1366]

(2) A second possibility is that Paul's hands were damaged. Modern parallels show how manual labor coarsens the hands; skeletal remains demonstrate how peasants' bodies were deformed by their hard labor.[1367] Working in unheated shops in winter could have affected Paul's *ability* to write in smaller letters, as some scholars have suggested. Yet Paul, unlike sources mentioning sickness affecting ability to write, nowhere attributes such inability to any sickness (cf. Gal 4:13–14). Also, Paul cites the letters' size, not their irregularity.

(3) One might write in large letters to invite a child to trace inside the letters.[1368] Paul could indeed treat the Galatians like children (Gal 4:19).

(4) Others suggest that Paul wrote large for emphasis. This is the most common view and one of the likeliest views. But surely this is not the only place where Paul wants to emphasize his thought, yet it is the only place where Paul mentions the large letters, an observation that may weaken this hypothesis somewhat.

(5) Others suggest that Paul was not accustomed to writing and thus wrote with large block letters rather than the smaller, thus faster, style of professional scribes.[1369] Thus Jerome suggested that Paul was acknowledging his poor handwriting.[1370] Even literate people of status usually did not have much practice writing because they could depend on scribes. Scribes actually wrote in variously sized letters, but Paul's were larger than his scribe's.[1371]

(6) Perhaps he simply draws attention to the script different from that of the scribe's so the Galatians will recognize his special effort here. A person's distinctive handwriting was often discernible to others.[1372]

[1365] As in Cicero *Att.* 8.13.
[1366] See Lightfoot, *Galatians*, 191–192n1.
[1367] Toner, *Culture*, 134.
[1368] Plato *Prt.* 326D; Seneca *Ep. Lucil.* 94.51; Plutarch *M. Cato* 20.5; Maximus of Tyre *Or.* 2.2.
[1369] G. A. Deissmann, *Bible Studies: Contributions Chiefly from Papyri and Inscriptions to the History of the Language, the Literature, and the Religion of Hellenistic Judaism and Primitive Christianity* (trans. A. Grieve; Edinburgh: T&T Clark, 1923), 348–49; Sanders, *Paul*, 4–5.
[1370] Jerome *Ep. Gal.* 3.6.11, in Soards and Pursiful, *Galatians*, 322.
[1371] Richards, *Letter Writing*, 166.
[1372] E.g., Cicero *Fam.* 10.21.3; Ovid *Tristia* 3.3.1–2; Pliny *Ep.* 2.16.2.

Still, Paul could have noted that the script was unusual or even large without the more emphatic "so large" (*pêlikos*). While view 6 (noting the distinctiveness of Paul's script) is likely correct, it seems best combined with either view 4 or view 5. Views 4–6 presuppose information available to the Galatians, namely Paul's handwriting style and ancient scribal practices.

Paul places his opponents' motives at the center of a chiastic charge in 6:12–13:[1373]

A They *want to make a good showing in the flesh*
B They *try to compel you to be circumcised*
C They do not want to *be persecuted for the cross of Christ*
C' They *do not themselves obey the law*
B' *They want you to be circumcised*
A' *So that they may boast about your flesh*

It was customary when charging someone to offer a credible motive,[1374] as well as to depict opponents in a bad light.[1375]

These interlopers *want to make a good showing in the flesh*, Paul warns (6:12). They are sowing with respect to the flesh, to their own damnation (6:7–8), but their interest is not simply their own flesh: their showing off in the flesh is clearly related here to boasting in the Galatians' flesh (6:13).

His opponents were not trying to *compel* circumcision physically (which would certainly have incurred the wrath of local gentile authorities), but rather by persuasion that Paul deems deceptive. Like Peter, who was effectively ready to "compel" gentiles to become Jews because he feared external pressure (2:14), Paul's opponents try to do the same because of their external pressures. Although "compelling" circumcision might appear among heroic exploits in an earlier period,[1376] educated Diaspora Jews would disapprove of forcing it on gentiles in the present.[1377] This depiction of Paul's rivals thus would characterize them negatively for almost any hearer in the Diaspora.

[1373] With de Boer, *Galatians*, 396.
[1374] Cicero *Rosc. Amer.* 22.61–62, noting standard procedure.
[1375] Cicero *Rosc. Amer.* 2.6. For the importance of *êthos*, or character, in making a case, see, e.g., Rhet. Her. 4.50.63.
[1376] Josephus *Ant.* 13.318.
[1377] Josephus *Life* 113. Maccabean literature applies this verb translated "compel" especially to gentiles forcing Jews to practice pagan customs (1 Macc 2:25; 2 Macc 6:1, 7, 18; 7:1; 4 Macc 4:26; 5:2; 8:2, 9; 18:5).

Paul emphasizes that he suffers persecution for proclaiming the cross (Gal 5:11); his rivals, by contrast, avoid persecution precisely by not proclaiming (the absolute sufficiency of) the cross.[1378] This is not the only time that Paul sets rivals in their place by citing his own credentials of persecution, credentials that his adversaries lack (2 Cor 11:23–33); suffering was essential to Paul's understanding of apostleship (1 Cor 4:9–13; cf. Matt 10:16–39), and those who avoided it at the expense of the truth or who exalted themselves were false apostles (2 Cor 11:13).

The specific source of the persecution that Paul's adversaries evaded is more open to debate. Here the source is not Paul's opponents themselves (as perhaps in Gal 4:29), since they are the ones fearing persecution. Some suggest that the persecution involves civic authorities or the local imperial cult (a major cult especially in Pisidian Antioch by this period). Gentiles could be exempt if they became Jews, i.e., if by circumcision they joined the people already tolerated as monotheists.[1379]

While such standardization of status would have been helpful, in most places in this period civic authorities would not have been enforcing the imperial cult.[1380] Moreover, it is not the Galatians but Paul's rivals, who are already circumcised, who are seeking to evade persecution here. All persecution elsewhere in the letter is Jewish in origin.

Others thus suggest that the persecution came from local Jews, who would disapprove of the Jewish Christian leaders (from inside or outside Galatia) if they did not circumcise gentile members of their community. This position is plausible and could well be correct. Luke reports that some local Jews in Galatia had strenuously opposed Paul and Barnabas (Acts 13:45, 50; 14:2, 4–5, 19), sometimes especially because of how they welcomed gentile sympathizers (13:45–48).

Others plausibly suggest that Paul's rivals were Judeans experiencing pressure from nationalistic sentiment in Jerusalem, which also affected the Jerusalem church. One form of this proposal speaks of pressure from Zealots,[1381] but the pressures could be from Judean nationalism more generally.[1382] The emphasis on Jerusalem in Gal 4:25–26 makes better sense if

---

[1378]   de Boer, *Galatians*, 398; Eastman, "Galatians," 831.

[1379]   B. W. Winter, *Seek the Welfare of the City: Christians as Benefactors and Citizens* (Grand Rapids, MI: Eerdmans; Carlisle, UK: Paternoster, 1994), 123–44; Hardin, *Imperial Cult*, 85–115; cf. already Jerome *Ep. Gal.* 3.6.12 (Edwards).

[1380]   Das, *Stories*, 179–215, esp. 197–200, 210–15.

[1381]   R. Jewett, "The Agitators and the Galatian Congregation," *NTS* 17 (1971): 198–212, esp. here 206.

[1382]   Cf., e.g., Josephus *Ant.* 20.200.

Paul's rivals came from there. These verses are not sufficiently explicit to rule out local pressures, but they likely weight the case toward including external ones. Jerusalem attitudes and local attitudes are not in any case mutually exclusive sources of pressure; although travel was slow, Jewish travelers to and from the mother land would bring news,[1383] and reports from either location could affect attitudes in the other.

Although the cross became a badge of honor for some Christians, through identifying with Christ (e.g., Gal 6:14), it remained a shocking scandal for outsiders (e.g., 1 Cor 1:17–18; Gal 5:11; 6:12).[1384] The cross represented shameful execution by slow torture, a penalty typically reserved for low-class criminals and slaves. Crucifixion could be employed by others as an example of the most awful sort of death.[1385]

Crucifixion was treated as appropriate for, among other offenses, cases of treason against the majesty of the emperor or for revolutionaries, i.e., for political cases.[1386] For Rome, preaching the cross was often the equivalent of announcing, "We are followers of a king you executed for treason, so we are treasonous too."

How did Paul know that his rivals did *not obey the law* (6:13)? This charge was familiar intra-Jewish polemic,[1387] but Paul charged that all sinned (Rom 3:20–23). (Paul's past experience also gives him high standards for law observance that few other people, including his rivals, met; Gal 1:13–14; Phil 3:5–6; cf. 2 Cor 11:22.) For Paul the law testified to the promise of Christ and the way of faith (see 4:21; Rom 3:21, 31); his rivals, then, fell woefully short. Paul's Christian understanding, which did not require him to excuse his own shortcomings, made clear that even desiring what was rightly another's was sinful (Exod 20:17; Deut 5:21), a sin that Paul likely assumed was widespread (Rom 7:7).[1388] Most importantly in the context, Paul's opponents did

---

[1383] For travelers carrying news, see, e.g., Euripides *El.* 361–62; Demosthenes *Ep.* 5.1; Seneca *Ep. Lucil.* 47.1; P. Oxy. 32.

[1384] See further discussion in, e.g., Cook, *Crucifixion*; comment on Gal 3:1.

[1385] E.g., Diodorus Siculus 34/35.12.1; Cicero *Verr.* 2.5.66.169; Seneca *Ep. Lucil.* 101.10–12.

[1386] This is its usual function in Josephus, hence probably in Judea (A. E. Harvey, *Jesus and the Constraints of History* [Philadelphia, PA: Westminster, 1982], 13; e.g., Josephus *War* 2.241, 253).

[1387] Jews differed among themselves on what it meant to be Torah observant; see K. H. Zetterholm, "The Question of Assumptions: Torah Observance in the First Century," pages 79–103 in *Paul within Judaism: Restoring the First-Century Context to the Apostle* (ed. M. D. Nanos and M. Zetterholm; Minneapolis, MN: Fortress, 2015), 80–81.

[1388] For this select commandment, but with a different expectation of those who had the law, see 4 Macc 2:5–6.

not keep the law because they were interested in showing off in the flesh rather than in suffering with the Messiah (Gal 6:12).

The verb translated *boast* is frequent in Paul, to whom belong thirty-five of the thirty-seven New Testament occurrences (as well as ten of the eleven instances of each of the two cognate nouns). The only two occurrences of the noun in Galatians appear in the present contrast in 6:13–14, but Paul elsewhere develops further the idea of one who boasts in the law while breaking it (Rom 2:17).

Paul's depiction of the rivals' desire to show off in the flesh (Gal 6:12) now takes a grotesque turn: they want to boast in *your* flesh, i.e., the flesh of your sliced foreskins.[1389] They wanted to boast in "their neighbor's work" rather than their own (Gal 6:4).

In contrast to his rivals' plan to boast in the Galatians' severed flesh (6:13), Paul boasts only in the flesh of Christ wounded in their stead (6:14). Whereas his rivals avoid being persecuted for the cross (6:12), it is the cross in which Paul boasts.

"World" (*kosmos*) in 6:14 refers to sinful humanity and its values (Rom 3:6, 19; 5:12–13; 1 Cor 2:12; 3:19; 5:10; 11:32; 2 Cor 5:19; 7:10). Paul's use of the perfect tense most likely suggests a finished act with continuing effects:[1390] with Christ, Paul has already died to the world (2:20). Identification with Jesus's crucifixion also meant the embrace of shame, of public degradation as a criminal; in embracing Christ, Paul counted the cost and sacrificed concern for his own honor.

The crucifixion of *the world* (Gr. *kosmos*) as far as Paul is concerned (6:14) entails not only death to the values of the present evil age (cf. 1:4) but also new life as part of the new creation (6:15).[1391] This new creation life involves a revolutionary new perspective on everything, viewing this age from the standpoint of Christ's eschatological act in history and its consequences for eternity.[1392] Although the old age continues, Paul belongs to the world to come, which has already invaded history in Jesus Christ through the power of the Spirit. On the new world's valuation, circumcision or lack thereof no longer are of significance in light of what

---

[1389] On the close connection between circumcision and flesh, Barclay, *Obeying*, 180, cites Gen 17:9–14, 23–25; Ezek 44:7, 9; Lev 12:3; LXX Gen 34:24; Jer 9:25; Sir 44:20; Jdt 14:10; Jub. 15:13–33; 4 Ezra 1:31.

[1390] Dunn, *Galatians*, 341.

[1391] With, e.g., Martyn, *Galatians*, 564–65 (noting the grammatical connection between 6:14 and 6:15); de Boer, *Galatians*, 401; Wright, *Faithfulness*, 478.

[1392] Cf. Gal 5:5; Rom 12:2; Keener, *Mind*, 153–55, 176–79.

God has done in Christ (6:15); fleshly concerns belong to the period of minority (3:23–4:11).

Paul's claim that neither circumcision *nor* uncircumcision matters (6:15a), which recurs in 5:6 and 1 Cor 7:19, presumably reflects his normal view when not writing polemically.[1393] Just as one should not think one is anything when one is nothing (6:3), so physical markers such as circumcision (signifying high status for Paul's rivals) and uncircumcision (a far better status from a gentile standpoint) are nothing in light of what really counts, the new creation. See fuller discussion on this phrase at Gal 5:6. The physical marks that matter now are no longer circumcision, but (ideally) marks of persecution that reveal participation in the Messiah's sufferings (6:17).[1394]

Early Judaism often spoke of "new creation," but not always in the same way. The earliest and best-attested use of the language applies to the coming new world, the new heavens and earth (Isa 65:17; 66:22).[1395] Jewish thinkers may have sometimes connected such language with God "creating" a new heart and spirit for his people.[1396]

Some later rabbis opined that one who converted someone was considered as one had created them[1397] (cf. Gal 4:19). Since conversion to Judaism is at issue in Galatians, this conversion background, if early enough,[1398] may be relevant here. A convert could be referred to as a new creature.[1399] Some thus construe *new creation* here as a matter of individual transformation.[1400]

Conversely, the biblical background, which was certainly available and widely evoked in Paul's day,[1401] includes individual transformation but as

---

[1393] With Sanders, *Paul*, 496, 551–52.

[1394] With Wright, *Faithfulness*, 1145.

[1395] Jub. 1:29; 4:26; 1 En. 72:1; 91:16–17.

[1396] Jub. 1:20–21; 4Q393 fiii 2.5–6, drawing on Ps 51:10 and Ezek 36:26. One who turned from sins would live (Ezek 18:30) and to get "a new heart and a new spirit" (18:31).

[1397] Said of Abraham and Sarah in Sipre Deut. 32.2.1; Ab. R. Nat. 12A; 26, §54B; Song Rab. 1:2, §3; see other citations in Davies, *Paul*, 119.

[1398] See fuller discussion on this point in Keener, *John*, 542–44.

[1399] J. Jeremias, *Jerusalem in the Time of Jesus* (Philadelphia, PA: Fortress; London: SCM, 1969), 324, citing b. Yeb. 22a; 48b, bar. (a proselyte as a newborn child, but unlearned in religious duties); 62a (again); 97b; Ger. 2:6; others cite Gen. Rab. 39:14; see also b. Bek. 47a. Cf. also B. D. Chilton, "Galatians 6:15: A Call to Freedom before God," *ExpT* 89 (10, 1978): 311–13; R. H. Charles, *The Book of Jubilees, or The Little Genesis* (London: Adam & Charles Black, 1902), lxxxiv, on Jub. 5:12.

[1400] See esp. helpfully M. V. Hubbard, *New Creation in Paul's Letters and Thought* (SNTSMS 119; Cambridge: Cambridge University Press, 2002), 11–25, for new creation in the Old Testament; 26–53 in Jubilees.

[1401] See, e.g., M. B. Stephens, *Annihilation or Renewal? The Meaning and Function of New Creation in the Book of Revelation* (WUNT 307; Tübingen: Mohr Siebeck, 2011), 46–116.

part of a wider transformation of the world. In light of Paul's death to the world in 6:14, a majority of interpreters envision the entire era of the new creation here.[1402]

In the present time, the new creation is expressed especially in believers, but it reflects the entire coming age. The promised Messiah has already come, so believers experience this new creation already although its consummation remains not-yet. Here, toward the end of his letter, Paul apparently recalls the truth he noted toward the beginning:[1403] Christ has freed believers from this present evil age (Gal 1:4). We therefore owe no allegiance to the elementary matters of this world (Gal 4:3, 9); we have been crucified to this world (6:14) and share in the resurrection life of the new one, the new creation.

Those who follow this rule (6:16) would be those who participate in the new creation that transcends circumcision or uncircumcision (6:15), an observation that obviously must affect how we understand *the Israel of God*. The word rendered *follow* in the NRSV here is the verb *stoicheô*, rendered *guided* in 5:25.[1404] In 5:25, it was an image of "walking" (corresponding to 5:16) in the path laid out by the Spirit. The rule believers *follow* is not the conventional understanding of the Torah, contrary to what Paul's opponents presumably taught.[1405] Rather, it is the law of Christ (6:2), the way of love (5:6, 13–14), the new creation (6:15) effected in believers' lives through the Spirit (5:16–23), the foretaste of the new creation (5:5). As walking by the Spirit (5:16, 25) is the truest fulfillment of the law (5:18, 23; Ezek 36:27), those who walk by *this* rule are God's Israel (Gal 6:16).

The term rendered *rule* is *kanôn*, which Paul elsewhere applies to proper spheres or geographic limits on ministry (2 Cor 10:13, 15, 16). Conjoined with *stoicheô* it probably connotes following the exclusive trail blazed for us by the Spirit (cf. Rom 4:12, walking in Abraham's footsteps regarding faith).

[1402] See esp. T. R. Jackson, *New Creation in Paul's Letters: A Study of the Historical and Social Setting of a Pauline Concept* (WUNT 2.272; Tübingen: Mohr Siebeck, 2010); cf. also Theodoret *Ep. Gal.* 6.15 (Edwards).
[1403] For some works repeating toward the end themes introduced toward the beginning, see, e.g., John 1:1, 18; 20:28–31; Rom 1:5; 16:25; examples in Harvey, *Listening*, 66–67, 104–6, 111–12, with Homer *Il.* Bks. 1, 24.
[1404] For *stoicheô* here referring back to 5:25, see also Martyn, *Galatians*, 566. Cf. also 2:14, in Barclay, *Gift*, 367n44.
[1405] Josephus speaks of Moses's rule or standard in the law (*Ag. Ap.* 2.174); for Philo, Scripture contains the "rules of truth" (*Conf.* 2).

Works sometimes closed with a benediction.[1406] The letter body falls between the curse for those who distort the gospel (1:8–9) and the blessing for those who adhere to it (6:16). Like the blessing of grace and peace in Gal 1:3 or of grace in 6:18, the blessing in 6:16 is a "wish-prayer" or blessing, invoking God directly in meaning though grammatically only indirectly.

Paul's rivals probably would have found the benediction's language familiar. The prototypical blessing for Israel was, "May the Lord bless you and protect you … and give you peace" (Num 6:24–26), or, in the common Greek rendering, "and give you mercy" (Num 6:26 LXX). It is thus not surprising that blessings often included, "Peace be on [so-and-so]," including in tomb inscriptions.[1407] Often they included, "Peace be on Israel" (see, e.g., closing benedictions in Ps 29:11; 125:5; 128:6).[1408] An inscription dedicated to a synagogue ruler in Antioch reads, "May peace and mercy be on all who …"[1409]

Jewish prayers for *mercy* were also common, including on "all those who love you";[1410] on Israel (e.g., "May the mercy of the Lord be upon Israel forevermore");[1411] or others.[1412] Scholars often compare the nineteenth benediction of the Shemoneh Esreh, which prayed for peace "on us" and on "all Israel"; Paul prays for *those who will follow this rule* and *the Israel of God*.

On whom does Paul intend this blessing? Grammatically, one can read this as either one blessing, *peace be upon them, and mercy,* even *upon the Israel of God,* or perhaps more simply two blessings,[1413] *peace* on *those who follow this rule* and *mercy* also *upon the Israel of God.* (The Greek word *kai* can mean "and," "even," or "also.") The identity of those *who will follow this rule* seems obvious enough,[1414] but who is *the Israel of God*?

[1406] E.g., Ps 41:13 (closing Bk 1 of Psalms); 72:18–19 (closing Bk 2); 89:52 (closing Bk 3); Ps 106:48 (closing Bk 4); 3 Macc 7:23; 4 Macc 18:24.

[1407] See, e.g., Carmon, *Inscriptions*, 79, §174; 176–77, §174; CIJ 1:273, §349.

[1408] CIJ 1:231, §293; 1:307, §397; 1:434, §599; 1:466, §650; 1:474, §661; 1:481, §670; 2:103, §866; 2:115, §884; 2:159, §973; 2:222, §1175.

[1409] CIJ 2:56, §804.

[1410] E.g., Ps. Sol. 4:25 (trans. R. B. Wright, OTP 2:656).

[1411] Ps. Sol. 11:9 (trans. Wright, 2:662).

[1412] E.g., Ps 25:6; 40:11; 51:1; 69:16; 119:77, 156; 123:3; 4 Ezra 8:45; 2 Tim 1:16.

[1413] Favoring the latter, see, e.g., de Boer, *Galatians*, 406; Das, *Galatians*, 648, noting that, "An uncontested instance of an epexegetical καί ('namely') is not available elsewhere in the undisputed Pauline corpus." The key word here, however, is "uncontested," since possible (though debatable) cases arise quite quickly on reading Paul's letters (e.g., Rom 1:5; 10:1, 21; 11:33; 15:19; 16:25; in Galatians, e.g., 1:4, 7, 13).

[1414] Unless even the future points toward the conversion of Israel; Paul has not hinted at that in Galatians, but we do not know what he may have told them before.

In favor of some reference to Jews in particular is the simpler assumption syntactically of two blessings and the consequently possibly separate appeal for "mercy."[1415] Favoring some sort of reference to Jesus's followers is the progression of argument through Galatians.

Some categorize the sorts of options as something like the following.[1416]

(1) Some argue that it means ethnic Israel.

(2) Others, Jewish believers in Jesus who observe the law. If this view is correct, one must exclude those who impose circumcision on gentiles, since Paul has already cursed them in 1:8–9.

(3) Still others, the Jewish people converted at the time of the end (as likely in Rom 11:26). Certainly the context of 6:16 is eschatologically pregnant; the new creation in 6:15 comes from a context (Isa 65:17; 66:22) that also speaks of the new Jerusalem (Isa 65:18; see comment on Gal 4:26). But Paul has not prepared for this sort of climax earlier in Galatians.

(4) Jewish believers in Jesus who do not impose circumcision on gentiles (cf. #2), though they are also included in (but do not represent all those in) the first blessing.

(5) The church (including Jews and gentiles), coinciding with those "who will follow this rule." This is by far the majority view and has been supported even by some Jewish scholars of early Christian origins.[1417] Because scholars contend that the Qumran sectarians and probably the Samaritans viewed themselves as the true Israel or the righteous remnant, analogies from the period exist for this approach.

(6) The church and ethnic Israel (perhaps coinciding eschatologically with those "who will follow this rule").

Paul elsewhere speaks of the "church of God" (1 Cor 1:2; 10:32; 11:22; 15:9; 2 Cor 1:1; Gal 1:13) or "churches of God" (1 Cor 11:16; 1 Thess 2:14; 2 Thess 1:4). *Church* translates the Greek term *ekklêsia*, which in the Greek version of the

---

[1415] A motif heavy in Rom 9–11; see M. Bachmann, *Anti-Judaism in Galatians? Exegetical Studies on a Polemical Letter and on Paul's Theology* (trans. R. L. Brawley; Grand Rapids, MI: Eerdmans, 2008), 101–23; S. Eastman, "Israel and the Mercy of God: A Re-reading of Galatians 6.16 and Romans 9–11," *NTS* 56 (2010): 367–95, esp. 368, 373, 385–90.

[1416] For surveys, see Matera, *Galatians*, 232; de Boer, *Galatians*, 405; Das, *Galatians*, 646–52.

[1417] See S. Sandmel, *The Genius of Paul* (New York: Farrar, Straus & Cudahy, 1958), 21; G. Vermes, *Jesus and the World of Judaism* (London: SCM, 1983; Philadelphia, PA: Fortress, 1984), 55.

Old Testament often translates the term for the *community* or *assembly* of Israel.[1418] To whom does "of God" apply here?

The consistent thrust of Paul's argument in the letter supports the inclusion of uncircumcised gentile believers here. Paul has argued that:

- Gentiles who receive God's Spirit in Christ are children of Abraham and of God in Christ (Gal 3:7, 16, 26, 29; 4:7, 28, 31).
- Differences between Jew and gentile make no difference before God in Christ (3:28).
- Paul has identified the present Jerusalem with Hagar (4:25) and Jesus's followers with the heavenly Jerusalem (4:26).

Identifying uncircumcised but Spirit-endowed believers as members of God's people would offer a fitting climax for the letter. Paul elsewhere identifies believers as spiritually circumcised (Rom 2:28–29; Phil 3:3; Col 2:11) and probably as spiritually Jewish (Rom 2:29), i.e., as faithful to God's covenant.

But Paul did not anticipate later anti-Jewish misappropriations of his work, counter-readings in which the (mostly gentile) church supposed that they had displaced Israel in God's plan.[1419] Indeed, later, "The Franks considered themselves to be the new Israel, and compared their kings to David and their bishops to Samuel."[1420]

Paul's entire theology is fuller than we would suppose if we had only Galatians. Paul was not prescribing, in this one polemical letter, a theological definition to be used in every setting; in 1 Cor 10:32 he distinguishes the church from both Jews and Greeks (cf. also 1 Cor 5:1; 1 Thess 4:5). Paul normally uses "Israel" to mean the Jewish people, but in at least one instance qualifies this label (Rom 9:6), and once he speaks of "Israel according to the flesh" (1 Cor 10:18).[1421] Calling anyone else Israel is not, then, Paul's *usual* language. It is, however, a fitting climax in this polemical letter.

[1418] E.g., LXX Deut 23:2–4, 9 (ET 23:1–3, 8). Another Greek translation of that term is *sunagôgê* (e.g., LXX Exod 12:3, 6). Cf. *laos* in A. Richardson, *An Introduction to the Theology of the New Testament* (New York: Harper and Brothers, 1958), 268.

[1419] Justin *Dial.* 11, 119, 123, 135; Apost. Const. 7.1.36; Augustine Expositions on Ps 53.8; 76.2.

[1420] I. C. Levy, "Introduction," pages 1–78 in *The Letter to the Galatians* (The Bible in Medieval Tradition; Grand Rapids, MI: Eerdmans, 2011), 3. He comments further on typical medieval supersessionism and anti-Jewish readings of Galatians (4–5).

[1421] Ethnic, physical Israel, obscured in the NRSV. Paul is not against "fleshly" ancestry (Rom 1:3; 4:1; 9:3, 5; Eph 6:5), but that is not the primary relationship (2 Cor 5:16; 10:2–3; 11:18, 22; Eph 6:9). See Hays, *Echoes*, 96–97.

Paul is not, however, adopting the later Christian supersessionist practice of a group claiming to *replace* ethnic Israel. Rather, he is thinking of believing gentile branches grafted into the single eschatological people of God (Rom 11:17, 24); these are the eschatological converts promised by the prophets (e.g., Isa 56:3–8; Zech 2:11).[1422] Granted, for Paul, unbelieving branches, whether Jewish (Rom 11:17, 19) or gentile (11:21–22), are broken off. But Paul also affirmed that in the end time Israel as a people would also convert to faith in the Messiah, convinced by the obedience of so many gentiles to their God (11:25–26; cf. 11:11, 14).[1423] Far from discarding historic Israel, Paul is seeking to anchor his gentile converts clearly in connection with it. As William Neil pointed out in an earlier Cambridge Bible Commentary more than half a century ago, "We are caught up, as Christians, in God's plan for the salvation of the world within the framework of human history. It links us with Moses, Amos, and Isaiah."[1424]

The NRSV's *From now on* (6:17) translates the same phrase (*tou loipou*) that is rendered *finally* in Eph 6:10 and the same term *loipos* may carry this sense in some other closing comments as well.[1425] The agitators who confused the Galatians (Gal 1:7; 5:10) have made trouble for Paul; in light of *the marks of Jesus branded on* his *body*, Paul calls on them to stop making trouble for him.

Paul, who identifies with Christ by the Spirit, has been crucified with Christ (2:20), and thus bears on his body *the marks of Jesus*. As noted later, he probably refers to his scars, but his particular way of describing them here may also allude to them by way of some known customs, since the term he uses (*stigma*) ordinarily referred to tattoo marks. Greeks usually limited actual *branding* to horses, but Greeks and Romans tattooed some criminals and misbehaving slaves; religious tattoos predominated more in Egypt and Syria.[1426] Tattoo customs varied from one culture to another; Greeks

---

[1422] Within the Old Testament, gentile adherents to Israel such as Rahab, Ruth, and, perhaps, David's Philistine bodyguard became part of the covenant people, whereas the Lord cut off those Israelites who broke the covenant of God. The size of those who kept covenant varied, from most of Israel (minus Achan) in Joshua's day to a small remnant in the northern kingdom in Elijah's.

[1423] Some might be tempted to think Paul deluded in this hope, but we should also note that the gentile "branches," instead of glorifying the God of Israel (Rom 15:9–12), through most of history has boasted against the natural branches (11:18), effectively obstructing what Paul envisioned as the divine plan.

[1424] Neil, *Galatians*, 88.

[1425] See 2 Cor 13:11; Phil 4:8; and 2 Thess 3:1; though cf. Phil 3:1; 1 Thess 4:1.

[1426] C. P. Jones, "*Stigma*: Tattooing and Branding in Graeco-Roman Antiquity," *JRS* 77 (1987): 139–55.

regarded tattoos as shameful, but reportedly Ethiopians, some Egyptians, and Sarmatians tattooed their children.[1427]

Some commentators suggest the image of slavery here; consistent with such an image, Paul is indeed Christ's slave, not a pleaser of people (Gal 1:10). This may not have been the first image to jump to hearers' minds, however. Slave tattoos[1428] appear but were not common.[1429] "Do not brand your slave," one moralist exhorts, "which would humiliate him."[1430] More often than brands or even tattoos a slave could bear wounds from beatings[1431] or on occasion leg irons.[1432] Moreover, Paul's term, *stigmata*, is plural, whereas a brand or even tattoo would probably be singular.[1433]

Others suggest a religious tattoo as background. Such tattoos marked one as property of or under protection of the deity; this would explain why no one should cause Paul further trouble.[1434] Israelites were forbidden to make tattoo marks, which recalled other peoples' superstitions (Lev 19:27–28; 21:5; Deut 14:1–2), but Scripture could also use the image of protective tattoos figuratively or spiritually (Gen 4:15; Isa 44:5; Ezek 9:4).[1435] In the familiar, pre-Christian work Psalms of Solomon, God spiritually marks the righteous for preservation (as in Ezek 9) and the wicked for destruction.[1436]

The Galatians had undoubtedly seen some of Paul's scars. Given the limitations of ancient medical practice,[1437] much of the physical damage he suffered probably had long-term effects. Paul's stoning (2 Cor 11:25), reportedly in south Galatia (Acts 14:19), could easily have left scars, as would his floggings (2 Cor 11:23–25; cf. 6:5). Scars could be used to identify a person.[1438]

Paul might refer to the effects of such injuries in Gal 3:1 and 4:13–14.[1439] Indeed, 6:17 probably includes all Paul's sufferings for Christ that affected

---

[1427] Sextus Empiricus *Pyr.* 1.148; 3.202; so also Thracians in Artemidorus *Oneir.* 1.8.
[1428] E.g., Herodes 5.28; Martial *Epig.* 3.21; Philo *Free* 10.
[1429] It appears in Italy during the Republic (Diodorus Siculus 34/35.2.32), but is reserved for the most disobedient slaves in Gaius *Inst.* 1.13.
[1430] Ps.-Phoc. 225 (my paraphrase). Non-branding of slaves seems presupposed in Philo *Spec. Laws* 1.58.
[1431] See, e.g., Theophrastus *Char.* 12.12; Apollodorus *Bib.* 2.8.2; Cicero *Fin.* 4.27.76; Quintilian *Inst.* 1.3.13–14; Martial *Epig.* 2.66.1–8; 8.23; Achilles Tatius 5.17.8–9; Plutarch *M. Cato* 21.4.
[1432] Ps.-Demosthenes *Nic.* 8.
[1433] Das, *Galatians*, 653.
[1434] Deissmann, *Studies*, 350; 3 Macc 2:29; Lucian *Syr. G.* 59.
[1435] With Deissmann, *Studies*, 351; Witherington, *Grace*, 454.
[1436] Ps. Sol. 15:6–9; the mark is a *sêmeion*, a "sign."
[1437] See discussion in Keener, *Acts*, 416–18. Surgery existed, but not for the cosmetic repair of wounds.
[1438] E.g., Homer *Od.* 19.467–73; P. Ryl. 174.6–7; P. Lond. 334.6; P. Oxy. 494.31; Luke 24:39.
[1439] With Longenecker, *Galatians*, 300.

him physically (*on my body*): e.g., travels, a night and day in the sea, heat and cold, hunger and thirst, anxiety about the state of the churches, as *well* as persecutions (1 Cor 4:11–13; 2 Cor 11:23–29). But commentators are right to stress *especially* persecution because persecution fits him being crucified with Christ (Gal 6:14). Here Paul "carries" the marks on his body, using the same term used earlier for bearing one another's burdens and each one carrying their own load (6:2, 5).

Paul's scars are the *marks of Jesus* (6:17).[1440] No mere mark of circumcision (6:12–13), these are marks of genuine and voluntary suffering for the Lord (6:14). Paul here identifies with Christ's cross not only by preaching it (6:14) but also by embracing the persecution that such preaching entails (6:12; cf. 5:11), at least in an empire committed to keeping its executions permanent. Although using a different Greek word for *carry*, Paul elsewhere speaks of carrying in his body the death of Jesus (2 Cor 4:10) by his apostolic sufferings for the gospel. The Galatians saw in Paul Christ crucified (Gal 3:1), for Paul died with Christ (2:19–20) and Paul's wounds were proof that he shared his Lord's sufferings (cf. 2 Cor 4:10–12; Phil 3:10; Col 1:24).

As *pathos*, or emotion, was valuable at the end of a speech, the preacher Paul may appeal to it also in his closing image: the image of wounds could be used to stir emotion. Some showed wounds to stir judges or juries against the accused.[1441] Others revealed wounds to invite sympathy, also a valuable emotion in persuasion.[1442] Wounds incurred nobly could, as here, be treated as signs of valor.[1443] They also could demonstrate loyalty to one's leader, nation, or the like.[1444] Sages also used their sufferings to demonstrate their sincere commitments to their beliefs.[1445]

Paul closes with a blessing of grace in 6:18, as he often does. That he is addressing a group rather than an individual does not require Paul to change *with your spirit* to "with your spirits"; the Greek term translated

---

[1440] For the scars identifying with Jesus's sufferings, see also, e.g., Jerome *Ep. Gal.* 3.6.17 (Edwards); Betz, *Galatians*, 324; Bruce, *Galatians*, 276; Matera, *Galatians*, 227; Allison, *Constructing Jesus*, 393–95; George, *Identity*, 186.

[1441] Quintilian *Inst.* 6.1.30; Cicero *Verr.* 2.5.1.3.

[1442] E.g., Seneca *Controv.* 1.4.2.

[1443] Silius Italicus 9.350–51; 13.825.

[1444] Valerius Maximus 7.7.1; Caesar *C.W.* 1.72; Suetonius *Jul.* 68.4; Plutarch *Alex.* 50.6; Josephus *War* 1.197.

[1445] See Diogenes Laertius 6.2.74; J. T. Fitzgerald, *Cracks in an Earthen Vessel: An Examination of the Catalogues of Hardships in the Corinthian Correspondence* (SBLDS 99; Atlanta, GA: Scholars Press, 1988), 43–44, 49, 59–65.

your here is already plural and Paul employs a distributive singular since each of them had a spirit.

After all this, Paul's final word is *adelphoi, brothers and sisters.* Despite the rebukes, Paul's affection for them, reaffirmed throughout the letter by this Greek title (Gal 1:11; 3:15; 4:12, 28, 31; 5:11, 13; 6:1), sounds the letter's concluding note.[1446]

Jewish books sometimes closed with "Amen."[1447] Some New Testament letters closed this way, but especially when they were closing with blessings (Rom 16:27; Jude 25; variant in Rev 22:21); "Amen" was, of course, a good way to close a blessing (Rom 1:25; 9:5; 11:36; 15:33; Gal 1:5), as here (Gal 6:18).

[1446] Even in levels of discipline short of excommunication, Pauline admonition emphasized treating others as brothers and sisters (2 Thess 3:15).

[1447] Whether this was added by the author or, more often, by an editor. See, e.g., 3 Macc 7:23; 4 Macc 18:24; *3 Bar.* 17:4; the ends of books of psalms, Ps 41:13; 72:19; 89:52; 106:48.

Selected Author Index

Ancient Sources Index